Metamorphosi

The Reality of Existence and

(Volume 3)

The Life Philosophy of the
Master of Existentialism

Shan Tung, Chang

美商EHGBooks微出版公司

www.EHGBooks.com

EHGBooks 公司出版

Amazon.com 總經銷

2023 年版權美國登記

未經授權不許翻印全文或部分

及翻譯為其他語言或文字

2023 年 EHGBooks 第一版

ISBN-13：978-1-64784-181-2

Chapter 4: Practicing the empirical law of existence 74

Chapter 5: The framework of Kierkegaard's existentialism 140

Table of Contents

Chapter 6: The Meaning of Life's Existence 781

Part 1: Kierkegaard's existentialist philosophical thought

Preface

Truth is a concept that philosophers cannot bypass when exploring the interpretation of the real meaning of the existence of the self, the existence of the universe and the existence of life.

Many philosophers claim to represent the truth, but their perceptions may not have anything in common with each other, and they may even be at odds with each other. In everyday life, many people also claim that their views are the truth.

The search for truth may be part of human nature, but the distinction between truth and fallacy is made consciously by the distinction between the "path of truth" and the "path of opinion" as described by Parmenides:

"Truth is considered to be eternal and unchanging," which is the most common description of truth.

According to historical records, the first philosophical reflection on truth was made by Aristotle, and in modern times almost all inquiries into truth, as well as into natural and social phenomena, are based on existing empirical knowledge, experience, facts, laws, perceptions, and verified generalizations and generalizations.

And the logical summation of inferences through generalizations and deductive reasoning, after verification. His footprints can be traced.

The following are his speculations and explanations of the natural phenomena under study and their regularity, based on logical reasoning and known scientific principles, and, after generalization and analysis, a tentative but acceptable explanation.

His famous words are recorded in the "Formal Science": "It is false that what is says that it is not, and it is false that what is not says that it is, and it is true that what is says that it is, and it is true that what is not says that it is not.

In human scientific activity and philosophical

research, the question of truth has always occupied an important place. And science (English: science, etymology of the Latin "scientia", meaning "knowledge") is a means of systematic cognitive system, which (things) for the future development of the need to

It is a systematic system of cognition that gradually gathers up useful things for future development, makes them grow slowly, refines and organizes them, and can test explanations and predictions about the universe. Science emphasizes the specificity and falsifiability of predictions, which is different from vague philosophy.

Science is not the same as the search for absolute truth, but rather a continuous search for ways to find (ways, experiences, etc.) to get closer to interpreting the truth, based on existing foundations.

Philosophy, on the other hand, is the study of universal, fundamental questions, including the fields of existence, knowledge, values, reason, mind, and language.

Philosophy differs from other disciplines in that it has a unique way of thinking, such as a critical, often systematic approach, based on rational argumentation.

In this sense, it can be said that philosophy is a knowledge formed by the application of thought and method.

Thus, all kinds of early Western knowledge were incorporated into philosophy as a discipline of analytic reflection to explore and reflect on fundamental questions about life, knowledge, and values.

For example, "Is there an objective standard of morality?" , "What is science?" and "Can artificial intelligence think? The study of philosophy has become something like a unified encyclopedia.

Most of the subsequent studies are based on the questions philosophers have explored, and the overall, fundamental and critical inquiry into the realm of reality and human beings, in order to gain a deeper understanding of the meaning of philosophy.

In the study of the universe and the principles and principles of life, it includes the conception and understanding of the universe as a whole, the discussion of the morality, duties and responsibilities of man in the group, the knowledge of the natural world and the ways of knowing it.

From this, man's ability to recognize his environment and self, and the clarity of his cognition, leads to more exchanges of opinions or debates on a certain issue, such as ideal and practical, rational and sensual, experience and thought, as well as will and freedom.

This kind of generalization and integration has led to a structured (mostly abstract) method of deduction, from a series of concrete facts to general principles, and gradually to three systems, namely, metaphysics, moralism, and intellectualism.

Some philosophers, under certain decided or certain premises, have applied the human mind to an "inward dialogue

After careful consideration of the evidence, they reason their way to a reasonable conclusion about the real world or about the people, things, and objects that are touched by any human activity.

In the process of active introspection, we analyze, synthesize, reason, and judge; or we focus our discussion on a particular area and a particular approach.

All these premises are predetermined for the purpose of searching for the truth, and can be more precisely revised. Thus, the question is asked: How is knowledge possible under determined, or certain, conditions?

How do theory and experience relate to and influence each other? To what extent does the statement require precision? What degree of effectiveness can be achieved by the actual application of the method? What is the nature of the object of study of knowledge?

In the process of exploring these questions, a number of propositions and subject names have emerged, in addition to the three aforementioned major systems.

In addition to the different schools of thought of philosophers, a particular argument that reflects the nature of things in the form of thought is, in logic, a judgment whose truth needs to be proven.

It is the opinion, the proposition, and the attitude of the person who creates the subject matter of the argument.

It is the center of the entire argument, the task of answering the question "what is being argued" and clearly indicating what the author is for or against. It is also a statement of judgment with a clear meaning.

Thus, there are many special terms used to identify a

particular body or group of bodies (persons or things). Examples include rationalism, realism, empiricism, pragmatism, positivism, criticism, etc.

The names of the categories according to the nature of things: those that appear before the word "moral" philosophy, "scientific" philosophy, "social" philosophy, "linguistic" philosophy, "historical" philosophy, "cultural" philosophy, etc.; and those that appear independently, such as "truth", "goodness", "beauty", "logic", "paradox", etc.

To summarize, there is a famous saying in ancient Greek philosophy, "I love my teachers and I love truth more", which embodies the pursuit of truth as a noble spirit above all.

The main task of philosophy is to examine a thought or idea (including concepts, concepts, arguments, etc.) again and again (including arguments for and against) in order to verify whether the reasons held are correct (the verification of truth and falsity).

Then we will judge whether the arguments are the purest and most realistic, that is, the correct reflection of objective things and their laws in the human mind.

Chapter 1: The Thinking of the Philosophy of Life of Chikegao

Kierkegaard's life and criticism of the times

From the point of view of Kant's existential thinking, we consider the situation where "phenomenon (subjective) and object (objective) are consistent", that is, the highest level of spirituality. According to Kant, human cognition can never reach the reality of the object, but remains in the phenomenon.

However, Hegel believes that human beings can use "dialectic" to obtain absolute spirit, so that the phenomenon and the object can agree, and in this way, they can understand the object (reality).

Therefore, according to Hegel's viewpoint, the connection between philosophy and philosophers' personal things should be kept in time or space, tangible or intangible.

But for a thinker like Kierkegaard, Hegel's position on which to analyze or criticize issues and events is not applicable.

The reason is that the whole of Kierkegaard's thought is closely related to his personal experience of life, to what he has seen, done, or encountered, either by himself or by others.

In his writings, one can not only observe the changing focus of his thought, but also find that his writings are almost a series of inner confessions of the individual in terms of his personal existence or physical spiritual reflections, as he wrote in his diary: "All my works are self-education.

In this chapter, we will look at the development and changes of existentialism under different historical conditions, the similar events that have occurred from ancient times to the present, and the overall context and connections. In this chapter, we will look at the development and changes of existentialism under different historical conditions, from ancient times to the present.

(I) Background of the Times (221-223)

The position of Kierkegaard in the history of philosophy is the father of existentialism. Existentialism was an important philosophical trend in the twentieth century, especially in the 1950s and 1960s, when the psychological level was relatively restless.

For example, the pursuit of personal feelings in the present, and the concept of life as nothingness and absurdity. This generally had a significant impact on the religious philosophy of the society at that time. However, what is the existence of a meaningful personal life? What is the value of life existence? This is the question of life's existence that deserves deeper reflection and exploration.

Kierkegaard is a very special philosopher who thinks dialectically, and his characteristic is that he is outside the mainstream of traditional Western idealist philosophy, which used to define existence in terms of "ontological" existence.

Aristotle defined existentialism as "the science of the existence of objects". Specifically, it is the study of the classification of objects, that is, the circumstances under which an object can be defined as "existing". This includes, for example, the question of the "universal" and the "specific".

Traditional Western philosophy treats human beings as rational animals, considers rationality as a mode of thinking, and constructs our world with such rational thinking. But when we think about life in this way, some problems arise.

First, we define what kind of nature a human being has, and then we see whether his existence meets this standard. In this way, the meaning and characteristics of a person's existence can easily be ignored.

For example, the question of scope is closely related to, but not identical to, the question of "being as being". Domains are often seen as the highest category or attribute. The domain system provides an exclusive, detailed classification of entities.

Each entity belongs exclusively to a category. Aristotle proposed such categories, which usually include substances, attributes, relationships, states of affairs or events, and so on. Central to the distinction between domains are various basic ontological concepts, such as particularity and universality, and the concept of the "universal".

For example, particularity and universality, abstraction and concreteness, ontological dependence, identity and modality, and so on. These concepts are sometimes regarded as domains themselves, used to explain differences between domains, or play a central role in describing different ontologies.

Therefore, it is easy to focus on universal, abstract, and common concepts by taking as a starting point the Western mode of thinking about social factors such as customs, morals, ideas, styles, arts, and institutions that have been passed down from generation to generation.

On the contrary, the specific, special, and individual things are not important and are intentionally omitted or not considered. It is not uncommon to think that individual things alone are ignored, and it does not matter at all.

For example, this dog and that cat belong to the dog category, which is dog-like, and the cat category, which is cat-like. It does not matter much if this dog is neglected, because there is no big difference between one more dog and one less cat in this world.

But what difference does it make if there is one more person and one less person? You may think it is too self-centered, but one more person or one less person does make a difference.

The human consciousness has a strong sense of self-love and thinking, and each person's existence is very special. If we take the collection of people into groups, races, and nations as the starting point for thinking, the rights of individuals will be easily affected.

It is easy to sacrifice the rights of the individual, that is, the group will give its life or rights to the individual for a certain purpose.

(II) Intellectual Background (223-226)

What were the characteristics of European philosophy in the nineteenth century? Hegel's position was absolute idealism, and his holistic thinking was based on spirituality, which eventually manifested itself as the will of the state.

After the Germans accepted Hegel's thought, they showed a strong national consciousness, and the national consciousness eventually evolved into racial consciousness.

In this case, the meaning of individual life will be lost. Kierkegaard was protesting against this background and trend of thought at that time and space.

In addition, Kierkegaard himself was a devout Christian and had many criticisms of the Danish state religion ---- Christianity at that time.

Once religion became the state religion, it became fully integrated with the society and politics of the time, and became secularized. There are various classes of vested interests in the religious community, and various superficial rules and regulations, and often the inner spirit of religion is ignored.

Many people have religious beliefs and go to churches or temples to burn incense and worship. But he only thinks of himself as a member of the community and does not really think about what he wants to achieve by believing in God, Allah, or God and Buddha to relieve his suffering.

He is only carrying out the responsibilities of an individual according to the rules of the community, one more or one less, it does not make much difference.

Therefore, Kierkegaard's existentialism has two

implications: first, he reverses the tendency of traditional Western philosophy to emphasize reason at the expense of individual life characteristics; second, he notes that the integration of Christianity into politics and society has obliterated the specificity of the individual in religious faith.

This means that we can pray together, but we cannot be saved together. Each person is special before God, and we cannot expect God to give each of us the same average score and then be saved together.

In fact, it is impossible for religion to calculate the debt of each person's original sin or the assets of the surplus of moral conscience by averaging them out as a group.

Otherwise, the meaning of religion becomes a social custom and a social group structure that can be inferred from social opinion or public opinion surveys to calculate the proportion to decide who can be saved.

As a child, he was weak and sickly, and had fallen from a tree in his childhood, resulting in a hunchback and suffering from a persistent spinal disease.

His nose was straight, his mouth was large, his upper

teeth were bulging outward, and his lower jaw was tucked in.

Despite this, Chikgo's precocious and perceptive temperament from an early age was due to his gloomy family atmosphere, where some of his siblings suffered from mental illnesses and died early, and where the combination of his parents' unethical behavior cast a lingering shadow over the family, causing him to be introverted and to indulge in personal thinking habits.

Kierkegaard's father became wealthy in business when he was young, and thus was able to provide the family with wealthy and regular material living conditions.

Influenced by his own religious experiences, his father chose to teach his children to be tough and religious, teaching them to fear God and to be committed to Him for the rest of their lives, according to the teachings of the Lutheran Church.

As an adult, Kierkegaard was unconcerned with his father's religious beliefs, but the solemn religious atmosphere he was exposed to from an early age provided a strong foundation for his future beliefs.

Compared to his upbringing, Kierkegaard's schooling

was a smooth ride. From an early age, he was a resourceful child who hardly ever achieved more than first place.

In 1830, Kierkegaard entered the University of Copenhagen and, at his father's wish, entered the seminary, but he also began a life of debauchery.

After a period of freedom and absurdity, Kierkegaard renewed his relationship with his father and began preparing for his theological exams, but his father died that same year.

Another major event that affected Kierkegaard was his engagement and dissolution of marriage to Regine Olsen, who met him in 1837 at the age of 15 and they fell in love.

In 1840, after presenting his dissertation, The concept of irony with constant reference to Socrates (1841/1989), he proposed to Olsen, but although he was convinced he would marry her, he broke off the engagement a year later.

Scholars who have studied Kierkegaard often attribute the breakdown of this marriage to Kierkegaard's restless nature or his unfortunate destiny, which prevented him from pursuing happiness, while his own account appears in books such as Kierkegaard's Diary and Either-Or.

Whatever the reason for this dissolution, according to Kierkegaard, "Olsen made me a poet".

After the dissolution, Kierkegaard moved to Berlin for a break and completed several pseudonymous books, such as Either/Or, Repetition (1843/1941), and Fear and trembling.

As a result of this family background, Kierkegaard went on to study theology and was a devout Christian.

He asked for the dissolution of his marriage, but when his fiancée married someone else, he repented and said he wanted to remain brother and sister to her.

This shows the indecisiveness of his personality. However, from his personal point of view, this is extremely natural, because Kierkegaard believes that being a human being represents a kind of physical pain or spiritual suffering that is torn apart.

Man has freedom of will, and the word freedom is a terrible experience of life, a wild and untamed horse. If we really think about the meaning of freedom, we will feel that being a human being is very painful and annoying, fortunately, Kierkegaard had a devout faith, so he pushed this pain to the extreme.

Chapter 2 : The Modern Problem of Life Existence

Almost all philosophical thought reflects the condition or crisis of a certain time or society, and Kierkegaard was no exception. Copenhagen in the nineteenth century was known as a product of the Golden Age, a period of political, economic, and intellectual prosperity in European society (Kirmmse, 1990: 24).

But instead of being confused by the appearance of prosperity, Kierkegaard actively criticized the entire social situation. The targets of his criticism were three.

The first was the Hegelian philosophical system that ruled at the time.

The second was the Christian world in which he lived.

The third was the degradation of values in society.

These three are not only the source of his reflection, but also the target of his fierce attack. It is also based on his reaction to these three that Kierkegaard developed his unique and infectious existential thought.

1.The Hegelian System of Humanization

Since the ancient Greek philosophers, Western thought has been pursuing the ideal of scientific unity. Plato (427~347 B.C.) further developed the Pythagorean view that the essence of everything is "number".

The universe is arranged in a well-ordered order that can be grasped and understood through the numerical order of arithmetic.

The medieval R. Lull (1235-1315) in his [great art] attempted to establish a grand unified academic discipline to unify various other disparate academic disciplines.

More recently, G.W. von Leibniz (1646-1716) also attempted to establish a unified science by combining numbers.

This idea of a unified science gradually developed into a movement of scientific integration in the 19th and 20th centuries as human science and technology advanced by leaps and bounds.

This movement eliminated the original metaphysical assumptions of Plato's thought and focused instead on a common language, common working assumptions, common methods, and even on a unified theory across disciplines.

The Vienna Circle of the early twentieth century is representative of this view.

In 1929, the Vienna Circle published a common vision of the scientific worldview, which not only showed a strong anti-metaphysical orientation, but also devoted itself to the analysis of scientific language in order to establish empirical standards of verification and to achieve scientific unification.

In their minds, the language of science (especially the language of physics) is the universal language of all other sub-domains, and the different languages of other sub-domains can be directly translated into the language of physics without changing their own meanings.

All science is a single system, with no barriers between psychology, sociology, and natural science.

Similarly, in the nineteenth century, Hegel was the model of thought for all of continental Europe, and even the science of the time was based on it. Hegel's famous statement, "All that is reasonable is real, and all that is real is reasonable (Hegel, 1819/1967: 10)." His thought equates reality with reason, believing that the essence of existence is reason or concept.

For Hegel's philosophical view, the individual is the instrument for the realization of absolute spirituality and world rationality, and the expression of the individual is in the connection with the universal relationship.

Hegel always believed that the subject of philosophy is "reason" or the Absolute, the unconditional presupposition of all human expressions and evaluations.

Thus, philosophy is the understanding of the "whole", the holistic, fundamental and critical inquiry into the real world and man.

The true meaning of philosophy is as a way of inquiry, not just as a specific, specialized body of knowledge.

In other words, the most important spirit of philosophy is to "break through the sand", to inquire into the meaning of life as a whole or into the existence of human beings themselves, and this inquiry is not done or dealt with in a piecemeal, disconnected manner.

This kind of inquiry is not done in a piecemeal, disconnected way (or processed), because it must be done in the face of the whole reality, and the whole person, in a learning context by observing, reading, discovering problems, collecting data, forming explanations, obtaining answers, and communicating, examining, and investigating.

Kierkegaard calls Hegel's philosophical thinking "speculative philosophy," which he criticizes for making people think that thought and existence have unity and that one can use an objective and non-objective approach to learning.

He criticizes "discursive philosophy" for making people think that thought and existence are uniform and that one can seek universal truths in an objective and impersonal way, as if to tell people that universal concepts have real meaning.

In the age of reason, the public, and scientism, Kierkegaard is the only one who can point out the crisis of his time, and the crisis of one's "inner being".

He believes that the truth of existence is revealed only through determination and action, and that this truth is not conceptual but realized.

In "The Final Supplement to the Non-Scientific Nature of Philosophy in Brief", Kierkegaard said, "Abstraction is not relevant to existence, but to exist is the highest goal for a person who exists (Kierkegaard, 1846/1944:313).

Kierkegaard believed that the society of his time was one in which reason and discernment reigned supreme, in which people were good at calculating possibilities and ways but lacked the courage to decide, in which they were good at marketing and propaganda but lacked the enthusiasm to act.

For Kierkegaard, the only way to create a real existence and a subjective truth is through the action of existence. Thus, his view of the philosophical task is this.

Our work is not to banish the individual as a victim of others, but to describe a situation in which each individual is equal and to unite them: and the mediator of this union is existence.

Each being has two paths before it: either the individual tries to forget that he or she is an independent being, which makes the individual ridiculous, because being has the feature that being drives the being to be, whether the being wants to be or not.

Or the individual can concentrate on the fact that he is an independently existing individual. For Kierkegaard, Hegel's ridiculous choice is the former, while he personally prefers the latter.

In contrast to objective truth, Plato's rationality, and Hegel's vast system, Kierkegaard is convinced that man is a spiritual, concrete being, and that those who emphasize the existence of rationality and system are merely trying to rationalize the world.

Truth is not a theory, but a task of life, to be achieved through lifelong struggle. If systems and reason were to replace existence, then human action and passion would become sacrifices to discursive philosophy.

2. Formal Christianity

In fact, all of Kierkegaard's thinking points to one purpose: religion. He said: "The reason why I decided to be a religious writer is to be a human writer who pays attention to the individual, because in the individual, the whole life and worldview are brought together. After being established in the philosophy of religion, he asked people to rethink Christianity, the meaning of human life, based on the belief in the connection between religion and the integrity of life.

Kierkegaard expected to use a true religious view to deal with life problems, but when he put himself in the shoes of a deep understanding and comprehend the general religious attitudes in the society at that time, he once put forward opinions on shortcomings and mistakes: people's tactics for a long time are Do everything possible to get as many people as possible into Christianity - and yet pay no attention to making sure that what they're getting into is really Christianity.

After about two thousand years of development in Europe, Christianity has become a kind of cultural tradition, social system and living customs, and it has almost become a blind obedience to life order. In other words, when these people claim to be Christians, they do not know what this means. what. Kierkegaard also said that it is more difficult to reintroduce Christ to the Christian kingdom and the pagans, because contemporary Christians always have the illusion that they are already in the Christian kingdom.

Kant wrote this: If we take a thing as something under the idea of another object, and this constitutes a principle to understand and determine its consistency with it; then we do it dogmatically this concept. When we take it only as a reference to the cognitive faculty, and thus turn to the (subjective) conditions of the subjectivity of thinking about it, without lightly committing to deciding, anything about its object;

As such, we simply deal with it critically. Christianity, which was popular in Danish society at the time, to Kierkegaard was nothing but an empty shell composed of a church that deceived the masses and a group of blindly obedient people. Therefore, from Bishop Minster to ordinary people, he pointed out things Negatives or shortcomings of the object, thus as a proposal to improve things, although sometimes it is expressed as criticism, only pointing out the situation of the object's shortcomings.

Religion is the category through which this age, all history, and all mankind must pass. Faced with the loss of religious essence, Kierkegaard believes that it is caused by too many external forms. People forget the most direct spiritual relationship between themselves and God, and they just go to church mechanically, pray and even repent. People perform these ceremonies just to prove that they are educated and civilized. In order to retrieve the essence of Christianity, Kierkegaard emphasizes inward contact with God. The self before God is called the theological self, which is the self before God;

God is not a thing-in-itself outside of people as it is commonly thought, and our ego has the concept of God. In other words, God exists in man's self, so why should man believe in God in an external form? Formalized religion makes people lack the soul, because people who don't understand seek dialogue with God. The ideal believer needs to seek himself through solitude. His personal experience is hidden and subjective, and it is also experienced through personal mysterious consciousness God exists, and Kierkegaard reminds people to look into their sins, prompting people to return to a direct connection with God from the reflection of sin.

3. A depraved society

The third focus of Kierkegaard's criticism is: the general public. After observing the phenomenon of the times, Kierkegaard mainly criticized two phenomena of the masses: one is the excessive expansion of the mass force; the other is the spiritual degeneration of the middle class. Aristotle (384-322 B. C.) once said, "Man is the animal of society." But in Kierkegaard's eyes, once people integrate themselves into the crowd, the crowd becomes a beast.

Kierkegaard himself was severely attacked by the beast of the "Crowd", and was ridiculed by the magazine "Pirates" at the time. Not only did the roadside children see him and shouted at him: "Either one or the other. , either one or the other." Even the Danish fairy tale master H. C. Andersen (1805-1875) once described a parrot that would only repeatedly shout: "Let's be like a human being!" gram fruit.

Judging from the background of the times, Denmark is politically changing from a dictatorship to a democratic system. People are generally full of confidence in the new century of democracy, but Kierkegaard is worried about such a social situation. Affected by political trends, many people think that when they do one thing together, they will not go wrong. Make a personal choice.

The crowd that Chikegaard refers to is not a

"collection of people" in the sociological sense, but refers to the way people live. Decisions made by the individual, and instead of the responsibility that the individual should bear, when the individual no longer needs to make a choice for himself, then the individual's existence disappears. The anonymity, abstraction, and impersonality of the masses are the highest manifestation of lack of reflection and sense of responsibility, which is the root of the moral corruption of the times.

Individuals should have the purpose of the inner meaning of life, and regard themselves as their own responsibility, rather than pass the responsibility on to the blindly moving masses. Qi Keguo believes that the era should cultivate complete and responsible people. Not a runaway beast. In addition to the attacks of the masses, he was particularly touched, and he also observed the phenomenon of spiritual deprivation and barrenness among the middle-class secular people in the society at that time.

These people use their abilities, run businesses, accumulate wealth, and they may leave results, but spiritually, they are a group without self. This group of middle-class people with knowledge and money, they pursue fashion, go to church, talk about culture, and live a seemingly tasteful life, but in the eyes of Qi Keguo, they are confused and dead, and they do not understand the importance of spirituality. The Wangyoucao, when they are busy with mundane affairs, their spirits are also silent.

Kierkegaard argues that one has the self only if one has the freedom of will, and that no matter what one's intelligence or upbringing is, everyone is an individual who exists alone in the presence of God. However, their lack of spirituality is not because of lack of education, but because of lack of will. Because of the weakness of will, people cannot listen to their own hearts and blindly follow the decisions and values of others. This is simple and reassuring. path of.

Kierkegaard believes that what people really need is complexity and obstacles. Out of love for humanity, out of desperation for my own embarrassment, and not being able to make anything easier than it is now; I realize that it is my task to make trouble everywhere. It is human nature to be afraid of trouble and pain, but the easy way of blind obedience is an escape that trades the mind for short-term peace. Kierkegaard believes that people are not born without a soul, but in the process of rolling around in mundane things, forgetting or deceiving them. The trials of the mortal world, so when he saw people's confusion and sinking, he felt that he had a mission to awaken the sleeping hearts of everyone.

Chapter 3: The philosophical thinking of Kierkegaard's life

In 1830, Kierkegaard began to study psychology, philosophy and theology, and in 1834, his religious beliefs fell into a low ebb and his life became rotten, and he went through four years of absurdity until 1838, when he gradually recovered.

In addition to being the epitome of German conceptual philosophy, Hegel boldly asserted that his philosophical system represented the historical sum of all previous philosophical thought.

The most enduring aspect of his philosophy is his view of history, society, and the state as they fall within the realm of the Objective Spirit.

Hegel saw his work as an expression of the self-consciousness of the World Spirit of his time.

At the core of Hegel's social and political thought are

forms of thought that reflect the essential nature of the object, such as freedom, rationality, self-consciousness, and recognition.

There is an important connection between the metaphysical and discursive elaboration of these concepts and their application to social and political realities.

We can say that the integrated meaning of these concepts can only be grasped through their social and historical manifestations.

Kierkegaard is also committed to reflecting on the theology of the past, drawing lessons from experience. In the eighteenth century, Christianity was challenged by Enlightenment philosophy and science, which gradually gave rise to liberal theology.

The term refers to the various types of theological thought that have counteracted traditional theology, and has become a general and ambiguous theological term that can have different meanings.

However, from a historical perspective of religious philosophy, liberal theology was a popular theological trend in European and American Christianity in the nineteenth and early twentieth centuries.

At the other end of the spectrum, however, is traditional Protestant orthodox theology (Protestantism), which originated from the Reformation movement led by the 16th century theologians Martin Luther, Calvin, and Tzu-Yun-Li, and is one of the three major branches of Christianity, along with Catholicism and Orthodoxy.

Some churches that are not Catholic and have no historical connection with the European Reformation, such as the Independent Churches, are also considered Protestant. Protestantism emphasizes "justification by faith" and believes that people are saved by God through faith alone, not through good works.

Protestantism takes the Bible as the sole basis of faith and opposes the Catholic pontificate, believing that all believers have a role in worshipping or venerating the God they believe in during religious activities or rituals, conducting rituals, and serving as altar servers or officiants.

Depending on the faith, priests are considered to have different degrees of sacredness. Whether in the practical social function or in the mystical religious level, priests have irreplaceable responsibilities within the scope of their duties.

The Protestant denominations differ in their views on theological issues such as the Eucharist, but generally agree on the "Five Solitudes" as the core of their beliefs.

Sola Gratia: The salvation of the human soul is only by divine grace, a gift from God.

Sola Fide: Man receives God's forgiveness of sins and salvation through faith alone.

03. Solus Christus alone: As the atonement for mankind, Jesus Christ is the only mediator ("mediator") between man and God.

04. Sola Scriptura: The Bible alone is the ultimate authority of faith.

Soli Deo Gloria: God alone is worthy to be praised and glorified.

The Christian Church has long been immersed in soteriological philosophy, with an emphasis on the interpretation of Scripture. In the midst of these two theologies, the Christian church gradually lost sight of what Christianity was about, and even lost focus of what it meant to be a Christian.

At that time, Denmark had made Christianity the

state religion, and it seemed to Kierkegaard that he was surrounded by titular Christians. Kierkegaard was a devout Christian, and the central idea of his philosophy was basically "how to be a Christian".

He believed that one cannot obtain the purest and most realistic truth through objectivity, that is, the correct reflection of objective things and their laws in the human mind, and that truth can only be presented through subjectivity, personal ideology.

The ideas, cultures, morals, customs, arts, institutions and ways of behavior that have been passed down through history. The philosophy of invisible influence and control over the social behavior of people, the pursuit of truth as if it were objective knowledge.

What Kierkegaard means is that, in the past, many people's concept of the so-called truth, to be in line with the observation or evaluation of things as they are, without adding personal good or bad or prejudice true, but, people look at things in an attitude, not to a particular person's point of view, to see things, that is, the properties of things themselves.

An overview of multiple perspectives reveals the

nature of things, without the inclusion of personal subjective consciousness of the real, by whom is it determined? Isn't it also up to people to determine? And the person who determines it, doesn't he also determine it by his subjectivity?

How can man explain in detail who has the right opinion and viewpoint on objective things? No one can be sure. What man can be sure of is to express his own opinion. Everyone is free to express his opinion, and this is closer to the truth.

He also opposes the religious creedalism that demands absolute adherence from the faithful, so he does not want to write his thoughts as philosophical theories, but expresses them in the form of creative works in literature and art, and publishes them in books and newspapers under different pen names.

By "truth", Kierkegaard meant spiritual, moral, and life purpose, not scientific, because there was still a lot of linguistic and psychological misconceptions in scientific facts at that time.

Kierkegaard described human existence as having three different levels: sensual, rational, and religious (or aesthetic, ethical, and religious).

Sensual people are either hedonists or people who are passionate about life experiences, who are subjective and creative, who do not have the courage to take responsibility for the world, and who feel that the world is full of expression and infinite possibilities.

People with a rational point of view, on the other hand, are aware of the facts and conditions that exist in front of them, are full of responsibility and obligation to the world, and clearly understand the norms and standards of behavior that should be appropriate when human beings live together in the world, and the various moral rules and regulations for human relationships.

Therefore, unlike sensible people, rational people know that the world is full of impossibilities, doubts, and problems that they do not understand, and when faced with impossibilities and doubts, rational people usually just choose to give up or deny the paradox.

However, the rational person's thesis is that a paradox is an apparently identical proposition or reasoning that implies two opposing conclusions, both of which are self-justifying.

The abstract formula for a paradox is that if event A occurs, then non-A is deduced, and non-A occurs then A is deduced.

Paradox is the confusion of different levels of thinking, meaning (content) and expression (form), subjective and objective, subject and object, fact and value implied in proposition or inference, the asymmetry of thinking content and thinking form, thinking subject and thinking object, thinking level and thinking object, the asymmetry of thinking structure and logical structure.

Paradoxes are rooted in the limitations of perceptual knowledge, perceptual logic (traditional logic), and paradoxical logic. The root cause of paradoxes is the formalization of traditional logic, the absolutization of the universality of formal logic, i.e., the use of formal logic as a way of thinking.

All paradoxes are generated by the formal logic way of thinking, and the formal logic way of thinking cannot find, explain, or solve the logical errors.

To solve paradoxes is to find and correct the logical errors in paradoxes by using symmetric logic.

Although rationality is based on existing theories,

through reasonable logical deduction to obtain a definite result. The opposite is anti-rational. The essence of rationality is negation and doubt.

However, in his Critique of Pure Reason, Kant points out that one cannot prove that there is freedom of will in life, but one cannot prove that there is no freedom of will in life either.

The finite reason of man cannot know the existence of life, freedom of will, soul and God.

The freedom of the will to exist is not an object of theoretical reason and has no cognitive significance, but the freedom of the will to exist has positive significance for practical reason.

Therefore, the freedom of the will to exist is the bridge from the Critique of Pure Reason (batch 1) to the Critique of Practical Reason (batch 2).

In the Critique of Practical Reason, Kant reaffirms the distinction between theoretical and practical rationality of the free will to live.

While theoretical reason deals with the capacity to know, the Critique of Practical Reason deals with the capacity to desire, and the highest form of expression of desire is the freedom of the will to exist.

Therefore, Kant's Critique of Practical Reason explores the role of freedom of will in moral practice.

(1) The Dialectic of the Meaning of Life Existence

Knowing how to deal with the connection between one thing and another is indeed a lovely and powerful way to discover and help find the revered absolute, which exists independently of any conditions and is constant and unchanging, which cannot be seen in itself, but which leads one to understand the truth of what is in things and to understand it to the absolute.

01. The Dialectic of Life Existence

Although Kierkegaard attacked or denounced Hegel's system of thought on a large scale, his way of thinking was still influenced by the Hegelian dialectic when he grew up in the mainstream of the Hegelian system.

K. Popper (1902-1994) divided Hegel's dialectic into three steps: thesis, antithesis, and synthesis.

Kierkegaard's existential dialectic, a philosophical

method for resolving disagreements, is a process of resolving contradictions between two opposing parties, and consists of only two steps: thesis and antithesis (Theunissen, 2005: 106).

Since the object of Kierkegaard's exploration cannot be grasped absolutely by rational inference, it is considered that there is no "thesis" stage. In fact, Kierkegaard wants to prove that God is still an independent concept that does not depend on any conditions and is constant and unchangeable through the discussion of one positive and one negative.

In addition, the scholar H. Diem (1900-) believes that Hegel's treatment of dialectical examination is to describe the problem of seeing the problem in a comprehensive way.

It refers to the correct reflection of the dialectical development process of objective things through concepts, judgments, reasoning and other forms of thinking, i.e. the reflection of objective dialectics.

It is to inquire into how a loaded experiential self is transformed into a purely thinking subject, while the question of continuous dialectical movement points to the process of regulation.

However, for Kierkegaard. The most fundamental feature of dialectical thinking is to examine the object as a whole, in terms of its intrinsic contradictory movements, changes and interconnections of various aspects, in order to know the object systematically and completely in its essence.

It is the contemplator of living existence who enters deeply into the question of the reflection of existential consciousness, so that its potential can be released into the organic entity (Diem, 1959/1978: 25).

Thus, in contrast to Hegel's view of dialectic as a process of regulating the positive and the negative, Kierkegaard focuses on the reflection of the meaning of life existence through dialectic.

In other words, after acquiring certain experience and knowledge through observation and study, different people have different views on the same issue, so they come together to expound their ideas in a similar way to debate, and in the process of communication, they eliminate the illogical parts of their original ideas.

This has two effects: on the one hand, they "try to

make others accept their own viewpoints", and on the other hand, they "abandon their original viewpoints in the discussion because they feel that they are incorrect and accept others' viewpoints instead".

The essence is to analyze and reject wrong or reactionary thoughts, words, and deeds with justification, both for oneself and for others.

Those who participate in the debate eventually arrive at a common result, which is more objective and systematic than their original ideas.

The process of dialectic is the growth process of individual's life metamorphosis, through the individual's reflection on the consciousness of life existence, thus making a choice; here the dynamic change characteristic of dialectic is transformed by Kierkegaard into the motivation of individual's inward thinking to face the existence.

02. Intrinsic Value of Dialectical Philosophy of Existential Thinking

Existential dialectic is the most common discursive technique used by Kierkegaard because of the state and condition of the activity of the dialectic itself.

It evokes paradox. In "Either/or", the sensual stage is contrasted with the ethical stage, and the ethical stage with the religious stage.

In "The Disease of Death", the despair of being caught in the finite time of life is contrasted with the despair of being caught in the infinite, and through the negative nature of despair, it leads to positivity, and through the dialectical relationship between faith and despair, "despair" constitutes the beginning of faith.

In fact, from the above-mentioned opposites, the most important thing that Kierkegaard does is to bring out the paradox and contradiction of the meaning of life existence through this dialectic of positive and negative life existence.

In his book The Philosopher's Toolbox, he analyzes paradox as a form of thinking that reflects the nature of things: reason against experience, reason itself leading to paradox, and experience against reason (Baggini & Fosl, 2003: 107-108).

On the basis of perceptual knowledge, people generalize the attributes specific to the same thing from the many attributes of the same thing and form concepts expressed in words or phrases.

Concepts arc abstract and universal. The third way is chosen by Kierkegaard, because Christ himself is an absurd, contradictory and paradoxical concept.

Both the Christian doctrine and the reincarnation of God can only reveal the limited nature of reason and systems, and underline the power of faith, which is the only way to reach God.

This technique of pointing from paradox to paradoxical supreme being (God) can be said to be an important element of the dialectic of existence applied by Kierkegaard.

03. The truth perception of dialectical philosophy of life existence

What is truth? There are probably many people who have never thought about this question carefully in their lives, but only rely on a feeling, a bclicf or a point of view that they must think is right, and assume it to be the truth.

In fact, when we ask, "What is truth?" when we need to solve a contradiction or a problem, we are asking what is truth. we are asking about the fundamental nature of things themselves: "What makes a correct belief correct? These correct beliefs must have something in common that makes them correct.

So, what is the measure of things that proves a belief or viewpoint must be correct?

This is a contradictory and difficult question in the Western philosophical field, which has been debated and debated from time immemorial, and is still unresolved.

And there is no definite conclusion yet. In the history of Western philosophy, there are two main types of truth-flap arguments.

First, the theory of truth: this kind of induction from actual practice, or by the concept of deduction and get a systematic, organized reasoning or argument.

The reason why a state of mind that trusts, has confidence or relies on someone or something is correct is that the belief is the same or consistent in nature, character or role, and can be objectively true in the case of one thing and another.

Second, the fusion of truth: this kind of systematic, organized reasoning or argument derived from actual practice, or from conceptual deduction.

The reason why a state of mind that trusts, has confidence or relies on someone or something is correct is because the belief is consistent with other beliefs, and a particular belief can be integrated into the whole belief puzzle, that is correct.

Let's look at what's wrong with the truth-conformity theory. Since this is a cognitive difference for each person, we will not go into it here, because it is clear from the previous section that truth-conformity theory holds that

What is right is that the belief is consistent with and corresponds to objective reality. The question here is: What is true when things are examined as they are, independent of any personal feelings, prejudices, or opinions?

Is the objective reality that is caused by the direct reaction of the human mind to the external objective environment or things through the sense organs? In fact, if we analyze it carefully, we will find that it is not true at all.

What human beings perceive is only the reproduction of the external world in the brain as perceived by their own senses, similar to "imaging", not objective reality. For example, you see a mango, oval-shaped, with a reddish color of egg yolk.

But this information is only the signal received by the "real mango" through the eyes and senses, through the nervous system in the brain "image", not the real mango.

In other words, human beings can only get the "image" of the external world through their senses and cannot evaluate the "reality" of what they perceive.

Therefore, we cannot determine what the objective reality looks like. According to truth conformity theory, if we cannot determine what objective truth is like, then we cannot confirm whether any belief is consistent with objective truth, that is, we cannot determine what must be truth.

(2) Principles of Dialectical Thinking

According to Socrates' view, "the more truth is debated, the clearer it becomes", truth is considered to be the most important and only based on reason (similar to logic, also called Abstract thinking) logical thinking is the process of reflecting reality through concepts, judgments, and reasoning in the process of knowing.

It is the only way to convince others and to discover the right way of truth, and is the decisive factor of one's behavior. He believes that truth can be discovered in the search for inquiry, in the reasoning and logic used.

01.The dialectical philosophy of thought is explained by quotations

In classical logic, anything can be deduced from a contradiction; this is called ex contradictione quodlibet (ECQ), also called the explosion principle.

Subcoherent logic, rejects the law of non-contradiction and is a logical system in which ECQ does not hold. Two-sided truth theory is one of the sub-coherent logics, a philosophical position that holds that there are real contradictions.

Two-sided truth theory is particularly interesting in logic because it challenges the orthodoxy of classical logic, even though classical logic is still dominant even today.

The correct reflection of the dialectical development of objective things through concepts, judgments, reasoning, and other forms of thought, i.e., the manifestation of the nature of objective things through objective dialectics.

The most fundamental meaning of human life or the unique place of dialectical thinking is to consider the object of thought as a whole, to reflectively examine the movement, changes and interconnections of its inner contradictions, in order to know the object systematically and completely from its essence.

The intention of truth-seeking has three main interpretative meanings.

(1) The assertion that any complex phenomenon can be explained by analyzing the underlying physical structure within the phenomenon.

(2) The effort to simplify complex concepts, events, states, etc., which have the effect of underestimating, misinterpreting, and obscuring the truth of things.

(3) The main consensus is that the dialectical method does not violate the law of non-contradiction of logic, tries to simplify one kind of scientific logical thinking into another kind of scientific logical thinking, defines the key words used by one kind of scientific logical thinking in the language of another kind of scientific logical thinking, and its conclusion can be derived from the propositions of another kind of scientific logical thinking.

02.The meaning of dialectical philosophy of thinking

"Dialectic" is a method of investigating research problems in order to dissolve different opinions. The word "dialectic" is a Japanese translation of a Western word, which means "to argue and to prove".

Its English translation "dialectic" can be split into the initial "dia" (interactive, between the two) and the root "elect" (to speak), which means "the exchange of opinions between different people".

After acquiring certain experience and knowledge through observation and learning, different people have different views on the same issue, so they come together to expound their own ideas in a similar way to debate, and in the process of exchange, eliminate the illogical parts of their original ideas.

This has two effects: on the one hand, they "try to make others accept their own viewpoints", and on the other hand, they "abandon their original viewpoints when they feel that they are incorrect and accept others' viewpoints instead".

The essence of this is that individuals are critical of

themselves and of others at the same time. Those who participate in the debate eventually arrive at a common outcome that is more objective and systematic than their original ideas.

Historically, there are different forms of systematic thought about dialectical reasoning. Dialectical philosophy of Eastern thought is a general term for the field of philosophy of the Eastern countries (China, Japan, India, and sometimes the Islamic countries).

This refers to the fact that, unlike the Western philosophical system formed under the influence of the ancient Greek dialectical philosophy, the Eastern dialectical philosophy is not a unified philosophical system, but has similar cultural characteristics.

Influenced by Western dialectical philosophy, Eastern dialectical philosophy has been classified and discussed using Western dialectical standards for more than a hundred years.

All regional dialectical philosophies of thought can still be divided into the categories of metaphysics, cosmology, logic, religious philosophy, social philosophy, political philosophy and cultural philosophy.

These include: Socratic Methodology, Hindu Dialectic, Buddhist Dialectic, Medieval Dialectic, Hegelian Mindfulness Dialectic, Marxist Materialistic Dialectic, Talmudic Dialectic (Judaism) and Protestant Dialectic.

03. Basic content of dialectical philosophy of thinking

Dialectics (English: dialectics, Greek: διαλεκτική, dialektikḗ; related to dialogue, also translated as dialectic, dialectical method) is a method of philosophical argumentation for resolving disagreements, a process of resolving contradictions involving two opposing parties.

Ancient Greek dialectic involves dialogue between two or more people who hold different views on a subject, with the aim of building up a knowledge of the truth of things through such well-founded dialogue, in the use of reasoning and logic to be discovered.

Dialectical thinking has been central to Indian, and European philosophy since ancient times. The term is used in many different fields, including philosophy, natural science, and history. Dialectic originated in the ancient Greek process of logical debate and is well known and understood by Plato's account of Socrates' "Dialogues".

Socrates believed that "truth" is the most important thing, and that only rational (similar to logic, also called abstract thinking, logical thinking is the process of reflecting reality through concepts, judgments, and reasoning in the process of knowing.

It is the only way to convince others and to discover the right way of truth.

The ancient Greek dialectic method of questioning and answering is derived from the Greek word "dialego", which means conversation, skillful and difficult to grasp argument, and refers to a form of logical argumentation.

It is now used in three fields, including thinking, nature and history, as an evolutionary concept of dialectical philosophy of thinking.

Since ancient times, various forms of dialectical reasoning have been documented in ancient India and in the West. The three basic forms are: Socratic anti-cogitation, Hegelian teleological dialectic.

Marxist materialistic dialectic. The core of Marxist dialectic is mostly derived from Hegel's dialectic, which conveys an idea, impression, or understanding of the nature and characteristics of certain intangible things, and modifies it into a philosophical doctrine of oppositional unity, universal connection, and evolutionary development.

Other dialectical reasoning includes: Hindu dialectic, Buddhist dialectic, medieval dialectic, Jewish Talmudic dialectic, and Protestant dialectic.

Debate is different from debate, rhetoric, or sophism, in which the debater insists on his or her point of view and aims to win the debate.

The debaters either refute their opponents and prove their own reasoning correct, or prove their opponents' reasoning wrong.

In rhetoric, the person using rhetoric uses logos, ethos, and pathos to convince the reader of his or her claims;

In sophistry, the purpose is often to deceive by deliberately introducing illogical fallacies into the argument, making a deceptive appearance, which is in essence a false deduction from a known or assumed premise, or from the result of a known answer to a counterfactual and the reasons and evidence used to support or deny something.

03-1 Ancient Plain Dialectic

In ancient Greek thinkers, dialectic had a wide range of meanings, from a refutation technique in debates, to a method of systematic evaluation of definitions, to the study and delineation of the connection between particular and general concepts.

Heraclitus, one of the founders of the ancient Greek simple materialistic dialectic, is famous for his philosophical view that "everything flows and nothing abides".

He is known for his philosophical view that "everything flows and nothing is permanent". He famously said, "One cannot step into the same river twice" and "The sun is new every day".

Socrates, Plato, Aristotle, etc. are also representatives of ancient dialectic. They were mostly based on idealism and contained many reasonable dialectical cores, such as the belief that truth is always concrete, relative, and can be transformed to the opposite under certain conditions.

Many ancient Chinese schools of thought have a simple dialectical approach. For example, the Taoist thought represented by Laozi, who had such famous quotes as "there is no one, difficult and easy, and short and long are comparable", "everything is negative yin and hold Yang, and the air is in harmony", and "blessing is the ambush of calamity, calamity is the dependence of blessing".

Another example is the doctrine of yin and yang and the five elements. In the I Ching, there are also concepts such as overcoming strength with flexibility, mutual transformation of yin and yang, and the endlessness of all things. All of these explain the relativity of things; that things are in motion, changing and developing; that there is no absolute and unchanging thing in the world except the change itself.

03-2 Contradiction and Transformation

The basic properties of contradiction: the sameness of contradiction and the opposition of contradiction.

03-2-1 Contradiction of opposites and unity

Opposition and unity are the basic properties of contradiction. The unity of opposites is the unity of a contradiction. The unity of contradiction is the property of interdependence and mutual affirmation of both sides of the contradiction, which keeps things unified in themselves.

It is a necessary prerequisite for the development of things to maintain their own unity temporarily, so that the two opposing sides can coexist in a unity. Due to the role of mutual unity between opposites, the two sides can draw on each other and use the factors that are beneficial to them to develop, thus preparing the conditions for the abandonment of the contradiction to be resolved immediately.

Contradictory identity refers to the organic, inseparable link between the contradictory opposites, embodying the nature and tendency of mutual attraction and transformation between the opposites. Contradictory sameness has the following manifestations.

① The sameness of contradiction refers to the interdependence and mutual continuity of the contradictory parties.

The sameness of the contradiction refers to the interdependence and mutual continuity of the two sides of the contradiction.

There are various ways to express the interconnection, the main ones are mutual transformation (under certain conditions) or mutual penetration. In a nutshell, sameness has two meanings.

One is coexistence, which means that the two sides of the contradiction coexist in a unity under certain conditions, and the other side does not exist if one side is lost; the other side can be transformed into each other under certain conditions.

The antagonism of the contradiction refers to the mutual rejection, conflict, and conflict between the two parties.

The antagonism of a contradiction is the property of mutual rejection and negation of both sides of the contradiction, which makes things change continuously and eventually destroy their unity.

When this change reaches the limit that the old unity of contradiction cannot allow, it causes the disintegration of the old unity of contradiction and the creation of the new unity of contradiction.

The struggle between opposites is the decisive force that makes new things negate old things. The antagonism of the contradiction refers to the tendency of both sides of the contradiction to exclude, conflict, negate and dissociate from each other.

Opposition and unity are the two fundamental properties of contradiction. The opposing property of contradiction is called opposition, and the unifying property of contradiction is called identity.

To deeply understand the contradiction of material dialectics, it is necessary to clarify the meaning of the identity and opposition of contradiction and the interrelationship between them.

03-2-2 Interdependence and Transformation of Contradictory Identities

Contradictory opposites and unity can be transformed into each other. The struggle between opposites does not draw an absolutely clear and fixed line between them.

In the mutual struggle between opposites, there is interdependence and interpenetration; the result of mutual struggle can lead to mutual transformation and mutual transition. Similarly, unity always presupposes differences and opposites, and there is no unity without struggle.

In the mutual unification of opposites, there is mutual opposition and mutual rejection; the mutual transformation of opposites that occurs as a result of struggle is the clearest manifestation of the inner unity between opposites. Contradiction and Unity.

The materialistic dialectics of contradiction is the dialectical contradiction, the objective contradiction of contradictory sameness, which refers to the organic, inseparable connection between contradictory opposites, embodying the nature and tendency of mutual attraction and transformation between opposites. Contradictory sameness has the following manifestations.

First, the two sides of the contradiction are interdependent and mutually conditional, coexisting in the unity.

This means that the two opposing sides of any contradiction cannot exist alone, but under certain conditions, each takes its own opposing side as the premise of its own existence, and without the other, it would not exist.

"You can't leave me, I can't leave you." For example, a magnet has two poles, north and south, and these two poles are inseparably linked.

Even if it is cut off and broken, it still has both north

and south poles at the same time. It is impossible to get a single magnetic pole with only the south pole and no north pole, or only the north pole and no south pole.

If the magnetism of one pole is eliminated, then the magnetism of the other pole will also disappear at the same time. As the saying goes: "Not the enemy does not get together.

"This is precisely the problem of paradoxical sameness. It is because they are enemies and opposites that they can come together to maintain the existence of a unified whole.

The forces of action and reaction in nature, the genetic heritage and variation in biological evolution, the truth and fallacy in knowledge, etc., are all manifestations of the identity of the two sides of the contradiction.

Chapter 2 of the Tao Te Ching, a masterpiece of ancient Chinese philosophy, states: "When all the world knows that beauty is beauty, it is already evil; when all the world knows that good is good, it is already not good.

Therefore, if there is no one, there is no one; if there is difficulty, there is ease; if there is length, there is shape; if there is height, there is inclination; if there is sound, there is harmony; if there is front, there is back. It means that if the whole world knows the absolute standard of "beauty", then "evil" which does not meet that standard will arise.

Likewise, if the absolute standard of goodness is known throughout the world, then the badness that does not meet that standard will also arise. But can we really find an absolute standard for beauty, ugliness, goodness, and evil?

So, out of nothing, something comes into being, and in the end, something comes back to nothing. What is the absolute standard of nothing? What is the absolute standard of something? If you start with the easy part before dealing with the hard part, the hard part will become the easy part.

What is the absolute standard of difficulty? What is the absolute standard of ease? The length is known by comparison, and the long one becomes shorter when it meets the longer one.

What is the absolute standard of length? What is the absolute standard of short? The higher one will be tilted downwards, and the lower one will become the higher one after tilting. What is the absolute standard of high? What is the absolute standard for low?

The lead singer and the chorus sing together. One day, when the lead singer is absent, the chorus becomes the lead singer. What is the absolute standard for the lead vocalist? What is the absolute standard for the chorus?

The person in front walks after the person in the back, and after the former, the former becomes the latter. What is the absolute standard of the former? What is the absolute standard of the latter?

In fact, the above differences are only comparative relative appellations, not the true nature. But people confuse the truth with falsehood, causing unnecessary troubles in life.

There is and there is not, difficult and easy, long and short, high and low, sound and voice, front and back, all these opposing sides are interdependent.

Second, the contradictory opposites are interpenetrating and interconnected.

This is a more important layer of the same meaning of the contradiction. The interpenetration of contradictions is expressed as mutual penetration and mutual inclusion.

Each side of the contradiction contains and penetrates the factors and attributes of the other side, you have me, I have you, there is one in the other, there is one in the other. For example, there is repulsion in attraction, and there is attraction in repulsion.

In assimilation, there is dissimilation, and in dissimilation, there is assimilation; in heredity, there is variation, and in variation, there is heredity.

There is rational knowledge in perceptual knowledge, and there is perceptual knowledge in rational knowledge. There is relative truth in absolute truth, and absolute truth in relative truth, etc.

The interpenetration of contradictory parties is a manifestation of the mutual penetration of contradictory parties, the mutual inclusion and intersection of contradictory parties in terms of molecules, factors or parts.

It is the interconnection from the form of interdependence to the content of interconnection. Thus, it is the state and stage of sameness that is one step further than interdependence.

Third, the conflict between the two sides under certain

conditions of mutual transformation.

You can become me, I can become you. The transformation of things is always towards their other, their opposites, which also shows that the opposites are interconnected and have an inherent sameness.

For example, an egg is transformed into a chick but not into a stone; war is transformed into peace and peace is transformed into war; success is transformed into failure and failure is transformed into success, and so on.

The mutual transformation of the two sides of the conflict is the state where the union of the two sides of the conflict reaches the extreme or the peak, and is the overall change prepared by the two sides of the conflict in the mutual penetration.

It is a dynamic form of interdependence in which both parties continue to depend on each other on the basis of the new unity.

(3) Absolute command

The law of freedom of will and reason in life is different from the law of nature in the existence of species, which dominates things at all times.

Although it comes from human reason, human beings also have the desire to love and cling to their senses, and the desire of the senses will interfere with the reason of the free will of life.

Therefore, the law of the free will to live, the law of reason, is not necessarily implemented, but is only a social matrix command for the free will to live. Kant distinguishes two types of commands.

The first is the hypothetical imperative, where P is a necessary condition for Q, which means "if P is false, then Q is false". By negating the latter, it follows that "if Q is true, then P is true".

Example 1: For an integer greater than 2, an odd number is a necessary condition for a prime number. If an integer is greater than 2 and is prime, it must be odd.

This is expressed formally as "If I want A, then I must do B." It expresses a moral practice of limited responsibility and conditionality. For example, to be a U.S. Senator, one must be at least 30 years old. If he is a senator, he must be at least 30 years old.

The second type of categorical imperative is a

condition that must be met.

For example, 520 is a categorical imperative for admission to a university, which means that 520 is an absolute condition for achieving a particular standard. p is a categorical imperative for q, which means "if p is false, then q is false". By negating the latter, it follows that "if Q is true, then P is true".

Example 1: For an integer greater than 2, an odd number is necessary to become a prime number. If an integer is greater than 2 and is prime, it must be odd.

An absolute condition is a specific event condition that is immutable, irreversible, and can be violated, expressed in the form "you must do A", which expresses a form of responsibility that is unrestricted, unconditional, and unconditional: for example, it must be carried out.

Example 2: Being at least 30 years old is a necessary condition for becoming a U.S. Senator. If he is a senator, he must be at least 30 years old.

Similarly, if you suddenly see a child about to fall into a well, no matter what kind of person he is, he will immediately feel fear and compassion for the pain.

It is not a desire to befriend the child's parents, or to

win the praise of friends in the neighborhood, or to earn a reputation for cruelty. Rather, reason tells you that "you must save someone," and that is an absolute imperative.

All "hypothetical necessity" is based on absolute necessity, but if it is one of the social ideologies, and if it is the standard and norm of people's common life and their behavior, it should be kept in its pure form, not a morality to be fulfilled for other purposes.

Therefore, in order to be purely moral, one cannot adopt "hypothetical necessity", but must adopt absolute necessity.

Absolute necessity is the pursuit of universal validity, with absolutely no exceptions.

Chapter 4: Practicing the empirical law of existence

(1) The Trial of Incarnation

Kant goes on to discuss the concept of the highest good. Although Kant esteems morality as the highest good, the highest good is not the same as the highest good. In his view, the highest good should include happiness and virtue.

But if happiness is included in the supreme good, does this lead to the possibility that people can be virtuous only for the sake of happiness (which would be in conflict with the second theorem)?

In Kant's view, the key is the condition that morality is worthy of happiness, and not the other way around. It is the effort to practice morality that makes a person worthy of happiness, not happiness for its own sake.

Kant argues that morality and happiness should

coincide in order to be considered complete and free of defects. Reason always thinks that a good person should have good reward, even if he does not have good reward in this life, he should have good reward in the next life.

If a good person does not receive good reward, our general concept will be considered a tragedy. There are two famous schools of ethics in the Western philosophical tradition, the Stoics and the Epicurean school.

The Stoics believe that morality is the greatest happiness and advocate morality, which is already happiness in itself; the Epicureans advocate that happiness is the most important, and that if one is responsible for the meaning of life, then the meaning of life is the morality that makes one happy.

Kant argues that the two schools are in contradiction because they both see morality and happiness as analytical propositions, that is, "morality (the subject) is happiness (the predicate)" and "happiness (the subject) is morality (the predicate)".

Each of these two schools of thought believes that the predicate in a proposition is already included in the subject, and that the predicate in traditional grammar is inspired by ancient Greek propositional logic (as opposed to the more modern first-order predicate logic).

In ancient Greek logic, the trinomial term "κατεγορωυμενον" (κατεγορωυμενον) was the counterpart of the "subject" (ὑποκείμενον).

In a trinomial argument, the two presuppositions lead to a concluding proposition in which the big word (P) is the predicate; the predicate is regarded as a characterization or attribute of the main word, which is logically taken as true.

This classical understanding of the predicate was more or less directly adopted by the grammar of ancient Greek and Latin, and then into traditional grammar.

Kant believes that happiness and morality should be composite propositions, meaning that the preposition is not included in the subject, that the preposition extends the meaning of the subject, and that both the subject and the preposition are combined by a higher third, i.e., a variety of different but related things.

First, the three axioms of practical reason

Morality and happiness are states in which there is no conflict between emotions, ideas, opinions, interests, or regulations, and require two conditions: the immortality of the soul and the existence of God.

Regarding the immortality of the soul, Kant argues that life is finite, and that it is difficult for a person to achieve moral perfection in this life.

Moreover, good people often do not receive good rewards in this life, so it is necessary to set his soul to live on after his death, so that he can receive the reward he deserves. Finally, the existence of God is necessary because the good man can receive good rewards, and it is necessary to establish the existence of a meta-just judge who can guarantee that the moral behavior of man will be worthy of happiness.

The immortality of the soul and the existence of God are fundamental propositions that are based on the self-evident facts of human reason, which have been tested by human beings over time and do not require further proof. As a guarantee of Telford's unanimous axiom.

For the Kantian view, we also need the axiom of free will. Although we cannot know free will, we need freedom of will in order to establish moral behavior, because freedom is a necessary condition for morality.

Only a person who freely performs moral acts is considered moral. For example, if a person is forced to give up his position to another person, people will not consider him a moral person.

It can be said that the ideas of freedom of will, immortality of the soul and existence of God, which are considered unknowable in the critique of the Critique of Pure Reason, in this case mean not only viewpoint, concept, opinion and idea, but also vision and picture.

In summary, whether in Chinese or English usage, "idea" is, in fact, our viewpoint, opinion, and belief about something. In many cases, ideas and concepts can be used interchangeably.

For example, one is that the new educational concept is external to information technology, so there are two separate objects: educational concept and information technology, the former overriding the latter, and educational concept has a dominant effect on information technology, and the informatization of education becomes a combination of education and modern information technology.

In fact, the opposite is true. In fact, the opposite is true. In today's rapidly developing information technology, there are already new concepts of education that we need to understand, and it is information technology that provides us with new educational concepts and stimulates our educational imagination, rather than educational concepts that provide the direction of information technology.

Information technology-based educational reform is about revealing the new concepts embedded in information technology and making them manifest as the basic concepts of curriculum reform.

This is the transformation of information technology-based education. Therefore, Kant regards them as necessary axioms in the practical rationality of life existence.

The above three have no subjective cognitive meaning, but they have the meaning of the moral practice of life existence.

At this time, man can only rely on the "Leap of Faith" to enter the unknown exploration of nature and to express man's desire for immortal liberation, and then to believe in the existence of a supernatural mysterious power or entity outside the real world.

The belief in the existence of a supernatural mystical force or entity outside of the real world leads to awe and worship of that mystery, which leads to a system of faith cognitive and ritual activities, and the power of faith to overcome doubt and what is normally regarded as impossible.

Only faith in an idea or religion and in someone or something else can restore the hope that "all things are possible". The "metamorphic leap of faith" is a strong spiritual will that demonstrates faith, not a pretentious belief in or admiration for a particular idea, doctrine, or religion.

As mentioned earlier, in Fear and Trembling, Kierkegaard emphasizes a deeper, more thoughtful approach to Old Testament activity: it mentions that Abraham, the "father of faith," followed God's advice.

The story of Abraham, the "father of faith," following God's advice to kill his son as a sacrifice and not to leave any flesh for anyone, is considered the best kind of sacrifice and a "sacrifice" that Judaism allowed non-Jews to offer at the temple.

He believed that if Abraham did not care about the life and death of his son, there would be no moral conscience thought behavior expressed by a certain standard of society, customs, habits. Virtue, beauty is the beauty of things ethical, and even the psychological struggle of emotions between family members or relatives.

Or that if obeying God and killing his son is a moral code, then what he did is meaningless. In the former case, there is no strong emotion and attachment to a person or thing, derived from strong feelings and psychological states of love, loyalty and goodwill between relatives.

For example, affection. contains a range of strong and positive emotional and mental states, from the most noble virtues or good habits, the deepest interpersonal relationships, to the most simple pleasures.

The latter, is foolishly faithful, without regard for consequences, without thinking about reasons, without weighing the pros and cons, knowing only to do something according to orders, without any thought of its own.

The nature of Abraham's actions, worthy to be chosen, pursued, and preserved, or of things and objects of this nature, lies in his leap from reason to the supernatural dominion, to the supernatural power, to the supernatural power of the universe.

The existence of a creator and controller of the universe, which gives a soul to man and continues to be a belief system after death, a belief in the omnipotence of God, a belief that everything is possible, that miracles will happen (which resulted in God sending an angel to stop Abraham from killing his son at the last moment).

Kierkegaard also believes that people in a normal state of mind have the confidence and courage to face the present situation calmly in order to get a date before something happens.

And quickly and fully understand the reality, analyze a variety of feasible options, and then judge the best to carry out the work of the specific plan, or the planning of a problem, and the ability to effectively implement it, then there will be no faith.

Kierkegaard's faith from Abraham is found in the practice of feeling and perception; it is felt and explored in action, and the emphasis is on physical action.

Human beings do believe that there is a condition, a

talent, that can transcend many fixed, subjective and objective perceptions of things, the limitations of a systematic collection (or habit), and the final outcome of unexpected personnel.

In his book "The Disease of Death", Kierkegaard believes that "despair" is the "disease of death", a common feature of things that human beings perceive in the process of cognition.

It is a disease that must be understood in a special way. It literally means a disease that ends in death.

We can also call it a "terminal" or "fatal" disease, but the meaning is the same.

In the context of what is expressed in this language or other signals, "despair" cannot be said to be the disease that kills. However, in the Christian understanding, "death" is "entering into life" with itself as the center.

Therefore, in the view of things or problems from a certain Christian position or perspective, secular, physical diseases are not considered to be lethal diseases, because although "death" is the end of disease, "death" itself is not the end.

If we are talking about a disease that causes death in

the narrow sense, then the disease should end with "death" and "death" itself is the end point. To hold such a view is to fall into "despair".

But in another sense, "despair" can be identified as the disease that causes death. In a literal sense, one cannot die from this disease, nor does it end in physical death. On the contrary, the pain of "despair" lies in the fact that one cannot die.

Therefore, it is more like a person who is seriously ill, lying on his death bed and fighting with death, but cannot die at the same time.

Therefore, the "as for" disease that kills is that there is no way to die; but that does not mean that there is still a chance of life, no, the real hopelessness is that even the last hope, which is death, is not available.

If death is the greatest danger, then we instinctively try to survive by any means possible.

But if we know that there is an even more frightening and embarrassing danger, then we wish we could die immediately.

When a disaster is so great that one would rather wish to die, then "despair" is the hopelessness of wanting to die but not being able to do so.

It is in this second sense that "despair" can be said to be the disease that kills. This pain comes from the struggle and grip of the ego psychologically between the objective things and the internal opposites of human thinking, which are mutually dependent and mutually exclusive.

The saddest thing that can happen to a person is to lose his conscience and soul, to become insensitive, and to die without dying, which is the "death" (at døe Døden).

For death means the end of everything, but "death" is the heaviest experience of death for the living person; and if man experiences this death in a moment, he will experience it for the rest of his life.

If man dies of "despair," as he dies of disease, then what is eternal in him, that is, the ego, will also die as the body dies of disease.

However, this is not possible. The death of "despair" keeps reviving it (itself). The person of "despair" cannot die, just as "the sword is not attached to the mind", so "despair" does not destroy that which is eternal.

The ego in the depths of "despair" will not die, and its

unceasing vitality will not be extinguished.

However, "despair" is a kind of self-destruction, although it is a weak and powerless self-destruction, unable to do what it wants to do.

It wants to destroy itself but cannot do so, and this weakness becomes a new form of destruction in which "despair" still cannot do what it wants to do, cannot destroy itself.

This is a kind of Potentsation, or a matrix of spheres of influence.

This is the gangrene in "despair", or the non-stop inflammatory symptoms that keep eroding to the depths of weakness and self-destruction.

It is no consolation to the one who feels "despair" to say that "despair" cannot destroy him.

On the contrary, this consolation is a kind of destruction, which continues to contribute to the corrosive pain, to the erosion of life, because it is for this reason that he feels "desperate" (not "was desperate"): he cannot destroy himself, he cannot destroy himself.

He has no way to destroy himself, no way to get rid of

himself, no way to turn into nothingness. This is the self-propagating formula of "despair," the fever that rises in the disease of the ego.

A "desperate" person feels "desperate" for something. It appears to be so for a moment, but only for a moment.

In that moment, the real "despair" will appear, or "despair" will appear in its true form. Because he was "desperate" for something, he was actually "desperate" for himself, and now he wants to get rid of himself.

For example, a person who is ambitious and whose motto is "To be president or not to be anything at all" ends up not being able to be president and therefore feels "desperate" about it.

But there is another interpretation of this: because he couldn't be president, he can't stand himself now.

The result is that he does not feel "desperate" because he cannot be president, but "desperate" for himself because he has not become president.

On the contrary, this ego, if it had become president, would have been complacent (in another sense, it would have been a "despair").

But this ego is the most unbearable thing for him in the ongoing existence of life.

In a deeper sense, it is not the failure to be president that makes him unbearable, but the ego that does not make him president.

Or, more specifically, the thing he can't stand is the fact that he can't get rid of himself. If he did become president, he would be desperate to get rid of himself.

But in the end, if he doesn't become president, he won't be able to get rid of himself desperately. Basically, the "despair" in his mind is the same because he doesn't have the self he wants, he's not himself.

If he does become president, he will not own himself, he will get rid of himself; and if he does not become president, he will feel "desperate" about not being able to get rid of himself.

So to say that a "desperate" person is destroying himself is a very superficial statement (they probably have never seen a "desperate" person, including themselves).

But this is exactly what the "desperate" person wants to do but cannot do, and thus feels miserable because "desperation" ignites something in the ego that neither can burn nor be destroyed.

Therefore, I lovc to cling to "despair" of something, but it is not really "despair". It is just the beginning, or as a doctor would say when talking about a disease, a medical term, it is still in latency.

The next thing is that there will be a preview of the onset of the disease, that is, the idea of clinging to what you want to have. A young woman feels obsession with love because of the loss of the person she is attached to.

It may be because of his death, or because he cheated on her, and she feels the obsession of losing something. This cannot be interpreted as a symptom of an attack; no, she is just clinging to her own love, an obsession that is hard to let go.

This ego of hers, if she had become his "lover", she would be happy and unwilling to abandon it, but now this ego has become an ego without "him", and it has become a kind of psychological torture for her.

This ego, which would have been her treasure (although in another sense it may also be a source of "despair"), has become a "void" that makes her sad and unhappy because "he" is dead.

Or it can be a disgusting nuisance, because it reminds her of a society in which men and women deviate from normal moral standards in order to seek illicit emotional and sexual interests.

Feeling "desperate" for herself and wanting to get rid of herself in "desperation" is the formula of all "desperation".

Therefore, the second form of "despair", wanting to be oneself in "despair", can be extrapolated back to the first form, that is, not wanting to be oneself in despair.

Just as we previously included the form of "not wanting to be oneself in despair" into the form of "wanting to be oneself in despair".

A person who is in despair will desperately want to be himself. But if he desperately wants to be himself, he certainly does not want to get rid of himself.

This may be true on the surface, but if you look closely, the contradiction here is clearly the same.

The self he "desperately" wants to be is not his present self (because wanting to be the real self is the opposite of desperation), that is, he wants the self to resist the force that is setting it up at that time.

However, no matter how much he "desires", he cannot do it; no matter how hard he "desires", the power is still stronger than it is, forcing him to be dominated by fame and fortune, and to be the self he does not want to be.

But this is how he gets rid of himself. He gets rid of his present self in order to be the self he dreams of being. If he could be the self he wanted to be, he would be complacent (although in another sense, it would still be like 'despair').

But now he is forced to be the self he does not want to be, and this is his suffering: he cannot get rid of himself.

Socrates, in proving the immortality of the soul, says that unlike the disease of the flesh, which destroys the flesh, the disease of the soul (sin) has no way to destroy the soul.

Therefore, if one says that "despair" cannot destroy one's ego (which is the paradoxical pain of despair), then it proves that there is something eternal in the heart of a person.

If there is nothing eternal in a person's heart, he cannot be "desperate"; and if "desperation" would destroy his ego, then there would be no "desperation" at all.

This is the disease of "despair", this obsession with

self-love in the ego, this disease of "death". The person who is "desperate" is terminally ill.

This meaning is different from any other disease. This disease attacks the most important organs of the human body, and the person cannot see but cannot die. Death is not the end of the disease, but it is often the end of the existence of life.

It is impossible to get rid of this disease by death, because this disease of love and clinging and the pain of not getting it (and death) is precisely because one cannot die without getting it.

This is the state of "despair". No matter how much the "desperate" person dodges it, no matter whether or not he is lucky (lykkes) to lose his ego (especially the kind of "desperation" that does not know that he is in "desperation"), and loses it unknowingly.

Eternity will still prove that he is in a state of "despair", pinning his ego to him, and the pain of not being able to get rid of his ego will always be a pain in his bones, making him understand that what he thought he had managed to get rid of was in fact only his illusion.

"Eternity" has to be done because having a free willed

ego and yielding to the ego to seek the possibility of returning to one's true self is the most meaningful metamorphosis of the existence of life in the universe, an endless sublimation and metamorphosis, but it is also the eternal demand of the truth for man.

According to Kierkegaard, "despair" is not accepting one's unwanted self, or clinging to one's present self, and eventually "losing oneself", which is the original sin in Christianity.

"Despair" is original sin. From despair comes faith that transcends the status quo, which is the "leap of faith" that can remove original sin. Those who are born in a state of confusion and die in despair do not necessarily know that they are "desperate".

Nor do they necessarily feel pain. The lowest level of "despair" is the person who is ignorant of the fact that he or she is born and dies in a state of confusion and is preoccupied with worldly things.

Others realize that they are "desperate" for certain worldly things, but still do not have the awareness of the eternity of the self.

Others become aware of the self, eternity, and the

weakness of their "despair" for worldly things, and for this reason they do not want to accept this self and fall into another kind of "despair".

Further, some people decide to give in to the weakness of self-acceptance, to let God take its course, while acknowledging their eternal nature (similar to the immortality of the soul).

Further, they must be willing to accept themselves as they are; they may choose to regain hope and escape from "despair" by a "leap of faith".

However, they may also choose to take "despair" as the ultimate truth and place themselves in eternal "despair".

Thus, people have different "despairs" at different "levels" of existence. A sensual person feels "despair" for worldly people, things, and events.

Rational people are "desperate" for rejecting themselves or not finding the ultimate truth. Belief is the only way out of "despair". Choosing to believe in and respect a certain proposition, doctrine, religion or someone is the only way to realize oneself.

The "faith" of Kierkegaard is a "metamorphic leap of

faith", a faith that transcends the boundaries of the self, a faith that believes that the self has unlimited potential and can be realized.

Second, the leap of faith metamorphosis and sublimation

Kierkegaard considers himself a prophet of counter-cultural Christianity, and he abhors Hegel's ideas, believing that Hegel has distorted the facts and images of the Bible and the prophets of authentic Christianity into a cultural Christian faith.

From his point of view, this cultural Christianity was not authentic Christianity at all. From the description and analysis of his late book, "The Crusade Against Christendom," it is clear that in a society where everyone is a "Christian

The true respect for the Christian religion has apparently disappeared. Hegel's influence on Christianity in Germany and the Nordic countries was twofold.

First, Hegel merged religion and philosophy, rationalizing Christian faith and theologizing it.

Secondly, Hegel's theory of statecraft adapted to the social trend of the national church. Kierkegaard was strongly opposed to the ideological trend of theological discernment and the social trend of nationalization of the church.

Therefore, he is not only recognized as a pioneer or leader of existentialist philosophy, but also respected by neoconservatism as a pioneer in thought and action.

In "Fear and Trembling," Kierkegaard says that the value of Abraham's son's sacrifice was his leap from reason to religion, his belief in the power of God, his belief that all things were possible, that miracles would happen, and that God sent an angel at the last moment to prevent Abraham from killing his son.

He said, "There is no faith without reflection through rational thinking. This "metamorphic leap of faith" opened Abraham's spiritual eyes to see the salvation that God had prepared, which was invisible to the human eye.

Kierkegaard describes and analyzes the anxiety that arises when a person is faced with a choice, and that this decision is a metamorphic leap that cannot be deduced by logical thinking.

Kierkegaard believes that the fall of man is also an irrational metamorphosis. However, there is another kind of metamorphic leap, the metamorphic leap of faith, which also cannot be deduced from life or work situations.

When one is faced with a deadly disease or insurmountable anxiety, the metamorphic leap of faith can help one overcome the situation and get through it.

In Kierkegaard's theory of metamorphosis, there are three stages of the metamorphosis of faith, but these stages are not the kind of stages that have a beginning and an end, a moment in time, but include aesthetic, ethical and religious, and these three stages interact with each other and influence each other in a state that cannot be clearly separated.

For example, in the final religious stage, ethical thought and aesthetics are still present. In particular, his view of ethical religion as a subjective reference is based on his unique aesthetic view, while the sense of beauty cannot be reasoned with the study of the nature of thought and the process of science.

And 'God' is a judgment that can be deduced from the ultimate reasoning of all actions and thoughts, therefore, it is even more impossible to prove the existence of God by reasoning and logic.

The aesthetic stage is a very noteworthy position in his study of the analysis and criticism of problems and events.

The aesthetic phase is characterized by a difficult entanglement with human existence, which is difficult to unravel or clarify, and the aesthetics he speaks of here does not refer to the course of aesthetics itself or to art, but to a "standard" of measurement.

The "standard" is whether each person and each thing satisfies his or her own aesthetics, that is, the biblical description of the "beauty" of what the Jews call good and beautiful in terms of what is good or right, which is the stage of aesthetics.

Thus, he criticized the Roman pope for having had an inner love that had reached the point of indulgence in pagan customs and the morally corrupt Greek Roman art.

In the ethical stage, Kierkegaard proposed the demonic form of thinking that reflects the nature of the object, which means "self- seclusion", that is, not coming out of oneself.

The opposite of this "self-seclusion" is love, which can lead one out of the "self-seclusion" situation and overcome the "demonic".

This characteristic of love can lead to a certain nature of connection between man and man or between man and love. In other words, in the ethical stage, love overcomes isolation, which leads to responsibility, and through responsibility, the ethical stage can be reached.

The religious stage transcends the aesthetic and ethical stages, and can be divided into two types, "Religion A" and "Religion B", whose representative figures are "Socrates" and "Jesus" respectively, both of which have in common their views on God and are existentialists.

The religion of "Religion A" or "Socrates" believes that "truth" can be found in human existence, that is, the basic "truth" exists in human beings themselves.

"Socrates wanted to use dialectic and existentialism to call truth out of human existence, and he did so in two ways: one is irony, which means searching for truth through radical inquiry.

The other way is midwifery. The teacher does not simply teach the truth directly, but helps people to discover the truth that is in them, and to bring forth knowledge that is in them.

From the existential difference, each individual being can no longer be considered merely as an existing being in the present (existence). It will be transcended and associated with the whole.

In the vision of the future, in the source from the past, its being is defined intrinsically and temporally. Socrates can be regarded as the founder of humanism, which can be considered as one of the quasi-religions.

But Socrates did not transform the total state of human existence, because such transformation can only be achieved in "Religion B".

"Religion B believes that truth cannot be found in man, so God must enter from outside of man and teach him, and so God enters into man in the form of Christ.

This is another metamorphic leap that God made through the incarnation of Christ, producing a metamorphic leap across time. For there is an "infinite difference in quality" between God and man, and man is not only finite, but sinful.

Therefore, in the final analysis, man must embrace the "truth" with inner passion through determination, that is, the "metamorphic leap of faith".

Without the metamorphosis of faith, we would become a religion of reason, but this is definitely not authentic Christianity. The way of God is higher than the way of man, and the incarnation is absolutely paradoxical and irrational.

The incarnation is indeed a great mystery, and it is a fact that no one has understood the truth of the incarnation for thousands of years. It was only when Jesus came back in the last days and opened up the mystery of the incarnation to mankind that we came to understand the truth of the incarnation.

Here are a few excerpts from God's Word: "The incarnation is the manifestation of God in the flesh, and God in the image of flesh working among the created ones.

Therefore, if it is said to be incarnation, it must first be flesh, and it must be flesh with a normal human nature, which is the minimum.

In fact, the meaning of the incarnation of God is God who works in the flesh and lives in the flesh, and the substance of God became flesh and became man. (From "The Substance of the "Incarnation" Where God Is")

"The incarnate God is called Christ, and Christ is the

incarnation of the Spirit of God, and this incarnation is not like any other fleshly man.

The difference is that Christ is not of blood but is the incarnation of the Spirit, and he has a normal human nature and a full divine nature that no man has.

His normal human nature was for the maintenance of all normal activity in the flesh, and his divine nature was for the work of God himself. (From "The Substance of Christ is Obedience to the Will of the Father")

"The Christ who has a normal human nature is an incarnation with a normal human nature, a normal reason, and a normal brain.

The so-called 'actualization' means that God became man, the Spirit became flesh, and to put it more clearly, God Himself dwelt in a fleshly body with normal humanity.

This is 'actualization', that is, the Word became flesh. (From "The Substance of the "Incarnation" Where God Is")

"Because he is a man of the substance of God, he is higher than any created human being, higher than any human being who can do the work of God.

Therefore, among all those who have the same human shell as him, among all those who have human nature, he alone is God himself in the flesh, and all others are created human beings.

Unlike the incarnate God, in whom the main thing is the divine nature in addition to the human nature.

Humanity can be seen in the appearance of the flesh and can be found in daily life, while divinity is not easily found.

It is because the divine nature is published under the premise of human nature, and it is not as transcendent as human imagination, so it is the divine nature that is the least discoverable by man.

Since it is said that God became flesh, His essence is the union of humanity and divinity, and this union is called God Himself, and it is God Himself on earth. (From "The Substance of the "Incarnation" Where God Is")

From the Word of God, we see that the incarnation is the Spirit of God, and that when the incarnation is put on, it is the Spirit of God materialized in a body with normal humanity and normal thinking, and becomes an ordinary, normal human being to work and speak among people.

This incarnation has a normal human nature and a full divine nature. Although this physical body is normal in appearance, it can perform God's work, speak God's voice, lead mankind, and save mankind because it has a full divine nature.

This complete divinity refers to the original nature of God, the essence of God's holiness and righteousness, all that God is, and the all-powerful wisdom of God, which the Spirit of God possesses.

This incarnation is Christ, the actual God who came to work on earth to save mankind.

Outwardly, Christ is an ordinary, normal son of man, but he is substantially different from all created human beings.

The indoctrinated man has only a human nature, without any divine substance; but Christ not only has a normal human nature, but mainly he has a full divine nature.

Therefore he has the substance of God, and is able to represent God completely, to speak all truths as God, to express the nature of God and all that he is, and to give truth, the way, and life, which no created human being can attain.

No matter how He speaks the word of God or the works of God, He is still living in His normal human nature, a normal flesh, and not supernatural at all.

This proves that God has come in the flesh and that God has become an ordinary man. It is this ordinary, normal flesh that accomplishes the fact that "the word was manifested in the flesh", which is the actual God who became flesh.

It is because Christ is fully divine that He can represent God, that He can speak the truth, and that He can save mankind; it is because Christ is fully divine that He can speak the Word directly and not convey it.

It is because Christ is fully divine that he can speak the truth at all times and in all places to provide for people, to pour it out, to shepherd people, and to lead the whole human race; it is because Christ is fully divine that he possesses the identity and substance of God, and we can say that he is the Word made flesh, the actual God himself.

Third, the incarnation of the Word

The greatest mystery of the incarnation is not whether

he was tall or normal, but that inside this ordinary man, there was a hidden divinity.

This hidden divinity is what no one can discover or see, just like when the Lord Jesus came to work, no one could know that the Lord Jesus is the Christ, the Son of God, if they did not hear His voice and experience His words and works.

Therefore, the incarnation of God is the best way for God to come among people in secret. When the Lord Jesus came, no one could see from the outside that the Lord Jesus was the Christ, the incarnation, and no one could discover that the divine nature was still hidden in his humanity.

It was not until the Lord Jesus spoke the truth and worked for the salvation of mankind that people began to follow him when they discovered the authority and power of his word; when Jesus rose from the dead and revealed himself to man, then people really saw that Jesus was the incarnate Christ, the manifestation of God.

If he does not speak the truth and work, no one can follow him, and if he does not testify that he is the Christ, the manifestation of God, no one can know him.

In man's conception and imagination, if God is really incarnate, it should be a superhuman incarnation, like a great man, majestic and tall in appearance, with power and authority in speech and miracles, that is the incarnate God.

If you look like an ordinary person with normal human nature, that is definitely not the incarnation. Let's think back to when the Lord Jesus came in the flesh and spoke.

No matter how much he spoke the truth and the voice of God, people did not know him, and when people witnessed Jesus, they were saying, "Isn't that the son of Joseph? Isn't that the Nazarene?"

Why do people say this about him? It was because Jesus had a normal human appearance, an ordinary man, not the image of a great man, and people did not accept him.

In fact, since the incarnation was made, it was necessary to have a normal human nature, so that people could see that the incarnation that God put on was a normal human body, a normal human being in appearance.

If the incarnation is a transcendent person, a special person, not a person with a normal human nature, then the meaning of the incarnation is lost.

Therefore, Christ had to have a normal human nature in order to prove that he was "the Word" made flesh.

Therefore, Kierkegaard advocates "subjective truth" and lays the philosophical foundation for neo-orthodox theology, a theology that rediscovers the Word of God and places faith in an exalted position, treating reason as a mere tool for understanding the Word of God.

It is because of the paradoxical nature of the fundamental truths of God's Word that the law of non-contradiction $(A \neq -A)$ of logic does not work in Christian theology, because God's will (thought) is higher than man's will (thought), and God's way (method) exceeds man's way (method).

In this respect, Kierkegaard was the pioneer of neo-orthodox theology, so apologetic theologians made him their ally.

Kierkegaard's definition of truth, especially as it relates to God and human existence, is an objective unknown that man seizes through his deepest passion and holds on to it.

But when the subjective, inner truth is the truth, the objective definition of truth becomes paradoxical. The Incarnation is an "absolute paradox," so it can only be disclosed and understood by faith.

Hegel's attempt to place paradox as a logical concept in a universal, harmonious, rational system of truth is contrary to the true meaning of paradox, and turns it into a symbolic representation of abstract philosophical concepts.

For Kierkegaard, Jesus is indeed God and indeed man, but the concentration of truth in one person is a logical contradiction.

He therefore rejects Hegel as a new and revealed truth, asking us to decide whether to accept or reject Jesus Christ as Lord. For a person to have a relationship with God, it must be a personal decision, not an abstract reasoning.

As emphasized earlier, Kierkegaard's Fear and Trembling, The Metamorphic Leap of Faith, speaks of the anxiety that arises when one is faced with a choice; and this decision is a metamorphic leap that cannot be logically deduced.

According to Kierkegaard, the fall of man is at the same time an irrational metamorphic leap. However, there is another kind of metamorphic leap, the "metamorphic leap of faith", which cannot be deduced from the situation.

When one is faced with a deadly disease or insurmountable anxiety, the "metamorphic leap of faith" helps one to overcome with strength of will and power (defects, mistakes, difficult and dangerous situations, unfavorable phenomena, etc.).

For the apostle Paul, the most important things in life are: faith, hope and love. Among them, love surpasses all others (1 Corinthians 13:13).

Paul saw faith, hope, and love as Christian virtues, and therefore faith, hope, and love became important symbols of Christianity. Faith is the foundation of faith, hope comes from faith, and with faith comes hope, and with hope comes love.

Jesus said, "A man who receives a prophet in the name of the prophet will receive the reward of the prophet; and a man who receives a righteous man in the name of the righteous will receive the reward of the righteous.

But whoever gives a cup of cold water to one of these boys to drink in the name of the disciples, I tell you the truth, this man shall not receive a reward. (Mt 10:42)."

The practice of love may be easy, as Jesus said, but there are very difficult practices of love, such as loving your enemies, which is beyond the reach of ordinary people, and most difficult of all, laying down your life for your friends.

Jesus said, "Greater love hath no man than this, that a man lay down his life for his friends. If you do what I command you, you are my friends. (John 15:13)."

Jesus Christ set a wonderful example for us by His example of redeeming love on the cross. Paul believed that of faith, hope and love, love is the greatest power.

For faith and hope benefit themselves, but love glorifies God and benefits both man and self.

"Faith" is the first step to an attitude of complete trust and dependence or belief in supernatural things (such as God, God), but it is also the most difficult commitment to fulfill, and that is why there are lukewarm believers.

From a certain position or perspective, Kierkegaard's view of faith or questions is that rational people know that the world is full of unknowns and impossibilities, with boundaries and limits set everywhere.

In the face of the unknown and impossible, the rational person can only choose to give up or deny, and feel sad about what is lost forever.

At this point, people can only rely on the "metamorphic leap of faith" to make use of the amazement and awe of the mysteries of the universe and life, to form a doctrine of exhortation and punishment for good and to teach the world, to make people devoutly faithful, and to use the power of faith to overcome doubt and reason, which are usually considered impossible.

Only a seemingly absurd faith can restore the hope that "all things are possible". The author of Hebrews explains faith as follows: "What, then, is faith? Faith is the assurance of things hoped for and the certainty of things not seen (11:1)."

Faith is central to the beliefs of all religions, and Christianity is no exception.

In addition to the Gospel of John, which uses Abraham as an example to discuss issues related to faith (8:31ff), several epistles also emphasize the importance of faith, including the Romans of Paul and the Hebrews, both of which use Abraham as a model of faith.

Abraham was the ancestor of the Israelites and the model of their faith. He was the first person to whom God spoke; he was uniquely chosen by God.

As soon as he heard God's call, he decided to abandon Harran, also known as Huron, formerly known as Carrhae, an ancient city in southeastern Turkey, which was easily accessible by land and water.

It is an ancient city in southeastern Turkey, located 38 kilometers southeast of the provincial capital of Şanlıurfa, now a small Arab village, on the eastern bank of the Beylih River, a tributary of the upper Euphrates, about 10 kilometers from the mouth of the confluence.

He traveled to the land of Canaan (today's Palestine), where water was scarce, with a simple bag and a religiously devout heart, clinging to God's promise: "If you will have faith and take this great risk, you will become the founder of a great nation.

He did not argue, he was not in a state of mind where he was caught between two or more contradictions and could not decide which one to choose, but entrusted himself completely to God and embarked on a new pilgrimage.

The first thing he did in every place he visited was to build an altar to worship God. God asked Abraham to give up his wealthy life, which on the surface was an extremely difficult request.

But in the Promised Land, a greater and more tangible blessing awaited him. People always think that it is more than worthwhile to sacrifice fame and fortune for the sake of truth.

In fact, behind the correct reflection of objective things and their laws in the human mind is often a wider sky.

After these things, God wanted to test Abraham, and called to him, "Abraham! Abraham answered, "Lord! Here I am." And God said, "Take your son, your only son, your beloved Isaac, and go to the land of Moriah, and offer him as a burnt offering on the mountain which I have shown you to reach.

Early one morning, all the preparations for the journey were made in Abraham's house. After Abraham said goodbye to Sarah, the faithful servant Eleazar followed him until he had to return.

Abraham and Isaac rode in unison on their donkeys, and came to the mountain of Moriah.

Although Abraham was calm and prepared for the sacrifice, when he turned to draw the knife, Isaac saw him clench his left hand in pain and a shudder spread through his body - but, nevertheless, Abraham drew the knife.

Abraham pulled out the knife anyway. ...... After that, they returned to the house and Sarah ran to meet them, but Isaac had lost his faith.

They didn't say a word about it, and Isaac didn't tell anyone about his encounter, nor did Abraham ever suspect that anyone had seen it.

On the third day, Abraham lifted up his eyes and looked into the distance. And Abraham turned to his servants and said to them, "Wait here with the donkeys; I will go there with the boy and worship, and then I will come back to you.

And Abraham put the wood for the burnt offering on his son Isaac, and he took the fire and the knife in his hand, and they went together.

And Isaac said to his father Abraham, "Father! And Abraham said, "My son! Here I am." And Isaac said to him,

"See, we have fire and wood, but where is the lamb for the burnt offering?

Abraham said to him, "My son, God himself will prepare the lamb for the burnt offering. So they walked together.

And they came to the place which God had shown them, and Abraham built an altar there, and laid the wood, and bound his son Isaac, and laid him on the wood of the altar. And Abraham stretched out his hand and took the sword, and prepared to kill his son.

And the angel of the LORD called to him from heaven, saying, "Abraham! Abraham!" And he said, "Here am I." And the angel said to him, "You shall not lay a hand on this boy, nor do him any harm at all.

Now I know that you fear God, because you did not leave your son, your only son, unto me.

And Abraham lifted up his eyes, and beheld, and behold, a ram with its two horns fastened in a thick little tree. And Abraham took the ram, and offered it for a burnt offering in place of his son.

And Abraham called the name of the place Jehovah Elohim[a], and to this day men say, "In the mountain of the LORD there will be a preparation.

Abraham's test of faith reached its peak in the killing of his son for sacrifice. It was not God's purpose for Abraham to kill his son and sacrifice him; He simply hated the burnt offering of human sacrifices.

Kierkegaard interprets the story of Abraham from a very unique perspective, "not so much to make Abraham easy to understand, but to make his interpretation more comprehensive".

Because Abraham hides himself, his paradox is that he is not only irreconcilable with universality, but he even rejects any possibility of disclosure.

In other words, in Kierkegaard's view, Abraham is inherently incomprehensible, and "it is impossible for the knights of faith to understand each other".

Abraham, the father of faith, if not misunderstood by later generations, stood on an absolute other side, "he reflected God".

God's purpose was to raise up Abraham's faith and obedience to God, so that he might become a model of faith for future generations.

If Abraham did not have enough faith in God and would have disobeyed God's command, there would have been no killing of the son and sacrifice, and certainly no question of ethical violations.

If Abraham had faith in God and was willing to obey God to kill his son, God's purpose of testing Abraham was achieved, and there was no need for him to commit an unethical act.

In Fear and Trembling, Kierkegaard says that the value of Abraham's sacrifice was that he leapt from reason to religion, believing in the power of God and that all things were possible and miracles would happen.

In the end, God sent an angel to stop Abraham from killing his son. He said, "If you don't go through reason, you can't have faith.

This "metamorphic leap of faith" opened his spiritual eyes to see the salvation that God had prepared, which was invisible to the naked eye.

The central thread of all Kierkegaard's explanations focuses on these concepts: aesthetics, immediacy, concealment, ethics, universality, disclosure, infinite abandonment, and faith. Faith is not the opening immediacy, but the final immediacy. The directness that is the beginning is aesthetics.

Man prefers to rest in the present and not to face a strange and unknowable future, but life extends every second towards a future full of variables.

Abraham was able to face the future with courage because he entrusted his life to God. Just as we pray for the hearts and souls of many brothers and sisters in morning prayer meetings and Sunday services, the pastor often leads us in "resurrection" in our prayers.

We can often boldly say out loud, "I believe in the resurrection! But it is not easy to maintain the hope of resurrection when you are physically and emotionally wounded and your life force is weak.

The Sickness unto Death (ET, 1941) talks about what he considers to be a truly deadly disease.

For human beings, what Kierkegaard called "deadly disease" refers to conditions that cause pain, abnormal behavior, and even death.

(2) Four theorems of the existence of freedom of will

The first theorem: Empirical objects are not the motives of good will.

The empirical object cannot be the motive of the good will. Kant believes that the universal basis of moral law cannot come from empirical objects.

Since empirical objects vary widely and change constantly with time and place, it is impossible to formulate a universal and necessary moral law based on empirical objects, so it is impossible for people to decide moral actions based on empirical objects.

Second theorem: "Moral laws" are not constructed according to personal happiness.

A "moral law" cannot be based on personal happiness. According to Kant, happiness is always related to a specific "empirical object", and the happiness that an "empirical object" can bring varies from time to time and from occasion to occasion.

Moreover, everyone's definition of happiness is different, and sometimes people's happiness is even based on other people's misfortune, so personal happiness cannot be a "moral law.

The third theorem: autonomy is the principle of universal legislation.

The freedom of the will to exist in life requires that the norms willed by the will of man can at all times be regarded as principles of universal legislation.

This means to make your standard a universal law that everyone can willingly accept. When a law is found in people's minds, Condor believes that its universality can be verified by a "generalizability test".

Think about this: If every rational person uses your standard, will it create a contradiction in perception or desire?

If there is a problem, it means that your standard cannot be universalized and thus cannot be a moral law. A moral law is a law of obligatory moral standards.

Like rules, a moral code is a codification by a special creator of moral requirements that reflect the natural development of a society's moral conscience.

A moral code is composed of standards of behavior

practiced by the overwhelming majority and those that are often violated but still valued, such as obligations. Thus, the codifier of the moral code is faced with a contradictory task.

The codifier must respond to the same forms of standards of behavior that have been handed down through the history of that society, as well as to the requirements that could be implemented before they were practiced.

The Moses' Laws and their typical counterpart in Hebrew society can provide examples of moral law. Jean Jacques Rousseau (1712-1778) composed the moral law in a positive form agreeable to all, and in a negative form objectionable to all.

However, all attempts to establish a universal moral law were doomed to failure because they were based on a false premise.

The idea that those rules, once formed, can be applied in all circumstances and in all historical situations (dogmatism, formalism).

The impossibility of establishing a universal moral law led some thinkers to look for a general norm that would abolish the rules of conduct and moral imperatives (rationalism, supreme imperative).

According to Kant, there are two kinds of imperatives of conduct: one is the absolute imperative, also known as the supreme imperative, which is unconditional.

The absolute command is the command to obey practical reason, and the act governed by this command has no purpose other than the act itself.

Kant argues that morality is moral because it is innate, universal, and necessary, and that in order to achieve this standard, we must look to the innate rule of reason, which is the moral categorical imperative.

The moral law is a criterion of self-discipline, which is contingent, and is an end in itself, without any conditions.

The moral law is inevitably related to the concept of obligation, and must be born purely out of obligation, morality for morality's sake, and obligation for obligation's sake.

The other is a hypothetical command, a command to pursue a certain purpose. The behavior governed by such a command is not subject to reason itself, but to some purpose, i.e., the concept of otherness.

For example, if one wants to be rewarded, one should obey the commands of one's parents. However, this is simply not possible in the life of a human group.

For example, if everyone borrowed money and did not return it, no one would be willing to lend money to anyone in the future, so it cannot be a moral law to borrow money and not return it.

In the first and second theorems, we can see that Kant opposes to base the moral law on empirical objects (qualities), and he advocates to base the moral law on forms, that is, on the moral law itself.

He argues that the moral law is based on form, i.e., on the moral law itself, rather than on its empirical content, which varies widely and is therefore not universal and necessary, while form, by leaving out the empirical content and retaining only the pure form, is universal and necessary.

The fourth theorem: Self-regulation of morality is the true morality

Freedom is self-discipline, and only self-discipline morality, not other-discipline morality, is true morality. This theorem means that the above-mentioned moral law is not imposed on you externally by others, but is provided to you by your own free will.

Self-discipline is the highest principle of freedom, and free will legislates for itself. What is valuable about morality is that one does it of one's own volition and is not forced to do so. If a person gives up his place to an old man only because he is forced to do so by the eyes of others, we generally do not consider him to be a moral person.

(3) The Three Stages of Life Experience

According to Kierkegaard, there are three stages of existential life experience that a person may go through on the way to believe in and respect religious ideas, doctrines, religions, or people enough to use them as a guide or example for his or her actions.

The aesthetic, ethical, and religious stages. The difference and transition between the aesthetic and ethical stages is explained more clearly in Either/Or, while the distinction between the ethical and religious stages is explained in more detail in Fear and Trembling.

Kierkegaard summarizes three different stages of life:

the first is the aesthetic stage, the second is the ethical stage of responsibility, and the third is the faith stage of total commitment.

The aesthetic stage is the initial and direct stage in which the individual envisages his or her situation, while the ethical stage is the intermediate stage in which things gradually develop from one stage to another.

The final religious stage is the highest ideological awareness and spiritual cultivation of life, i.e., cultivation, and the sense of life.

The three stages of life can be seen as the process of personal experience toward God.

1. Aesthetic Development Process

The aesthetic stage is a special or particular aspect of a person or thing that is governed by various feelings, impulses and emotions in the life of the individual.

In this stage, people "live for themselves" and individuals adopt a way of life that aims at directly satisfying their own desires, so they tend to fall deeply into the wrong quagmire and cannot extricate themselves from the pleasures of the flesh.

Life is full of corruption, moral decay and shameless behavior. In other words, it can be said that people at this stage are hedonists.

Sometimes people in this stage will be moved, happy, and other positive meanings for loved ones or objects, and can be remembered for a period of time or longer by the actions or words of one or more people, in order to glorify their own degradation.

For example, the artist would say that this is a way of life, that this kind of life will bring people some kind of pleasure. Don Juan is a typical representative of the aesthetic stage, according to Chicco.

Don Juan is a well-known legendary figure in Spain, and many people regard him as a synonym for the "Saint of Love" and the "Sire of Love".

Don Juan liked to pursue young and beautiful women and was eager to have sexual relations with them, but never thought of making a commitment to a woman, to be with her for life, and to assume moral responsibility.

Kierkegaard says that Don Juan's lifestyle eventually leads to emptiness, despair and boredom. For the repetition of pleasure is tiresome, and it is unlikely that people will be able to live a life of pleasure without stopping.

The goal of the aesthetic class is to maximize pleasure, to counteract the boredom of life's repetitive, uninspired existence through the constant pursuit of happiness.

Kierkegaard uses love as an example, pointing out that love in this class is romantic, sensual, direct, and immediate. It does not require any rational explanation, does not seek consistency of decision, and is purely impulsive and contingent.

It seeks pleasure and freedom, but is unwilling to commit itself to love, believing that responsibility will bring about the loss of true self and love.

But Kierkegaard points out that this life is not immune to anxiety. The aesthete's emotions and reactions are dependent on external things such as the environment, beauty, and wealth, and they do not know that there is a self, that their self is fragmented.

When their freedom allows them to see more pleasures, they are overwhelmed by the infinite possibilities. They are afraid of discovering other greater pleasures that they "should" pursue, afraid of moral responsibility to reduce enjoyment.

When the elements that make them happy are removed, they become unhappy and want to try to change the environment. But when the environment cannot be changed, they feel they can no longer be their own free selves and are reluctant to be themselves.

Kierkegaard believes that what the aesthete lacks is the inner subjectivity of self-recognition brought about by choices. Ultimately, the body or mind feels very uncomfortable and hopes are not fulfilled.If one wants to get out of the dilemma, one needs to pursue an alternative way of life, i.e., an ethical way of life.At this point, the individual wishes to be guided by universal ethical and moral laws, i.e., to move from the aesthetic stage to the ethical stage.

2. Ethical development process

The special or peculiar feature of the person or thing in the ethical stage is the individual's willingness to be guided by reason, to restrain one's passions, and to combine one's desires with social obligations.

In this stage, the individual "lives for others", assuming that he or she is in the same situation as others and thinking about them, and no longer only about his or her own interests.

Since this stage requires the individual to assume certain responsibilities for others, the individual forms an ethical relationship with others, and no longer ignores the ethical responsibilities of the individual to others, as in the case of Don Juan in the aesthetic stage.

In the wording and intent of Kierkegaard's writing, this stage is represented by the character Judge William in "Either-Or," who emphasizes his struggle for freedom, his struggle for others, and reminds himself to be a good husband.

At first glance, Don Juan in the aesthetic stage and Judge William in the ethical stage are two very different and opposite poles, and may even be unrelated.

In fact, the ethical stage is sublimated from the aesthetic stage, emphasizing that this state already exists in practice, and that romantic love in the aesthetic stage is elevated to marital love through a certain personal metamorphosis and a choice to assume ethical responsibilities.

The ethical hierarchy described by Kierkegaard is a

universal, rational ethical system that unifies the confusion, instability, and personal disorientation of the aesthetic hierarchy.

The ethical person is determined to realize the self through the ethical life, to establish a stable self through the consistency of speech and action, the implementation of commitments and future plans, and to become a real being in society.

The ethicist responds to the aesthete's view of marriage by arguing that romantic love is difficult to sustain unless it is given an ethical relationship such as marriage.

Only when two people are united by marriage does it have the possibility of lasting a lifetime. This does not diminish the freedom and mutual need of love, but rather in marriage, these originally physical pleasures become eternal.

Responsibility is not given because one does not want to do it, but only because society expects one's role to be fulfilled.

The responsibility that society expects from both partners in a marriage is precisely to love each other, so that responsibility is actually complementary to love, and beauty can still exist in responsibility.

This ethical view states that the individual is part of a universal moral community, and that the individual's desires do not conflict with the moral community, the public good, because moral responsibility in this system is given by the community.

The individual is not repressed in the community, but through his participation in the rules of the community, he achieves a more virtuous self. Thus, the goodness and responsibility that exists in the individual is the public goodness and responsibility, and thus the individual can be justified in doing good.

Therefore, the ethicist, responding to the aesthete's fear of losing his own self by having to pay a great moral responsibility, points out that the moral law provides the individual with a satisfying model of life, with only a few opportunities to ask the individual to sacrifice for others.

In society, the responsibility of the individual is limited, so the moral life is not strenuous, unintentional, or unattainable; the social morality can be shared by the community.

In response to the ethicist, Kierkegaard points out that the ethicist thinks that moral responsibility can be easily achieved by simply fulfilling the responsibilities assigned to him by society.

Moreover, reliance on the moral standards of the group becomes an excuse for people not to take responsibility for their own decisions. Kierkegaard points out that in practice the system of the ethicist is equally unstable and ultimately desperate.

He asks how the ethicist can be sure that the standards of morality set by society will remain unchanged?

If the law can change from time to time, how can the ethicist be sure that his limited self is living a moral life at the moment?

Even different societies have different moral standards, so which set of standards should one follow and whose standards should one follow? However, the moral stage is not yet the highest stage of life.

At this stage, although the individual subordinates himself to the universal ethical and moral laws, ethics and morality are universal and individual behavior is individual, and sometimes there is inevitable incompatibility between the two.

In this case, the individual will develop a sense of guilt. Kierkegaard believes that the sinfulness of the individual can no longer be explained by ethics and morality, because sinfulness belongs to the realm of religion, and the way out of sinfulness is to go to God.

In the transition from the ethical stage to the religious stage, Kierkegaard believes that one needs to make a leap of faith, i.e., you fully embrace your faith, which is often considered to be formed by external factors.

Most are influenced by parental, social, political, religious, and traditional ideologies. Only the process of faith must be internally responsive, involving personal experience and the search for human meaning, and then choosing a faith that suits you and being willing to do anything for it, even if it requires a great deal of effort.

3. Religious Development Process

The special feature of people or things in the religious stage is that their lives are guided by their beliefs and are no longer governed by the desires of the aesthetic stage, nor are they governed by the universal ethics and moral laws of the ethical stage.

It can be said that in the religious stage one "lives for God". In the concept of religion, faith can be divided into two types: faith and trust.

Those who believe in religion often take faith as their confidence and see it as self-evident, while others who have doubts about faith and do not recognize the existence of a deity tend to see faith as a creed without evidence.

When distinguishing between faith and belief, it is common to give an example that is easy to understand, such as: If I tell you I have a hundred dollars in my pocket and you tell me to take it out and look at it, that is faith.

If you believe in me, you will not ask me to take it out to see that is faith. Faith is the choice and holding of one's own view of life, values and worldview.

But philosophical accounts and discussions of faith are almost exclusively confined to theistic religious beliefs, i.e., belief in God.

And usually, they deal with faith as understood in the Abrahamic traditions of the Christian branch, though not to the exclusion of other aspects of faith.

In other words, a firm belief and faith in a person, an object, a thing, or a concept, including a belief in and reverence for an idea or religion.

At this stage man stands in an absolute relationship with the Absolute, placing God in the highest position, faith over personal enjoyment, and universal moral obligation.

Kierkegaard refers to the religious stage as being higher than the ethical stage, as the multitude, which is tense, frightened or excited by unexpected stimuli, says with certainty. If the ethical stage is the rational stage, the religious stage is the irrational stage.

God may test an individual when he wants to establish a one-to-one interconnection with God, between people, between people and things, and between things.

These tests may sometimes cross the line of universal moral law and become as if God has called man to do something unethical. It is easy to see that this stage is represented by Abraham.

The reason why Kierkegaard considers Abraham great is because of his devout religious beliefs, which put aside the laws and validity of worldly moral codes and chose to kill his son for the sake of God. He had to make the most difficult choice between the moral command "Thou shalt not kill" and the religious test "Love God".

Kierkegaard did not completely reject human sensibility and reason, but he believed that faith was higher than the first two.

In other words, faith in God cannot be manipulated by logic, scientific method, or other rational methods. In the case of God, man can only have an unwavering faith in the divine object of his faith (including specific doctrines and teachings), and a wholehearted conversion.

This ideological conviction and total conversion are expressed in specific religious rituals and activities, and are used to guide and regulate one's behavior in the secular society. It is a special kind of social ideology and cultural phenomenon.

Religious belief is an ideology, as a spiritual custom, is extremely complex, with human production, life, work and learning and other aspects of a myriad of ties.

Even if one believes in and reveres a certain proposition, doctrine, or religion of God, and takes it as an example or guide for one's actions and words, or if God gives absurd demands.

Belief in God means the possibility of going beyond reason into a mystical and absurd spiritual realm. That is why Kierkegaard says, "It is because of the absurdity that I think it is so and do not doubt it.

Finally, from the perspective of faith, Kierkegaard suggests that "all men are not right before God". He cites Jesus' temple cleansing passage, which states that a person thinks that practicing civil society values means that he is living in God's righteousness.

In reality, all men are not right before a God who is all good. The distance between man and man is relative and insignificant in the absolute gap with the Lord, and no one can justify himself as more holy than another.

One cannot claim to have done all that one can do, to be complacent about the moral responsibility one has achieved, but rather, when faced with the immense and infinite responsibility of morality, one should imagine that one can do more, and be terrified and desperate for what one has not been able to do. This is the despair of the ethical person who knows the self, but cannot have the self.

Chapter 5: The framework of Kierkegaard's existentialism

The existentialism advocated by Kierkegaard emphasizes that philosophers should explore the problem of the existence of life in reality.

He opposes the German concept of the ideal, and believes that the main thing is to grasp the existence of individual autonomy in a very concrete way.

In the process of contacting things in the outside world, Kierkegaard's personal feelings or experiences about his own "solitude" and "exceptions" have led him to create a philosophy of concern for himself - existentialism.

Kierkegaard's philosophy can be said to make use of the simplest and most sensual methods of our daily life.

In other words, he wants to use ordinary, practical, and concrete methods to interpret the existence of his own life and to dispel the boredom and absurdity in his own mind.

"Existence" refers to the "existence" of this time, this place, and this person, a flesh-and-blood personal "existence". There is joy, anger, sorrow, and happiness in personal existence, and it is through joy, anger, sorrow, and happiness that one can experience language, reason, and logic.

It cannot reveal the unique personality of each individual, and it cannot reveal the true meaning of life existence - existence.

In the latter case, the true meaning of life's existence can only be experienced through each individual's own internal, unique and subjective life experience.

According to Kierkegaard, this is an individual who is dominated by fear, trembling, pessimism, despair, and other negative emotions. This pessimistic and negative emotion is the most genuine experience of an individual facing his or her own existence.

It is this negative emotion that drives the most direct response to survive, the "either/or" choice.

Kierkegaard also emphasizes the view that rational thought alone is not enough to trigger action, and that this choice is described as a leap.

There must be a determination to end the thinking process, and this determination must be driven by a strong, explosive, and short-lived emotional state.

This emotional state is usually caused by an event of great significance to the individual. For example, the ecstasy after a major event, the despair after a tragic failure, the sudden death of a loved one, the extreme sadness caused by

The abnormal fear brought about by sudden danger, etc. The passions that form a person's ego are referred to as the inwardness or subjectivity of the individual.

The most important thing is that the intensification of passions, like love and faith, does not just happen by chance, but they must be based on the realization of the truth of the matter, and on a deep understanding of it.

They are cultivated and nurtured on the basis of a deep reflection and a careful understanding of a particular thing.

Kierkegaard clearly contradicts his philosophy with traditional philosophy, especially his criticism of rationalism represented by Hegel, as the fundamental direction of his philosophy.

He believes that the fundamental error of Hegel's philosophy is to take necessity, which is in accordance with the general laws of nature, as the highest principle of practical unity and the guarantee of the unity of reason and reality, and thus to fall into the confusion of "objectivism" and to be at a loss as to what to do.

The world is nothing but a necessary manifestation of the objective spirit, and all concrete and particular existence is an instance of this universal existence, a certain component of a certain stage of this whole.

In this way, man actually loses his own autonomy and independence, the possibility of making decisions and choices.

Most importantly, one loses one's individuality and freedom of will, which in turn makes one forget one's responsibility for the events that occur and removes the possibility of treating oneself and the world ethically.

The Hegelian philosophy is a philosophy that sacrifices the individual to the whole of thought, dehumanizes the human being, and is a disdain for the status and dignity of the human being.

(1) Dialectical thinking in Western philosophy

In Western philosophy, dialectic has many different meanings.

1. Classical Period

In classical Greek philosophy, dialectic (διαλεκτική) was formed by many dialogues (dialogue), including argument, counter-argument, proposing proposition (theses) and opposing proposition (counter-propositions, antithesis). counter-propositions, antithesis).

The result of a dialogue can be a refutation or integration of related propositions, a combination of opposing propositions, or a qualitative improvement of the dialogue.

The influence of the term dialectic is also related to its role in the philosophy of Socrates and Plato in the classical Greek period (5th-4th centuries BCE).

Aristotle says that the term "dialectic" was coined by the pre-Socratic philosopher Zeno of Elea, and Plato's dialogues are examples of Socratic dialectic.

Regardless of what Immanuel Kant says, the ancient

Greek dialectic simply means a logic of falsehood or similarity in appearance. For the ancient Greeks: "These are only illusory logics, nothing else.

01. Socratic Method

Socratic dialogues, also known as Socratic interrogation, are a special type of dialectic in which a series of questions is used to make a more accurate statement of an ambiguous belief, identifying the logical consequences of the statement and its contradictions.

Socratic dialogue is often destructive because it reveals errors in beliefs, and it is constructive only when what is discovered allows for further investigation of the truth.

The detection of error is not considered proof against the proposition. Just as the definition of a word creates a contradiction that does not provide a correct definition.

The main purpose of Socratic dialogue is to allow the talker to avoid errors that are not identified, or to teach them the essence of inquiry, which in turn raises the talker's mind.

For example, in the Euthyphro, Socrates asks

Euthyphro to define "piety".

Euthyphro believed that piety was a favorite trait of the gods. However, both Socrates and Euthyphro admit that the gods quarrel with each other, just as human beings quarrel, because of the object of their love or hatred.

Thus, Socrates argues, there must be some qualities that some gods love and some gods hate. Euthyphro also recognizes this.

Socrates concludes that if Euthyphro is right, there must be certain qualities that are both pious and impious (loved by some gods, but hated by others).

Euthyphro admits that this is absurd. Thus he knew through Socratic dialogue that his definition of piety was not good enough.

02. Plato

Plato has another interpretation of dialectic, written in the Ideal State, which is dialogical and intuitive.

In both Platonism and Neoplatonism, dialectic has an ontological and metaphysical role, taking wisdom from the rational to the intelligible.

From one concept to another, until it finally grasps the supreme concept, the first principle, which is the origin of everything. Thus, the philosopher finally becomes the "dialectician".

In this conception, dialectic is the process of inquiry that eliminates the assumptions in the process of reaching the first theorem (Republic, VII, 533 c-d) and slowly accepts the unity of pluralism.

Simon Blackburn writes that, by this definition, dialectic is used to understand "the whole process of enlightenment, in which the philosopher is educated to the knowledge of the highest good.

03. Aristotle

Aristotle emphasizes the close relationship between rhetoric and dialectic, and he gives a number of reasons for their relevance.

First, rhetoric is the "antithesis" of dialectic (Rhet. I.1, 1354a1), and second, rhetoric can be said to be the "outreach" (paraphues ti) of dialectic and textual studies (Rhet. I.2, 1356a25f).

Finally, Aristotle mentions that rhetoric is a part of

dialectic and also like dialectic (Rhet. I.2, 1356a30f.).

In saying that rhetoric is the "antithesis" of dialectic, Aristotle is clearly referring to the Gorgias of Plato (464bff.).

In Palato's narrative, he uses the word antistrophos to express the analogy between the two. It is likely that Aristotle also intended to express an analogy.

Argumentation is the practice of arguing (publicly or academically) for or against an argument, while rhetoric is the practice of defending one's position (in public) and refuting the other.

The analogy of dialectic has great significance for the orientation of rhetoric. In his Gorgias, Plato states.

Rhetoric cannot be an art because it has nothing to do with a specific subject. A real art is defined by a specific subject, for example, medicine or shoe-making is defined by its product (health or shoes).

2. Philosophy of the Middle Ages

Logic (which should include dialectic) was one of the three arts taught in medieval universities, the other two being rhetoric and grammar.

The first medieval philosopher to study dialectic was Boethius (480-524), mainly based on Aristotle's doctrine.

After him, many philosophers of the scholastic school also used dialectic in their works, such as Pierre Abelard, William of Sherwood, Garlandus Compotista, Walter Burley, Roger Swyneshed, William of Ockham, and Thomas Aquinas.

The form of the dialectic at this point is as follows.

Definitive question (to be asked at ......)

Provisional answer to this question (it looks like ......)

The main argument of the provisional answer

The argument against the provisional answer, typically an argument from an authority (the opposite of ......)

The answer to the question after evaluating the evidence (my answer is ......)

The answer to the objection (for the first argument, for the second argument, my response is ......)

Modern Philosophy

01. Kantian Dialectic

From the time of the Stoics until the end of the Middle Ages, dialectic was quite closely connected with formal logic.

Later, Kant used the term "a priori dialectic" to denote the effort to reveal falsifications that arise when trying to apply the scope and principles of knowing outside the realm of phenomena and possible experience.

02. Hegelian Dialectic

About half a century after Kant's birth, Hegel (1770-1831 A.D.) was born in Stuttgart, Prussia. When one thinks of Hegel, one thinks of "dialectic", but this philosophical term has been around since the ancient Greek period. The meaning at that time was as follows.

To ask a question about a person's claim and keep answering it, so that the other person can discover the error of his claim and gradually lead him to the right one.

This is called dialectic or question-answer method. This is also known as Socrates' method of questioning and answering, as mentioned earlier. In contrast, Hegel's subsequent basic theory of dialectic is as follows.

All finite, non-permanent beings have an internal incompatible contradiction. This contradiction consists of a thesis (positive) and an antithesis (negative). Contradictions do not remain static, but generate opposites.

When the thesis and antithesis are combined, they become the next stage of existence. This new stage of existence is called synthesis, and this new stage also contains new arguments and antitheses.

In Hegel's dialectic, reaching a new stage is called "aufheben", which means "to cease to exist, to abolish, and to ascend to a higher level".

It is not simply discarded, but develops a new state in itself, which eventually leads to a higher level, to a higher unity.

All existence contains arguments (positive) and counter-arguments (negative), which, after continuous opposition and movement, will reach "unity" and then be discarded.

This cycle will go on forever and existence itself will continue to develop itself. Hegel's dialectic is probably structured in this way.

That is the situation in which Kant contemplates "the agreement of the phenomenon (subjective) with the object (objective)," the highest level of spirituality.

According to Kant, human cognition can never reach the reality of the object, but remains in the phenomenon; however, Hegel believes that human beings can use dialectics to obtain the absolute spirit, so that the phenomenon and the object agree, and in this way, there is a way to understand the object (reality).

In the first part of his Encyclopedia of Philosophical Sciences, Hegel gives the most extensive overview of his dialectical method. Hegel's dialectical method is usually expressed in a threefold way, as described by Heinrich Moritz Chalibos, as consisting of three stages of dialectical development: the positive topic, which elicits a reaction; the negative topic, which contradicts or negates the positive topic; and the syllogism, which is a tension between the two.

The synoptic, in which the tension between the two is resolved by synthesis. In simpler terminology, it can be considered as follows: problem → reaction → solution. Although this model is often named after Hegel, he never used this particular formulation.

On the other hand, Hegel did use a "three-value logic model" very similar to the antithesis model, but the terminology most commonly used by Hegel was.

"Abstract-Negative-Concrete. In many of his works, Hegel uses this mode of writing as the backbone of his argument.

Chalibos'   formula   of "Proposition-Antithesis-Concrete" does not explain why a proposition needs an antithesis.

However, the "abstract-negative-concrete" formula implies that there is a flaw or possible incompleteness in any initial proposition, for example, that it is too abstract, untried, erroneous, and inexperienced.

For Hegel, truths with concreteness, synthesis, and absoluteness must always pass through the stage of negation in the process of moving toward completion, which is the stage of mediation. This is the essence of what is commonly known as Hegel's dialectic.

To describe the activity of overcoming negation, Hegel also often uses the term "Aufhebung" (translated as "sublation" or "overcoming" in English), which corresponds to the Chinese term "abandonment", to conceptualize the operation of dialectic.

Roughly speaking, the term means to retain the useful parts of ideas, things, societies, etc., while transcending their limitations. Hegel states that the purpose of dialectic is "to investigate the existence and movement of things in themselves, and thus to demonstrate the finiteness of the partial domain of understanding.

Hegelianism, the philosophy of G.W.F. Hegel, can be summed up by the maxim "Reason alone is real," which means that all reality can be expressed in the realm of reason.

His goal was to restore reality to a more integrated unity within a system of absolute idealism. Hegel applied dialectics to his idealism, creating a dialectical idealism. Hegel's dialectic is considered to be a teleological dialectic.

03. Marxist Dialectic

Marxist dialectic, also known as materialistic dialectic, was formed gradually by Marx's first systematic and critical reform of Feuerbach's materialism and Hegelian dialectic. The dialectic is mainly derived from the Hegelian dialectic.

There are three basic laws of materialistic dialectics, namely, the law of unity of opposites, the law of reciprocity of qualities, and the law of negation. The relationship between these three basic laws is generally considered.

The law of unity of opposites reveals the source and power of development, the law of interchange of masses reveals the state of development, and the law of negation reveals the trend and path of development. Many people advocate that there is only one fundamental law of materialistic dialectics, namely the law of opposition and unity.

It can be seen that the Law of Oppositional Unity is essentially Hegel's Abstract-Negative-Concrete method of discernment, and the other two laws are only extensions of the Abstract-Negative-Concrete method.

Marx and Engels, on the other hand, used the principle of materialism and considered the dialectical law as the internal law of development and change of objective things, and applied it to their explanation of social and economic processes.

In the Marxist philosophical system, dialectics is considered to be a worldview and methodology opposed to metaphysics, a doctrine, and theory of universal connection and eternal development - it understands and depicts the world as

It understands and portrays the world as the whole of universal connection and the process of eternal development, and understands development as "the result of various contradictions inherent in things themselves, which change under the influence of external factors", i.e., determined by internal factors and influenced (promoted or delayed) by external factors.

04. The difference between dialectic and sophistry

Dialectics (English: dialectics, Greek: διαλεκτική, dialektikě; related to dialogue, also translated as dialectic, dialectical method), is a method of philosophical argumentation for resolving disagreements, a process of resolving contradictions between two opposing parties.

Or rather, sophistry itself is a methodological approach. More precisely, sophistry is a method of argument, and its fundamental characteristic is a distorted argument, sophistry being different from arbitrariness and from rumor.

A sophistry is different from an arbitrary assertion

and from a rumor. But sophistry, when arguing for reason, always presents a large number of "grounds", so that, on the surface, it can always confuse some people who are not reasonable.

In the history of Western philosophy, Hegel was the first philosopher to systematically criticize sophistry. He pointed out: "The word sophistry usually means to move a truth in an arbitrary way, on the basis of false grounds, or to shake it and deny it.

Or to make a false truth sound so beautiful that it reverses right and wrong and becomes as if it were true. This passage of Hegel's exposes the characteristics of sophistry, which is the intentional reversal of right and wrong and confusion of black and white.

The Method of Argumentation

It belongs to the realm of debate, but it goes beyond the definition of reason and even truth in the science of debate.

The Difference between Dialectic and Fallacy

First of all, what is dialectic? Dialectic is based on totality, where difference is the entity of the totality (or Hegel's absolute spirit, or Marx's practice), and then the difference is seen as the entity itself, denying the self-difference that it produces.

In contrast, the sophistic debate does not obey the law of identity; it adds multiple perspectives externally to the discussion of the problem. For example, when we say that the atomic bomb killed a lot of people, someone says, "But we have the atomic bomb.

This is a typical sophistry debate. We are talking about the number of deaths (which is one perspective), while he is talking about the atomic bomb, which is a technological perspective.

He is moving between different perspectives. This is the nature of the so-called sophistry of splitting the issue into two. He adds multiple perspectives and then externally combines them, so we are asked to divide them into two and not just focus on the bad side.

This is the core of the sophistry debate. In the history of philosophy, this is embodied in Leibniz's Monadology. According to Leibniz, the monad is both one and many.

At first glance, it looks like dialectic. In fact, it is a sophistry. For by one, he means that the monad is one in its own right.

In terms of its sequence of monads, it is composed of many monads, which is many. He is moving between two perspectives, not obeying the same law. And here he cannot deal at all with the harmony between the monads, which must be added externally to God. These are the remnants of the intellectual thinking.

"You think that this thing is X, but X will inevitably lead to Y, and Y will become Z on a certain occasion, and it is well known that the probability of Z is very small, so X must not happen.

You're wrong, I'm right. Oh yeah I win." The two are not comparable. The mode of thinking of the dialectic method, which has been clearly explained in my column, is to examine the proposition p and its negative proposition non-p.

For example, if we talk about the value of high-speed rail, set "high-speed rail is useful" as p and "high-speed rail is not useful" as non-p.

The movement change is examined through the propositions p and non-p. For example, if we say that the high-speed rail is useful at present, then p is the main aspect of the contradictory proposition. But at the same time, the proposition non-p cannot be ignored, because with the accumulation of quantities, p and non-p will transform each other.

Let's take another example. If "the dress is red" is p, then the corresponding negative proposition non-p is "the dress is not red".

A red dress is dyed black, and this is the transformation of the proposition p and non-p, that is, movement. In fact, the dialectic method is very simple: to see what can be seen and to prevent what cannot be seen.

The unseen does not exist at the moment, but it has the possibility to emerge at any time. The human eye has limitations, so we must be aware of the existence of the invisible as much as possible.

The former is a common saying "prevention is better than cure", which is for development. The latter cloud "perspective to comprehensive", is for the connection. So that you see here should know. The method of debating is not for debating at all, or rather, the materialistic method of debating is not much concerned with debating at all.

Because you can win or lose the debate, most of the objective world will not be shifted by two people's debate.

And there is nothing to say about sophistry. Confusing concepts, slippery slope effect, etc. etc.

Just to win the debate and win the thing. Finally, an analogy. Argumentation is a telescope, something you use to recognize your own limitations and to keep examining the unknown.

Debate is a kind of blindfold, designed to confuse the other side's thought patterns, to try to shift the focus of the other side and win the debate. What many people understand as dialectic is not dialectic.

For example, "look at the problem in two parts" and "look at the problem in its entirety" do not reflect the essence of dialectics, but are merely a kind of totalism.

In fact, totality is inherent in dialectics, but it is not dialectics itself. In other words, totality is not necessarily bound up with dialectics.

In the above example, the two contradictory parties are still understood as two monads (atoms), and when we need to split them, they are two monads, or "contradictory parties" as they are called in the textbook.

But what if we want to look at them together? It is to create a content without content, and to bring it together from the form.

We can see that this sameness is not a specific sameness in the Hegelian sense of content, but a sameness of form. This sameness can be found to be dispensable under analysis.

This dialectic, which treats both sides of the contradiction as singletons and atoms, is in fact a kind of mechanism. In the history of philosophy, this kind of mechanical way of thinking must be generalized by introducing a big book (the generalization of "metaphysics").

In this way, the dialectical method is no different from the previous philosophical thinking, which is to erase the fundamental spirit of the dialectical method, or not to try to understand it.

And how does "dialectic" become a sophistry? It is very simple. Whatever is good and right.

I can tell you through a lot of explanations that it is the work of my dialectic, that I have seen it before it happened.

Or I can say that I want to emphasize what I want according to my own needs, that is, I can say some nonsense in a plausible way, and I can say whatever I want.

Because the contradiction between the two sides of the opposition unified well, the contradiction has a primary aspect secondary aspect well. This kind of talk is total nonsense, it does not reflect what is the main thing that we should pay attention to, and what is the secondary.

Some people rely on this kind of talk to emphasize something and ignore something at will according to their own needs. In addition to arbitrary definitions of what is "the point," textbook dialectics (sophistry) teaches us to divide into two, or to look at things holistically. Again, this is nonsense.

However, it is the philosophical basis for the dialectic: we need to look at the whole picture! The phrase "look at the whole picture" is, like most of the philosophical maxims in our textbooks, pure nonsense.

The core of the technique of sophistry is that A is talking about one thing and B is talking about another, but B has to find a way to deceive, or temporarily deceive, A and the audience that the two things are actually one and the same, or are very intimately related.

There are similarities and differences between apologetics and sophistry.

04-1 Similarities.

Sophistry is the method of reasoning from a given argument to a given contradiction in a generally accepted former argument. The same is true of sophistry.

04-2 Differences.

The objective purpose of sophistry is to deceive, and the objective purpose of sophistry is to introduce fallacies in the arguments that defy logic, and to make deceptive and specious reasoning and arguments.

The dialectical method does not aim at deception subjectively, and objectively tries to avoid fallacies that defy logic.

Dialectic functions beyond classical logic and science, while sophistry violates one or the other of classical logic or science.

In other words, what dialectic reveals is complementary to classical logic and science, and therefore dialectic should not behave in a way that contradicts classical logic or science, while sophistry contains fallacies that violate classical logic or some scientific (or metaphysical) principle.

The misuse of the name apologetics, and even the masquerading of sophistry as apologetics, is ubiquitous in life. So much so that communities sometimes perceive these sophisms as apologetics, eroding people's sense of justice and righteousness, unaware of the negative effects of this practice.

Sophists believe that "arete" is the most important and decisive factor in a person's behavior throughout his or her life. They believe that the artistic quality in speech is indicative of a person's talent.

Speech is considered to be an art form, which entertains and infects the audience through a brilliant presentation. Nevertheless, the sophists taught their students to seek talent in various ways, not just in oratory.

Socrates opposed the sophists and their teaching of "eloquence as an art and an infectious speech, without logic or proof".

(2) The two main points of Kierkegaard's existentialism.

First, existence is prior to nature

The idea that existence precedes nature means that man's existence is passive and predetermined (man cannot decide whether he is born male or female), but man can use his predetermined life existence to create his own nature.

Therefore, what makes a person valuable is not his or her destined existence, not his or her historical background, family background, nor his or her status of birth, but the freedom to choose to transform his or her own nature, how he or she chooses to be the person he or she wants to be and what he or she wants to do.

Secondly, existence is divided into three levels.

(3) Kierkegaard divides the existence of life into three levels.

01. Sensual existence.

A type of personal style. This type is characterized by

a sympathetic attitude and a kind heart to observe things. It is easy to show emotions and values the harmony of interpersonal relationships. As opposed to rational.

In the process of dealing with people, they follow their own consciousness, that is, they are accustomed to thinking from their heart and do not consider objective conditions more, if they are dominated by subjective views, they will become materialistic and religious.

Usually pursuing one's own happiness, pursuing a lighter life, pursuing one's own selfish side, existence from maintaining life to pleasure.

02. Rational existence.

A type of personal style. This type is characterized by logical reasoning to observe things. It is not easy to show emotions, is not sympathetic, and does not care about the harmony of relationships. Relative to sensuality.

In a normal state of mind, in order to get the desired result, have the confidence and courage to face the situation calmly, and quickly and fully understand the reality to analyze a variety of feasible options, and then judge the best solution and the ability to effectively implement it.

It is a serious and responsible life, solving one's own problems in a rational and philosophical way, making oneself ethically responsible to others, and conforming to the moral existence of society.

03. Religious existence.

Due to the unknown exploration of the universe and the pursuit of immortality, we believe that there is a supernatural mysterious power or entity outside of the real world, so that people have reverence and worship for this mystery.

This leads to a system of beliefs, cognitive and ritual activities, and like folk myths, it also has its own mythology, which is interconnected with each other and is essentially a spiritual trust and ultimate care.

It is a system of belief based on the existence of supernatural power, the creator and controller of the universe, and the continuity of the soul after death, a life of prayer and love, a life of consciousness and reverence for God, and thus a spiritual existence.

In the last 12 years of his life, Kierkegaard wrote many articles and books, and published books on religion, philosophy, psychology, and even humor.

Before Sigmund Freud (1856-1939), one of the most influential thinkers of the twentieth century, he also wrote a book entirely devoted to anxiety, The Concept of Fear, and was praised by Freud for his innovative ideas in psychology.

(4) The situation in which Kierkegaard's life exists

The existence of human beings is different from that of birds, animals, or trees, and is unique because of the phenomena of the mind. Before we begin to explore the concept of despair, this paper will first explain what he considers to be the basic human condition.

It is generally accepted that there are three anthropological premises to Zicke's concept of existence: first, that man has a self, second, that man is a synthesis, and third, that man is made by God (Theunissen, 2005: 4).

However, the above presupposition of the human condition is a static view; in fact, these three are indeed Kierkegaard's presuppositions of man, but their presuppositions should include a stronger notion of dynamic realization.

In other words, these three presuppositions do exist, but they must be achieved by human effort before they can be truly realized, and with human self-awareness and choice, they generate different meanings for individual life levels.

01. Man has an ego (self)

Before discussing the composite form of the human being, it is important to understand what Kierkegaard identifies as the human self. Kierkegaard offers a simple analogy to illustrate this.

It is like a house with a cellar, which is designed to be lived on the ground. If a man lives a sensual life and forgets his spirit, it is like living in a cellar and leaving the floor empty, which is a ridiculous thing.

(Kierkegaard, 1843/1957: 176).

Man is constituted as a spirit, a spirit united with the body, and this spirit is man's ego, so that man's ego includes both soul and body. In other words, man is different from animals and plants because of the combination of the body and the soul.

Kierkegaard also says, "Man is spirit, and spirit is ego, and ego is a relationship that connects ego to itself, or in a relationship, connects the relationship to itself, and ego is not this relationship, but the connection of this relationship to itself (Kierkegaard, 1849/1980: 13).

The so-called spirit is the consciousness that one forms about oneself, and this consciousness has an identity with oneself, which forms the "ego", while the relationship in the second sentence is the relationship between the spirit and the body.

Consciousness is the power of self-reflection that grasps the spirit and the body as a whole (Chua Mei-chu, 2002: 38-39). In The Deadly Disease, the "self" consists of two elements: the relationship between the self and the ego, and the state of establishment (Theunissen, 2005:26).

When the ego is related to the self, the ego develops a relationship in this relationship and forms the person's sense of self.

The spirit is the ego of man, and man has the ego because he has the spirit, that is, the ego really arises when he becomes aware of himself and recognizes the whole of himself.

02. Man is a synthesis

Kierkegaard believes that "every human being is created to be a self, to be himself." The highest morality and responsibility is not to be a "good" person, but to know oneself and become a "person" through the choice of whole-person commitment.

True morality does not lie in a generalized moral law, but in the unpredictable decisions that one makes within oneself about the various possibilities of life. Kierkegaard reminds us that "truth is subjectivity" and that the highest good and truth are not in the mass, but belong to the individual.

"Faith is a paradox, the individual is higher than the universal." When one places oneself in a group, one cannot accept the unique sacredness of each individual, cannot repent and turn to God independently.

God "made man and woman in His own image" and "placed eternity in the human heart", so man is essentially spiritual.

But Kierkegaard points out that man is not purely

eternal and infinite, as God is, but paradoxically "a synthesis of the infinite and the finite, of the transient and the eternal, of the possible and the necessary.

In short, he is a synthesis". Finite and transient means that man lives in a particular time, space, and environment; without finiteness, man lives in abstraction and imagination.

Infinity refers to the power of imagination that transcends one's finiteness. This imagination helps one to imagine different realities, to formulate and develop different plans. Without limitlessness, man is confined to the world and goes with the flow.

Possibility means that man chooses himself in freedom, that he is his true self and not at the mercy of destiny.

Necessity means that man is his true self only when he integrates finitude and infinity, otherwise he is lost in possibility.

But "synthesis is the relationship between two factors; in this way, man is not yet the self" means that even if one understands that man is a paradoxical synthesis, what one presents is only a negative third party.

Only when the self chooses, commits itself to a relationship with this self-consciousness, "I am the connection that links the self to the self," does this positive relationship truly constitute a complete self.

Only when one comes face to face in faith with the One who knows what I am, the Infinite One, can one understand the necessity of man, his unique construction by the Lord, and his own divine image, original uniqueness, and His predetermined purpose for each single self.

Man's ego is a correspondence with the Lord, and the Lord is the measure. To know oneself is to know the Lord, and to know the Lord is to know oneself. The Lord does not reveal Himself in the objective world for us to observe and understand, but He reveals Himself as the foundation of our subject.

Kierkegaard points out that only when one is in a healthy balance between these two poles does one complete the unity of the self and overcome the loss of unity and desperate domination.

Of course, Kierkegaard does not mean that the completion of this synthesis will free one from all anxiety and struggle. Man is still a paradoxical synthesis, and therefore faith is an ongoing struggle and task throughout his life.

When man turns inward in the midst of all the circumstances of life, faces God and his own existence, and chooses to submit to God, he passes through eternity into his present and receives the reality of his existence.

The new self becomes absolutely related to the Lord, and this relationship connects the self with the Lord with absolute responsibility

After the establishment of the human ego, how does the human self-consciousness arise? In Kierkegaard's existential thought, he proposed that "man is a synthesis of finite and infinite, temporary and eternal, free and necessary (Kierkegaard, 1849/1980: 13)".

As we can see, Kierkegaard believed that human beings have two factors at the same time, and that these two factors determine human consciousness, so that the human self becomes itself in the harmony of finite/infinite, temporary/permanent, and freedom/necessity.

If one looks at the human being from the point of view

that he is a synthesis, one can see that he has not yet become his true self (Kierkegaard, 1849/1980: 13).

To become a synthesis, two factors must be combined, and the coordination of these two factors does not exist as a matter of course, but is only possible through human choice and practice.

Becoming the self involves the process of infinitization, that is, the infinite withdrawal of oneself and the return to oneself in a finite process.

The length of life is finite, but the contribution of life can be infinite. The human intellect may be limited, but the imagination may be infinite.

If man cannot become himself, he will fall into despair. Whether he knows it or not, as long as the ego exists, he is in the process of generation, so the ego may not really exist, because when the ego does not want to generate the ego, the ego does not exist.

Taken together, being a composite in this context represents two meanings.

First, that man himself has two opposing qualities at the same time.

Second, human existence is the process of reconciling the two.

In other words, the reason why human beings have various forms of existence comes from the awareness of these two opposing factors and the process of how to adapt to them.

03. Man is made by God

In the introduction to "The Disease of Death," Kierkegaard begins with a religious story. There is a man in the Bible named Lazarus who rose from the dead because of the miracle of Christ. According to the Bible

Christ came to the tomb of Lazarus and cried out, "Lazarus, come out! And Lazarus came out of the tomb wrapped in a gauze (John 11:4). Jesus said to him, "I am the resurrection and the life, and whoever believes in me, though he die, will live again (John 11:25).

Kierkegaard uses this story to illustrate that God is the creator of mankind and that death is the end of life for mankind, but from a Christian perspective, death is not the final destination, but only a small part of eternal life (Kierkegaard, 1849/1980: 7-8).

The point of this story is not that God has the power to raise man from the dead, but that man was created by God.

As long as God exists and man believes in God, death is not the end of life; man is an eternal being and death is only a form. Kierkegaard points out the following themes to be discussed.

As long as one believes in God, one should not be afraid of death, but what one should be afraid of is the disease that causes death while living. And what is the real deadly disease? It is what Kierkegaard calls the disease of the spirit - "despair".

04. "Suspending ethics" to the desperate

Kierkegaard reveals the fears, absurdities, relationships, and responsibilities involved in moving from the ethical to the faith level by re-reading the account of Abraham's sacrifice to Isaac in Gen. 22:1-10.

Abraham is called the father of faith, or, according to Kierkegaard, the knight of faith, because of his total reliance on God and his "suspension of morality" into absurdity.

The highest sacrifice one can make in the moral stage of ethics is to become a tragic hero. Tragic heroes know clearly their place in society and the responsibilities required of them.

Therefore, they are considered moral when they sacrifice their children for the common good, leaving the responsibilities of the family above the common good.

This morality is capable of being spoken about and of withstanding rational discussion. Abraham's duty as a father, as understood by social roles, was to love his son.

As a husband, he was also expected to speak openly to his wife. But Abraham's actions are unknown, uncertain, and cannot be spoken or explained to others.

His actions were not communal, and he did not even know why God's command was good. His actions cannot be explained or legitimized by the framework of reason or social ethics, whether for Conde or Hegel, and Abraham inevitably becomes a murderer, not a "father of faith.

However, in the midst of the "either/or" violation, he became a knight of faith. The test Abraham received from God did not expect others to be convinced or to follow him.

Only he, as an independent individual, could ask and

decide whether he was in temptation or a knight of faith. In fact, Abraham's role as a knight of faith itself implies a violation, a transgression.

Faith is an instantaneous decision, yet the long journey to Mount Morley implies a struggle, yet relies on absurd suffering.

If the "suspended ethics" proposed by Kierkegaard were to be replaced by absolute responsibility, as opposed to morality, then Abraham should not fear and tremble in fulfilling the call of God.

Kierkegaard describes the intersection of aesthetic and ethical strata that still coexist in the hierarchy of faith.

Even when Abraham stood before God, he could not shed his human nature, his inability to abandon, his actual experience, his fear of the unknown.

At the same time, Abraham, as a father, had the highest obligation to his son, and naturally felt an immediate fear of such an anti-ethical action.

What is more, Kierkegaard shows that Abraham, as an individual, did not hate Isaac. It was precisely because Abraham loved Isaac deeply, even in faith, that Isaac's existence was a manifestation of God's love for Abraham, the blessing and honor promised to Abraham, and a deepening of his responsibility in faith for Isaac's love, that he was placed in such a tension between disobedience, violation, faith and ethics.

The "second, new inwardness" of Abraham in the face of this tension is the confession that "I believe because it is absurd".

True faith lies in the courage to face the fundamental impossibility in the midst of the pain of abandonment, to know that God himself, not in any sphere of knowledge, refuses to make reasonable calculations and explanations for the things he has to face.

In contrast to the tragic hero's infinite abandonment, Abraham is at the same time perversely convinced that the goodness of God will restore him to the promised Isaac in this world, not in the next.

Abraham made a leap of faith through absurd and endless renunciation. But in terms of regaining, through this leap, Abraham changed from active to passive, committing himself to the miraculous guidance of God.

It was this close responsibility and connection to

God's miracle that made possible the love that Jesus taught and that transcended ethical relationships. According to the sinful nature of man, sensual love can lead to disappointment, pain, loss of motivation to love, and can even turn into hatred and jealousy.

And when confronted with the Lord's strict demands of love for each person, it only leads to avoidance, denial, and resistance to the commands one needs to bear.

Kierkegaard points out that if there is no higher being than the ego, how can I bring myself under control to fulfill the love that transcends the limited nature of man?

When there is an absolute responsibility and relationship with God, the life of love is derived from the life connected to the eternal God, which has eternal meaning.

It does not fall into the chaos of self-regulation, and there is no more excuse to escape, and the Lord gives strength and comforts and forgives those who are willing to fulfill the commandment of love.

Such love and responsibility are not part of the universal norm, but must be presented in a sacrificial ethic. In the absolute singleness of man and in the absolute responsibility of God, no one can replace the role of the individual in fulfilling this responsibility to the earth and to the self.

Summing up the above discussion, from the aforementioned analysis of the situation of human existence, it can be concluded that Kierkegaard believes that the situation of human existence is: "Man is an individual with an ego, because he exists in finite/infinite, temporal/permanent, free/necessary, forming a synthesis of two opposites and yet reconciliation.

As a creature of God, the only thing one should do is to believe in order to obtain eternal existence.

(5) The Development of Priscilla's Life Existence

The aforementioned dynamic process of existential dialectic is also shown in the development of life as proposed by Kierkegaard. The process of how one transcends from a shallow existence to a more profound existence is the dialectic of existence (Chua, 2002: 17).

Kierkegaard emphasizes that human beings have a

free nature, and through the manifestation of self-consciousness, they are able to choose and practice for themselves, thus developing three stages of life with different experiences and different values.

In his book Stages on Life's way, published in 1845, he proposed that the various stages of life are, in order, the aesthetical stage, the ethical stage, and the religious stage.

In either/or, the meaning of the aesthetic and ethical stages is explained separately in two parts, and in fear and trembling, the highest state of existence, the religious state, is further explored.

01. The Development of Sensibility

In "Either/Or," Kierkegaard uses the literary character Don Juan17 as an example to illustrate the sensual life of man.

Kierkegaard describes Don Juan as a character who may exhibit two specific or co-existing qualities, according to some specific legendary interpretations.

According to some accounts, Don Juan is a simple, lustful playboy, a man who simply wants to play with any woman.

In other accounts, however, Don Juan is seen as a man who truly enjoyed every woman he seduced, and who was gifted with the ability to see the true beauty and intrinsic value of each woman.

In the early legends he was always described as the aforementioned point of view. The original intention of Tiso was to use such a character as a warning to the world that good and evil will be punished, and that even a man like Don Juan will not escape punishment.

He is a flirtatious man who is in the sensual stage of indulging in sensual pleasures.

The characteristic of the sensual stage is that they act according to their feelings, impulses, and emotions, and are deluded by material things.

Since they do not realize the meaning of existence, they do not see existence as a responsibility and avoid entering into the fetters of life. In short, they are committed to the pursuit of momentary pleasures, and for them all relationships are transient and without continuity.

Because the experience of life is constantly repeated

and has no permanent value, the inner world has no reliance or guarantee, so they can only live in the "present moment", which is also the phrase that people often use today, "Today there is wine and today there is drunkenness, tomorrow's sorrow is tomorrow's sorrow".

It is a philosophy of mortal life derived from this fast-changing world, and the argument is probably like this: "Look how fast the world is changing, how unpredictable all fortunes and misfortunes are, how powerless it is to live! Instead of worrying and being anxious, why not live in the present moment and grasp what is true and unmistakable? "I'm not sure what to do.

However, this understanding of "living in the present" is far from the original meaning of "living in the present". Although this stage may seem to be free, there are times when Kierkegaard spends a lot of money to satisfy his immediate desires, but in the end, he feels guilty in confusion and degradation (or is it because he cannot see any other meaning in life that he simply considers enjoyment as the primary reason for existence?) The reason is that

Therefore, it is described as "like a plant that does not have a rapid motor response; a being that lacks obvious nerves and sensory organs (although with a special stimulus response of the directive sense) without its own mobility, limited by the land, because it is lost in an ever-present longing.

They endure or experience everything for a long time, but still feel hungry, and the result of the constant race towards desire eventually brings melancholy.

The scholar W. Lowrie believes that the sensual stage was the experience of Kierkegaard's life as a young man, who lived in school and lived the life of a rich boy, spending his money on tailors, booksellers, tobacconists, and cafes, but in his book The Concept of Melancholy

However, in his book "The Concept of Worry", he confessed that it was "fear" that brought him to such a stage. Because of his worries, sorrow and fear of nothing, he chose to live a life of debauchery and happiness to avoid the seriousness of life experience.

However, life is confused because we have not found the direction of life, and we do not know the real meaning of living in the world now.

The goal does not have to be ambitious, it can be a happy benchmark, each time the goal is very simple, but not within reach, so that it will be satisfied in the progress, and will not cause a sense of loss because it is within reach.

Personally, Kierkegaard is aware that through sensual happiness, one may be able to satisfy one's intention and desire for something or purpose, but with it comes a more empty and meaningless depression, and with one's self-consciousness, one may be led into a state of despair.

In short, the perceptual stage is an experimental stage, where the perceptual person only tries to explore various possibilities, but is not willing to devote his life to make a sincere choice, and can only perform on the basis of predictions and future development of the object of study and the relationship between internal and external factors.

The lack of scientific theories is considered to be objectively correct and erroneous due to their consequential nature, independent of the reality of existence. This is the most fascinating, but most painful feature of this stage.

02. Progress of ethical development

In the second half of the book "Either/or",

Kierkegaard quotes the virtual character Judge William to illustrate the characteristics and importance of the ethical stage.

What is the meaning of life, the confusion and uncertainty of life and death in this world? Is it just to fill my stomach with three meals a day, or to wake up and see the sun in the morning, why does a long life of eating, shitting and sleeping seem so dull day after day?

But I know to be satisfied, satisfied with what I have already got. Behind the materialistic desire and luxury competition is emptiness and vulgarity, and if you cannot find the direction of life, you cannot live the taste of life, and you do not know the meaning of life.

Therefore, people in the ethical stage have recovered from the desire (mental) from the confusion and degradation of normal, we are always awake, only when we know that the past ridiculous years like a dream, at this time, from the confusion, wrong situation, just awakened already, from the desire of the shock after awakening, bring people a purpose of the existence of life: the purpose of the meaning of life.

Only when desire exists, the goal exists. The spiritual

awakening of the individual begins at the ethical stage, when the awakening of desire means that man begins to link desire with the goal of life, and to focus on the continuity of life, to become a person who is committed to carving out a history of life, not a person who is drunk today.

At this time, man no longer lives only for his desires, but has a personal or systematic understanding of what he wants to achieve in his life, and will try to achieve it for this plan, the experience of life existence.

From the sensual stage to the ethical stage is the expression of the individual's "choice of self" and "rebirth of self", which is the process of discovering the ability of self

This is the process of discovering one's ability to point out or clarify the personal situation that is not easy to see the nature of things.

After entering the ethical stage, the individual raises the level of his or her life, focusing on moral consciousness, responsibility, and the pursuit of self-choice and willpower, which obviously manifests itself as the stage of realizing obligations.

At this stage of development, the individual begins to connect himself/herself with others, to assume responsibility and accountability in society, marriage, and career, to face the trend of development and change, and to be willing to commit to the nature of things that can continue to exist, and to choose and pay for the uncertainty of the future.

The ethical individual's knowledge of oneself is not only a silent meditation, but also a reflection of an action from oneself, replacing the knowledge of oneself with an autonomous and intentional choice of self.

To choose oneself is to become aware of one's past actions because one feels guilty about them. Realization due to regret is a personal commitment to the past.

If the individual continues to attribute to others or to circumstances the causes of his limited self, he will not accept his true self until hc is able to attribute to himself the causes of his limited self, and then he will be able to take responsibility for his self.

Therefore, the prerequisite for making ethical decisions is to become aware of one's self through repentance. As opposed to sensual love, which is a momentary flutter of emotion, the ethical stage seeks a constant, stable love between husband and wife, by committing to important occasions, life and death situations? Important decisions and choices.

Sublimation of romantic metamorphosis into commitment and responsibility. The Hedonist is rich in emotion, sentimental, and experiences the absolute change of emotion in everything, and recognizes the autonomy of life with sensuality.

The "ethicist" is engaged in the conscious activity of transforming society and nature, and sees romantic love as lacking or absent, and that it can only become marriage through transcendental ascension.

The ethics at this stage is not entirely regulated by society or tradition, and Kierkegaard emphasizes that such ethics should be a choice of "inwardness," in which the relationship between the individual and the individual, society, and others is realized.

The individual is willing to face everything by taking responsibility, because the transition from the emotional stage to the ethical stage is the repentance of the latter to the former, and it is an either/or choice that allows one to truly enter the ethical stage.

By understanding the importancc of choicc, his choice is made with passion, will, and practice, and he commits himself to ethical behavior with true inner virtue.

03. The Development of Religion

The metamorphosis from the ethical stage to the religious stage requires two steps of practical action: first, repentance of sins, repentance of one's past faults, and the cessation of all worldly attachments, including human relationships, love, family, wealth, fame, etc.

The second step is true faith. Having faith in a certain idea or religion and in a certain person or thing, one must then embrace unlimited enthusiasm to escape from the "city of destruction" and embark on a journey to find "eternal bliss", to reach the mountain of happiness and the city of heaven through dangers and various tests.

People in the religious realm are called by God to open their own path of faith. The characteristics of Religion A.

It is the establishment of a connection of some nature between man and the eternal God, or between man and God, in an attempt to solve the problem of sin. In the book

"The Religious Philosophy of Kierkegaard", it is mentioned that

The consciousness of sin is an intermediary of existence.

For Christianity, man has a sinful nature from the moment he is born, and this sinful nature cannot be eliminated, and it is passed on from generation to generation without ceasing, which is "original sin".

The origin of "original sin" comes from the ancestors of mankind, Adam and Eve. The only way to be redeemed is to believe in Jesus Christ as Savior and Son of God.

Religion A, as proposed by Kierkegaard, is about man changing and adapting to his relationship with God in order to be saved from sin, so the focus is on man's internal concept of trust in God.

Religion B, on the other hand, is a divine revelation, an explicit or covenantal standard that entrusts everything about the individual to God.

Abraham's sacrifice is the best proof of this. In the Bible, Abraham obeyed God's instruction to kill his son for a burnt offering, and Kierkegaard refers to Abraham's act as "suspension of ethics to achieve a purposeful purpose".

Ethically speaking, this kind of behavior is against human nature and also against the moral norms of society, and is a kind of murder.

However, from the point of view of using the mystery of the universe and life to form a doctrine of exhortation and punishment of evil, and using it to teach the world and make people believe, it is a religious ritual "sacrifice" (sacrifice).

The Christian's behavior is to observe ethics and morality, but ethics and morality are not absolute standards, and they must sometimes be suspended in order to achieve higher purposes.

Religion B is the highest form of religious expression that Kierkegaard holds in high esteem, and he preaches his religious thought, modeled on Abraham's devotion to faith.

He believes that true faith is a leap from rational adherence to ethical norms to faith in God.

Therefore, reason must be abandoned in order to reach the final stage of religion in a fully committed way.

In ancient times, due to man's unknown exploration of the universe and his desire for immortal liberation, he came to believe in the existence of a supernatural mystical force or entity outside the real world, so that he would be in awe and worship of that mystery.

This leads to a system of beliefs, cognitive and ritual activities, and like folk mythology, it also has its own mythological legends, which are interconnected with each other.

In essence, it is the highest stage of spirituality and ultimate care in life, and at the same time, the most difficult to reach.

The only way to reach this stage is to return to the deepest part of one's heart in prayer and seek a dialogue with God, not just through social fellowship.

It requires the abandonment of ties to organizations or groups of like-minded people, and the freedom from the bonds of people bound together by common interests, which means that to experience God one must rely on oneself.

In other words, after experiencing the norms and standards of behavior that are appropriate when living purely in one's own selfishness and in the public life of mankind, after experiencing the sensual life of life and the ethical and rational acts of salvation, one must finally return to the individual.

This spiritual level of generation is the relationship with God, and man needs a transcendental existence, which is the most incomprehensible, but also the purest choice of man for himself: faith.

Chapter 6: Appearance, shape and nature of the existence of Qi Keguo

In the process of moving logic from traditional formal logic to modern dialectical logic, Kant proposed a whole new field, including three sets of logical judgments: possible and impossible, existence and non-existence, and necessary and contingent. Background of the concept.

In the 18th century, Kant taught the Logic 28 times during his 41-year teaching career. During this time, Kant used Professor Ehr's Logic, and his lectures generally followed the chapters of the original book.

However, he not only made some additions and deletions to the original book, but also openly debated some of its arguments.

It is also in this process that Kant has created a new approach to the traditional areas of logical judgment, such as "entity," "quantity," "nature," and "relation. In this process, Kant created "pattern" in addition to the traditional areas of logical judgment. The influence of "pattern logic".

As Kant pointed out, the old formal logic in the "field of metaphysics" of the laws of neutrosophic, contradiction, and identity was not content-independent in its deductive logic.

With the addition of a new column for style in the field, logical judgments of possibility and impossibility, existence and non-existence, necessity and contingency must involve the concrete content of logic.

Thus, Kant's "Stylistic Logic" has given birth to the transformation of modern logic from formal logic to dialectical logic.

The two most important themes in Kierkegaard's published works are the call to be truly Christian and the description of human existence.

The first theme is clear from Kierkegaard's autobiography.

The second theme can also be grasped from his publications. In almost six years (1843-1849), Kierkegaard completed three books, Fear and Fright, The Concept of Fear, and The Disease of Death, which deal with the concepts of fear, sorrow, and despair, the psychological terms that appear most frequently in Kierkegaard's other writings.

W. Lowrie and A. Dru, important figures in the study of Kierkegaard, regarded these three books as a trilogy of Kierkegaard's research on human psychology (Lowrie, 1965: 3).

Although Kierkegaard himself never clearly states the connection between fear, worry, and despair, he often uses these three words together in his books, sometimes pointing to the same state.

Sometimes the three words refer to the same state, but the differences between them are obvious from the text, and scholars who have studied Kierkegaard in the past have partially explored the meaning of the three words.

This paper attempts to clarify the similarities and differences, and presents the researcher's viewpoint as follows.

1. The Common Significance of Existence Modes

Although we can only imagine from the literature left by Kierkegaard, based on what is already known, the three do not know how things are the same and how they are different.

But it is certain that the connection of some nature between human and human or human and things formed by the three is generated through human existence.

Kierkegaard's exploration of human emotions, such as fear, sorrow, and despair, is in fact intended to prove the existence of human beings.

Psychological symptoms such as fear, worry, and despair are generally referred to as psychological states caused by neurophysiological changes in human beings, related to thoughts, feelings, behavioral responses, and a certain degree of pleasure or displeasure.

Kierkegaard, on the other hand, establishes human existence in terms of emotions, which can be understood in terms of its reaction against rationalism. Kierkegaard argues that between concepts and facts, concepts are impotent.

Human existence is a realized fact that cannot be fully explained by rational concepts, unlike rationalism from Plato onwards, which is accustomed to reason as the basis of human existence.

Kierkegaard criticizes rationalists who are good at building magnificent temples but do not live in them.

In particular, fear, anxiety and other emotions that are generally regarded as negative. Just as a doctor would say that no one is perfectly healthy, no one who truly understands human beings would say that anyone is truly free from despair.

No one can confidently claim to have never been affected by fear, anxiety or despair, and these psychological symptoms are the best proof of a person's existence. Emotions are the true indicators of the facts of life, so Kierkegaard chose to illustrate the facts of existence by referring to the emotional states of human beings.

Moreover, these psychological symptoms are also the human response to existence. Psychological symptoms such as fear and despair are states of human spiritual development. In exploring fear and despair, Kierkegaard begins with the idea that "man is a complex" and "man is spirit", and in "The Concept of Fear" Kierkegaard says

If the two cannot be closely connected in a person or a thing and become a spiritual body, then man is only an animal and will never become a human being, that is, only a manifestation of the spirit, and since the spirit exists by the manifestation of self-love, it exists in a power of resistance that constantly interferes with the relationship between the soul and the body.

Man possesses the ego by possessing the spirit, and man truly exists by possessing the ego. It is because human existence is a process of struggle as a complex that almost no one can escape the pain of this struggle.

These psychological states, which Kierkegaard explores, arise when the individual self consciously strives for a certain ideal or goal in violation of human nature, and when the two conflict, human nature naturally reacts with fear or reluctance.

Based on this potential for syndromic uneasiness, Kierkegaard makes the individual encounter difficulties on the path to becoming an ego, and manifest existential states of fear, apprehension, and despair.

In other words, psychological states represent the fact of human existence, and are also the reaction of human existence, so they can be described through these states. In the study of Kierkegaard, his analysis of human psychological symptoms is often regarded as the greatest contribution of Kierkegaard, but what cannot be forgotten is that

We should still regard these psychological symptoms as observations and descriptions of human existence, and they are a series of bright lights pointing to the path of "existence".

2. The distinction between the appearance, form, and nature of existence

01. Different objects

In "The Final Supplement to the Non-Scientific Nature of Philosophical Fragments," Kierkegaard says, "Fear and trembling are the psychological states that a person has when he is tried by God, when he suspends ethics to achieve the teleological purpose.

In the case of Abraham's sacrifice, for example, Abraham, a knight of faith, still felt fear when confronted with God's command.

Kierkegaard describes this fear as coming first out of curiosity: we are as curious about the outcome of our faith as we are about the ending of a book.

It is not always possible to choose the path of faith with total commitment from the beginning, and sacrifices are often made with a hint of skeptical awe, not to mention the fact that the sacrifice is made to the son of Abraham, so it is only natural that skepticism and fear should fill the heart.

Fear and trembling are a state of purpose suspension or uncertainty as the believer walks toward God with awe and fear in his heart.

Fear is the uneasiness that arises when the object of fear is unknown. Fear is a deep sense of foreboding, and the foreboding of the existence of life is fear.

In "The Concept of Fear," for example, Kierkegaard treats fear as a sin that precedes original sin, and he explores why Eve was tempted to pick the forbidden fruit.

Kierkegaard argues that God does not tempt nor is

tempted by man, but each man is tempted only by himself. Chicco argues that both Adam and Eve chose to eat the forbidden fruit out of their own depravity, not because of external temptation.

Although the source of fear does not necessarily lead to the fall, the fear of nothingness makes people choose to fall in order to escape from the fear of nothingness.

If fear is not viewed from a theological perspective, death becomes the main cause of the emptiness of life. When one realizes the inevitability of death, one's knowledge of death triggers fear.

Existential thinkers have always regarded death as the main cause of the emptiness of life, because death represents the dissipation of physical life, the ultimate death of man, and this attitude toward death, which places man in a state of emptiness, is also the main cause of fear.

When we further put despair into the consideration of the object, we can find that despair is also a psychological symptom that arises when the object of fear becomes the self.

Despair is the withdrawal of oneself from the

relationship. From fear to despair, it can be said that the fear of an individual's anxiety about nothingness turns into the discovery that what really drives an individual's anxiety does not come from the outside world, but from the sense of nothingness of one's existence.

From the above discussion, it is clear that the most fundamental difference in existence patterns is mainly the difference in the object. The concept of fear is different from the concept of fear and other fear-like concepts.

The positive meaning of emptiness represents freedom, that is, the more freedom one has, the higher the degree of fear of possibility.

In other words, fear is about something certain, while fear is about the feeling of the unknown of emptiness. When an individual finds out that the main cause of emptiness is oneself, the painful reaction that occurs when one wants to but cannot escape from oneself is despair.

02. Different degrees

There are three constructs that influence the existentialist thinking of Kierkegaard: one in dialectics, one in Hegel's inspirational influence, and one in religion.

He believes that each person has a great responsibility for his or her environment.

Although the world is constantly evolving, it still cannot liberate people. Authentic existence means that an individual with free will will make a decision for good or evil.

In the decision making process, because human beings are finite, the generation of "fear" - "worry" - "despair" is predictable.

However, one can also have faith beyond "fear"-"worry"-"despair" and have the potential to turn the situation around. However, we must clearly distinguish that "fear" and "sorrow" are two different states.

He uses the incident of Adam and Eve eating the forbidden fruit to explain it in words or in writing, and in this incident he clearly discovers the nature of the deep psyche.

There are two aspects of "fear": on the one hand, there is the anxiety of "unfulfillment", the anxiety of not being able to realize oneself because of limitations. On the other hand, there is the "fear" of wanting to realize oneself and fearing to realize oneself.

Individuals with free will need to make decisions and participate in their own hands, not just in abstract thinking activities such as analysis, synthesis, reasoning, and judgment in their minds.

It is not enough to talk about a certain proposition, doctrine, religion or someone's extreme belief and respect for orthodoxy; one must make up one's mind and determination, and the decision one makes is for the realization of one's own self, which is the problem that occurs simultaneously with the fall.

After the fall, there is another internal emotional conflict in the psyche, which leads to irrational feelings of worry or fear, which in turn leads to guilt, which leads to anxiety, and the limit of anxiety is despair.

When man's spirit clashes with matter, he experiences the conflict within himself because of his limited spirit, so he has the idea of trying to leave behind the things that hold him back and to be free of himself.

In the books "The Concept of Fear" and "The Disease of Death", Kierkegaard systematically describes the relationship between the concept of self-centeredness and the hope and imagination of future things.

In short, both are conditions or psychological attitudes of physical and mental disorders, but there is still a difference in the order of precedence. Fear precedes despair and is a precursor to despair, and everyone may have an ideal goal or objective.

But because we all have the possibility of freedom of will, this unknown brings people the feeling of "fear".

"Fear" is a person's insistence on facing the ideal, the uneasiness of not being able to satisfy the present, and the resistance of basic defenses, but "despair" is deeper than "fear".

Despair is not a passive acceptance, a load, but an active action, as Kierkegaard said: "Despair is no longer a passive suffering, but an action"; "Despair" is a form of psychological expression of the difficulties that arise when an individual faces the efforts that he or she has built up.

"Fear" is a state of adjustment according to the depth of mental understanding, and may produce the fear of being completely unable to face the "ideal".

In addition, the fear of the unknown leads to the development of a state of "despair" of incompatibility. The uncertainty brought about by the feeling of "emptiness" leads to anxiety, sadness, and fear.

"Despair" is a response to this uncertainty, so "despair" is more intense than "fear". When a human being faces the unknown "emptiness", the attitude of "fear" arises.

When the effort to regulate the attachment of love fails, the behavior of "despair" arises, which is the difference between passive and active in the process of negative emotions.

In addition, we can also say that "fear" is an emotion that arises from the ignorance of the existence of life based on the resistance of the basic defense of the awareness of life existence; "fear" is the "fear" of the emptiness of life existence; "despair" is the feeling that arises from the frustration of the action of developing countermeasures in the face of "fear".

Although there is no definite formula for the development of these three, the theme of Kierkegaard's exploration is to focus on the inability of human beings to adjust themselves smoothly, as a balanced complex, thus forming a state of "fear" - "fear" - "despair" negative emotions continue to increase.

Kierkegaard classifies things, phenomena, and concepts of life existence into categories, separating out the essence and its inner connection, which often makes people feel that it hinders the development of things, or impedes the existence of things.

However, Kierkegaard believes that through the awareness of these psychological symptoms, one can help one understand the existence of the self and discover the situations in the existence of life where it is possible to be free from the relationship with the self, and then find a way to be free from the pain of the existence of life, to be free from the worries, to be free from the fetters, and to become an autonomous and true self.

Chapter 7: Keguo's Consciousness

Born in Copenhagen, Denmark, in 1813 and died in 1855, Kierkegaard was a melancholic and prolific writer, once called the "Danish madman," who wrote countless works in his short 42-year life.

The Danish writer Søren Aabye Kierkegaard (1813-1855), known as the "father of existentialism," said in his diary, "The greatness of Socrates was that, even when he was accused and had to face the People's Assembly, he saw no group but the individual; the superiority of his nature was that he saw only the individual. , and

"But, alas, we mortals all act according to our senses, so that once we are gathered together, our impressions change - we see only abstract things and groups, and we become different".

He also says in the diary: "But in the eyes of God, the infinite number of souls that millions of people have had and have now does not form a group; He sees only each individual.

Kierkegaard lived only 42 years, but he had already published many works before he was 30 years old, and he walked around Copenhagen as a writer.

In 1846, the Danish sensationalist newspaper The Corsair published drawings and articles mocking Kierkegaard, portraying him as a comical eccentric, walking down the street and being gossiped about, pointed at, and implored and ridiculed by people, "dying from the slow trampling of geese," he joked.

This unpleasant personal experience made Kierkegaard more aware of the dangers of blindly following the "crowd. He called these ignorant masses "mobs" and "opinionless rabble".

In his mind, the "crowd" brings with it a lack of discernment, a lack of opinion, a lack of agreement with others, and a risky style of action that ignores subjective conditions and practical possibilities, and only the "individual" enters the religious stage as the way to the truth.

As a devout Christian, Kierkegaard says, "In God's

eyes, the infinite number of souls that millions of people have had and have now does not form a group, but He sees only each individual.

He believes that true faith must come from the heart of the "individual" and reach directly to the God of his faith, not from external indoctrination and social pressure.

Diary of Kierkegaard, Reflections of a Church Revivalist - The Tamed Goose / 1854: "Imagine what it would be like if the geese could speak - they would have arranged things so that they would have their own worship and worship God.

They would get together every Sunday and listen to a male goose preach a sermon. The male goose will talk about the ultimate destiny of the goose, the ultimate goal given to them by the Creator.

Their wings will carry them to the faraway land, the land of blessings, where they truly belong.

On earth they are like strangers in a foreign land. This is true every Sunday. At the end of the service, the crowd would rise and the geese would waddle home.

The next Sunday they come back for worship - and

then go home - and that's it. They will grow big and fat, plump and beautiful, and finally they will become the food on the plate on St. Martin's night - that's it!

Kierkegaard's work covers theology, literary criticism, psychology, and religion. He made many discoveries or pointed out errors in the social and Christian reformation of his time, and made more significant breakthroughs in philosophical understanding and opinion.

In particular, he laid the groundwork for the development of modernism by providing a reasoned analysis of Hegel's and Romanticism's erroneous or reactionary ideas, words, and deeds, and thereby rejecting them. He also gave a modern meaning to the role of the Bible and had a great influence on theology and religious philosophy in the twentieth century.

On the one hand, philosophy has been ridiculed for its lack of practical utility; on the other hand, when social and historical problems come to the fore, people often feel the need to reflect on reality from a philosophical point of view and seek ideas to solve the problems.

In today's increasingly utilitarian age, this dilemma and wandering state of mind seems to be more and more obvious. This further motivates people to ask: What is the meaning of philosophy? What is the mission of philosophy?

Philosophy is the study of universal and fundamental issues, including existence, knowledge, values, reason, mind, language, and other fields. Philosophy differs from other disciplines in that it has a unique way of thinking.

For example, it has a critical, often systematic approach, based on rational argumentation. In everyday parlance, philosophy can be derived as the most fundamental beliefs, concepts or attitudes of an individual or group at the time of its creation, when philosophy originally meant "love of wisdom".

At a time when knowledge was not yet differentiated and the social structure was relatively simple, philosophy, as love of wisdom, was itself knowledge, the key to insight into the world and the mysteries of life.

In "Dream of the Red Chamber", the so-called "worldly matters are all learned, human feelings are essays" is the primary stage of this state, and the realm of Laozhuang and Buddha is the advanced form of this state. Thus, for ordinary people, the concern is to relate philosophy to knowledge for practical use.

For philosophers, philosophy represents the state of walking on the wind, the most harmonious and beautiful state of seeing through the bonds of life and death and living with nature.

So, with the change of time, does the original meaning of philosophy still exist? In its original meaning, philosophy is

It seeks to realize a general perspective on social life and life experiences, and to point to a higher realm. As long as human beings exist, this realm will continue to emerge.

Lao Tzu's "The Great Way of Wu Wei", More's "Utopia", and Marx's "Communism" all point to the ideal realm of social life.

Those who have a grateful heart will accumulate an emotional complex; those who have a righteous act will accumulate a moral responsibility; while those who have a depressed mind will only have a cynical and resentful heart.

This kind of reflection on the present life in order to seek transcendence is already an intrinsic character of philosophy. When Kant opposed the solipsism of his time in the Critique of Pure Reason, he already saw the limitations of English empiricism and French solipsism from the level of discernment, and his re-exploration of reason meant a re-exploration and rearrangement of the world.

In fact, this is also the rational examination made by German intellectuals in the face of the history of the time. This is the transcendent side of philosophy, and also its living side.

Thus, it has become an intrinsic character of philosophy to reflect on the present life in order to seek transcendence, which we can only truly understand if we do it ourselves, and it is useless to rely on imagination.

Experience is the precious wealth of life, only experience will let you grow, and only experience will let you mature. Philosophy is an ability to imagine the future, and philosophical thinking is to perfect and perfect this ability to imagine. This is the beauty of philosophy.

When human beings lose this imagination, it is also the time when human beings' ego is destroyed. The operation of philosophy is to cultivate this transcendent insight and ability, but it is not enough to stop there.

Not only do we need this ability, but we also need to realize this ability, which is to "decide" and "do", to "practice". This "practice" is not a reckless impulse, but a choice and action made on the basis of insight into society and life, a change of the present.

Without such practice in the sense of change, philosophical insight would be a cynical helplessness, and this cynicism is actually another kind of submission to the current reality, another interpretation of the real world.

When philosophy is confronted with social history, its direct form of existence is a social-critical theory. In this case, the direct mission of philosophy is to see through the social existence and its inner contradictions and explore a path to another kind of social reality.

In this way, an abstract "ought" is transformed into a realistic "possibility", from the "not yet" of the present society to the "could be" of the future.

Therefore, we should return to the existence of human life, understand the limited purposes that human beings can achieve, understand human worries, fears, and sensibilities, and find the possibility to live in peace.

His philosophical writings are full of literary excitement, or emotions of tension, surprise, and excitement, and are not at all like the serious and restrained philosophical writings that are commonly thought of as detailed and elaborate. Since the age of 22, he has been writing and writing day and night, and has spent 20 years of his life reading or concentrating on writing.

Kierkegaard, who lamented that he "never had a confidant," was not recognized by the intellectual community during his lifetime, but was honored with the title of "Father of Existentialism" years after his death.

The reason for this title is that he shifted the focus of philosophy from the process of seeking answers to the external world and the construction of knowledge systems to the existence itself, which is the meaning of human life.

Existential Being refers to the existence of the meaning of human life. If we ask: Does the sun exist? Does the moon exist? This question is meaningless because whether you ask it or not, these things will remain the same and will not change.

The existence of human life is not rigid, but a stage

with vitality that I love to take and can choose freely with my own will. In other words, existence is the choice of self-love, the possibility of choosing to become autonomous.

When making a choice, there are two possibilities: the first is to choose not to be oneself, and the second is to choose to become oneself.

The first choice is obviously easier. In this case, we are used to pretending to be ourselves, hiding our true feelings and playing the role expected by others.

We never make a sincere choice because we are afraid that a sincere choice will bring us into conflict with others.

Kierkegaard brings out the connotation of free choice in the "existence" of human beings. He argues that although humans are the only ones in the universe who are qualified to use the word existence, few people actually use it.

Kierkegaard once gave a vivid example as an analogy: life is like a drunken farmer driving a wagon home, apparently the farmer is driving the wagon, but in fact the old horse is dragging the farmer home.

Because the farmer is drunk and has no sober

consciousness at all, but the old horse knows the way, so it can drag the farmer home.

A person's life is like a drunken farmer driving a carriage on his way home, most of the time in a drowsy state. Only when one is awake can one decide what path one wants to take and be true to oneself.

Many contemporary issues, such as living for yourself, being yourself, etc., are inspired by existentialism.

In the Chinese translation of the "Diary of Kierkegaard", the first one chosen was written in 1836, as follows: "I have just returned from a party, of which I was the vitality and soul

I am a party vigor and soul, I am a party vigor and soul, I am the word, everyone laughs and reveres me for it - but I go away, I really need to use in this diary, a dash as long as the earth's orbit - I want to shoot myself.

The 23-year-old Kierkegaard wrote this diary as a full expression of his melancholy and pessimism, his weariness and impatience with people and worldly values.

After returning from a very popular and respected party, he "wanted to shoot himself," disgusted and angry with himself because of his enjoyment in the group. He described his mood as "the same as a eunuch's libido, a pool of stagnant water.

He wrote in his diary: "I have a close friend - my melancholy - who follows me around ...... She is the most faithful mistress I know.

The new edition of the Chinese translation of the diary is a selection of the most representative chapters from the nearly 10,000 pages of the diary, organized in a chronological framework into four major themes: the labyrinth of the mind, interpersonal relations, philosophical thought, and the interpretation of Christianity.

The four themes outline the image of Kierkegaard as a son of man, a writer, and a Christian, and present the whole picture of Kierkegaard's inner world.

It begins with "The Labyrinth of the Mind" and ends with "Life and Death". A diary he wrote a year before his death says: "Listen to the cries of women in childbirth, gaze at the struggles of dying men in their final moments, and tell me, is there a single thing in the beginning and end of life that is intended for human enjoyment?

Thus, Zichenko sees life in this way: "Man accepts life without choice, then spends it under conditions of helplessness, and finally surrenders it under an irresistible struggle.

Conclusion

The ethics of faith proposed by Kierkegaard is not to establish a solid system of universal ethics, but rather to emphasize the dynamic two-way ethics of the individual in faith.

By "individual" he means individual, not isolated. A person can only be himself before a higher power, God, and a person can only be a self-reliant person before all people.

His emphasis is on the need for the individual to maintain the integrity of the individual, the true morality, in the congregation as well as in the religious life, the reality of the subject. The individual, in the midst of the "either/or" choices he faces in life

The individual, in the midst of life's "either/or" choices, constantly seeks to choose himself or herself with a whole-person, passionate commitment, choosing to be in absolute relationship with the absolute God as a unique individual, with absolute responsibility and obligation.

"In the face of the intellectual, political, religious, and social erosion of human subjectivity, Kierkegaard advocates a return to his own inwardness, where only in the realm of the individual can man see himself clearly, understand himself, and discover his deepest relationship with God.

However, Kierkegaard's individuality focuses on purity and integrity in relation to oneself, rather than isolation from the "other".

This "suspended ethical" obligation is not to abolish ethics; the life of faith will only deepen the love of the other through the love of God, not suspend it; rather, it is to abandon human rational judgment and calculation, and to leap from the finite existence of life to the metamorphosis of unknown, infinite possibilities.

Therefore, Kierkegaard does not want people to live the isolated life of Thoreau, nor does he preach atomic individualism, or an individual who exists alone to the exclusion of all others, but he believes that the existence of God brings out the existence of the individual.

In other words, it is natural for each person to be

alone or to identify himself as an individual, but it does not follow that he naturally becomes an independent individual.

This is because the individual that Kierkegaard requires is an individual who, in the process of interaction between the environment and the outside world, develops the inwardness to turn to himself.

It is the pursuit of a truth of personal subjectivity that is developed in the world of others, and the gradual "emergence" of an individual through individual introspection and action.

Kierkegaard's view that human beings can only become individuals through generative efforts echoes that of the German philosopher of history, Herder, who believed that every animal develops according to its own internal mechanism, but human beings are not such animals; they are not born perfect, but must develop their own perfect personality and humanity.

The existential psychologist Rollo May (1909-1994) also supported this view, stating that if the self is to be realized, it must have a clear affirmation and determination of itself, and that plants or animals grow by instinct, and that the nature and being of these creatures are identical.

However, to become a true human being is only by personal choice, and the decisions that people make every day will give meaning to their existence. Therefore, the purpose of being a human being is to become a free and complete human being, a "conscious individual" with a complete inner nature.

Part 2: Martin Buber's Philosophy of Dialogue

Preface

The philosophy of religion (English: philosophy of religion) is a fictitious reflection of the objective world. It is the belief that what dominates nature and society is a supernatural, superhuman mystical realm and power, and therefore infinite awe and worship.

The philosophy of religion is a philosophical consideration of the problems and concepts it contains. The philosophy of religion studies topics such as the existence or non-existence of God, the nature of God, the relationship between religion and science, the relationship between religion and morality, and the nature of good and evil.

The philosophy of religion differs from the philosophy

of religious belief in that the former is a study of religion from outside of it. The latter, on the other hand, is based on the belief in a particular idea or religion or pursuit, and therefore the religious views of the 20th century are more diverse than those of the previous two or three centuries.

This is related to the great changes in cultural reality on the one hand, and to the deepening of humanistic research on the other. In the last hundred years, religious issues have received a great deal of attention in the liberal arts, and many prominent thinkers have put forward a great deal of new ideas and doctrines from a variety of fields, making people increasingly aware of the importance and complexity of religious issues.

Judaism, by far the oldest monotheistic religion in the world, is confronted with the same questions as other religions in the 20th century. And as a people who have lived and died with Judaism, the Jewish people

Some of the more prominent Jewish philosophers of the 20th century include Herman Cohen, Franz Rosenzweig, Martin Buber, Abraham J. Heschel, and Mordechai M. Kaplan.

Martin Buber is the most famous of them, and his

thought is a prominent and typical part of 20th century Jewish theological philosophy that consists of parts or individuals that are combined into a whole.

The development and evolution of the concept of "relationship" in 20th century Jewish religious philosophy, encountering verbal dialogue. Martin Buber is a prominent representative of 20th century Jewish philosophers, and his philosophy of dialogue is the most powerful interpretation of the concept of "relationship".

Martin Buber's "I and You" encounters the philosophy of verbal dialogue "relationship" as a single or inductive, detailed and in-depth statement of the issues, events, and studies of "I and You" or "I and He".

It also presents the "existential" problems, or solutions to them, and describes them in its own interpretation. The first and the second involve Hermann Cohen, Franz Rosenzweig, and Emmanuel Levinas.

Hermann Cohen (German: Hermann Cohen, July 4, 1842 - April 4, 1918) was a German Jewish philosopher, one of the founders of the Marburg School of Neo-Kantianism, and is often called "the most important Jewish philosopher of the nineteenth century".

Hermann Cohen devoted himself to explaining Kant's theory of experience, the foundations of ethics, and the foundations of aesthetics, and in 1902 began publishing his own major works on systematic philosophy in three volumes: Logic and Pure Knowledge (1902), Ethics and Pure Will (1904), and Aesthetics and Pure Feeling (1912). The fourth volume of the project on psychology was never written.

Franz Rosenzweig, the famous Jewish thinker and philosopher of the 20th century, whose life was a great spiritual quest and whose profound philosophical ideas were perfectly integrated with the study of Judaism.

Franz Rosenzweig is one of the great thinkers of the twentieth century who can be ranked with Wittgenstein and Heidegger, whose life is even more bizarre than Wittgenstein's, and whose importance is not yet widely recognized.

But just as the solitary Kafka was destined to receive his time, so too is Kafka's time bound to come. Although he left behind few writings in his short life, every step he took in his thoughtfulness was well thought out.

From writing "The Star of Salvation" on postcards in

the trenches, to translating the poems of Judah Halevy, to collaborating with Martin Buber on the translation of the Bible during his illness, the trajectory of his life was the realization of thought, and the perfect unity of knowledge and action was achieved during his fatal illness.

For Hermann Cohen, religion begins with the establishment of a mutual verbal dialogue "relationship" between the individual human being and God, and his discovery of the concept of "correlation" opened up a new approach to the construction of Jewish philosophy.

Franz Rosenzweig argues that although man cannot know the nature of God or the world, he can enter into a verbal dialogue with them, that is, a dialogue with them.

This is what he means by "the new thinking". Hermann Cohen's "interrelationship" and Franz Rosenzweig's "the new thinking" have had a subtle effect on Martin Buber's philosophy of dialogue.

In Daniel, Martin Buber suggests that the two attitudes of "I and you" and "I and it", which are fully presented in I and you, are always clearly identifiable and show a strong recognition of the dialogical "relationship" between the "I and you" encounter.

Levinas criticizes the "symmetry" of Martin Buber's "I and you" encounter speech dialogue "relationship", arguing that the relationship between the "I" and the Other is asymmetrical and proposing the concept of the "absolute Other".

James C. Livingston once said of Martin Buber: "Martin Buber is the most important, and certainly the most influential, Jewish religious philosopher of the 20th century.

Martin Buber's great contribution to modern thought, and to Christian theologians such as Brunner and Tillich, was his book I and Thou (1923).

Leaving aside the fact that the phrase (I and Thou) has become an idiom, this book has had a wide impact not only in theology but also in the various social sciences, psychotherapy, and education."

Chapter 1: The era background of the formation of the dialogue philosophy of "I and Ru"

In 1923, Martin Buber published his acclaimed book, I and Thou. In that book, he distinguished between "I and you" and "I and it" and presented his "philosophy of dialogue" or "philosophy of relation" in poetic language. Martin Buber claims that his philosophy is "atypical", that there is no system, that his life is his philosophy.

I must reiterate: I don't teach. I just point to something.

I point to the real, I point to what is not seen and is rarely noticed in the real. I take the hand of the person who is listening to me and lead him to the window. I open the window and point out the window.

I don't learn to speak, but I talk. Martin Buber's life was a life of dialogue, and the philosophy of dialogue was an intrinsic theoretical support for almost all his activities.

He actively participated in the Cultural Zionist movement, studied Jewish Hasidism, and collaborated with Rosenzweig in the translation of the Hebrew Bible, making a great contribution to the revival of the Jewish people and the promotion of Jewish culture.

It can be said that the Cultural Restoration Movement is a dialogue between Jewish tradition and reality; while Hasidism advocates entering into a state of ecstasy and realizing direct communication between man and God.

The Hebrew Bible is a dialogue between God and man, and the translation of the Hebrew Bible is a dialogue with the original text; there is a need for dialogue and communication between people, and these dialogues are themselves a kind of relationship.

This shows that the "philosophy of dialogue" is the most important part of Martin Buber's thought. Martin Buber's philosophy of dialogue is one of the responses of Judaism to modernity. The philosophy of dialogue already answers the question of "what is Judaism", that is, Judaism is a religion in a traditional-modern dialogue, a religion in relationship to other pluralistic factors.

The concept of "dialogue" indicates one of the possible relationships that can take place between religions and even cultures, and therefore an organization of the concept of "dialogue" is urgent and very important and necessary.

Since it is only in Martin Buber that the concept of "dialogue" begins to take a mature form and clear expression in the Jewish philosophy of analytic thinking and reflection on fundamental questions of life, knowledge, and value, this paper takes Martin Buber's philosophy of dialogue as the main axis of discussion.

Martin Buber (1878-1965) was a man who, in the 19th century, conducted a relatively advanced search for and pursued the purpose of social activities, science, and religious and cultural groups that directly affect the physical and mental development of human beings at all levels.

In particular, his philosophy of dialogue, the point of view or social consciousness of the interconnection between people and things, is sufficient to establish a system of thought, and is ranked with Kierkegaard and Nietzsche as the founding fathers of existentialism.

In his time, his religious philosophical thinking reflected the socio-political aspirations of the general public and the trend of thought in the study of the universal, fundamental questions of life itself, including the fields of existence, knowledge, values, reason, mind, and language.

Born into a Jewish family in Vienna, Martin Buber studied philosophy, history, and art at the Universities of Vienna, Leipzig, Berlin, and Zurich, and was fascinated by the work of Wilhelm Dithey (1878-1965). (He was fascinated by the philosophy of Wilhelm Dithey and Simmerl. His life's research and activities are divided into four parts.

(a) Religious philosophy

(2) Biblical translation and related treatises

(Hasidism (Hebrew: חסידות; or Hasid), a branch of Jewish orthodoxy influenced by Jewish mysticism, was founded in the 18th century by Rabbi Baal Shem Tov in Eastern Europe to oppose the overemphasis on legalistic Judaism of the time. The Hasidic sect was founded in the mid-18th century by Rabbi Baal Shem Tov in Eastern Europe to oppose the overemphasis on observant

Judaism. The Hasidic sect was a religious mystic group among Polish Jews in the mid-18th century that opposed the orthodox laws and supreme authority of Judaism and emphasized union with God through fervent prayer and piety.

(4) Participated in meaningful Jewish propaganda for nation-building among the masses.

His field of study is very much related to his book "I and Thou," which is devoted to the state of interactions and interactions between people and things.

His translations of the Bible are obscure and difficult. He believes that the Bible cannot be studied in depth without seriousness, and that people should acquire wisdom and experience in the process of learning and practice through reading, listening to lectures, studying, and practicing.

Translation is an effort to explore the author's heart and soul, a conversation between the translator (reader) and the author, just as the author leads the people to point out and explain, to understand, comprehend, awaken, and realize from the removal of doubts.

So, strictly speaking, Martin Buber's religious

philosophy of "I and you, I and it", the "philosophy of dialogue", also begins with the "confession" of the religious who, for his own faults, expresses his repentance to the priest alone, who then, on behalf of God, forgives his faults.

Section 1. How to repent to God?

According to Wikipedia, the Sacrament of Confession is one of the seven Catholic sacraments. The confessor comes to the confessional in the church, confesses his sins to the priest through a partition, and seeks absolution.

Catholics believe that the confessor confesses directly to God and that the priest is the intermediary, but that the priest can ultimately forgive the sins of the faithful.

Don't worry about confessions being leaked

In any case, the most important aspect of the whole sacrament of confession is that the confessor's confession to the priest should not be disclosed because of the priest's obligation of confidentiality.

Excommunication for breaking the confession

Under the law of the Catholic Church, if a priest

breaks his obligation of confidentiality, he is excommunicated, which is the most severe punishment for a priest, and only the Pope can allow him to return to the Church.

Moreover, not only could a priest not reveal the confession of a penitent, but he was also forbidden to reveal who had confessed, a rule that had existed in the Catholic Church since at least 1215.

One day a young man confessed to a priest: "Father, when I was carrying a bucket of water across the street, I saw people coming and going and it was difficult to pass, so I raised my voice and shouted, 'Urine! Urine! Some people say I am a genius, some say I am a fool, in your opinion, what am I?

The priest asked back, "Brother XX! How do you see yourself?"

The young man looked confused: "......? .

The priest said, "Brother XX! For example, a bag of wheat can also be flour, in the West it becomes bread, in China it becomes buns, in the eyes of a baker it is bread, in the eyes of a winemaker it is wine, in the eyes of a homeless man it is food that can be used for a meal, but wheat is still the same wheat".

The young man was enlightened: "......? The young man realized: "?

The priest gently and calmly asked, "Brother XX! What is the lie that you have told today? What was the lie you told today?

The young man said calmly, "Father! Don't you already know everything?

The priest smiled and said, "Yes, Brother XX! When you said that these were the two lies of the day, was it already the first lie? . ...Why? The priest knows the first lie. ....

As one person reads a book, a hundred people have a hundred thoughts and opinions, and a thousand people have a thousand thoughts and opinions, so Martin Buber's translation of the Bible is like that of a priest who knows very well in his heart that he is a priest.

In the mind of the general public, people are self-centered, from the perspective of their own bodies and minds, from the perspective of society, from the perspective of mountains and rivers, and even from the perspective of the entire universe, as if the eyes of the whole world are on them.

This is where Martin Buber (1878-1965) began his translation. The early church fathers also retained the meaning of "liturgy" in worship.

In the Didache, it is affirmed that the office of bishop and deacon is fulfilling the "Liturgy" of prophet and teacher, the word Liturgy, which is the same word now used by many of the present churches, was originally a Roman term of life and was later referred to by Christians as a church term, while the original term of life disappeared and became a Christian term.

A series of public forms of ritual or modes of worship of any religious community, occasionally referring specifically to rituals that are routinely used (whether recommended or prescribed) by the Christian congregation or the Christian denomination.

Liturgical renewal truly corresponds to the fundamental expectation of the Council: "The liturgy is most adequate to enable the faithful to express the miracle of Christ and the pure nature of the true Church in their lives, and to make it known to others. And there are three elements that make up the liturgy.

First, the role of Christ.

The Vatican II Constitution on the Liturgy defines the liturgy more fully, including the presence of Christ in the celebration of the Mass, the celebration of the sacraments, the celebration of the Word, and the Divine Office. At Mass, Christ Himself "offered Himself on the cross, and He still offers Himself by the hands of the priests".

St. Augustine said, "Whoever baptizes, baptizes Christ Himself. The active role of Christ in carrying out His priestly duties. He performed this duty in preaching the gospel, healing the sick, releasing the captives, bringing this duty to its peak, and completing it.

Second, the role of the Church.

Christ connects the Church with Himself and makes it a powerful executor of the office. These expressions: "by the hand of the priest", "whoever pays the baptism", "when the Bible is read in the Church", "when the Church prays and sings" all point to the role of the Church in the liturgy as an executor of the office.

And as an act of Christ and of the Church, the liturgy is "the most excellent divine act, and no other act of the Church can be compared, in the same name, with the utility of the liturgy.

Thirdly, the Bible.

It is an essential component of the liturgy. The Scriptures are of great importance in the celebration of the liturgy because the Scriptures read and explained in the sermon and the psalms sung are derived from the Scriptures; the prayers, collects and liturgical hymns are also inspired by the Scriptures.

The prayers, collects and liturgical hymns are also inspired by the Bible; the movements and symbols are also inspired by the Bible". Therefore, the celebration of the liturgy, whether it be Mass, the sacraments, the ordinances, or the hourly prayers, must include the proclamation of the Word of God.

At that time, people lacked sincerity or were impractical, and the sacraments such as Christian worship, Mass, or baptism were merely formal and superficial.

The liturgy is "the most outstanding sacred action", and all of this is inspired by the Bible; there are also actions and symbols that are taken from the Bible, therefore, to carry out the emphasis on the sacred meaning of the spiritual food, it is necessary to read and understand it seriously as a guide, so that the general public can read and understand the sacred meaning of the Bible.

Once they understand the true meaning of the Bible, they will not have a self-centered and biased perception, and they will not become a living prop in the rituals of the Church. Only then can we truly understand the true meaning of "conversation," "dialogue," "relationship," "encounter," "I and you" and "I and it.

The content describes Martin Buber as a thinker who valued the relationship between "I" and the outside world, valuing "I and you" rather than "I and it" (the world of experience).

Therefore, he respectfully believed in the Bible as "you". This is an "encounter" that transcends time and space and the spirit of history.

It is not difficult to find in it a change in the objective existence of Dilthey's consciousness, reflected in an indirect or invisible way, of Martin Buber's consciousness, through the activity of thought.

Although the main part of the "encounter" with the

origin and foundation of things carries the psychological overtone of judging things according to one's own perceptions without trying to conform to the actual situation, Martin Buber's (and his) consciousness is not as strong as his own.

But Martin Buber, from his life to his death, always had a passionate and sincere expectation of human beings, and devoted his whole life to the "encounter" with other people, which contains accidental and unexpected encounters.

Strictly speaking, for devout followers, both religious believers and personal worshipers, Martin Buber was inspired by the Hasidic religious life from his childhood.

He broke the gap between religious thought and moved from the Old Testament to the New Testament, listening intently to the Sermon on the Mount of Jesus and the revelation of the Gospel of John.

According to his doctrine of the "encounter" with the worldview, which is a generalization and summary of natural and social knowledge, he injected a new spirit into the Jewish Founding Movement: and changed being "Jewish" to being Jewish "human".

From the standpoint or starting point of Martin Buber's existentialist philosophy, it is clear that the book "I and Thou; Ich und Du" is based on Jewish thought, which is a study of the universal and fundamental problems of modern Western idealism since the 16th century, including the fields of existence, knowledge, values, reason, mind, language, etc., and the wrong or He is also an expert in the analysis of wrong or reactionary thoughts, words, and deeds, and thus rejects them with reason.

In his view, it is not Descartes' idealistic philosophy of "I think, therefore I am" that really determines the existence of one's ego life.

Nor is it anything perceivable or imaginable that is hostile, repulsive, or in conflict with the self, including both things that exist objectively and can be observed (e.g., people, trees, houses, abstract things such as prices, freedom) and things that are imagined (e.g., deified figures).

Rather, it is a way of "dialogue" between oneself and the various existences in the world, and the way in which events occur in a state of interaction and mutual influence between people and things.

This kind of "life existence" for the ego itself has to be established and generated in relation to the life existence in the world of "Being" and "It", but the existence of the human ego life existence itself.

But the existence of the human being's self-existence itself, which is an intense hope for "you", makes the human being constantly and informally resist and transform "beyond" the present situation according to the pre-determined idea, and it is because of this resisting relationship that the human being's spiritual, moral and interactive action or influence on things is cultivated.

It is precisely because of this antagonistic relationship that one cultivates and practices one's spiritual, moral and interactional role or influence on things.

I and Thou is one of the most important books of the famous Israeli religious philosopher Martin Buber (1878~1965). It was published in Leipzig, Germany, in 1923 and translated into English in 1937.

It is the mature work of Martin Buber's "philosophy of dialogue". In this book, Martin Buber reminds us of the state of interaction and mutual influence between I-Thou things, which are the subject of each other.

This view has had a significant and far-reaching influence on later theology, ethics, philosophy, education, and other aspects.

Martin Buber's philosophy of dialogue, which began in the first decade of the twentieth century, is a progressive process of change from the small to the large, from the simple to the complex, from the low to the high, a constant renewal of things.

This book can be said to be the maturation of the philosophy of dialogue. He started this book in the general concept of including knowledge and skills. It is the experience or observation of a certain event or a certain event after the acquisition of the mind and apply to the subsequent work.

These previously acquired knowledge and skills are crucial to the mastery of work or the teaching of learning.

Instead of abstract, universal ideas that act as categories or classes of entities, events, or relationships, the starting point is neither metaphysics nor theology, but philosophical anthropology; this approach to philosophy has led Martin Buber to be regarded as one of the contemporary thinkers of existentialism. This approach to philosophy is why Martin Buber is considered one of the contemporary thinkers of existentialism.

However, his emphasis on the between with G. Marcel (1889-1973) and F. Rosenzweig (1886-1929) is significantly different from the emphasis on the existential subject of other existentialists.

In philosophy, the term "existential subject" refers to a being with a unique consciousness or a unique personal experience, or another entity external to and related to itself.

The subject is the observer and the object is the observed. The subject is the central term for the discussion of its own nature. The nature of the subject also plays a part in the dominant or central role in the discussion of subjective experience in Anglo-American analytic philosophy.

The sharp opposition between the subject and the object corresponds to the opposition between thought and the extended object in Descartes' philosophy.

Descartes believed that thought (subjectivity) is the essence of spirit, while the extension (occupation of space) is the essence of matter.

Res extensa is one of the three entities proposed by René Descartes in his Cartesian ontology (also known as "radical dualism"), the other two being res cogitans and God. In Latin, "res extensa" means "something that extends".

Descartes, too, often referred to this form of thinking as reflecting the nature of things. On the basis of perceptual knowledge, people generalize from the many attributes of the same thing, forming a concept expressed in words or phrases, which is translated as "corporeal substance".

In Descartes' ontology of the "entity-attribute" model, extensiveness is the main attribute of material entities. In the Second Meditation, Descartes analyzes a block of wax (see the block of wax argument).

A solid piece of wax has certain sensory properties. When the wax melts, however, it loses every property of appearance that it had in its solid form.

However, Descartes believed that the idea of wax could still be found in the melted substance.

The second section, the main principles of the core thinking of "I and Ru"

This is the principle of the "philosophy of dialogue" presented by Martin Buber, the famous Israeli religious philosopher, in his famous book "I and Thou; Ich und Du".

Martin Buber sees I and Thou (I and it) and I and Thou (I and you) as two ways in which people and the world communicate or communicate with each other, which together construct the "being" of the existence of self-life itself.

"I and Thou" is the influence and involvement of something related. It means that all the people or things (it) that are involved with and influence each other are things or means to satisfy the interests, needs, and desires of "I" in order to achieve a certain purpose.

Therefore, what "I" and "it" establish is only a partial, one-sided interpersonal thing, and the situation of interconnection and influence occurs between them, and the "I" at this time does not have or keep the part that it should have, and there is no damage or mutilation.

The relationship between "I and Thou" is a certain nature of connection between human beings and human beings or human beings and things: that is, "I" regard "Thou" as the whole, all, everything, as the fundamental condition for life.

It is not a situation in which we establish a connection and influence between people, things and things with "you" in order to satisfy "my" personal interests, needs and desires.

Therefore, it is necessary to approach "you" with the "existence" and the whole life of the "self" being itself.

At this time, the "I" that exists in the "existence" of the "self" is the real "existence" that exists in the "existence" of the "self" and is truly capable of self-awareness.

The so-called awareness is a state of being in which "the ego can choose to live itself". It means to be aware of the present moment.

It is, for example, about what is happening and why; about all the possibilities and most likely consequences of any choice or action.

It is about being keenly observant of what is so and why, and of how it can be kept from happening and why.

In short, the "I" of "I and you" is the selfless, unconcealed, unconcealed, public I. The "I and it" of "I" is the individual, self-serving, one-sided I, as opposed to the "public" I.

Martin Buber's principle of dialogue between "I and Thou" as it relates to the influence and involvement of related things is extremely important for educational theory and practice, i.e., the ideas, truths, or insights gained from enlightenment.

This is because the process of mutual communication and feeling between people, especially the development and change of education, is experienced.

There is always a certain level of interaction and dialogue between teachers and students, as well as influence and involvement in related matters.

Martin Buber expands on this mutual dialogue by arguing that the fundamental or starting point for the development of education is the mutual dialogue between teachers and students.

Therefore, the principle of dialogue is to express the sincerity and honesty between "me and you" in order to touch others from the bottom of their hearts and eventually gain their trust.

The principle of mutual respect, trust, and love between "I and you" (not I and it), with the hope that the desired goal will become a reality, and the conceptual understanding that both teachers and students can adhere to each other.

The laws or guidelines by which this is said or done also apply to things in general, not only to bring to mind things forgotten or hard to recall, but sometimes by cautioning teachers not to overestimate the reality of the situation because of their high self-esteem.

To cause many teachers with cognitive biases to mistake themselves as authorities of knowledge, titans specializing in a particular discipline or profession, and to treat students as machines (It) in the process of acquiring knowledge or skills through reading, listening, thinking, research, and practice.

At the same time, students are also reminded to respect teachers and not to hold certain concepts or attitudes. For example, the mentality of exchanging money for learning and experience gained in the process of learning and practice.

Rather, we should regard a competent person who is worthy of learning and who is able to bring certain correct knowledge and guidance to everyone.

They are regarded as machines that automatically accept coins and sell knowledge without human control. Not every student has the ability to communicate and exchange ideas directly and satisfactorily.

Therefore, it is one of the tasks of the teacher to educate and train students for a long period of time in accordance with certain objectives, so that they can grow in their ability to converse.

For students who have difficulty in communicating in language with two or more people, they should be given a good environment and conditions to impart their ideas, character, and knowledge without discrimination.

In order to positively influence the student's ability to converse, and to motivate him to be sincere and honest with his own life, so as to touch others from the bottom of his heart, and eventually to gain their trust and answer.

Although the teacher and the student are often in contact with each other in general concepts including knowledge, skills, or experience or observation of a particular event or situation, the teacher and the student are often in contact with each other.

The teacher and the student are often working with

each other on general concepts including knowledge, skills, or what they have gained from experiencing or observing a particular event or incident, and applying them to subsequent assignments.

These previously acquired knowledge and skills are not sufficient for work or teaching the critical gaps in knowledge that are important for mastery, and for the direct exchange of meanings.

However, the teacher can continue to understand and appreciate the joy of "teaching and learning" through the whole process of dialogue.

In other words, through this continuous dialogue between two or more people, the more mature person (the teacher) can guide those who are changing from young to old, from simple to complex, from ignorant to mature, a process of metamorphosis "beyond" the current situation, and constantly progressing and renewing themselves (the students).

The teacher acts or changes the student in an indirect or invisible way, in a state of interaction and mutual influence between each other's dialogues.

The feedback from the students to the teachers is also

a sharing of life between the teachers and the students in their own existence. Therefore, in the social activities whose direct purpose is to influence the physical and mental development of human beings.

The main point is that in the process of cultivating students in schools, if both teachers and students see each other as people who have or maintain the parts that they should have, without damage or defects, they try to achieve, within a certain range, the greatest possible "we and our students".

If both students and teachers treat each other as persons who have or maintain the parts of each other that should be there, without damage or defects, and try to maximize the extent to which the rules or guidelines according to which "I and you" speak or act are also applicable to each other in general, the development of the role or influence of both parties on the matter in question will be better promoted, and the mutual connection, interaction and influence of both parties will be more effective.

Chapter 2: Contents of the Dialogue Philosophy of "I and You"

The content of Martin Buber's book "I and Thou" is divided into four parts: Volume I, Volume II, Volume III, and an afterword.

The first volume illustrates the two contradictory and unified properties of things in the world itself and the two opposing natures of life at the same time; the former refers to the opposition between the world of Thou and the world of It, and the latter refers to the opposition between the life of I-Thou and the life of I-It.

The second volume explores the emergence and manifestation of I-Thou and I-It in human history and culture.

The third volume explains the eternal thou, i.e., the connection between God and human things.

The first part:

In the first volume, Martin Buber argues that man himself is situated in two world environments or contexts, and therefore has two distinct lives.

On the one hand, people live in a certain area or sphere of activity of "it," and in order to sustain life and desire and demand things, they must treat the existents surrounding the self, including other people and living things, as separate and apart from the "I," and think or judge the rationality of something from a different viewpoint or perspective in opposition to it.

In this way, I can obtain the knowledge and experience that I have acquired in the process of learning and practice. And to make others or things available to me. This is a situation where the "I" is related to the "it".

In addition to the whole, all, and everything of "it", man also dwells in the whole, all, and everything of "thou", and in a certain field or area of activity, man meets (encounter) with other "thou" as a being without prior appointment, and the "I" that meets unexpectedly or by chance is no longer just something in the same objective thing.

The "I" is no longer just a subject who, in the process

of direct contact with objective things, acquires through the sense organs, the awareness and application of the phenomena and external connections of the objective things.

It is also a being with a unique consciousness and/or a unique personal experience, or another entity external to itself and in relation to it.

"The Thou is no longer a thing in a certain time and space. "I and Thou are not separate from other parts or wholes or subjects; Thou is the whole, all, everything, life, even the divine.

The unexpected encounter or chance meeting between "I" and "Thou" is a way to face the bright light of "Thou"'s existence with one's whole life, and to feel the deep and heavy torture and pain and suffering of the body or spirit.

Martin Buber argues that the two contradictory attributes inherent in the things of life itself are that one must dwell in all, all, all of Thee, but one must also return at all times to all, all, all of Him, which is the true condition of man.

This is the true condition of man, who must at all times resist and metamorphose out of dissatisfaction or unwillingness to submit, "beyond" a certain limit that cannot be crossed by the present itself, and this is where man's achievement is remarkable and influential.

Second part:

In the second volume, Martin Buber argues against two kinds of transcendence, a view of things or issues from a certain position or perspective.

The first is the use of the immense and eternal universe to swallow up the entire life of the "existence" of the self, so that there are separate living persons, beings, or other entities with different social status, abilities, and roles in the interconnection between persons, persons, and things in a certain society.

By putting the finiteness of the "existential" life of the self into the infinite process of the universe, the self is transformed "beyond" the present situation, so that the situation that did not exist becomes a fact that lasts forever.

Secondly, the finite nature of the "existent" life of the "self" is expanded to swallow up the universe and other existents, and the universe, which resides in an infinite process of time, is taken as the "self" life itself.

The second is to expand the finiteness of the existence of the "self" to swallow the universe and other existents, and to treat the universe, which resides in an infinite flow of time, as the "existent" life of the "self", and to complete the essence or meaning of the existence of the self.

The absolute nature of truth is the absolute truth, which means the unconditional and unlimited nature of truth; while the relative nature of truth is the relative truth, which means the conditional and limited nature of truth.

Therefore, for these two kinds of metamorphosis "beyond" the present situation, the view of things or issues from a certain position or perspective. The former is the positive meaning and usefulness of the object to the subject, and the metamorphic "beyond" situation.

It points to the universe beyond human beings, depriving single human beings, creatures or other indivisible entities of their moral subjectivity, especially the meaninglessness of "love" in it.

The latter directs the positive meaning and usefulness and metamorphosis of the object manifested to the subject "beyond" the status quo, to a being with a unique consciousness and/or with a unique personal experience, or another being external to itself.

Or another entity external to itself and related to it, so that morality loses its absoluteness and all self-sacrifice is just another form of self-satisfaction.

The third part:

In the third volume, Martin Buber further attends to the positive meaning and usefulness of the object in relation to the subject, and the transformation "beyond" the present situation, in its "action or influence on the thing in question".

It is presented in the "state of interaction and mutual influence" between the "I" that "exists" in the existence of the "self" and the "things" that exist in the existence of other beings in the universe.

Only in a certain nature of connection between man and man or man and things can man be introduced to the sublime divine totality, all and everything, and only then can the existence of the "self" and the existence of the "thou" simultaneously undergo a change in form or essence, a metamorphosis, a "transcendental" state of being.

In this book, Martin Buber further explains the discipline of religious study of universal, fundamental issues, including existence, knowledge, values, and reason, through the clarification of the two contradictory properties inherent in all, all, everything, and life itself.

This includes the core concepts in the fields of being, knowledge, values, reason, mind, and language, namely, the concept of the metamorphosis of the "transcendent" present, and the clarification of the fundamental spirit of Christianity's "love".

It also clarifies the fundamental spirit of "love" in Christianity, that is, a strong emotion and attachment to a person or object, an emotional and psychological state derived from strong love, loyalty, and goodwill between relatives.

For example, maternal love. It contains a range of strong and positive emotional and mental states, from the noblest virtues or good habits, to the deepest interpersonal relationships, to the simplest pleasures.

Such emotions and attachments drive those who feel them to seek physical, intellectual, and even imaginative proximity to the object of their love.

More importantly, Martin Buber reads "I and Thou," a certain nature of connection between a person and a person or a person and a thing, a special attention to or a solemn representation of a certain thing or idea.

There are five levels of education, which are summarized in a certain way to clarify examples and to make the other person think and understand.

First, at the level of the teacher-student relationship, both the teacher and the student are a being with a unique consciousness and/or a unique personal experience, or another entity external to and related to themselves, in their "I and Thou" influence and involvement in the matter in question.

Enjoying a set of accepted norms in the process of exchange between parties, i.e., when one party provides help or gives a resource to another party, the latter has the obligation to reciprocate the emotional and intellectual exchange of help given to him or her.

Instead of teachers treating students as external things that do not concern them, as objects of knowledge and activities of the subject.

Therefore, students should not be under great

external pressure, contrary to their own wishes, and submit to the conditions of pressure, bound to the will of the teacher, with the idea of stagnant and unchanging, and unable to develop the teaching materials and teaching methods.

The teacher should not build on his or her own will to force others, or himself or herself, to submit to students to accept knowledge that is not human and different from the nature of other animals.

Second, at the level of teaching, the teacher should achieve the maximum mutual communication with the students, telling each other their own ideas and reasons why they do so, and the other side telling you back their own ideas and reasons.

In short, it means that teachers and students talk to each other and let others know what's on your mind! Thus, teachers help students get out of a learning rut through dialogue or take them on a collective journey toward a goal.

The teacher's forward thinking is always ahead of the students, so the dialogue can be advanced in behavior, action, thought or technology, etc. A real dialogue between students and teachers has an abstract, but absolutely existential, connotation.

At the same time, it is also a person to a person or something, a cognitive feeling of the content of the discussion, so that students can automatically and spontaneously, according to their own meaning, to trace the search (or the pursuit of the ideal) with the degree of contact with the nature of things, the most pure, the most consistent with the actual truth, that is, objective things and their laws in the human body.

The teacher's own cognition or ideas are not the basis for the teacher's closed judgment of things, without seeking to meet the actual situation, unilaterally asking students to adopt the teacher's understanding of things, the interpretation of views.

Third, at the level of materials for teaching, including textbooks, handouts, reference materials, videos, pictures, and so on.

Communication between teachers is the act of telling others what they think and why they do it, and others telling themselves back what they think and why they do it. And in the materials for teaching purposes

In the material for teaching, the subjective or objective self-impressions of the value of the discipline should be considered important and taken seriously in those individual persons, creatures, or other entities in which the self can find opportunities to make situations that did not exist, a reality.

Humanities are disciplines that are divided according to the content and nature of learning. For example, mathematics, physics, chemistry, etc. The subjects of theory of knowledge, such as the events and actions of human society in the past, and the systematic recording, interpretation, and study of these events and actions.

History is an important achievement of human spiritual civilization, along with ethics, philosophy, and the arts, and provides the present with a basis for understanding the past and acting in the future.

Literature is the art of using language as a tool to reflect objective reality and express the writer's spiritual world, including poetry, prose, novels, plays, fables and fairy tales.

It is an important form of cultural expression, which expresses inner feelings, reproduces social life of a certain period and a certain region, and studies universal and fundamental issues in different forms, i.e. genres.

It includes the fields of existence, knowledge, value, reason, mind, and language, as well as a culture that reflects reality and emotions by shaping images and creating atmosphere with the help of some means or media, as opposed to the three subjects of sports, music, and art.

In addition, it is important to explore the existence of the self, the real meaning of the existence of real life, and the existence of a single person, biological or artistic. The study of the human, biological, and other indivisible entities.

A series of questions that require answers or solutions in order to understand something new, or in an uncertain situation, or to control the relative or combined situation of various situations in a certain period of time.

It is a series of questions that require an answer or an answer in order to be studied and discussed, or to be solved. After a dialogue, individuals have positive emotional and cognitive attitudes toward teachers and students, and are therefore willing to accept each other's ideas, behaviors, and values, and to emulate them, so that they can become more consistent with others or groups.

For example, in the case of religious philosophical metaphysics and science, to distinguish the similarity and difference of attributes or the superiority of things: assuming that the sacredness of theology exists in a certain way of expressing content (as distinct from "content").

For example, it exists in physical, supernatural, psychological, or social reality, and finds evidence for it through personal spiritual experience, or through the historical records of such experience as recorded by others, and rationalizes this hypothesis through the power of faith.

The study of God, deities, moral standards, and religious texts is often not an in-depth study of faith. Theology often does not delve into the rationality of faith itself, and theological beliefs assume stereotypical empirical impressions and contradictory test results.

Although, in ancient times, the study of metaphysics, in the broad sense, included theology, modern metaphysics delves into the nature of things, laws, reasoning, etc., without recognizing the discipline of God in the discourse.

It does not recognize the assumption of contradictory beliefs in the discipline of God, which is based on experimental and logical reasoning, and the study of a certain object as the scope of study, and the practice of objective laws and truths that are unified and certain.

In the philosophy of modern metaphysics, the apparent phenomena that do not correspond to the nature of things are also the things that are the object of study and debate in action or reflection.

Although its assumptions may not be proven by scientific practice through one or more objective existences to prove the truth of a thing, i.e., to show or conclude with figures or facts.

But it must not be contradicted by the practice of experimental and logical reasoning for the unification of objective laws and truths based on a certain object as the scope of study, which is completely different from theology.

The author of the Stanford Encyclopedia of Philosophy states the following proposition or point of view about theology and philosophy: "From the point of view of both disciplines, the process or linguistic form of a point of view, if certain reasons are applied to support or refute it, usually consists of a thesis, a thesis, a thesis, a thesis and a thesis.

The premise, usually consisting of a thesis, a thesis, an argument, and a way of arguing, is that, at least from the dialogue between the two disciplines, after looking at something

The theological process or form of language usually consists of a thesis, an argument, an argument, and a form of argumentation. Then the argument belongs to the realm of theology; otherwise, it falls into the realm of philosophy."

The events and actions of human society in the past, and the systematic recording, interpretation, and study of these events and actions.

Metaphysics is an important area of philosophy for the study of academic thought or social activity, and focuses on three types of questions that require answers or solutions: (1) the fundamental principle of all existence, i.e., the question of the nature of existence; (2) the question of the root of all kinds of existence; and (3) the fundamental presuppositions of all kinds of knowledge. Therefore, the scope of the study of metaphysics includes cosmology, ontology, or ontology; some people also discuss theology and the theory of knowledge together.

The main topics of metaphysics include being, substance, reality, the nature of universal existence, properties, laws of change, God, soul, freedom, and the ultimate basis of knowledge.

This epistemological and rational method of analysis was also borrowed by theology and used by philosophers and theologians to study the rationality of faith itself, comparing the descriptions of religious texts with historical, archaeological, and scientific findings.

The result was the birth of natural theology in Europe, where natural religion or theology is not limited to empirical inquiry into nature, nor is it combined with the results of pantheism.

However, it does seek not to make a situation occur that attracts special unnatural talents (telepathy, mystical experiences) or supernatural sources of information (sacred texts, theological revelations, creedal authority, direct supernatural communication).

Natural theology, aiming to adhere to the same standards of investigation as other philosophical and scientific undertakings, generally refers to the ability of people to form concepts, make judgments, analyze, synthesize, compare, reason, calculate, etc., and to accept the same standards of investigation based on predetermined criteria.

It accepts the same criteria for measuring the effects of programs that have or will have, according to predetermined criteria, in order to determine their feasibility, for reference in choosing or improving them, and for advising on shortcomings and errors.

The metaphysics of reason in the mind, which breaks down things or objects from the whole into their parts, or attributes and rules of careful thought, makes it impossible for human beings to fully understand God's truth at once.

Therefore, when God reveals the truth, fewer and fewer people will take into account the understanding of mankind at that time. In the article "Leading Scientists Still Reject God" in Nature, one of the world's most authoritative and prestigious academic journals, it is reported that

The religious beliefs of American scientists have been controversial since the turn of the century. A recent survey found that among top natural scientists, non-belief in religion is greater than ever before.

This means that the comparison of metaphysics and theology is usually controversial and inconclusive.

This is partly because the accumulated data of empirical facts, the largest body of human knowledge, usually fails to resolve the debate over the comparison between metaphysics and theology.

The other part is that the terms used by metaphysicians and theologians are often confused, and their arguments are therefore only a discussion of their own views without intersection.

The saying "teachers of scripture are easy to find, but teachers of men are hard to find" means that teachers who can teach you lessons and study are everywhere and easy to find, but teachers who can teach you the philosophy of life and the truth of being human are rare and hard to find.

Therefore, including the religious philosophy of death, teachers should not deliberately avoid or conceal it in the classroom, deliberately make people ignore or neglect it, pretending not to see it.

Fourth, on the level of dialogue attitude: attitude is potential, mainly reflected through people's speech, expression and behavior.

It refers to the individual to the surrounding environment of people, things and objects to uphold a fairly long-lasting and consistent behavior performance. From a psychological point of view, attitude consists of three important components.

The cognitive component, in psychology, refers to the process of acquiring knowledge by forming concepts, perceptions, judgments, or imagination, which is the mental function of the mind to process information.

The cognitive process can be natural or artificial, conscious or unconscious; cognition uses existing knowledge and generates new knowledge. It is also the understanding of things or beliefs; it is mainly intellectual and rational in nature.

2. The emotional component, used in psychology to

describe the feeling (Feeling) the human brain's response to the individual properties of objective things that act directly on the sense organs and the perception of the sensory system.

It is the concept of unpleasant emotion experience, which is the psychological reaction of the inner mind, the degree of emotion, joy or dislike of something; it is the emotional and sensual side.

Behavioral components, which are controlled by the individual's internal will and are specifically expressed in external actions, such as: making movements, making sounds, and making reactions.

The part of behavior that is manifested outwardly; the action that belongs to a certain thing or thing that is not abstract, not general, and the details are very clear.

Attitude contains the positive meaning and usefulness of the individual to the subject's performance and the criteria and norms of people's common life and their behavior in the judgment, is part of the personality, there is no certain standard; and the three components of attitude, may not be consistent.

Due to the expectations of the social environment or

the influence of family upbringing, the attitude held by an individual may not always be truly expressed, and often hides his or her true intentions, conceals himself or herself from reality, and expresses himself or herself in a socially acceptable way.

Another reason for internal and external inconsistency is that the individual is facing some conflict or distress, so knowing is one thing and acting is another.

Experts and scholars generally believe that individuals' consistent behavior toward people, things, and objects in their surroundings is learned through dialogue, socialization, imitation, and model learning.

In addition to the intentional strengthening of social will, it is gradually learned. For example, students usually hold respectful attitudes toward teachers and derogatory attitudes toward delinquents, both of which come from education through dialogue learning.

Fifth, at the level of teaching and learning benefits: In general, the way of thinking that identifies the similarities and differences between teachers and students provides an important avenue of dialogue for an objective and comprehensive understanding of things.

For example, in terms of the above-mentioned identification of similarities, dissimilarities, or higher and lower attributes between teachers and students in terms of metaphysics and theology, and in terms of the critique of the educational system.

If theology is assumed to be true, after a series of correct reasoning, it is clearly false; if theology is assumed to be false, after a series of correct reasoning from known or assumed sources, it is clearly false.

If theology is assumed to be false, then after a series of correct deductions from known or assumed premises, or after the results of a known answer, and after a counter-reasoning, then it is obviously true.

Thus, dialogue has stimulated the search for knowledge and explanation - delicate and detailed thinking that has attracted the attention of many thinkers and enthusiasts throughout the ages.

The solution of paradoxes, which are not easy to solve, requires creative thinking, and can often be achieved by teaching each other in a way that brings new ideas.

The contents and methods of teaching philosophy of dialogue explain and present in detail and in depth the teaching and learning of each other, and the progressive development of the teaching experience of perfecting the good and remedying the lack. Therefore, through the practice of dialogue teaching, teachers and students understand each other deeply that learning leads to knowledge of deficiencies and teaching leads to knowledge of difficulties.

Knowing the inadequacy of learning, they can then know how to reflect on themselves. Although a sword is sharp, if it is not sharpened, it will keep cutting things; although a person has good qualities, if he does not study, he will not achieve anything. Though there is good wine and food, if one does not taste it, one cannot know its deliciousness; though there is the way of beauty and goodness, if one does not study it, one cannot reach the state of perfection and goodness.

Therefore, only after learning do I realize that I am still inadequate, and only after teaching others do I realize that I still do not thoroughly understand. Knowing that I am not enough, I feel ashamed and try my best to learn; knowing that I do not understand deeply enough, I try to seek advice from others in order to attain proficiency.

Although the blade of the sword is sharp, it cannot cut

other objects without sharpening; although the human nature and temperament are gifted with intelligence, the process of acquiring knowledge or skills through reading, listening to lectures, thinking, research, and practice cannot be seriously pursued.

It is not possible to improve the cultivation and connotation to make the learning and morality to be exquisite and perfect. Although there are fine wines, fine meals, and delicious foods, one cannot know their taste unless one discerns the taste carefully with one's own mouth.

Although there are truths and laws of the right things, if we do not try to acquire knowledge or skills through reading, listening, thinking, studying, and practicing, we will not be able to realize their usefulness. Therefore, by absorbing knowledge through understanding and practice, we discover our own shortcomings.

By teaching knowledge and skills to others, one realizes that one has not explored deeply enough the nature, laws, and reasons of things. When one discovers one's own deficiencies, one feels guilty and strives to learn; when one knows that one's research is not deep enough, one seeks out teachers from all over the world and learns the truth.

From this, it appears that teaching and learning are mutually reinforcing dialogues. Thus, both teaching and learning act or change in an indirect or invisible way on each other and contribute to the advancement and improvement of both. Teaching is the interaction between teaching and learning, a fundamental social process between people, and the basis of human organization and cultural development.

Teachers and students tell each other what others want to know and what they do not understand, and answer what the other does not understand, exchange or clarify each other's opinions, give each other guidance or clarify examples, and cause each other to associate and understand, and add to each other's deficiencies or losses.

In this philosophical process of dialogue, teachers and students communicate with each other emotionally to reach consensus, share, and progress together, and to realize mutual development and teaching. Therefore, it is only through learning that we can know our own shortcomings, and through teaching others that we can know what we are confused about.

We know that we have deficiencies, and then we know what we don't understand. Knowing that you have deficiencies, you can ask yourself in return; knowing that you are confused and don't know what to do, you can work hard to improve yourself. Therefore, teaching and learning are mutually conducive to the development and advancement of each other, and teaching others can also increase one's own learning and knowledge.

The fourth part, in the postscript:

Martin Buber's denial of "self-submission" is that it expresses the phenomenon of separation and even opposition between two things that are originally naturally interdependent or harmonious in modern and modern Western societies, and that only when unity is achieved (for others) will the self be free and sound.

When Heidegger characterizes the ego in everyday coexistence by sinking, the personality, once the ego is forced to act against its inner will as some kind of socially specific phenomenon of natural interdependence, or the separation or even opposition of two things in harmony with each other, or much

The phenomenon of separation or even opposition

between two things that are naturally interdependent or harmonious is, to a greater or lesser extent, also in contact with the "true ego life existence" itself under the condition of separation or opposition between two things that are naturally interdependent or harmonious.

The true "existence" of the self is often trapped in an abnormal, powerless and meaningless feeling, and will succumb to the "going with the flow" of the self in all things, and the existence of the self disappears in the infinite and vast value and meaning of the universe.

Martin Buber's negation of "self-transcendence" lies in the fact that it is confined to the fact that my life existence cannot transcend the experience of death, and that it creates "isolation or the feeling of being alone and meaningless".

The transcendence of man begins with the reflection of the true meaning of life existence, but the a priori does not exist in the control of 'I', but only in the affirmation of 'I and you', 'I and it', in the interaction between man and man or man and things.

Only in the affirmation of "I and you", "I and it", in the interaction between people and people or people and things, in a certain nature of connection, does transcendence arise.

Martin Buber explores the "encounter" in the interaction between people and people or between people and things of a certain nature, affirming the search for a "sense of being", for example, in Descartes' famous saying "I think, therefore I am".

What does it mean? It means that, because I am the subject of thought, in order to think about existence, I must first exist. Conversely, if I doubt my existence, then doubt itself is also a kind of thinking, so I must first exist as well.

However, there are a number of psychological doubts about this statement that need to be clarified. The philosopher Berkeley made a similar statement when he said that to exist is to be perceived.

Berkeley agreed with Locke's view that all human concepts come from experience, but disagreed with Locke's doctrine of first and second nature. He argues that both the first and second natures are sensations (as opposed to perception or awareness), and that

All knowledge is a function of the person who is

experiencing or feeling, meaning that only what is felt by the other can prove its existence.

That is, only when others respond to our actions can we prove that the signals we send exist. The existence of a signal proves that we exist too.

This includes the related principles of "conversation", "dialogue", "relationship", and "encounter". His book "I and You" describes Martin Buber as a thinker who valued the state of interaction between the "I" and external things - a connection of some nature between people and people or people and things.

The emphasis is on "I and you" rather than "I and it" (the world of experience). Martin Buber Buber argues that man has two distinct lives when he is in a world in which things have two opposing natures at the same time.

The world presents itself to him as a double world of contradictory things, of two properties. By establishing the duality of the world, the principle of the relationship between the world of experience of "I and it" and the world of "meeting", "conversation" and "dialogue" between "I and you" is established. Martin Buber Buber believes that "I and it" and "I and you" are two ways of communication between human beings and the world, and that they jointly construct the existence of self-life itself as human existence.

First, the objective relationship between "I-It" (I and it)

The first mode is the I-It observation of things as they are without adding personal opinion to them.

All the people or things (it) that are associated with "I" are tools to satisfy the interests, needs, and desires of "I", so "I" and "it" establish only a partial and one-sided relationship, and "I" is not complete at this time.

Under this model, the individual treats external things as if they are selfishly used and manipulated for the purpose of satisfying selfishness.

For example, if a teacher and student view things in a "me and it" manner, and do not view things from the perspective of a particular person, that is, the attributes of things themselves, then the relationship between the teacher and the student is not complete.

If the teacher and the student are not looking at things from a particular person's point of view, that is, the nature of things, the nature of the connection between people and people or people and things, there is no feeling between the teacher and the student, and the teacher selfishly focuses only on achieving his teaching goals.

Second, the subjective relationship of "I and you" (I-Thou)

The second model is the "I-Thou" (I-Thou) relationship of judging things according to one's own perceptions or ideas, without seeking to conform to the actual situation, and the "I-Thou" (I-Thou) relationship of a certain nature between people and people or people and things.

The relationship between "I and you" - between a person and a person or a person and a thing - is of a certain nature: I see "you" as the whole, all, everything, as survival and development, and I do not establish a relationship with "you" for the purpose of satisfying "I love to hold on to" personal needs.

In this model, the individual must acknowledge that each person has an understanding of natural or social things that is unique to him or her, while giving meaning to the object, whether in the form of symbolic transmission and communication, or the spiritual world of spiritual content.

This means that the individual is judging things

according to his or her own perceptions or ideas, and does not care whether they are in accordance with the actual situation.

Therefore, it is only when the entire existence and life of the "I" is close to the "You" that the autonomous "I" truly feels the real existence of freedom of will and becomes a truly self-aware person.

In short, the "I" of "I and you" is the common, unconcealed and unhidden I that belongs to the public; the "I and it" is the individual, selfish, unpublicized, secret and illegitimate I that belongs to the individual.

Thus, Martin Buber argues that Buber argues that "I and Thou" creates a "dialogue," a mode of association of a certain nature between man and man or man and thing in the world, which is used not only in the relationship between man and man, but also in the state of interaction and mutual influence between man and divine things.

A process of behavior that can be realized through various carriers by the subject of behavior different from others, the two-way flow of information, forming the perception of the subject of behavior to achieve a specific goal.

And in practice to know things, to a mutual subjective basis of self-knowledge or ideas, the judgment of things, does not require whether the actual situation, and can make a person's life, more full of spiritual spirituality.

This kind of connection between people and people or people and things, a certain nature of "meeting" the world, is manifested in three kinds of relationships, to a certain degree of connection.

(1) The life related to human interaction is the process of mutual communication and feeling between people. Such as cooperation, interaction, competition, conflict, etc.

In other words, people can interact with each other to increase mutual understanding. This is the "meeting", "conversation", "dialogue" open relationship, with a complex communication system, mainly consists of its formation, acquisition, maintenance and application, especially the mutual sense of both sides, more than the same meaning deeper.

In life, it is the relationship between our own concepts, words and deeds, and the human ability to communicate in the same way as others' concepts, words and deeds, in which we dedicate and accept the life of "I and you" and "I and it".

(2) Life in relation to nature, a relationship that is "difficult to comprehend in the quiet silence and mystery of the world order refers to ethical events and systems of relationships, or systems of values, or ideals.

In particular, the ethical aspect tends to be the moral purpose, often referring to justice and obligation. The relationship between the ethical order and the natural order belongs to the field of metaphysics and moral philosophy.

The early Greek philosophers, such as the Stoics, considered morality and the cosmic order as one, as the Taoist advocates of the unity of heaven and man, and as the expression of universal reason.

I. Kant (1724~1804) believed that the moral order is the physical order, which is prior to the empirical or phenomenal order.

G.W.F. Hegel (1770~1831) believed that moral order is a part of natural order. The moral order is a proof of the social order.

It means that there is order and sequence in society,

that is, there are certain norms, there is no unrest and disturbance, and the lives and properties of the members of the society are not threatened; the existence of social order means the sound and proper operation of social norms and social components.

The existence of social order means the soundness and proper operation of social norms and social components.

In the case of the social and natural orders, one of the earliest views was that the natural and social orders were created by a transcendent God or gods, and that there was a correspondence between the two orders (e.g., the Son of Heaven, the highest order in the social order, is the highest order in the natural order).

The other argument is that the natural and social orders are naturally formed; they are not created by God or gods, but through human interaction and a series of human decisions.

In this view, human reason is considered to be insignificant in the formation of the social order. After the rise of scientism, some Westerners in the eighteenth and nineteenth centuries had great faith in human reason, believing that a new order could be formed through the action of human reason, and that the new order was openly presented, revealed in its true form, and void of any depth.

Although no precise content can be obtained from them, their power penetrates human creation and human understanding, and pours into the ordered world, dismantling it again and again, which is presented in personal history and human history.

(3) Life associated with spiritual beings literally means "something in the mind", "the object to which the mind corresponds", and psychologically refers to the ontology of consciousness, thought, or general mental states.

It is a relationship that cannot be grasped clearly, that is vague and subtle, that is difficult to understand, but that is open and unobscured.

In this world, any kind of rhetorical technique is used to visualize the spiritual essence. The rhetorical devices include metaphors, similes, exaggerations, double entendres, and prose, and other colorful language.

No rhetorical technique, including metaphor, simile, exaggeration, double entendre, and proverb, can explain the "transcendental realm" in an appropriate way. In the face of the "transcendental world," human language is so limited and inadequate that it is unable to discuss its profound philosophies in any detail.

Martin Buber's According to Buber's philosophy of dialogue, the value of human beings is presented in the relationship of "encounter," "conversation," and "dialogue," and in the influence and involvement of the "I" and other beings in the universe on related things.

As the saying goes, "I am blinded by the sky but do not know the human being", I am blinded by the happiness of living beyond the human world, and I do not know the reality of people's suffering.

Only "encounter," "conversation," and "dialogue" have a spiritual a priori foundation and can lead people into the sublime world of the divine, and the influence and involvement of exchanging related things with each other is divine, but "dialogue" is the realization of the meaning of life existence between people and the divine.

"Love" is not an attribute that is the target of action or thought, nor is it an overflow of the emotional liberation of "I", but it is a relationship between "I and you" and "I and it" that reveals itself in the experience of life.

Chapter 3: Humanism Discourse

Section 1, Background of the Times

In his essay "Humanism in Hebrew", Martin Buber systematically analyzed the potential dangers and dangers of humanistic thought in the world at that time.

Under the guidance of modern realism and philosophical thinking, people believed in the myth of "opening up the world", "innovation", and "conquest" as the invincible myth of progress, and human beings engaged in the activities and processes of creating social wealth by working with labor, earning money, and making a living.

The creation of material and spiritual wealth has gradually shifted to a new manufacturing process, with the trend of replacing human and animal power with machines, and replacing "individual workshops" and "manual production" with large-scale factory production.

Due to the invention and use of machines, the material production methods and economic life progress. This era has become a symbol of the continuous departure from the traditional nest.

It means that the farther mankind leaves the barbaric state, the less it relies on nature, and the stronger its ability to control nature. The result is the opposite of what mankind originally expected from science and technology, which brought the benefits of material civilization.

Wherever man brought civilization, he also brought barbarism; it was as fierce as a flood of wild animals, sweeping away the formerly pure and simple folk and the peace of ancient simplicity and harmony.

It seems logical that before the nineteenth century, mankind had experienced the scourge of war, plague, and bubonic plague, and that it would have learned from its deeply torturous failures or mistakes that

It would seem that mankind would have learned from deeply torturous failures or mistakes that were caused by things beyond their control or that they were unable to remedy, and thus would have felt dissatisfaction, remorse, resignation, and regret.

However, due to the proliferation of materialistic desires at that time, people's latent desire for dissatisfaction has exploded, and it has become a reality that human beings are constantly destroying nature, almost overflowing, indulging, and destroying the ecology of nature.

Ironically, after the excessive use of pesticides, chemical fertilizers, antibiotics, and other environmental hormones, species are gradually dying one by one.

It is ironic that after the destruction of environmental hormones through the excessive use of pesticides, chemical fertilizers, and antibiotics, the species are dying one by one.

On the other hand, in the industrial revolutionary economic society, individuals were reduced to the gears of the "collective" machines, human beings were separated from their loved ones, and values such as moral and ethical responsibility were gradually degraded.

In the field of faith, man and the divine will have been separated from each other for a long time, and the inner heart is unable to bear the reliance of faith; therefore, the meaning of the world exists only in the symbols of material civilization, and the world has become a world without foundation support.

This was a peculiar time in history when scientists

inherited the spirit of the Renaissance and the Age of Reason (Enlightenment), which valued science, against the backdrop of realistic utilitarianism, laissez-faire lifestyles, and a depleted sense of morality.

The means or methods of controlling and changing the natural environment in the West were thus significantly developed. Important inventions and discoveries made a positive contribution to the Industrial Revolution.

However, this was a continuous development of various material means, methods, approaches, and technologies created or invented based on scientific principles rather than general practical experience.

Since then, mankind has rapidly moved from the agricultural age to the industrial age, and various technological civilizations have spread rapidly around the world, and the whole world has been swept into the wave of industrialization, from which almost no one can remain unaffected.

In order to satisfy their own desires, people exploit nature to the best of their ability, and because of their selfishness, behind the seemingly bustling and prosperous scenery, there are many lost souls hidden.

The alienation of interpersonal relationship between people is manifested, and the distortion of the original mind, which is constantly squeezed, is pushed by the passage of time in the vicissitudes of the sea and the sea, and a sense of powerlessness that is beyond human control.

Under this premise, the pursuit of fame, fortune, and materialism has become an inevitable destiny for human beings, although many people have become rich overnight.

However, due to social change and urban industrialization, people have lost their original harmony and intimacy when facing their living environment, and as a result, modern people feel a sense of meaninglessness and powerlessness when facing their living environment.

The result is that modern people feel a sense of meaninglessness, powerlessness, social isolation, and self-separation when facing the environment around their lives, but they have lost their original nature and purpose of being human.

The result of this excessive servitude to the outside

world has led to the growing emptiness of the human mind, which was not anticipated by industrial civilization.

American sociologists have placed more emphasis on the psychological aspect of alienation and neglected the social structural aspect. For example, Melvin Seeman and Robert Blauner have divided the content of alienation into four categories: (1) powerlessness, (2) isolation, (3) meaninglessness, and (4) self-alienation.

First, the sense of powerlessness, said to do things, there is a feeling of powerlessness, there should be two reasons.

One, either you want to get what you do not get, and very far away from you, you see the reality, suddenly feel very low depression.

Second, either you are living a life you do not want, but can not afford to get rid of it, to pursue what you want, you do not dare, timid and cowardly, afraid to go out of the current circle of comfort. Simply put, life has not reached the way you want it to be.

It is the feeling that an individual does not have control or influence over his or her living environment (including the production process). The frustration of disappointment when one's hopes, dreams, and expectations are blocked and cannot pass or develop smoothly, or when one's abilities and talents cannot be fully developed.

Secondly, loneliness is a feeling that arises when workers do not have a sense of belonging to their work group, do not share their work goals, and feel alienated from the values and norms of the social environment.

Loneliness is often referred to in real life as a subjective state of social isolation, accompanied by the painful experience of not being accepted because of the individual's perceived isolation or lack of contact with others (Jeny de Jong-Giered, 1987). Perlnen (1982) defines the symptom of loneliness as

Loneliness is an unpleasant, distressing subjective experience or psychological feeling, and most people experience the pain of loneliness. Statistics show that loneliness has become a common problem among modern people.

Psychologists estimate that as society becomes richer, this concern for loneliness and human relationships will continue to grow.

Third, a sense of meaninglessness refers to the lack of a sense of purpose; workers feel meaningless when they are unable to achieve social and cultural values in a way that makes sense to them.

Many people now feel unhappy, unhappy, and uninterested in life precisely because they cannot devote themselves to the "most ordinary daily life" and instead set obstacles for themselves with their great materialistic desires.

Life is indeed meaningless, meaning is given to us later in life, and life does not have a purpose, but is not called life, but physical or mental work for a certain purpose or under compulsion.

There is no unified and ultimate answer to life and living, which is why it is worthwhile for all people to keep dreaming and exploring. The meaning of life is in the most ordinary daily life! If you don't use your body and mind, no matter how you live, it's a monotonous and boring life, and you won't live an interesting life.

Fourth, social isolation means that people work only to make a living, not for the purpose of self-fulfillment, and it is difficult to find the fulfillment of participation in the work environment. Social isolation (English: Social isolation) or social isolation, social isolation, social isolation, refers to the complete or near complete lack of contact between people and society.

Social isolation is different from loneliness, which is only a temporary lack of connection. Social isolation can occur in individuals of any age, although symptoms may vary by age group.

Social isolation can be a temporary, episodic state or a lifelong cycle that occurs over a lifetime, and the characteristics are similar in both cases.

All forms of social isolation can include staying at home for long periods of time without contact with family, acquaintances, or friends, or deliberately avoiding any contact with people when the opportunity arises.

Alienation

In philosophy, it is generally translated as alienation, which means that in the process of development, the subject separates itself from the opposing object by its own activity, and this object gradually alienates itself from the subject, thus becoming an external alien force against the subject itself.

In sociology, alienation, in a broad sense, means the alienation of an individual from the main aspects of his social existence. In economics, it refers to the various antagonistic relationships that arise between people in the economic sphere.

The concept of Alienation has evolved considerably, i.e. it is an increasingly rich concept in sociology and psychology. Thus, Alienation appears in various disciplines, including sociology, socio-political philosophy, psychoanalysis, existential philosophy, etc.

Melvin Seeman, an American social psychologist, constructs alienation from a psychosocial perspective as a hierarchy of five distinctly different components and structural forms of things, namely

(1) Labor detachment: the loss of the desired goal or result in labor by mental or physical effort and activity.

(2) Sense of powerlessness: the feeling of frustration that arises when the wishes of the mind are obstructed or when the ability to perform fully cannot be realized, so that it cannot have an impact on others and on society.

(3) Social isolation: The complex emotions of anxiety, loneliness, and boredom that arise when a person is

isolated from the outside world or lacks a partner, which means a sense of loss of intimacy with others, the community, and society.

(4) Sense of alienation from values: Due to social change and urban industrialization, people lose their original harmony and intimacy when facing their living environment, which eventually leads to a complex state of mind in which modern people feel meaningless, powerless, socially isolated, and separated from themselves when facing their living environment, and lose the sense of meaning in the activities of life experience.

(5) Feeling of alienation: It is difficult to find a sense of participation and fulfillment in the work environment because work is only for the purpose of earning a living and not for the purpose of self-realization. It can also be described as a state in which people become alienated from themselves and others. The feeling of being a stranger to oneself.

Alienation, also known as alienation, is a term with an uncertain meaning that varies depending on the user.

Basically, it refers to an eternal attribute or set of attributes of a person that make an entity or substance its very essence and that necessarily exist, without which it would lose its identity.

That is to say, the fundamental attributes inherent in things themselves, which determine their nature, appearance and development, are usurped by something, by improper means, from the rights or possessions of others, resulting in the phenomenon of deprivation or loss of humanity.

In the face of this absurd picture of the world, Martin Buber insists that life must be lived in the face of God, but that this God is not a transcendent God who exists in our external world.

Based on the teachings of Hasidism, which was popular in Eastern Europe in the 18th century, he argues that God is omnipresent, possesses all things, permeates all worlds, and is even present in the present, in sensual things.

This mystical doctrine rejects mere ritual obedience to God and emphasizes the presence of God in everyday life.

The human being, on the other hand, is a force of mediation or negotiation between two parties, a person or thing that can serve as a communication link between the secular and the sacred.

How can this mission of man be realized, how can it be linked to the divine and the sublime? Martin Buber believes that this does not exist in the sense of not blaming others for internal setbacks, but rather in the sense of turning around, identifying the crux of the problem in oneself, and trying to correct it.

It does not exist in the experience of a solitary and contemplative life, but in an 'encounter', a 'dialogue', a transcendence in the interpersonal divine self.

For "the state of interaction and mutual influence with human things is originally a situation related to the human things of God, a real conversation of heart and soul.

The union between the secular and the sacred, starting from a new and separate beginning, is not a specific presentation of a theory or an elaboration of its essence, but an exchange of physical encounters, and a relationship of mutual conversation with the transcendental realm that expresses the nature outside.

Since the destruction or extinction of the Mycenaean civilization in the 12th century B.C., until the submission of the Roman Republic by force in 146 B.C. in Greece, and especially since the Hellenistic period.

It has been a tradition, especially since the Hellenistic period, that one should not blame others for a setback, but rather look back and find out what is wrong with oneself and try to improve it. Inner peace is not to hope for anything, not to be happy when you gain, not to worry when you lose, and not to pursue fame and fortune.

To let go of desires is like being able to hold on to one's personality without interference in a polluted environment. It is the fundamental way to follow the word of God in our lives, the way that every believer must seriously pursue (1 Peter 1:15; Hebrews 12:14).

Augustine, a Christian patristic philosopher and apologist, followed the path of "inner experience" in the Christian faith.

He taught that man should not look outward for God, but should turn back to himself and consider the purest and most realistic truth, that is, the correct reflection of objective things and their laws in the human mind.

It resides in the human mind or feelings. Because the mind is the main body of thought, and both are inside the body.

In the form of the process of generalization and indirect reaction of the human mind to objective things, initially by means of language, Augustine's inner turn is influenced by Neoplatonism, which acts or changes in an indirect or invisible way.

Augustine's theoretical description, i.e., the single or inductive elaboration of a problem, event, study, etc., and the presentation of its problems or solutions, with its own interpretative narrative, does provide Descartes with the means to establish a first philosophy.

For the great enlightening pointers or elucidating examples that evoke and enlighten the subject, Descartes' "I think, therefore I am" and his ability to speak or write about a subject to others.

As a result of contemporary concerns and reflections on language, it has become clear that words and expressions do not have a universal meaning, but are given different meanings depending on the speaker's intellectual background, social system, subjective position, and the field to which the discourse belongs.

In Book XI of On the City of God, Augustine says: "If I

deceive myself, I exist. That is, if man does not exist, he cannot deceive himself; therefore, when I deceive myself, I precisely exist.

If I deceive myself, then I exist; and when I deceive myself, when my existence is certain, how can I deceive myself in my existence? For if I am deceived, it is I who am deceived, and if I have deceived myself, there is no doubt that I have deceived myself, not because I know that I exist.

Therefore, I do not deceive myself because I know that I know this. Likewise, as I know that I exist, so I know this: I know this.

The above quotation from Augustine, which deals with a heavy and complicated matter, is obviously very similar to the "doubt" of Descartes' methodology: "If a man does not exist, he cannot be deceived, and the fact that a man is deceived means that he exists.

A man doubts because he is afraid of being deceived, and if he doubts, he exists, so "I doubt, therefore I exist. (dubito, ergo sum) is the correct reflection of objective things and their laws in people's consciousness, which cannot be doubted."

Since the contemporary concern and reflection on the systemic problems of constructing materials and grammatical rules of organization, which is a combination of command and meaning, with sound (symbols) as the material representation and semantic connotation as the content, people do not perceive a universally consistent meaning of words and expressions.

Thus, "exposition" focuses on a structured analysis; the words contain lighter meanings; they meet the requirements of objective conditions and are suitable for a wider range of applications; and they are common to both written and spoken language.

For example, this speech is very detailed and in-depth in terms of the thinking and subject matter of an issue, and the seriousness of the issue, or the fact that it has yet to be resolved.

And "elaboration" refers to the explanation, explanation, analysis of profound truths or problems that are not easy to understand; the words contain heavier meanings; they meet the requirements of objective conditions and are suitable for a narrower range of applications; they are mostly used in written discourse.

For example, Bakhtin's "Exploration": "Do not build your happiness on the suffering of others".

In order to refute skepticism's interrogation of faith, Augustine proposed the "thesis" of "I doubt, therefore I exist", which is also based on self-seeking. This is a realistic and positive attitude. In real life, there are always situations when people do not understand or even misunderstand us.

In the face of such situations, it is not helpful to complain about others; rather, the foundation of one's standing in society lies in whether one has the morality and talent to be known and used by others. Therefore, "seeking the truth from oneself" is also the fundamental basis for establishing oneself in the world.

The semantics of this judgment sentence (the actual expression of the concept), the concept that can be defined and observed as a phenomenon, is the source of the modern Descartes' "I think, therefore I am" interpretation of things. The essence of these ideas is to hold on to oneself and to seek nothing else.

This is also the consistent view of freedom of will and happiness that has been used in many aspects of Western culture, whether correctly or not, including Western culture, materialism, industrialism, capitalism, commercialism, sexual hedonism, imperialism, modernism, and even the interpretation of Western civilization.

Martin Buber uses God as the ultimate purpose of the end, and explains in detail the endless trust, proposing "encounter", "dialogue", and facing the other, in order to open the self that is so tightly covered or closed that it cannot be uncovered at will.

They do not know that what they consider to be the ultimate trust is just like the ritualistic attitude of the mind and its words and deeds that must be valued because God is considered to be higher than oneself.

Therefore, such a person does not know for what reason he or she is like this, nor does he or she know for what reason he or she will not be like this, but can only insist on a certain point of view, not knowing how to change it, so that he or she is confused and does not know what to do.

If we respond to the other unknowns of life experience with a perception that produces certain limitations and is in a state of confusion, we will only be baffled and unable to control our own agitated emotions, and therefore we will not be able to investigate the root cause.

Martin Buber "proposes "encounter", "dialogue", facing the other", meaning that only "communication" grasps the root, the foundation or the most important part of things. It is only by 'communicating' and grasping the root, the foundation or the most important part of things that we can obtain a metamorphic 'transcendent' situation in the human God Self, because 'the state of interaction and mutual influence with human things

It is a dialogue with the wisdom, thoughts, and emotions that exist in the human heart, and the possibility of survival, which is the process of transmitting and feeding back thoughts and feelings between people, between people and groups, in order to reach a consensus of thoughts, and is an important tool for expressing thoughts and emotions, and is the main means of interaction with the interpersonal God Self.

It is an important tool for expressing thoughts and feelings, and is the main means of interpersonal interaction with the Divine Self.

It is only in this way that we can rely on a theory or an elaboration that does not manifest itself concretely, a communication of an actual existential encounter, a dialogue between the nature of manifestation and the transcendental world, an action or influence on the thing in question. It is really the culmination of it.

The biggest difference between this and the traditional Western view that insists on self-opinion and refuses to change the self is that the emphasis on the "other" in modern Western philosophy is quite similar in nature to the material and can be mutually inclusive.

Of all the various aspects of the philosophy of the Other, only Proust can relate to Martin Buber's basic philosophy and view of 'experience' in order to decipher the ideas and truths contained in all things.

Proust expressed it in a refined way: "There are two worlds: the world of time, where fate, vision, suffering, variation, delay and death are laws, and the world of eternity, where there is freedom, beauty and peace.

Everyday experience is in the world of time; in moments of contemplation, or by accident of unconscious memory, there is a glimpse of another world. It is the duty of art to provoke this epiphany as a light in the world of time.

Since the 17th century philosopher Descartes' rationalism, dualism in modern Western philosophy has generally meant that it does not lean toward either materialism or idealism, but rather presupposes a dichotomy between subject and object, with the exaltation of subjectivity as the backbone.

It is not until Kant regards knowing as the second stage of knowledge, which is interpreted as the stage of knowing that the scattered and united materials provided by the sense are integrated and unified to obtain the meaning at the level of knowledge, so that knowing becomes a meaningful thought from sense to knowledge, thus producing the scientific knowledge with universality and necessity.

Because of the completion of the construction of the phenomenal world by the a priori subject, only the material essence remains, which is too obscure, too deep and too wide, and cannot be glimpsed in its entirety, which is confusing.

Husserl wants to express the material essence more

thoroughly than Kang, using the phenomenological method, considering that every appearance is a representation of something, and consciousness is always a consciousness related to something.

At the same time, he also advocates the "truth itself", that is, the existence of the idea that transcends the absolute and universal objective being of time and space, and proposes the study of the essence of consciousness, or the description of the fundamental and absolute law of the a priori knowledge.

Its basic feature is mainly expressed in the methodological aspect, that is, by returning to the original form of consciousness, describing and analyzing the process of constructing concepts (including the essential concepts and domains), so as to obtain the actual proof of the specification (meaning) of the concepts.

We believe that only on this basis can we clarify the true meaning of those concepts in traditional philosophy, so as to re-explain the problems in traditional philosophy and to carry out in-depth research in various fields.

However, this way of thinking could not escape from the accusation of metaphysical egoism (the idea that the ego is the only real being and that all realities, including the external world and other people, are representatives of that ego and have no independent destiny of existence).

Recognizing that this is not the way to go, the later Husserl proposed the doctrine of mutual subjectivity, arguing that philosophy cannot avoid the problem of "other". Thus, reciprocal subjectivity is a requirement of the empirical scientific method; it means that the statements of observation in the empirical sciences can be accommodated only if they can be verified by the researchers of each discipline.

By observation, the researcher means that it must be repeatable, i.e., that it is not limited to one or a small number of individuals with special gifts, and that it can be expressed in words.

Strictly speaking, the first observation and its verification are not mutually subjective, because any observation is necessarily made by a subject. It is only through the medium of language and the communication between different subjects that observation can be verified as a mutual subjectivity.

Therefore, the existentialist philosopher Heidegger

believes that the crisis of modern civilization started from the modern social humanism, the clear delineation of subject-object orientation, and the excessive pursuit of freedom of subjectivity, without recognizing that human being exists in the world and co-exists with "others".

This also shows that the traditional subject's self-expanding and unique status has begun to waver in the modern "other" world, and thus appears in the philosophical consciousness of postmodern psychologists. Mutual subjectivity in phenomenology has another special meaning.

In the discussion of the origin of knowledge, phenomenologists believe that people live in groups in the world, and that there are different relationships between people, the most fundamental of which is knowledge, i.e., the relationship between one subject consciousness and another or more subject consciousnesses, each of which has a cognitive role, i.e., mutual subjectivity.

Not only is Levinas' "Facing the Other" the most obvious embodiment of the 'other', but modern holistic, fundamental, and critical inquiry into the real world and human beings seems to be better understood through observation or experience, and better grasps the theoretical discourse of 'mutual subjectivity' (intersubjectivity).

Some scholars believe that the a priori proposition of rationality has the validity of inter-subjectivity because in principle every subject of knowledge has rationality and can have insight into the universal validity of the a priori proposition of rationality.

Therefore, philosophical anthropologists often regard mutual subjectivity as a characteristic of human beings, because as a subject, human beings always point to others and depend on them. The unquestionably close relationship between "otherness" and "mutual subjectivity" seems to make it difficult to distinguish between the two in the study of this problem by strict criteria.

A. Schutz, by synthesizing the ideas of M. Weber and Ed. Husserl, the originator of phenomenology, constructs his sociology and exposes Husserl's statement of "mutual subjectivity"; emphasizing that each person has an a priori self in the cognitive subject, and has the ability to cognize [the other and the I].

This ability to cognize the social environment and the

self, as well as the clarity of cognition, is also a concrete manifestation of mutual subjectivity.

However, the difference of opinion and view on a certain issue already includes the difference of theoretical interest.

The theoretical connotation of the question of "otherness" is very different, whether from a general point of view or from the standpoint of the self; whether "overlooking" the relationship between people or "facing" the "other", the problem is particularly difficult to distinguish.

One can grasp the relationship between "mutual subjectivity", the structure and entity of each sign of existence, and also face the "other" from the "self" and appreciate the true meaning of this "other".

Of course, it is necessary to look at the "total", but it implies an inner contradiction. "There may be a limit to the 'total'. Either the 'total' has a limit, which means that there is a different 'other', or it is so large that the 'other' will not exist at all.

From this we can deeply understand that when Bamenides thought about the question of existence, he believed that reality is fluid, that all changes in the world are illusions, and that therefore one cannot know reality by the senses.

At that time, Parmenides opposed Heraclitus' view of universal change. He believed that the diversity and illusion of all things was only an illusion, and that there was only one thing in the whole universe, eternal and indivisible, which he called "one".

He argued that either the existent exists or the existent does not exist, but this argument that the existent does not exist is wrong.

If we accept Heraclitus' view of things or problems from a certain standpoint or perspective, we will think that things change in line with the phenomenon of birth, old age, sickness and death.

But, according to Parmenides, if we think that things will disappear, we are making the mistake of thinking that 'the existent does not exist'. Therefore, in proposing 'one' there is a pain or difficulty, but it is inconvenient to say so.

Therefore, the "existence" of Parmenides is achieved through the path of logic. Since 'being' as a coefficient ('is') is the definitive embodiment of any linguistic expression, it gives thought its own definite object; feeling is in 'non-being' due to flux and cannot be determined by thought.

Thus, Baldwin emphasizes that "existents" can only exist in thought and speech, and that those concrete things that are objects of sensation are in the flux of birth and death.

The concrete things that are objects of sensation, in the process of birth and death, are "non-existent" because they cannot be expressed and fixed exactly in words. From the point of view of his philosophical thinking, both the Miletus school, which takes the changeless "non-existence" as the origin of everything, and advocates the existence of "non-existence", and Heraclitus' fire origin, are all false and absurd "opinions".

The only "theory of truth" is to insist on the existence of "existents" and the non-existence of "non-existents".

Although this topic also deals with the issue of "mutual subjectivity", it is not defined under the name of "mutual subjectivity" because, as the title of the book suggests, "Facing the Other" is always discussed from the standpoint of "facing" the other.

The question of "otherness" is not only about the "other", but also about the other subject, and the relationship between "otherness" and the change of the whole Western philosophical tradition. The proposition has been elaborated to the best of its ability, and psychoanalytic philosophers have also discussed the problem of interaction with the world of the 'other' from within their inherited intellectual traditions.

Thus, it is in the postmodern philosophical landscape of existentialism that Martin Buber's ideas about "you," "encounter," "dialogue," and "relationship" have their distinct honor and prestige.

In "I and You," Martin Buber, in a reflective critique of recent Western philosophy from the tradition of Jewish thought, argues that what really determines the meaning of one's existence is not the "I-thought" or the various objects opposed to the self, but rather the way in which one relates to the various beings and events in the world.

Martin Buber In his early years, Martin Buber devoted himself to research and studied the history of Western thought and the mysticism of Hassidism and Jewish thought, and from time to time, in the process of creation, he experienced a state of high emotion, full concentration, oblivion, and divine assistance.

In other words, he had the experience of "ecstasy", so he paid great attention to the thought and the revelation of the meaning of life's existence. However, Martin Buber is not, after all, a hard-headed man. But after all, Martin Buber is not just talking about theories in a rigid and boring way, a universal religious philosophical language is still needed.

So Martin Buber began to work on the Hassidic philosophy. Inspired by the Hasidic religious life, Martin Buber began to break down the religious divide and move from the Old Testament to the New Testament, listening intently to Jesus' Sermon on the Mount and the revelation of the Gospel of John.

He tried to translate his intellectual experience into a unique concept of the divine, which might limit the value of Martin Buber's religious philosophy. But in order to have a solemn and sacred reference to the Western tradition, this "careful translation" is a necessity for the ideological pantheon.

Fortunately, Martin Buber was deeply aware of the value of his religious philosophy. Fortunately, Martin

Buber was keenly aware of the solemnity of the sacred at the time. Despite the traces of religious philosophical language in his "poetry," the power of "poetry" to shake people to their core can, after all, break the fetters of language.

Plato believed that it was impossible to be a poet by virtue of the art of poetry alone, and that without this "poetic fascination", whoever knocked at the door of poetry would always be standing outside the door of true poetry, and his work.

Thus, although the form in which Martin Buber expresses his thoughts in I and Thou gives us the difficulty of studying its obscure and difficult depth. While the systematization and systematization of doctrine is certainly helpful to understanding, the danger is that the true voice from the source of existence will be weakened.

However, a systematic account is necessary to highlight the transformation of Martin Buber's Western tradition of holistic, foundational, and critical inquiry into the real and the human, as well as his significance for the modern West's analytical reflection on and reflection on fundamental questions of life, knowledge, and value.

Chapter 4: The main ideas of Martin Buber's most important work, I and You

In Martin Buber's book "I and You", he takes as the essence of the world a certain nature of connection between people and people or between people and things. This view can be very useful in psychotherapy to understand the basis of knowledge of the life of the visitor. There are many masters in psychotherapy who have been influenced by his ideas.

The main ideas of Martin Buber's most important work "I and You

In Martin Buber's book "I and You", he takes as the essence of the world a certain nature of connection between people and people or between people and things. This perspective can be effective in existential psychotherapy in guiding others towards the recognition of the existence of the self-living being itself.

There are many masters in existential psychotherapy who have been influenced by his ideas. Psychodrama is a form of collective psychotherapy, the psychoanalytic school of psychotherapy, which is a kind of drama that allows the patient to give vent to his or her feelings and thus achieve therapeutic effects.

Role reversal: Role reversal is the core of psychodrama role-playing theory, which means that the protagonist and other people on the stage swap roles.

Patients can experience the emotions and thoughts of the characters, thus changing their previous behavior; soliloquy: the protagonist speaks directly in front of the audience, expressing some unconscious feelings and thoughts; doubling: a supporting character stands behind the protagonist and performs with the protagonist, or speaks for the protagonist, this supporting character is the doubling.

The double can imitate the inner thoughts and feelings of the protagonist, and often express the subconscious content. The stand-in helps the protagonist become aware of internal mental processes and guides him to express non-verbal thoughts and feelings.

The stand-in assists the protagonist and acts as a liaison between the director and the protagonist. The stand-in can play an integrative role, enhancing the interaction between the protagonist and the supporting characters. The goal of the psychodrama is to induce the patient's self-initiated behavior in order to directly observe his condition.

Moreno opposes Frode's study of unnatural dreams and the practice of verbally reproducing them in the clinic. In contrast, he placed great emphasis on activities or behaviors in the natural environment, including role training.

He believes that it is important to have an authentic two-way cohesion that "resonates" in the whole group environment, which is much more complex than simple empathy and communication, involving cognition, desire, desire, choice and behavior.

The first non-directive therapy, also known as client-centered therapy, emphasizes the person's ability to self-adjust to restore mental health. Carl Rogers believes that the self is how we feel about our experience of ourselves.

Rogers divided the ego into two faces: the actual self and the ideal self. The transition from the actual self to the ideal self is a process of upward growth. Carl Rogers believes that human nature is good and that people tend to do what is good for them. Even though there are differences in potential among people, they will still use their abilities to improve their own lives on their own initiative.

If a person is allowed to live in a good environment and is allowed to develop freely, he or she will develop a healthy and mature self.

Carl Rogers believes that the most fundamental human character process is the process by which an individual progresses toward growth, a process called "self-actualization. People generate experiences by interacting with their environment, and we evaluate these experiences as positive if they enable us to achieve our goals, or negative if they do not.

And people will always tend to be evaluated as good experience direction, and over time, people can achieve their goals. This is why the tendency to self-actualize is an effective force for self-healing.

A person who has achieved self-actualization can be seen as a self-confident person who can often do positive things and accept challenges in the face of various experiences, and grow. Once the growth is achieved, the person also has more self-confidence and has reached a positive cycle for a long time.

Friedrich Salomon Perls (1893-1970), a German psychologist and founder of Gestalt therapy, made a major contribution to psychology by developing a new approach to psychotherapy, which he called "Gestalt therapy," also known as completion therapy. Gestalt therapy

The basic premise is that if one is to reach maturity, one must find one's own responsibility in one's own way of life.

The theory of Gestalt therapy is derived from Gestalt psychology, which means "completeness" and emphasizes the integrity of the person and the sense of wholeness: the individual has a tendency to seek completeness, and an incomplete completeness will be noticed until the completeness emerges and stabilizes.

The individual will complete its perfection according to its current needs. Peirce believed that to satisfy a need, a completion must be formed. The behavior of an individual is a whole, greater than the sum of its parts.

The meaning of an individual's behavior is to be

understood in the context of the whole of his or her life. As for the understanding of human beings, they cannot be seen in isolation from the environment (the whole). The individual understands his or her environment through the principle of form and landscape.

Moreover, since phenomenology refers to "the immediate experience that the individual perceives with his or her senses," Gestalt therapy believes in "the immediate perception of the environment by the person concerned, without inferring the causes of a certain behavior.

Therefore, Gestalt therapy is phenomenologically oriented. Because the therapy is based on the here and now, it is also oriented toward the existence of the self in life itself.

In Gestalt therapy, "awareness," "responsibility," and "freedom and choice" are important triangles, i.e., the stronger the awareness, the greater the possibility of freedom, and the more responsible one is for one's own decisions and actions. This is the flavor of existentialism.

Some of the terms used in Gestalt therapy, such as "projection," "internalization," and "repression," are of psychoanalytic origin, so Gestalt therapy can be said to be influenced by many schools of thought.

The difference is that Freud's view of the person is essentially mechanical and functional, whereas Peirce emphasized a holistic view of the human personality, in which each part of the person is closely linked to the whole.

Second, whereas Freud focused only on the internal psychological conflicts that were repressed during childhood, Peirce emphasized the importance of controlling the situations that individuals deal with. This orientation places much more emphasis on the process than on the content, that is, what is experienced at the moment is more important than what is expressed.

Peirce believed that for the purpose of self-understanding, it is far more important to understand how a person is behaving now than to pay attention to why he or she is doing so.

From Jacob Levy Moreno, the founder of psychodrama, to Carl Rogers, who pioneered non-directive therapy, also known as case-centered therapy, to Friedrich Salomon Perls, the founder of completion therapy, and many others, all of their therapies are essentially the practice of Martin Buber's philosophy.

Martin Buber He believed that when a man is in the world, he is in a world where things themselves have two opposing and contradictory unities, and he has two different lives, and the world appears to him as a double world.

By establishing the two contradictory attributes inherent in the world itself, the article lays the foundation for thinking about the world of "I and it" experience and the world of "I and you" relationship.

The duality of the world and the duality of life: the world of "you" and the world of "it" contain two elements that constitute the nature or state; "I and you" and "I and it" contain two elements that constitute the nature or state of life.

The book is divided into three volumes. At the beginning of each volume, a quote is given as an introduction.

The first volume aims to identify the duality of the world and the duality of life, the opposition between the world of "you" and the world of "it", and the opposition between "I and you" and "I and it" life. "I and you" "I and it" "I" "you" "it".

The second volume discusses the events and actions of "I and you" and "I and it" in the past of human society, and the systematic recording, interpretation and study of these events and actions and their representation in culture.

The third volume clearly shows the state of the "eternal you", i.e., the mutual influence and effect of God and man on people or things, acting or changing each other in an indirect or invisible way.

Volume 1

The introduction to the first book: "O man, stand in all the majesty of the truth and listen to the message that man cannot live without it, but he who lives by it alone does not He who lives by 'it' alone is no longer human." The aim is to reveal the duality of the world and the duality of life, the opposition between the world of "you" and the world of "it", the opposition between "I and you" and "I and it" life. "It" rules the world of experience, which is also the world needed for the life existence of the self, life existence and life experience.

Man's life existence is in a dual world, so he can feel two different kinds of life. Man is situated in the world of "it". This means that for the survival and needs of his cosmic life, man must treat the co-existents around him - other people, living things - as objects separate from the "I" and opposed to me, and through the experience of them, he acquires knowledge about them, and then assumes the knowledge to make it available to me.

As long as I hold the concept or attitude of "I and it", this kind of personal behavior towards people, things, and objects in the surrounding environment is quite persistent and consistent, then the co-existents are the third party "it" for me, and the world is the world of the third party "it" for me. This naturally leads to two consequences.

First, any co-presence that is associated with me becomes an object of my experience, a thing to be used in action or thought, and a means of satisfying my interests, needs, and desires, of accomplishing or promoting something. Martin Buber called this state of interaction and mutual influence between things that exist the "I and it" relation.

When people try to explain an event, their understanding of the event usually depends on the framework. Thus, in order to achieve the goal of using co-presence, I have to put the co-presence into a spatio-temporal frame. For example, when a conversation partner closes and opens his or her eyes quickly, we may use a physical frame (judging it to be a physical blink) or a social frame (judging it to be a possible wink) to understand it and produce a completely different response.

The former might be an involuntary, not particularly meaningful response due to dust in the eye, but the latter might mean a voluntary and meaningful action, grasping it as one of the objects. For how can I successfully exploit objects if I have no knowledge of the many connections between them and their place in the spatio-temporal network? My attitude towards co-existents depends on the needs of any spatio-temporal location, on the shape and quality of their specific properties to be exploited.

Man perceives things by connecting with their surface, their material shape, from which he extracts information about their nature and acquires experiential knowledge (which is necessary for survival). Only by knowing the spatio-temporal nature of objects, their causal sequence, we can say that we understand them and use them. For example, if the output sequence of a system at moment n depends only on the input sequence at moment n and before, and has nothing to do with the input sequence after moment n, then the system is said to have a causal nature, i.e., the system is a causal system, otherwise it is a non-causal system.

For example, if I look into a glass: it is sitting on my table, and I just look at it, it will not run away to other places.

Therefore, the so-called co-existent is only one of the many third-party "it" (it), and it is also the thing that is the goal of two things that complement each other, that are indispensable, and that accomplish each other's limited, anticipatory actions or thoughts. People are also inhabiting the world of the second person "you". In the world of "you", there is no object relationship between subject and object, but only a state of interaction and mutual influence between the subject matter of "I and you".

During this period of the existence of the self-life itself, he is connected with the world of people and people or people and things of a certain nature, and the co-existent second person "you" sees each other at a certain place at a certain moment, two or several people at the same time, or, to put it differently, meets the co-existent person as the second person "you". At that moment, this and I no longer become (separate from each other) the object of action or thought in isolation. There are two layers of meaning here.

(1) When I meet the second-person "you"

I am no longer a subject who experiences and exploits the values of others, nor am I in "relationship" with them in order to satisfy any of my needs, even the most noble ones (such as the so-called "need for love"). This layer is also better to analyze along the lines or reasoning, that is, the process of analysis, synthesis, judgment, reasoning and other cognitive activities on the basis of images and concepts, without regard to desires, purposes, self-interest and so on.

The process of analyzing, synthesizing, judging, and reasoning on the basis of images and concepts. This is because the second person "you" is the world, in a broad sense, the whole, all, everything, the fundamental condition for the existence of things, and the general name of all the gods in heaven and earth. I will approach the second person "you" with the whole life of my entire being and the true nature of the self that exists in the life of the self itself, nicknamed "you".

(2) When the co-presence is presented to me as the second-person "you"

It is no longer one of the things that are the target of action or thought in the world of space-time, and contains a limited, expectant object. At this point, the "great power of uniqueness" of the Coexistence has become fully

I". The second-person "you" is the world, and there is no other object, and the second-person "you" does not have to depend on other objects, and does not have to expect other objects.

The second-person "you" is a being without any condition, without any restriction. I cannot distinguish the same attributes of the second-person "you" from other beings, and I cannot analyze the second-person "you" and know the "you" in a calm, rational and non-emotional way, because all this means is that I place the "you" in contingency, and try to impose on the human desires and qualities. I place the 'you' in contingency, managing and controlling human desires and qualities in such a way as to achieve scientific, social or political ends that do not have to be under the will of the manipulated.

The term 'contingency' has several meanings. The first meaning refers to the coincidence, the accidental coincidence and the opposition of purpose. For example, a person goes to the market to buy groceries and meets a long-lost relative, so they want to embrace each other in the street. The second meaning refers to the opposition between the individual and the universal. It means broad and common, and it corresponds to special and individual. For example, many people know that exercise is good for their health, but they pass up opportunities to improve their health or weight because they don't want to sweat and don't have enough free time.

The health media Prevention suggests that a short walk with 15 minutes of free time, without sweating profusely, can have the effect of controlling blood sugar and maintaining weight. The third is the possibility, as opposed to the inevitability. Therefore, for the "I and you" relationship, the inevitability that occurs in all daily life meanings, the cause and effect, is all chance, because it lacks the fundamental that transcends predestination and is prior to experience.

In the following, Martin Buber gives a case in point.

Buber gives an example that may convey part of the meaning of the doctrine of "I and you" and "I and it". When Andersen offered a scarlet rose to the little girl who washed the dishes in the inn (Bałostowska: "Golden Rose. When Andersen offered a scarlet rose to the ugly little dishwasher girl in the inn (Bałystóvsky: "Golden Rose. All pity is the expectation of the appreciation of others, the expectation of the beauty of the goodness of one's heart and the disregard for the ugliness of the little girl, the expectation of the contempt for her inferiority, the expectation of the comparison of her existence with other objects.

In short, there is hope for the future or waiting for a chance encounter with fate. But in this momentary encounter between "I" and "you", some phenomena caused by the non-essential connection between the co-existents, which may or may not appear, which may or may not appear (as distinct from "inevitability") in the process of development and change of things, produce an encounter that contains no intensified contradiction within things, which suddenly disappears. Her ugliness, her humility, is but an arbitrary trick of fate, and "I" meet her "you" beyond time and predestination.

For, although "it" is only a limited and expectant opponent, "its" "you" is a cold and ruthless absolute being who transcends the cause-and-effect constraints imposed by the universe. At this moment, the second person "You" is this inclusive world, and "I" meet "You" with my tormented and discriminated soul, my whole life, and "I" tremble with every pain and every joy of "You".

In the world of "I and You," Martin Buber distinguishes between love and emotion: emotion is a thought or idea in the mind of man, while love is freely present; emotion commits ideals, hopes, expectations, etc. to someone or something, but man commits ideals, hopes, emotions, etc. to loving someone or something. This is not a [rhetorical] method of referring one thing or reason to another thing or reason when describing things or explaining them, but the two things or reasons have something in common. It is a true, certain, unquestionable truth. Love is not so attached to me as to regard you as content, as an object.

Love stands between "me and you". Anyone who has not experienced life, who knows things, who has not been experienced, who has not realized this truth in his true nature, cannot know what love is, even if he has put himself in the position of knowing, understanding, experiencing, enjoying and expressing his feelings throughout his life, which means that after a long time or after a lot of effort, a certain wish has finally come true and he has a deep affection for someone or something.

Love is a strong emotion and attachment to a person or object, derived from the strong feelings and psychological states of care, loyalty and goodwill between relatives. In short, to love is to take the initiative to make the whole happy. Although a common language, a common territory, a common economic life, and a common cultural manifestation, a common psychological stability, and a common cultural difference among all human beings throughout history make a universal definition of love difficult, but not impossible (the Shapiro-Wolffian hypothesis).

Love can include love of the soul or mind, love of legal and social institutions, love of one's own body and skin, love of the delicacies of the sea, love of money and treasure, love of knowledge or skills acquired through reading, listening, thinking, studying, practicing, etc., love of power or authority to control, govern, dominate, etc., love of spiritual satisfaction and gaining greater respect from society, love of all people in general and love of all people in particular. It is difficult to count the number of people who love all people, especially friends or fellow citizens, and so on.

Different people attach different importance to the love they receive. Love is essentially an abstract concept that can be experienced but is difficult to express in words. Love, by its effect on people or things, pervades the whole world.

In a broad sense, it is all, all, everything. In the eyes that stand in love and look outward from love to the world, and see things with wisdom, others are no longer entangled in the toil of running around. All people, whether good or evil, wise or foolish, beautiful or ugly, are transformed into true reality in turn.

The most famous and explicit advocacy of existentialism is Schartre's maxim that "existence precedes nature". Morality and soul are created by man in his existence.

In the world of "I and You", Martin Buber distinguishes between the existence of the real and the existence of the object, which leads to the consideration of the past and the present: the present does not refer to the end of the "passed" time, the frozen moment in the flow of time, as we perceive it, but to the real and lively, full of the present.

The present exists only when the state of interaction and interaction between things that "meet" in the present moment occurs, and it is only when "you" become present in that moment that the present becomes visible.

However, in Martin Buber's view, the "I" is only present when the "you" becomes present in that moment. However, in Martin Buber's view, the encounter between "I" and "you", the state of interaction and interconnection between the pure existence of "I and you", both transcends and remains in time, it is only a moment in time.

When a person is absorbed in something, or in a situation or thought activity, deeply obsessed with it, and cannot extricate himself from what he is experiencing and using, it means that he is, in fact, still living in the past. There is no present in his time.

He has nothing except the things that are the goal of his actions or thoughts, and the things that are the goal of his actions or thoughts are stuck in time that has passed.

It is beyond the will of man or man's power, and the pre-determined slavery is in the infinite continuity of time.

Therefore, he cannot help but rest, reside, and temporarily dwell in the world of the second person "you", and cannot help but return from time to time to the world of the third person "it", lingering between the uniqueness of "I and you" and the inclusiveness of "I and it".

The real existence is standing in the present, and the existence of the object of life is huddled in the past, and the two opposing natures of one thing at the same time are the real situation of human beings. This is the sadness of the existence of life, the existence of life itself, and also the greatness of the meaning of the existence of life.

For although man has to stay in the world of the third-person "it" in order to survive, man's intense longing for the second-person "you" makes him resist it and transcend it, and it is this resistance that creates man's spirit, morality, and art.

Any single individualized "you" will definitely undergo a great metamorphosis towards better or more perfection, similar to a caterpillar in a chrysalis, completing the process of becoming a butterfly, breaking the cocoon and becoming "it", before spreading its wings again.

"There is no such thing as a free I. There is only the I of the first word "I and you" and the I of the first word "I and it". When someone says 'I', it is one of those two 'I's.'

If Descartes based the "I am" on the "I think", Martin Buber directly embedded the existence of the "I" in the "state of interaction and mutual influence between man and things".

In Martin Buber's view, "relationship" is a state of interaction between people and things. For Buber, there is one and only one kind of "relation" that has two opposing natures at the same time, the state of mutual use and influence between "I and it" and "I and you", the connection of a certain nature between people and people or people and things, corresponding to the world of feeling and the world of connection respectively.

In the world of feeling, "it" is the state of mutual use and influence between people and things as an object, where people are aware of the existence or happenings around them, "the world is felt, but not cared for"; in the world of connection, "you" is the real life of a certain nature of connection between people and people or people and things, "all real life is a dialogue in encounter".

This is the contradictory relationship between two properties inherent in things themselves, as Martin Buber repeatedly argues in his first words "I and You": "What is on the level of life is living in front of us. That which is in the aspect of life lives in the present, and that which is in the aspect of object lives in the past.

"If a person is attached to the things he feels and uses, he is living in the past, and there is no present in every moment of his life. All he has are objects." I met "you" and entered into a direct connection with "you," without desires in between, and without means in the way, "connection is the unity of the chosen and the chosen, the unity of the passive and the active.

However, the most difficult destiny to overcome with strong will and strength (defects, mistakes, bad phenomena, unfavorable conditions, etc.) is the constant change between life and the things that are the object of action or thought.

Culture, too, is always making unprecedented turns, either "going down through one gyroscope after another in the spiritual underworld" or "going up into the most subtle and intricate vortex".

Every "you" in the world has some kind of connection between people and people or people and things, and inevitably falls back into the state of mutual use and influence between "it" people and things again and again. But where the connection is withdrawn, only feelings remain.

The so-called feeling is that the "you" is gone. Martin Buber even takes the extreme change to mean a great metamorphosis in the midst of dormancy towards a better or more perfect aspect, similar to the process of a caterpillar in a chrysalis, completing its metamorphosis into a butterfly, the moment of breaking the cocoon is the moment of butterfly transformation, the moment of "transcendence". The moment when the cocoon is broken is the moment of transformation.

The metaphor of the present situation is "'it' is the chrysalis, 'you' is the butterfly. It's always entangled, and becomes a thing with two opposing natures at the same time. "Without the state of interaction and mutual influence between "it" and things, people cannot live.

But whoever lives only in the state of mutual use and

influence between "it" and things cannot be considered a human being.

Martin Buber repeatedly distinguishes between "I and you" and "I and it", but knows that the spirit of both originates in a natural reality.

From the initial natural "tight bonding" to the natural "breaking away", then realizing the limitations of "it", and then pursuing the bonding with "you", Martin Buber sees the tug-of-war between human beings and individuals, in which "it" and "you" grow and fall, and go through difficulties together. This is a process that is manifest in the history of the individual and in the history of mankind.

Man's ability to feel "it" is growing, while the energy to connect with "you" is weakening. It is as if Martin Buber, in his time, was dissatisfied with the so-called "public life of modern man", "the political and economic figure who leads the way ...... treats the people he wants to reach not as carriers who have no way to feel "you", but as performance centers and struggle centers, each with a particular capacity to be of a specific kind And that can be put to a specific use.

The existentialist thinker Martin Buber, nearly a

century ago, pointed out the inescapable destiny of human beings: "Every 'you' in our world, every connection of some nature between people and people or people and things, must become a state of mutual use and influence between 'it' people and things.

Both "you" and "it" are the initial words that Martin Buber's "I and You" repeatedly discourses, or more precisely, "I and you" and "I and it" are themselves, paradoxically, two unified properties.

Martin Buber cleverly uses the state of interaction between persons and things between persons and things as a primitive to further elaborate his argument: "One primitive is the pair 'Ich-Du' and the other is the pair 'Ich-Es'.

On this basis, Martin Buber constructs a set of religious philosophical ideas about connection, encounter, and dialogue.

It is as if a teacher who truly understands "I and you" will help the student to teach and grow, so that the best possibilities of his life will become a reality, and a true doctor will never treat the patient as an object, but will adopt the attitude of personality facing personality, so that a living body, which has been deserted, can be revitalized.

With "I and You", Martin Buber shows us that there is a certain nature of connection between people and people or people and things, and that only by establishing a genuine encounter and dialogue with each other can life be truly looked after and cared for, and individuals or societies be freed from painful and self-desired conditions.

Volume 2

Introduction to Volume 2: "Listen to the 'I'! How perverse and unpleasant is the 'I' of the nature! When man conceals his self-contradiction and recites the 'I' with sadness, it invites much sympathy and compassion...", in order to discuss the presentation of "I and you" and "I and it" in human history and culture.

(1)Beyond Self-Loss and Self-Sacredness

Martin Buber's work directly addresses the two dominant values in the history of Western thought, and aims to explain the core concept of religious philosophy, transcendence, and to clarify the fundamental spirit of

Christian culture, love. At the end of the second volume of I and Thou, Martin Buber likens the two transcendental views he opposes to two world pictures.

One is the use of the immense and eternal universe to engulf the individual's life, so that the individual can achieve self-transcendence and immortality by committing his finite nature to the infinite process of the universe.

The second is to engulf the universe and other beings with the infinite "I", taking the universe in the infinite process of time as the content of the self-completion of the "I", thus casting the "I" into eternity.

For the sake of convenience in discussing the presentation of "I and you" and "I and it" in human history and culture, let us call the former "self-submission" and the latter "self-transcendence".

Both begin with man's transcendence of life existence, or rather, the quest for the meaning of life existence with the intention of "saving life". Transcendence is based on man's fear of the absolute contingency and absurdity of existence (his own existence and the existence of the universe) and his reflection on the meaning of the existence of life in the universe.

This reflection on the true meaning of one's own existence is naturally linked to a higher consciousness and a more transcendent purpose.

For, to go back and rethink the past and to learn from it means in itself that the spiritual consciousness of man rebels against the physical existence of the material body. The difference is the point of transcending the metamorphosis and sublimation.

In other words, resistance only indicates the nature of the metamorphic "transcendence" from the negative side, but the value content of the transcendence itself in terms of what is the meaning of life and where one can get a place to live is still a question that remains unanswered or unanswered. This gives rise to the distinction between the "self-submission" theory and the "self-transcendence" theory.

It can be said to be a transcendental view that emerged from the same day as human reflection.

It can be found in Plato's philosophy, in the Stoics' asceticism, in Plotin's cosmology, in the philosophical system of the Academy, in medieval mysticism, in Hegel's cosmic rationality, in all places, in all aspects, in all places. To satisfy man's search for the meaning of life and his desire for immortality.

This doctrine places man in the universe, and the "existence" of the self-existence itself is transformed and sanctified, even transcending the mundane and divine, giving it a mysterious and super-conscious motive.

It proclaims that in this vast and magnificent cosmic order, there is a hidden purpose of supreme goodness, purity, and beauty. When one realizes that the physical and psychological limitations of the individual are but a moment in the infinite evolutionary process of the universe.

When one "surrenders" to the feeling of helplessness, powerlessness, and inadequacy, one loses something in one's heart.

(2)Self-surrender" has a long history, and it can be said to be a reflection with human beings

"Self-surrender" leads one to the spiritual realm of equanimity and equality, where life and death are transcendent to the net of the Indra. However, any kind of "self-submission" can hardly avoid some fundamental drawbacks.

The demand for transcendence of the ego begins with a meaningless rebellion against the existence of the ego life itself, but "ego submission" only asserts that the apparently meaningless cosmic order has some divine purpose. But "self-submission" only asserts that the apparently meaningless cosmic order has some divine purpose.

On the other hand, its effect on moral philosophy is simply destructive and catastrophic. If the necessary progression of the universe is the very process of the unfolding of the moral realm, then we are affirming that everything is good and pure, that everything is logical and rational.

Worse still, this doctrine implies the idea that all individuals are instruments of the cosmic process of "I and it" to realize their own content, so that "love" between I and you becomes a meaningless myth of the "existence" of self-life existence itself.

(3)"Self-transcendence

The "self-transcendence" theory places the point of transcendence on the completion of the "existence" of the individual's self-existence itself, but it cannot escape from the dilemma of the "self-submission" theory as well.

No matter how lofty the spiritual needs of human beings are, no matter how distant they are from material desires and selfishness, they are after all a kind of "love" needs that I love to cling to. Therefore, it is asserted that morality is the realization of a certain need of conscience, and it is unapologetically said that the original purpose of morality is for utilitarian purposes.

For example, humanistic psychology, which has been prevalent in Europe and the United States in recent years, has particularly exposed the fatal flaws of this doctrine.

For example, in order to reconcile humanism, which is centered on the self-fulfillment of the individual, with the Christian spirit of self-sacrifice, Fromm simply attributed the altruistic realm as a necessary part of self-realization (Fromm, "The Man for Himself," ch. 1). However, if the ultimate goal of self-sacrifice is self-satisfaction, then such sacrifice has lost its originality and the absoluteness of its moral conscience.

(4)"Self-submission" and "self-transcendence

Western religious philosophers have proposed the

"self-submission" theory and the "self-transcendence" theory from a superconscious point of view. "Self-submission" means that man feels small in the face of the infinite, i.e., God, to the extent that his insignificance is reduced to zero in comparison with the infinite.

However, when one devotes oneself to God, one gains a sense of sublimity and a great power that shocks one, just as a drop of water thrown into the sea never dries up. Western religions such as Judaism, Christianity, and Islam belong to the "self-submission" theory. The ultimate reality in Western religions is the personified God.

"Self-transcendence" means that one's own mind and spirit can expand infinitely, and finally become one with all things in the universe, at which point one gains a sense of sublimity and power. This is the case with the saints, the supreme beings, and the true beings of the East. The ultimate realities of heaven, Tao, and Brahman in Eastern culture are impersonal in nature.

The spiritual expansion of the sage in the "self-transcendence" theory is not exclusive, and the unlimited expansion of his spirit does not prevent others from doing the same. This expansion is similar to the quantum effect of a magnetic field, where the quanta of the field can be superimposed, unlike a physical body, which is already limited by its volume and cannot produce the benefit of quantum superimposition.

Once an entity occupies a position, it will prevent other entities from occupying that position again. The improvement of the state of mind and spirituality can be synchronized, and our improvement will not exclude the improvement of others; it is inclusive.

Martin Buber's doctrine directly addresses the two dominant values in the history of Western thought. The aim is to explain the true meaning of the central concept of religious philosophy - transcendence - and to clarify the fundamental spirit of Christian culture - love.

From the perspective of the ultimate transcendental ideology, the ultimate thinking of Eastern and Western cultures is similar, just like the taiji diagram, in which yin and yang form a complementary structure. "Self-transcendence" and "self-submission" are also complementary.

We are small in the face of all-wisdom, all-power, all-goodness, and all-God, but when we are firm in our faith and justified by faith, we gain great and incomparable spiritual power, which has the meaning of "self-transcendence".

We are constantly raising ourselves to a higher state of mind and spirituality, but we must respect nature, society, and human nature, not be headstrong and do whatever we want, which has the meaning of "self-submission".

Volume 3

Introduction: "Is solitude not also a doorway? Is it not true that in the depths of loneliness there is always a mysterious and direct view? Is it not possible that my communication with myself cannot be transformed into a divine communication with the mysterious? The purpose of this book is to show the relationship between the "eternal you", God, and man.

In the third volume of I and You, Martin Buber interprets the metamorphic "transcendental" status quo that advocates religious philosophy as a mysticism that dissolves into the oneness of the divine, the celestial, and the divine, as a representation of "submission to self".

The Mahayana Buddhist thinking, which asserts that everything in the universe is contained in the "I" body, is interpreted as the "existence" of the existence of the self and the transformation of the "transcendent" status quo.

From the viewpoint of Martin Buber's religious philosophy, the former mistakenly treats the infinite vastness of the universe in time and the sequence of cause and effect as the eternal immortality of the value theory.

Therefore, it can be said that it starts from the confusion of the meaning of "existence" that exists in the life of the self and the inability to understand the nature of life, and starts a rebellion with the wrong perception of the meaninglessness of the universe, only to end by bowing down to the latter. Martin Buber, in speaking of "self-transcendence," likewise failed to see the reasoning behind it.

The "existence" of the ego's life existence itself cannot have the root of value a priori, otherwise why would the ego need to reflect on the meaning of life existence and pursue the meaning of the real existence of life itself?

Rebellion is only the starting point of the metamorphic "transcendence", and the completion of the metamorphic sublimation of life transcendence can only exist in a higher realm than my body.

If the value of "existence" or the transcendence of the ego-being itself does not exist in the universe outside of man nor in the subject, then where can the "existence" of the ego-being itself reside?

This question leads us to the most subtle and profound part of Martin Buber's thought. His answer is that value is present in relationship, in the relationship between the "self" and other co-existents in the universe. Relationships are the house of spirituality.

All the doctrines that hide the contradictory unity and duality of the two attributes of subject and object themselves are stuck in the superficial world of "existence" that exists in the life of the ego itself, blinded by the happiness of the superhuman world, without knowing the reality of the hardened experience of human life.

It is only dialogue that can introduce the "existence" of the self-life existence into the sublime world of divinity, and only relationship has divinity and a priori roots.

Of course, we agree that we are familiar with the scene of life in which the "existence" of the self exists in itself, and we are familiar with it with our hearts. People are satisfied with the world of "existence" that exists in their own being, even if it is a world of "things that are the target of action or thought", and they let it shine and glow.

We even deliberately close the door to the depths of life, allowing our bodies to remain in the external world of our own existence, the "existence" of our own being, which is constantly objectified.

We know the sickness of being in it: the nobility and glory of being human are erased, lies are deceived, and violence is trampled on. There is a lot of capriciousness and distrust among people, and only ends and means are devised to maximize the "existential" benefits of our own existence.

In the words of Martin Buber, we are submerged in the world of "it" that only focuses on feelings and uses. The "I" in "I and it" gradually withdraws from the connection between lives, and thus loses its true self.

01. The single "you" calls for the eternal "you"

"If one continues to go back and forth to the world where I love and cling to the splendor and brilliance of the world, one will not find the transcendent divinity, and if one walks away from the transcendent divinity, one will not find the transcendent divinity either.

Whoever takes the life of self-submission to the whole and moves toward his "thou" and moves all the worlds of self-submission to "him" finds the divinity that is not found beyond the realm.

Martin Buber Buber believes that each person lives in the dualistic "I" of the subject-object dichotomy of self-life existence and self-existent "existence", and that if the "I" of the "I and Thou" is stronger, the person becomes more and more human, and vice versa, the more self-life existence.

On the other hand, the more one is swayed by the "existence" of one's own life, the more one is trapped in a virtual world of unreality. Only by fully believing and establishing a verbal dialogue can the personality become stronger and the reality no longer leave.

It is like Socrates, who made his personality stronger through constant dialogue with people, "the 'I' that talks endlessly, the air of conversation that blows on every path he takes, even in front of the judges, even in the last period of his imprisonment.

His 'I' lived in the same way as his 'I'. His 'I' lived in the connection of dialogue with people, and that connection was embodied in the conversation. It is through a "full, true, pure" conversation that the "I" can truly meet the "you".

But what is more important in "I and you" is neither "I" nor "you", but the "harmony" between them, the encounter, the conversation and the connection. "Whichever carrier is distorted in the connection, the connection is also distorted." Martin Buber emphasizes that the "I" and the "you" must be "I" and "you" in a relationship of encounter and dialogue, not separate "I" and "you".

Therefore, neither can the "I" be swallowed up by the "you", so that the "you" ceases to be "you" and becomes something that exists alone; nor can the "I" degenerate into the "self" and identify itself as something that exists as a separate "being" of the self-life itself.

These two diffcrent ways of "being" of the existence of the ego-being itself depart from Martin Buber's esteem of encounter. Both of these different ways of "being" in the existence of the ego's life itself deviate from the "relationship" of encounter with speech that Martin Buber esteems.

Martin Buber's In his philosophical view of dialogue, Martin Buber presents the meaning of each in two scenes, one of which is a cosmic scene in which "a small earth emerges from the swirl of stars, and a small man emerges from the bustle of the earth.

Then history carries people forward, passing through age after age, through cultures piled up in ant tomb after ant tomb, crushing over one pile and creating another.

On the other side of the painting is a soulful scene: "A weaver weaves long, thin threads of cotton: the circular orbit of the stars, the life of all creatures, the history of the world.

Everything is spun by a thread of cotton spun into a long, thin strip, and there are no more stars, no more creatures, but sensations, images, or even just experiences, states of the soul."

From the point of view of the "existence" of the self-life itself in Martin Buber's religious philosophical ideal, in the former "universe", the "I" is buried in the world, and there is no so-called "I" at all; in the latter "soul", everything is composed of all time and space.

In the latter "soul", there is no such thing as all things

made up of time and space. Both of these burials make it impossible to establish a true connection, and Martin Buber is convinced that everything is contained. Martin Buber is convinced that everything is contained in a "relationship" of encounter and dialogue with each other, and in the ultimate realization of the existence of self-life, the "being" that exists in itself leading to the eternal "you".

"An extension line of interconnectedness intersects with the eternal You. Each individual 'you' is a view to the eternal 'you'. Martin Buber's setting of the "relationship" between the "I and Thou" encounter in verbal dialogue occurs not only between man and man, but also between man and God.

He also points out in his postscript that many people "do not see a "relationship" of encounter with God and a "relationship" of encounter with the people around them.

There is in fact a close 'bond' between the two," and this is the core of Martin Buber's deep concern. This is the core of Martin Buber's deepest concern. "Belief in God means never referring to God in the third person.

In the fall of 1921, Martin Buber suddenly figured out this question that had been bothering him for years, that sometimes brought up certain emotional disturbances, that were still waiting to be answered or to be answered, and decided to refer to "God" by the word "you" in a straightforward manner.

"Even if someone feels that the name of God is too shy to be uttered and is willing to think that he is an atheist, when he brings his whole obedient life to call upon the 'you' of his life, the 'you' that cannot be limited by anything else, he is already calling upon 'God' in his heart, in a straightforward way.

"This is why Martin Buber insists on the use of the word of encounter. This is why Martin Buber insists on prayerfully approaching "God" and moving toward "God" through an encounter with a "relationship" of words, not as some theological theories teach.

This is why Martin Buber insists on approaching God and going to God through a dialogical "relationship" of encounter, rather than, as some theological theories do, examining the object of God's action or thought as anything perceivable or imaginable, including both objectively existing and observable things (such as people, trees, houses, and abstract things like prices and freedom) and imaginary things (such as deified figures).

That would fall into the unchanging pattern of "I and it". The eternal "you" cannot, by its very nature, be "it".

This is why Martin Buber refuses to meet each other. This is the reason why Martin Buber rejects the energy of the "relationship" between each other, of the encounter of words, and the reduction of the effect or influence on things between the self-living being, the "being" that exists in itself, and "God".

Martin Buber Buber's philosophy of encounter-verbal dialogue "relationship" emphasizes that "the regression of religion is in fact a regression of the prayer of encounter-verbal dialogue "relationship" in religion.

The energy of mutual access to the "relationship" of encounter-verbal dialogue is increasingly buried in religion by the objectivity of action or thought.

It becomes heavier and heavier in religion, so that it is difficult to say "you" to the "being" that exists in the fullness of self-existence itself, without division.

What Martin Buber cares about is the "relationship" of encounter with speech, the relationship of encounter with speech between "I and you" and each other.

That means the real encounter with the individual life,

and the whole life with the "existence" that exists in the ego-life existence itself in submission to the ego, and moving towards the transcendent "God".

The "being" that exists in the self-life of the human being surrenders to the "I and it" in the world of experience of the experience of duality, and the "I and you" create a world of interactions between human beings.

The value is expressed in the use of interpersonal resources that one possesses for political or economic benefit, in the state of mutual influence between the "being" that exists in one's own life existence, the "I" and other co-existents in the universe. The relationship of encounter and dialogue is the home of spirituality.

All doctrines that obscure the subject-object dichotomy remain in the superficial world of "being" that exists in the life of the ego itself, the world of "it," in the broadest sense of the word, is all, all, everything.

Only the connection of some kind of "relationship" between man and man or man and things can lead to a transcendent spiritual understanding and a root beyond the realm of the a priori.

Some people think that 'love' makes us vulnerable to

things that are the target of action or thought. Sometimes we may think to ourselves, "Why should I love someone who is indifferent and ungrateful? Or, "Why should I suffer because I am bound to love?

However, the apostle Paul tells us to pursue love, saying, "Now abide in faith, in hope, and in love; and of these three, the greatest is love. Seek after love. (1 Corinthians 13:13-14:1)

English New Testament scholar C. K. Barrett writes, "Love is an action, and all that God does is based on love.

When people love God or care for others, even though their love is not complete, they are learning what God has done. When the "presence" of our own being exists, we can please God by acting and behaving in a way that imitates God in our speech and dialogue "relationships".

The "being" that exists in its own being seeks to love by thinking about how to live out the teaching of 1 Corinthians 13:4-7.

For example, how do I treat my children with the same patience that God has shown me? How can I treat my parents with consideration and respect? How can I do everything at work without seeking my own benefit? When something good happens to a friend, do I rejoice with him or do I envy him?

As we "pursue love" in the "existence" of our own being, we will find that we need to always seek to meet God in a verbal "relationship" because He is the source of love.

We also need to turn to Jesus as the best example of love. Only then will we understand deeply the meaning of true love and gain the power to meet and speak in "relationship" to love people as God loves us.

Therefore, when we "love God and love others," we not only realize the key to the divine world that exists in our own being, but we also realize the true content of the value of our "being" that exists in our own being.

True existence, as a direct or indirect adjective in the new era, is mostly used to evaluate others; that is, the essence, the original, the pure, and the physical truth. The essence refers to the fundamental properties inherent in things themselves.

Soon after the "existence" of one's own being becomes the "temple of the Holy Spirit", the Holy Spirit will transform your finite life beyond the present into His infinite life, as if a limiting line has been erased and replaced with an endless long line. At this point, you will feel that you have lived forever.

According to the true existence, "eternal life" literally means eternal life. This life is the life of "divinity". The original life of man is love of sin, is short-lived, and will perish. In salvation, the "divine nature" gives us His life, so that we may have His life, that we may no longer love sin, and that we may not perish.

Does the "eternal life" of true existence refer to the future hope of man after death? The "eternal life" of the true existence is not only the future hope and fact of the "existence" of the existence of the self, but also the present fact of the "existence" of the existence of the self.

The reason why the believer does not sin as the unbeliever does is that he has the power of "eternal life" that exists.

The person who has the "eternal life" of true existence, the mind, words, attitude and behavior of his encounter with the "relationship" of speech and dialogue are all directed toward the transcendent divinity, and can exist forever to the "eternal life" of true existence.

Those who have the "eternal life" of true existence, the

"existence" of their self-existence itself becomes meaningful, no longer waiting for death, waiting for judgment, waiting for the guilt of unrealistic thoughts that human beings may or may not have, waiting for the feeling that they have done something bad to others, that they owe something to others, or that they have done something wrong.

Now the "existence" of the existence of the self exists for eternity, for hope, for a home.

Therefore, the "eternal life" of true existence is not a vague hope of the future or a self-soothing agent in the face of the fear of death, but the "eternal life" of true existence is today.

The "eternal life" that really exists is an inner life that can be experienced in the "existence" of our own being, so that a new vitality can be injected into our lives and our lives can have a different ending.

This is where the existentialist philosopher Martin Buber's philosophy of encounter with the "relationship" of speech and dialogue is really far-reaching and profound.

Therefore, before we discuss the differences and similarities between the true existence of Christianity and other religions, we must address the basic premise that Christianity does not believe that the "existence" of human life as a self-existence itself is only a combination of small and large chances, a chance or coincidence.

Martin Buber's philosophy of encounter with verbal dialogue "relations", the "eternal life" of true existence, does bring about a change in the mental image of things from external feelings to the "existence" of the human being in his own life.

But if this is all that exists in the "existence" of the self, then "Christianity" is only a religious philosophical idea that cannot really bring about a change of life for human beings.

However, Martin Buber's philosophy of encounter with the "relationship" of verbal dialogue always believes that whether human beings accept it or not, there is a transcendent Creator of the universe who is the most true, the most good and the most beautiful, and who gives to human beings the "eternal life" of true existence, so that they can enjoy the beauty of this creation "with Him".

Therefore, not only in this life does the "existence" of self-existence itself exist, and He is pleased to intervene in the daily life of man, but in the next life, those who believe in God will also experience the resurrection of the "eternal life" of true existence in the flesh.

As the Bible records in John 6:40, the Lord Jesus said, "For it is my Father's will that everyone who sees the Son and believes should have eternal life, and I will raise him up at the last day. Therefore, the "eternal life" that really exists refers to two facts: In Christ, we have new life in this life.

In the future, our flesh will be resurrected into eternity. The "eternal life" that really exists is available to us when we accept Jesus, because the Lord Jesus said, "Truly, truly, I say to you, he who hears my word and believes in him who sent me has eternal life and does not come into condemnation [note: the word condemnation can also be translated as judgment here], but has passed from death into life. "(John 5:24)

02. The "eternal life" that really exists

Let us return to the philosophy of "relationship" proposed by Martin Buber in his "I and Thou" dialogue, which goes beyond the viewpoint of "immortality" and engages in the exploration of exclusive "immortality", which means "death without death" in the usual human context, that is, a person's body decays and loses the phenomenon of life due to death.

In fact, the "life essence" is not extinguished or disappeared, but can exist forever. Therefore, the English word "immortal" can be translated as immortality or "eternal life".

The word "immortal" has different meanings in the Western and Eastern disciplines that study universal and fundamental issues, including existence, knowledge, values, reason, mind, and language. In Aristotle's (384~322 B.C.) trinitarian citation explanation: For example, all men are bound to die.

(Universal principle) Socrates is human. (Special statement) Socrates is bound to die. [By replacing the particular (minor) with the general (major), the major premise is that "all men must die".

That is, since ancient times, it has been said that the result is the same in all conditions, regardless of the West or the East.

This may be an option that human beings "do not like", but the fact is that there is no way to prevent death from happening, so religious philosophers imagine that human beings may die without dying, and thus find "words" to support this idea, which becomes a form of thinking that reflects the nature of the object of "immortality" or "eternal life".

Ideas, cultures, morals, customs, arts, institutions, and behaviors that have been passed down from generation to generation and through history. The social behavior of people have invisible influence and control role in thought.

Then the ghosts and gods will always exist, and immortal consciousness from the role of cognition, such as feelings, perceptions, hallucinations, imagination, concepts, etc.. After the death of their parents, they "believe" that they are not completely extinct and that their ghosts and spirits will always exist, thus establishing the rituals and customs of honoring their ancestors.

The Western view of immortality or immortality is based on a position or point of departure that either places hope in the soul, or refers to a way of expressing content, or the ability to analyze and judge, invent and create, solve problems, or the ability of human beings to use reason, and similarly explains the view that people die but do not die.

This can be seen from the early Greek philosophers. The earliest Western beliefs that man has eternal life are found in the Apology and Phaedo of Plato (427-347 B.C.).

The Greeks generally believe that the answer to the question of "who" is the "being" that exists in our (human) self-existence itself should be "our soul". In the preceding interpretation of the concept of immortality or immortality, although it is not explicitly stated, it is indirectly revealed that the words indirectly, it is revealed that the word we or "person" does not refer to an image with an external body, because it is not the "real" "I" or "person".

In what Plato often classifies as a kind of metaphysical dualism, sometimes called Platonic realism, the human body, like things in the phenomenal world, is a mere replica.

The "essence" is the world of concepts or ideas derived from thinking or reasoning, that is, the soul; the body has death, which is a phenomenon, and the idea that man "has no death" is the "essence".

On the other hand, Plato sees the human body as a

"temporary depository" for the soul. The death of the body is like a decaying, collapsing house, which can be discarded and found another place to live.

Therefore, when we say "I" is "who", we are not referring to the "body" that will sometimes die, but to the immortal soul.

Plato's other theory of the immortality of the soul is that the human soul, before it is reborn, has learned many concepts by thinking or reasoning, as opposed to the sensible cognitive world.

After reincarnation, the concept or idea obtained by thinking or reasoning is forgotten, and it is only when there is a suitable opportunity for recollection that the knowledge of the idea can be recalled.

The recollection of knowledge is possible because the soul retains material from previous lives (before this life) or from the world of truth for reference or study. The mental process of knowing and understanding things through the activity of the soul's consciousness has a very different effect on people or things than the sensory function of the body.

Just as the object of sensory action or thought decays

and decomposes, so does the body; but as the object of the soul's cognition is eternally pure, so is the soul eternally pure.

Aristotle, in his De Anima, asserts that the rational soul is eternally immortal, and that the difference between the animal soul, which is responsible for sensation, and the vegetable soul, which is responsible for nourishment, is that it can exist outside the human body after death. To be able to know and to think, or to be called pure intellect, means the immortal part of the soul.

St. Thomas Aquinas, as a church father, certainly believed in Christianity and recognized the immortality of the soul as an object or event that does not need to be known by the senses.

It is an important issue in metaphysics, as it is the opposite of the present. The ability to know things without having to be "material" is the influence or function or effect of the soul on people or things, and is therefore also called "intellect".

The philosophical view of R. Descartes (1596~1650) already separated "mind" from "matter", thus assuming that in the system of "mind", there is a living rational soul that dominates the activities of the mechanical physical body.

Therefore, this master must have the role of "knowledge". From this it is deduced that whatever cannot be seen in the body should be attributed to the soul, and the existence of the soul can be proved by the "activity of thought". Thus, it is established that all perfect reality has a prior "cause".

In other words, the existence of thought comes from the "pre-existent" soul, and by extension, since the soul exists before the body, it must not decay when the body dies, which means that the soul can live forever. Before the modern era in the West, the theory of soul was originally one of the arguments of philosophers and belonged to the field of philosophy.

Only in recent years, "parapsychology" has emerged, and from some factual experiences gathered together, it is thought that the existence of the soul is a "possibility", but it is difficult to make a precise and correct statement in the short term. Even some existential philosophers believe that the existence of relationships depends on the existence or absence of the basis of relationships.

The basis of a certain nature of connection between people and people or people and things is a passive objective existence, while the state of mutual influence is an active, dynamic process. The basis of a relationship between two people is not necessarily a relationship or a connection.

For example, if a couple has been divorced for a long time, even though there are still multiple bases of mutual influence between them, if they stop seeing each other, the state of mutual influence does not exist.

Conversely, a relationship can take place between two strangers who did not have any basis for a "relationship" of encounter and verbal conversation, only that the process of establishing a basis for a "relationship" of encounter and verbal conversation, a state of mutual influence, takes longer and sometimes requires the intervention of an intermediary than those processes that have a basis for a "relationship" of encounter and verbal conversation, a basis for a "relationship" of encounter and verbal conversation of some nature with people or people and things.

Therefore, the best definition of love may be the active act of treating a living being or object (which may be a person, an animal, an object, or a deity) with sincerity and making it happy as a whole.

In short, love is the active making of the whole happy, encompassing a range of strong and positive emotional and spiritual states, from the noblest virtues or good habits, to the deepest interpersonal relationships, to the simplest pleasures. Such emotions and attachments drive those who feel them to seek physical, intellectual, and even imaginative proximity to the object of their love.

At the same time, it is also the nature of the "relationship" between people or things to which all human activities are directed, and it is not the overflow of "I" emotions, which are presented in the "relationship" between people and people or people and things, in a certain nature of connection between people and things, which opens up and brightens itself.

It is here in the encounter of verbal dialogue "relationship" that "I" and "you" transform and sublimate themselves and transcend themselves at the same time. People resist the unreasonable, unjust constraints or oppressions of the world of "it" and move towards transcendence, and in the state of mutual influence, people realize communication beyond the boundary!

Postscript

Postscript: "Whoever tries to grasp the spirit or to know the nature of the spirit, after having received the spiritual breath, has disobeyed the Spirit. And if he gives himself credit for the gift of God, he is equally guilty of betrayal. This could be the summary of each volume. After analyzing the two values, Martin Buber presents his words of encounter. Buber presents his philosophy of "relationship" in the dialogue of words of encounter: he affirms the preciousness of "I and you".

Martin Buber's rejection of "self-submission" is that it expresses the phenomenon of alienation that is characteristic of modern and contemporary Western societies, and that it is when unity is achieved (for others) that the self achieves freedom and integrity of will.

Heidegger uses degradation as the characteristic of the "existence" of the ego's life existence itself in the daily coexistence. Once the personality is forced to act as a phenomenon of social alienation against the inner will of the ego's life existence itself, it more or less touches the conditions of alienation.

The "existence" that exists in the real self-life itself will often be confused and sink into the consciousness, the abnormal powerless and meaningless feeling, and the "existence" that exists in the self-life itself will yield to the "going with the flow" of all things and disappear in the infinite and vast value and meaning of the universe.

Martin Buber Martin Buber's denial of "self-transcendence" lies in the fact that it is confined to the fact that my life existence cannot transcend the prior experience of death, and that it creates "isolation or the feeling of being alone and meaningless.

The metamorphic "transcendence" of the human being begins with the reflection of the true meaning of "existence" that exists in the life existence of the self, but the a priori does not exist in the control of "I", but only in the affirmative encounter with the verbal dialogue "relationship" "I and you", "I and it", in the interaction of some nature of connection between human beings and human beings or human beings and things.

Otherwise, an "eternal life" that is born to exist, without a lack of I, does not exist in time and space, much less does it need to appreciate the reflection and transcendence of the true meaning of "existence" that exists in the life of the self.

Martin Buber explores the "encounter" in this interaction between people and people or people and things, in a certain nature of connection, and affirms the search for a "relationship" of "being" in an encounter with words.

For example, Descartes famously said, "I think, therefore I am". What does it mean? It means that, since the subject of thought is me, in order to think about being, I must first exist. Conversely, if I doubt my existence, then doubt itself is also a kind of thinking, so I must first "exist" in the existence of my own life.

However, there are many psychological doubts about the "relation" of the encounter with verbal dialogue, and the reasons for it. The philosopher Jean-Paul Berkeley made a similar statement when he said that the "being" of the existence of the self is perceived.

Berkeley agrees with Locke's view that all human concepts are derived from the experience of encountering verbal dialogue "relations", but disagrees with Locke's doctrine of first and second nature. He argues that both first and second nature belong to sensation (as opposed to perception or awareness), and that

All knowledge comes from the quenching of life existence in everyday experience, or feeling an encounter with a verbal dialogue "relationship" meaning that only what is felt by the "other" can prove the "existence" of the life existence of the self itself.

That is, only when others respond to our actions can we prove that the signals we send exist. The existence of a signal proves the existence of the "existence" of our egoic being itself.

An example of this is given in Martin Buber's "I and You" in everyday life. For example, when it snows, many children like to step on the snow to make their footprints.

"The action of "stepping" is a signal of our own existence, and "traces" are a response from the outside world. When a child sees his own footprints, he confirms his action.

In the case of a couple, lovers, or friends, they deliberately ignore each other during a cold war. This kind of anti-intimacy behavior is actually an application of the theory about the existence of a verbal dialogue "relationship" in the encounter.

Because the other party pretends to be indifferent,

ignoring and not responding, one cannot confirm the existence of one's own signal from the other party's response, nor can one confirm one's own existence.

Similarly, when we post a dynamic message about ourselves on an Internet social platform, it is not the action of posting a signal itself that gives us a symbol of presence, but whether others respond with positive encounter speech dialogue and enthusiastic comments, so that we can experience the real emotion of our own signal, and only then will we gain the joy of a sense of presence.

Therefore, the sense of presence in the encounter speech dialogue "relationship" is not about making actions or sounds, but about having an effective response to the encounter speech dialogue "relationship" from the external world.

This need for a sense of presence in the encounter-verbal relationship can be said to be an acquired habit from early childhood, which is why infants cry and scream to gain attention when they cannot get a timely and effective response to the encounter-verbal relationship.

Similarly, many people who see a psychiatrist complain that they lacked loving and caring encounter relationships in their childhood, so that now they do not know how to love others through encounter relationships.

The lack of love is in fact the psychoanalytic way of exploring the signals that some people send to themselves during their early childhood without anyone responding to them or responding to the quality of their conversational "relationships" that are not good enough or timely enough.

In the long run, my need to love to hold on can only be hidden, but it cannot disappear. Younger and younger children will have less and less need to respond to external encounters and conversational "relationships".

As the "being" of the self exists, it becomes less and less able to express itself to the outside world, and it does not respond to others effectively in verbal dialogue, and interpersonal relationships become worse and worse as negative things become the cause and effect of each other.

Therefore, the absence of the sense of existence in the "relationship" of encounter and conversation will lead to the alienation of the sense of meaninglessness in the existence of the self and the loss of the sense of value in the existence of the self. It is like a separate piece of jigsaw puzzle.

The absence of a sense of "relationship" with the outside world will make it difficult for us to establish a "relationship" with the outside world, and a separate puzzle will not be able to know the value of the "existence" of our own being.

This requires us to be in a state where the fullness and value of life exists in the "I-Thou" encounter and dialogue (in this state), where I approach "Thou" with my whole being, my whole experience of life, my true selfhood, and the continuous mutual attention with You.

Conversion to the "Eternal You

In human history and culture, including writing, language, architecture, food, tools, skills, technology, knowledge, customs, art, etc., "I and it" is gradually devouring "I and you", the ground of some nature of connection between human beings and human beings or human beings and things.

And treating people as objects, adopting an "I and it" attitude towards them, not only degrades them but also pays the price of their own humanity (the master treats his slave as an object, and the slave suffers along with the master's own dehumanization).

Martin Buber Buber calls for man to break free from the domination of "I and it" not only in the encounter of verbal dialogue "relations", social relations, but also in the encounter of verbal dialogue between man and nature, and to seek the relationship of "I and you".

The development of modern technology has not only led to the alienation of human beings, but also to the subjective anthropocentric ideology advocated by it, which has caused the deterioration of the living environment by the infinite seizure of nature.

Believe in the simplicity and magic of the "existence" of the self that transcends the existence of the self, and believe in the submission of the "existence" of the self to the compliance of the self with the existence of the self, and in the coexistence of each other without conflict in speech and dialogue, in order to realize the expectation and desire of the Creator.

This is like the eagerness of people to see their long-lost relatives and friends come to them, which contains the true meaning of the "existence" of the life of the self. The expression of ideology, language, and words obscures the true nature of existence.

In the world of meditation and wisdom, we see the truth, the existence and activity of beings around the "existence" of our own being, and the connection of a certain nature between people and people or people and things.

Everywhere there is a continuous mutual attention with the same being (people). Such a state of "I and you" interaction can (and should) exist not only between people, but also between people and animals, plants, and even inanimate beings.

If we look at the phenomena and movements of things in the forest, or investigate a tree, we can estimate the amount of wood it contains, and if we only care about using it or selling it for profit. However, this is not the only way for people and trees to meet, talk, and "relate" to each other.

It is also possible to recline under the shade of a tree, to meditate on the world and see things with wisdom, to be relaxed and happy, and even to be one. Thus, in Martin Buber's encounter with the dialogical "relationship" of words, God is present in these creatures.

Thus, the "I and Thou" relationship is through the creation encounter speech dialogue "relationship", which ultimately leads to a kind of I and eternal "Thou", i.e. God establishes a certain nature of connection between "I and Thou", between man and man or man and things.

Martin Buber Buber's "relational ontology" that encounters the verbal dialogue "relationship" and repeatedly pursues the initial words "I and Thou" and the primordial "I and Thou" in "I and It" theoretically helps people to construct a new vision of the ideal world under which they can emerge from the "crisis of faith".

Martin Buber argues that the real crisis behind the "existence" of self-life itself is the fusion of faith in God with realism, which advocates certainty of outcome if one follows the steps of certain social matrixes.

The real crisis of faith, therefore, is the conflation of faith in God with realism and the simplification of it into a "formula" that one can follow to achieve the results we want.

The fusion of faith and realism has led to the development of a meritocracy that includes the idea and practice of "good deeds will be rewarded", emphasizing that good deeds will be rewarded.

Under such a mindset, when we encounter setbacks and failures, we either feel resentment and anger toward God, thinking that God has not rewarded us for our good deeds, or we feel anxiety and self-condemnation, thinking that we must not have done well enough and that is why there is no good outcome.

The tendency to believe that "good things happen to good people" is very destructive when it is reflected in the interaction and fellowship with people and things. This mindset causes us to tend to condemn others when they face setbacks, thinking, "You must not have done enough, not good enough, to get this result.

For example, when a friend's child is in a crisis of faith, this mindset naturally blames the friend for not doing his or her part in leading the child, or the youth pastor of the church for failing to do his or her job and causing the child to leave the faith.

The collateral effect of this is that people hide their failures and are reluctant to share their frustrations. Yet the core of Martin Buber's faith in God is not based on the formula, "If I do something, it will happen," but on the formula, "What God wants to do will happen.

So I adjust myself to move forward toward God's determined future. The former is a disguised form of social matrix constraintism, which evolves into saving oneself by "acting or thinking on the things that are the goal".

The latter emphasizes the grace of the encounter with the "relationship" of words, and the renewal of the world is not based on human effort, but on the final act of God.

Whether the new heaven and earth that God will create will come or not has nothing to do with our efforts, but rather with His promises and acts, the grace of the encounter speech dialogue "relationship"; yet God invites us to encounter speech dialogue "relationship" to trust Him, to adjust our way of life, and to move forward now toward this certain future.

From the perspective of faith, the "relationship" of encounter and conversation is directed to God. So while we can interpret Martin Buber's "relational ontology" from a theoretical point of view, we can also interpret it from a theoretical perspective. But we must not forget the ultimate destination of Martin Buber.

The "eternal you" is Martin Buber's "relational ontology. This is the premise of Martin Buber's "relational ontology," and it is also the connection and attachment to the nature of a certain kind of "relationship" between "I and you" and people or people and things.

To convert to the "eternal you" of the encounter-verbal dialogue "relationship" is to abandon this objective and real attachment that exists independently of human consciousness. That is, the world in which man and things interact and influence each other, as the devotees of history have said.

But Martin Buber says, "That is for the sake of the world. But Martin Buber says, "How foolish and desperate is the man who forsakes the path of life in order to seek God! "For we can find God everywhere in all things by meeting in a "relationship" of speech and conversation.

It is clear that conversion to the Eternal You is not a renunciation of the world, in the broadest sense of the word: all, everything, everything. Rather, it is about transforming one's attitude toward the world and the interactions and interactions between people and things through the encounter of verbal dialogue.

From seeing everything as an object of "existence" that exists in the life of the self, to seeing everything as a connection of some nature between "you" and people or between people and things. From the encounter with the verbal dialogue "relationship" between "I and it" to "I and you".

"The one who is attached to the state of interaction and influence between people and things in the world is not close to God through the "relationship" of encounter with speech, and the one who has abandoned the connection of a certain nature between people and people or people and things in the world is not honored by God through the "relationship" of encounter with speech.

The only way to approach the unsearchable "God" is to move towards "I and You" with the whole "relationship" of encounter and conversation in life, and to consider the world's living beings as "You", the link of some nature of encounter and conversation between people and people or people and things.

God is only in the nature of some kind of encounter between people and people or between people and things, in the nature of a "relationship". If one clings to the state of interaction and influence between people and things in the world, one abandons the world.

It is a renunciation of the true existence of "eternal life" and of the nature of the "relationship" between people and people or between people and things, the communication between the conflicting parties within things and the relationship that occurs between things.

The former treats God as the "eternal" world of "true existence", where people and things interact and influence each other, while the latter pursues God as a "relationship" of encounter and conversation, where people and people or people and things are connected by a certain nature of encounter and conversation.

It is only in the connection between "I and you", between people and people or between people and things, that the existence of God can be realized.

"The ever-expanding field of the "relationship" between people and things, of a certain nature of encounter and dialogue, is gladly united in the Eternal You, and each individual You is an insight into the Eternal You.

Each individual You is an insight into the Eternal You, and each individual You is a statement of the primordial word "I and You" to the Eternal You. Therefore, the so-called "relationship" of the encounter speech, "I and You" and "I and It" of the "Eternal You", is the fundamental guarantee of our encounter speech "relationship" with the "I and You" in dealing with the world.

"The experience of human life cannot be divided into a "relationship" of encounter and dialogue with God, a certain nature of connection between human beings and human beings or human beings and things, and a state of interaction and mutual influence with the non-genuine human beings and things of the world, and one cannot pray to God with devotion and use the world ruthlessly.

If you treat the world as an object of use, you must also see God in the same way. The opposite is also true: to maintain some kind of "relationship" with God in the nature of an encounter between the real person and the person or the person and the thing, in order to maintain a relationship with the world in a state of interaction and mutual influence between the real person and the thing.

Martin Buber Buber is very clear here about the "relationship" between "I and you" and "I and it": conversion to the "eternal you" is the source of the "existential" meaning that exists in the very existence of the life of the self.

"The purpose of God's coming to man is not to make him yearn for him, to make him long for him, but to convince him of the real meaning of the existence of the self-life itself in the world. It is only in the connection of this genuine "relationship" between man and man or between man and things of a certain nature of encounter with speech that meaning exists, and this is the home that man seeks.

God's revelation is never a simple answer to life, but rather a gift of power that helps one to brush away the unbearable lightness of "being" that exists in one's own being, and to make the experience of living life meaningful and heavy.

"The meaning of "existence" that exists in one's own being is not of the next life, but of this life. So everything must begin with yourself here and now, loving, committing, and revealing the meaning of life existence in your own way, revealing its sacred meaning in every daily thing that you meet and speak and "relate" to.

You meet God when you meet the connection of a certain nature of encounter with a verbal dialogue "relationship" between people and people or people and things in the world with the whole existence of "being" that exists in your own life existence itself.

Martin Buber Buber's thought here is full of the mystery of Jewish thought, yet highly contemporary in meaning. The orientation of the "eternal you" was once accepted by the Western philosophical tradition from Christianity, but the historical progress of Western philosophy is moving towards the state of interaction and mutual influence between "it" people and things, and away from the "you" connection of a certain nature of meeting verbal dialogue "relationship" between people and people or people and things.

Martin Buber's The "relational ontology" of Martin Buber is to reconstruct the "eternal you" in Western philosophy.

It is only by transcending the degradation of "the state of mutual use and influence between "it" people and things" and converting to the "eternal you", the connection of a certain nature of meeting verbal dialogue between people and people or people and things, that the inflated and enlarged ego can be restrained.

The "existence" of the self exists in itself, and with the complementary state of interaction and mutual influence between the "Eternal You" and people and things, one can properly deal with the world of the connection between people and people or between people and things, where a certain nature meets the "relationship" of speech and dialogue.

Martin Buber He calls on people to devote themselves to "you", to perceive the world of connection between people and people or between people and things, and to get out of the crisis of the realist era.

Chapter 5: Conclusion

In the twentieth century, the theories of religious philosophy of anthropology, represented by the ideas of Martin Buber and Jaspers, essentially indicate the "existential" dilemma and cultural crisis that modern man is facing in his own life existence.

This means that "anthropology" is a product of human ideology that has been created over a long period of time, and at the same time is a phenomenon that records or discusses important events and developments in the past, and is a deposit of human society and history. To be precise, "anthropological culture" is condensed within and outside of material things.

It is the way of thinking, values, way of life, behavioral norms, art and culture, science and technology of a country or nation that can be passed on and disseminated, and it is the process by which human beings, through various carriers, realize the two-way flow of information to form the perception of the subject of the behavior.

It is a kind of ideology that can be passed on and is the

sublimation of the objective world's perceptual knowledge and experience. It is also the loss of individuality and the alienation of the subject.

Martin Buber's philosophy of "I and You" or relational ontology is a critique of the traditional philosophical state of mutual use and influence between "I and it" people and things, starting from the "I and You" encounter verbal dialogue "relationship".

Martin Buber suggests that man's true existence is realized in a certain nature of connection between man and man or man and things of "I and you", not in a state of mutual use and influence between man and things of "I and it".

God is the "eternal you" - God is the thing that meets in dialogue, does not act or think as an object of discernment, in a certain nature of connection between man and man or man and thing facing "you".

Martin Buber Buber's idea of encounter-verbal dialogue "relationship" is based on a reflection of the theological humanism of human existence, and is also a critique of the crisis of Western cultural realism and social romanticism.

"If the principles or theoretical systems of faith, which are held with passion and firm conviction, do not grow with the growth of human beings and exist with the existence of human life, then the state of mutual use and influence between human beings and things would have died out long ago.

The study of the philosophy of religion and the argument for God from "anthropological culture" is a characteristic of the Western view of religion in the 20th century, and the philosophical view of religion from "anthropological culture" is essentially a philosophical reflection on religion and the problems and concepts it contains in the sense of subjective reflection, as well as a rational expression of the philosophy of religion after profound reflection.

In terms of the position from which we observe things, we can say that "human beings are the beginning of religious philosophy, human beings are the center of religious philosophy, and human beings are the end of religious philosophy.

With the continuous development of secularization of religious philosophy, it has become one of the keys to decipher the mystery of religious philosophy to go beyond the narrow position of religious theology and to consider the cultural system linking human beings with gods or supernatural or divine beings from the perspective of "anthropological culture.

The religious view of "anthropological culture" in the 20th century conveys that man as a "transcendent being" is a "being" pointing to God, a "dialogue" with God, and that the connection between man and man or man and things, a certain nature of "relationship" of encounter and dialogue, is what Martin Buber intended to find in the "relationship" of encounter and dialogue between "I and you" anthropology and religious philosophy.

The "existence" of the self-existence itself

Existentialist philosophers of religion believe that "existence" is the most basic concept, and that many things can be said to "be", and that the verb "to be" has many uses and is therefore confusing, so there are many kinds of existence.

People may use different words, different phrases, or even different languages to describe the same thing, but the thing will not change because of the different descriptions.

For example, Information Engineering (IE), also known as Information Engineering, is a skill of "processing information by engineering means" and belongs to a branch of computer science. However, due to the confusion of the definition of "information" and the confusion of the two sciences of "information engineering" and "information systems", the subject is now commonly referred to as "information engineering" again.

Therefore, it is now common to rename this subject as knowledge and data engineering, where the correlation between words is often studied to find out how people describe the same thing differently, or to find out what is described as the target thing when they act or think together from the phrases containing related words.

The study of ontology has always been central to Western philosophy, from the cosmological ontology of ancient philosophy, through the divine ontology of the Middle Ages, to the rational ontology of modern times. Ontology, also known as existentialism and existentialism, is the study of concepts such as existence, being, becoming, and reality.

It includes the question of how to classify entities into basic categories, and which entities exist at the most basic level. Ontology is sometimes called existentialism and belongs to the main branch of philosophy known as metaphysics.

Ontologists often try to determine what the categories or highest kinds are, and how they form a system of categories that provides a catch-all classification of all entities. Commonly suggested categories include substances, properties, relationships, states, and events.

These categories are characterized by underlying ontological concepts such as particularity and universality, abstraction and concreteness or possibility and necessity. Of particular interest is the concept of ontological dependence, which determines whether categories of entities exist at the most fundamental level.

The disagreement in ontology is usually about whether there are entities belonging to a certain category and, if so, how they relate to other entities. Thus, ontological research cannot escape the constraints of the concept of entity. That is, no matter how much it changes, the existence of an independent and non-dependent entity is always fundamental to ontology.

Martin Buber's philosophy can be examined from various perspectives, including the philosophy of dialogue, the philosophy of encounter, the philosophy of the other, and so on. From the ontological perspective, Martin Buber believes that "ontology is relation", and that relation precedes entity, and entity emerges from relation, so his ontology can be called "relational ontology".

We can see from this how Martin Buber's approach to the transformation of Western philosophy is fundamental.

So what exactly is "relation"? We know that in Martin Buber there are two original terms. We know that in Martin Buber there are two initial terms, "I and you" and "I and it".

Martin Buber Buber tells us that "I and it", which represents the Western philosophical tradition, is not essentially a real connection of some nature between a person and a person or a person and a thing, and that only by recognizing the non-essential state of mutual influence of "I and it" can the real connection of some nature between a person and a person or a person and a thing of "I and you" be established.

The "I and it" connection of some nature between

person and person or person and thing is, in the view of Martin Buber's philosophy of encountering verbal dialogue "relations", only a state of mutual influence of experience and use. The "I" that exists in the life of the self is the center of the world, and the "I" perceives the world.

In the broad sense, it is all, all, everything. "The world around us is only an object of perception. The "existence" of the life of the ego itself, my experience of it, shows that I perceive the world only outside the world, while the experience itself is within me, which constitutes a gap between consciousness and existence, between the ego and the world, that modern Western philosophy cannot cross.

This is a kind of contradictory and unified opposition of two properties in the thing itself, rather than an intermingled connection of a certain nature between man and man or man and thing. In addition to the aforementioned things or situations, the "existence" of the self-living being itself, the state of mutual influence of "I and it" is not equal.

"I" is the active one, "it" is the passive one, "I" is the subject who experiences "it" and uses "it". The "I", the subject, has the ability to objectify, while the "it" is merely the thing that is the target of action or thought. Modern science has pushed this to the best possible level, leading to the over-exploitation and exploitation of nature by man.

Furthermore, the "existence" of the self-living being itself, "I and it," is not a direct, human-to-human or human-to-thing connection of some nature that meets a verbal dialogue "relationship.

Whether I know it or use it, I need to use mental representations (or mental images) in order to represent the means of things that are not experienced by the individual or do not exist, and this weakens the state of intimate interaction between I and it.

Heidegger's later twist on "man is the caretaker of existence" is also to have restored the intimate connection between man and the world, between man and man or man and things of a certain nature.

In contrast to the state of "I and it" interacting with each other, Martin Buber emphasizes that "I and you" is a real "relationship" of some nature of encounter between man and man or man and thing, a verbal dialogue.

It is a fundamental relationship, which Martin Buber calls "the original relationship", that is to say, a relationship in its ontological status, where the original word "I and you" creates a world of connection between people and people or between people and things, where some nature meets a verbal dialogue "relationship".

It is only in this "relationship" between people and people or people and things, where words of a certain nature meet, that everything is alive and real.

To break the crisis of alienation in the Western modern world, it is necessary to return to this real connection between things, as Martin Buber said, precisely in the realm of the connection between people and people or between people and things, of a certain nature of meeting verbal "relations".

Human beings exist as persons, they are not conceptually rigid, and it is the original and most general concepts of human reality that reflect objective reality, the fundamental nature and regularity of phenomena, and define the characteristics of scientific theoretical thinking of an era.

In this worldview of "the connection between man and man or man and things, a certain nature of meeting verbal dialogue", the recent Western religious philosophy lingers, and all kinds of questions that demand answers or solutions are solved.

In the interaction between the "I and it" encounter and the "relationship" of speech, the question of how the subject "I" can go out of the inner realm and enter the outer realm of "it" is a major problem of modern religious philosophy.

In philosophy, the more emphasis is placed on the interaction between "I and it", the more urgent it becomes to clarify the question of the state of mutual influence of subject and object.

However, if the subject is regarded as the "I" in the state of mutual influence, then the "I" is in the connection of a certain nature of meeting speech dialogue "relationship" between people and people or people and things from the beginning, and the problem of how to overcome the "I" in order to enter the object does not exist anymore.

If we consider "existence" as "you", then "I and you" meet in a kind of mutual communication, in a "relationship" of some nature between people and people or people and things, which is to return from the "epistemological" level to the level of "living experience of the world".

It can be said that Martin Buber understands the original "world of lived experience" from the body of "the connection between people and people or between people and things, the "relationship" of a certain nature of encounter between speech and dialogue".

It is an ontological world from which our cognitive and scientific worlds are derived. Martin Buber Buber portrays this world of origin on many levels, i.e., his world of "interactions between people and people or between people and things, of a certain nature of encountering verbal conversational "relations"".

In Martin Buber's In Buber's "I and You", the world, the world that "I" face, is definitely not an "it" world, but I see the world as "you".

One of the primary characteristics of this connection of some nature of encounter-verbal dialogue "relationship" between an original person and a person or a person and a thing is that it is "direct". Martin Buber Buber says: "The connection of a certain nature of encounter verbal dialogue "relationship" between a person and a person or a person and a thing with "you". Directness is the absence of any conceptual system, innate conscience, or dream image that crosses between "I" and "you"; all intermediaries are obstacles.

"The emphasis on "directness" is to negate the mental representation (or mental imagery) in "the connection of a certain nature of encounter verbal dialogue "between a person and a person or a person and a thing", and to be able to express those things that refer to a person or a group of people in which the particular subject has no knowledge or skill from many practices, or that do not exist as a means to achieve an end.

I see it as a means to my end in the interaction between the thing with which "I" and "it" meet in a verbal dialogue "relationship". In theory, concepts are mental representations (or mental imagery) that can also represent things that are not experienced or existed by individuals.

It is only a means of fixing perceptual concepts in existence. Martin Buber Buber demands the abandonment of all mental representations (or mental imagery) that are also capable of representing those things that are individual, unexperienced, or non-existent.

To achieve a real direct connection of a certain nature of encounter with a verbal dialogue "relationship" between a person and a person or a person and a thing, because once a pure relationship is mixed with something else, the connection of a certain nature of encounter with a verbal dialogue "relationship" between a person and a person or a person and a thing is degraded.

We become lost in mental representations (or mental imagery) that can also represent things that individuals do not experience or do not exist, and forget our original closeness to the world.

Likewise with the "directness" perspective, "mutuality" is another fundamental feature of an ontological encounter with a verbal dialogue "relationship" of some nature between persons or things.

The connection of

Another essential feature: 'the connection between persons and persons or between persons and things, a certain nature of encounter with the "relation" of speech, is mutual and must not be ignored in such a way that the power of the meaning of the state of mutual influence is lost'.

In Martin Buber's view, we live in a "relationship" of encounter-verbal dialogue

Mutuality, "inhabiting the vastness of life in a state where everything complements each other and affects each other".

The mutuality of "I and you" is not only between human beings, but also between human beings and things, and between human beings and God. Martin Buber draws on the biblical interchange between God and man to show that the "mutuality" of a certain nature of encounter between man and man or man and things in a "relationship" of dialogue is a characteristic of the "existence" of all self-living beings themselves, and that we cannot ignore other messages from outside ourselves.

After emphasizing "immediacy" and "mutuality", we can grasp with some certainty what Martin Buber calls "human and human being". What Buber calls "the connection between people and people or people and things, the "relationship" of a certain nature of encounter with speech".

This state of mutual influence is the "between" of the "relationship" of encounter speech dialogue, which is the most basic doctrine of Martin Buber. This is the most fundamental doctrine of Martin Buber.

The "between" is a mark of distinction from the field of subjectivity in previous modern philosophy, because the "between" cannot be found in the "I", in intentionality, in the subject's interiority, or in the world as I understand it, in objecthood.

Martin Buber Buber emphasizes the encounter with verbal dialogue "in relation to" "between". It is necessary to show that mental representations (or mental imagery) are able to represent things that are not experienced or existed by the individual.

The point of departure is not in the "I" or in the "other", but in the "relationship" between me and you. "The spirit is not in the "I", it is in the "relationship" between the "I" and the "you".

In this way, the "relationship" between me and you is united, but it does not become an object of action or thought. The best manifestation of the "between" of the "relationship" of meeting verbal conversations is "conversation.

There is always a tension of mental representation (or

mental imagery) between the "conversation" that allows you and I to maintain our own special or unique characteristics, and the "relationship" that binds us to each other.

The ability to represent those individuals, who have not experienced or existed, is a reversal of the previous philosophical statements aimed at overcoming the recent philosophy of subjectivity. But never to return to a collectivist methodology, to take the whole body as the base of research, as Hegel did.

The "I" is connected to the "you" in meeting the verbal dialogue "relationship", but it cannot be submerged in the whole and lose itself.

If we analyze this kind of connection between people and people or people and things, some kind of nature of the "relationship" of encounter speech, in terms of "dynamics", it is the "encounter" (croiser). One enters into the realm of the "between" of the "relationship" of encounter speech, that is, the encounter between me and you. Martin Buber Martin Buber says: "All real life is an encounter".

In the "relationship" of encounter and dialogue, I and

you come closer together to see each other, and encounter is the guarantee of mutuality and equality of mutual communication.

In encounter, although the person or thing to which all human activities are directed is external to me, I can have a sympathetic insight into him/her. "When we walk along a certain path and someone walks on his/her path and meets us, we can only know our path, but in the encounter we can appreciate his/her path".

In this way, the encounter with words creates the opportunity for communication, and the encounter creates the opportunity for "conversation". Encounter is a prerequisite for "conversation". In encounter, the person or thing to which all human activities are directed meets me, and this allows me to go beyond myself, to be in the world, instead of being fixed in my inner self.

A real encounter does not depend on my existence, but it is not separated from the "I" in the state of mutual influence.

Therefore, in the "relationship" of encounter speech dialogue, "it is not the "I" that should be eradicated, but the delusional instinct of the I alone, which leads one to avoid the world of connection between persons and persons or persons and things of a certain nature of encounter speech dialogue "relationship", and to enter the world of "mutual influence on persons or things among the possessed things of the object".

"The notion of "encounter" verbal dialogue further frees Martin Buber from egoism, and opens me to the world, to the state of mutual influence of things encountered in life, thus forming an infinite world of connection between people and people or between people and things, of a certain nature of encounter verbal dialogue.

Through the above concepts of "immediacy," "mutuality," "between," and "encounter," Martin Buber depicts for us a world of intrinsic relations. Buber depicts for us an ontogenetic world of connection between people and people or between people and things, of a certain nature of meeting verbal dialogue "relations". All other worlds are derived from it.

This includes the "me and it" world. But the problem is that people often get caught up in the world of interaction between "I and it" things and forget about the original "I and you" world.

Martin Buber Buber tells us that "I and you" originate from natural integration, and "I and it" from natural separation; but there is a connection between the two, i.e., the interaction between "I and it" things is generated from "I and you".

"In our world, every "you" is destined to evolve into an interaction between "it" things, which is the celebrated sadness of our destiny.

Although the "I and it" relationship is a departure from the original "relationship" between human beings and human beings or between human beings and things of a certain nature, it is also essential for people to survive in the world, and people depend on it for their survival and development, and "people cannot survive without the interaction between the "it" things, but those who survive only by the interaction between the "it" things are no longer human beings.

Note that in the second half of the poem, Martin Buber is emphasizing that "I and it" are only the relationship between things that interact with each other, and that only "I and you" are the connection between the essence of life, between man and man or man and things, a certain nature of meeting verbal dialogue.

One must not be so engrossed in the "interaction of things" that one forgets the "I and Thou" of the life essence, the connection of a certain nature of the "relationship" between people and people or between people and things.

We call the notion of an abstract set of ideologies, the "I and you" connection between people and people or people and things, a certain nature of meeting verbal dialogue "relationship", Martin Buber's "relationship ontology". This is called Martin Buber's "relational ontology".

It opposes the a priori status of "I think" established by Descartes' "I think, therefore I am" and the principle of modern subjectivity established by it. In philosophical terms, this refers to a being with a unique consciousness, or a unique personal experience, or another entity external to itself and in relation to it.

This is because most existentialist philosophers since Plato have considered essence to be prior to existence. For example, when an artisan who specializes in casting glass wants to make a beautiful piece of glass, he must first design the shape of the glass in his mind.

The idea and practice of the sculpture is preexisting in his mind according to the prototype of the designed sculpture, and then he makes it according to this idea.

In this example, in fact, in the process of making glaze, the color of glaze is one of the important elements of expression, which can bring people a visual feeling and is better than the form. Therefore, when making glaze, we must rely on its crystal material and the delicate casting technique.

The unique charm and individuality of glaze can be manifested through the delicate expression of the casting technique and the unpredictable color effect, which is the essence of the true existence of glaze.

However, in their eyes, it is impossible to have an essence that is common to all human beings, because the God of true existence does not exist.

Otherwise, the real God would be created by the abstract consciousness of man, and man would not exist before essence. As the saying goes, "Man accepts life without a choice, then spends it in a hopeless condition, and finally returns it with an irresistible struggle.

No one can make any decision for him, no one can

"live" for him, no one can "grow old" for him. No one can "live" for him, no one can "grow old" for him, and no one can "die" for him.

Therefore, from the standpoint of the "existence" of the existentialist self-existence itself, one's own sins can only be borne by oneself, and there is no room for redemption or grace. In addition, "existence precedes nature", meaning that man is completely independent of any predetermined moral principles.

To paraphrase Schart, man is his own master, not God's slave, and he is to shift all responsibility from God's shoulders to his own. Nietzsche, who proclaimed that God is dead, further pointed out that Christian mercy, grace and salvation are a strong emotion and attachment to a person or something that

It makes man vulnerable and greatly undermines his dignity; it is when man renounces God that his self-life can truly exist.

But this is not true for Martin Buber. But in the eyes of Martin Buber's existential theists, "it is impossible to find "I think, therefore I am" in the primordial nature of knowledge-seeking; there is no such thing as a primitive and simple concept of the subject.

According to the ontological analysis of ontology, how does the "I" that constructs the philosophy of "I and you" and "I and it" of "encounter" come into being? Martin Buber says that "man becomes "I" through the encounter of speech and dialogue "in relation" to "you".

That is to say, the connection of some nature of encounter verbal dialogue "relationship" between man and man or man and thing precedes the emergence of "I", and the idea of "I" as "entity" comes after the connection of some nature of encounter verbal dialogue "relationship" between "I and you" man and man or man and thing.

"It is only when the original word "I affect you" and "you act on "me"" fall apart, when both "act" and "affect" are reduced to objects, that "I" is freed from the original experience and steps out of the infinite original word "I and you" and "I and it" into one entity.

Martin Buber The discussion here by Martin Buber is quite consistent with Hegel's "theory of self-consciousness". Self-consciousness is not a product of self-reflection, but is generated only in the face of others. From the above analysis, Martin Buber firmly concludes that "I am not the product of self-reflection. Buber firmly concludes that "I and you" are essentially prior to "I", and that "I and it" only arise after "I" has arisen.

That is to say, after the original "I and you" have met with people and people or people and things, the connection of a certain nature of verbal dialogue "relationship" and the creation of the concept of subject, there will be a modern worldview of the state of mutual influence between subject and object.

"I and it" starts from the combination of "I" and "it" meeting in a verbal dialogue "relationship", because "it" is by nature later than "I", and there is no doubt about this, because "it", as a product of objectification, must be later than the subject "I".

Martin and Buber here use "relational ontology" to dissolve the foundation of modern philosophy "I think, therefore I am", thus establishing the status of "relational" links between people and people or people and things, some kind of nature of encounter with verbal dialogue.

In the different ontological meditations on the world and the wisdom to see things as they are, the world takes on different, mutually influencing states of consciousness. Martin Buber understands this.

The establishment of "relational ontology," that is, the ability of mental representations (or mental imagery) to represent things that are not experienced by the individual or that do not exist, reveals the true nature of the world and does not allow it to be obscured by the worldview of the interactions between mundane things. It is because "experience is not enough to show the world to people".

The world view that is popular in society, that is, the interaction between "I and it", and the state in which "I and you" meet and "relate" to each other, is the true world that is revealed.

"The two opposing attitudes that a man has when he holds a thing at the same time, and therefore the world presents to him the two contradictory and unified worlds of attributes that the thing itself has", where "you" and "it" are not another world that exists outside the world.

"You" and "it" represent the attitude of mutual influence on the world, and any thing can be "it" or "you". Here both "you" and "it" are forms of connection that present a certain nature of encounter verbal dialogue "relationship" between people and people or people and things, which depends on the initial use of the words "I and you" and "I and it" to meet verbal dialogue "relationship".

It is important to note that such a statement does not mean that the attitude of "I meet you" and "I meet it" precedes the connection of a certain nature of "relationship" between people and people or people and things.

Rather, it is the attitude of the "being" that exists in the existence of the self that determines the state of interaction of the "relationship" between the encounter and the verbal dialogue. The connection between people and people or people and things, a certain nature of the "relationship" of encounter and dialogue, is still innate, and it is guaranteed by the innate you.

"The innate "you" is realized in the personal experience of the encounter with the encounterer, in the connection of a certain nature of the encounter speech dialogue "relationship" between a person and a person or a person and a thing.

One can find "you" in the encounter of the encounter of a verbal dialogue "relationship", one can grasp "you" in uniqueness, and finally, "you" can be described by the initial words "I and you" and "I and it" in the encounter of a verbal dialogue "relationship".

All this is based on the fundamental, a priori root of a certain nature of the connection of meeting verbal dialogue "relations" between people and people or people and things".

"You" is not, of course, the object of action or thought, the person or thing to which all human activity is directed.

"When I say "you" in a high or low tone, the person or thing to which all human activities are directed ceases to exist.

What is the new face of the world?

First of all, it is the understanding of language.

Language is a complex system of communication that consists mainly of its formation, acquisition, maintenance and application, and especially the corresponding ability of human encounter dialogue. The use of language is deeply rooted in human culture. Therefore, language is used not only for communication, but also for many social and cultural purposes, such as strengthening group identity and social class, as well as for social grooming and entertainment.

Here, we understand Descartes' "I think, therefore I am" language to mean that from the fact that I am thinking, I can deduce my existence.

Through the language of Kant's "Being," we understand it to mean: "Time does not pass, but only the existence of things in time; and what corresponds to time, which is unchanging and permanent in itself, is the immutable thing in existence, that is, the entity."

By understanding the meaning of the term "intentional" phenomena in Husserl's phenomenology, it means "things that are present in consciousness". Phenomenology thus calls for a shift from a concern with external existence to a deeper reflection on consciousness.

Here Husserl accepts his teacher Brentano's notion of intentionality, asserting that the present is the object of an intentional act, and that all consciousness is intentional, or more directly, that consciousness itself is intention, and therefore consciousness is the origin and mother of all phenomena.

To "return to the thing itself" is to "allow the nature of the object to appear naturally in the intuitive view of the phenomenon of consciousness". The object does not have any meaning (object is not equal to "reality").

Unless the consciousness is directed toward it, for Husserl, the prerequisite of the theory of knowledge is to keep the phenomenon of the object (that is, the object as it appears) in its original form in the cognitive faculties of the subject.

The meaning of the phenomenon is not to show its own appearance, but to show the essence of its own existence. "In one sentence, Husserl found the interface between subject and object and revealed the possibility of "subject-object unity".

Traditional philosophies have been constructed from the aspect of consciousness, following a lineage or a structure to analyze the world. He says that "language is the home of "you"" and that "man dwells in language, not language in man".

It is evident that language, as interpreted by Martin Buber, is something completely beyond the "you". What Martin Buber interprets is completely beyond the realm of subjective consciousness, and the world appears as a double perception when one has a double life experience.

But it is only because man speaks the double initial words "I and you" and "I and it" that he holds a double attitude. This is the double cognition of language as interpreted by Martin Buber, which allows one to deepen the "relationship" of a certain nature of encounter between people and people or people and things, from the subjective level.

Through the interpretation of language, we can further understand the connection between "I and you", between a person and a person or a person and a thing, a certain nature of encounter with the "relationship" of speech.

Although, Martin Buber's Although Martin Buber's "I and Thou" connection between man and man or man and thing, some kind of nature encounter with the "relationship" of speech includes the state of mutual influence on nature, man and God, the most complete and real of them is the "I and Thou" connection.

But the most complete and real "relationship" between man and man or man and things of a certain nature is found in the "existential" life of the existence of the self.

The state of human interaction is in Martin Buber's three realms. The state of human interaction is primary among the three realms of Martin Buber, as Heidegger focuses on it.

The "existence" of the self-existence itself meets the "eternal life" of the true existence of the "relationship" of the verbal dialogue.

One: Beyond "Relationships

Modern society is full of crises, and everyone seems to be able to grow stronger through the power of assistants. However, when we rely too much on the power of reason and become independent and arrogant, human beings lose their original vitality and keep slipping into the abyss of sinking.

Therefore, Martin Buber proposes to transcend the "I and it" relationship by using the "I and you" relationship to help human beings escape from the destiny of unfreedom, from the cage of loneliness, and from the situation of sinking in modern society. This is not only the transcendence of the state of interaction and mutual influence between things, but also the transcendence of the world.

Second, the three realms of relationship

In his book "I and You", Martin Buber proposes to transcend the "I and It" relationship with the "I and You" relationship. The word "You" has three meanings - the Other, the natural world, and the existence of the eternal God. Thus, there are three realms in the world where the "existence" of self-life itself exists and meets the "relationship" of verbal dialogue.

The first realm is the relationship between "man and nature".

This "relationship" of encounter and dialogue exists in an abstract concept, an unfathomable nothingness, and a realm that language cannot attempt to reach. There are countless creatures in the world that exist together with you and me, but are not really close to us. When we refer to them as "you," we are often constrained by the framework of language.

Because "the connection between people and people or people and things, the "relationship" of a certain nature of meeting verbal dialogue", the mutual response needs to be conveyed through language, but grass, wood, and stone do not have language, so we can understand that.

In a world where "heaven and man are united" and where things are intertwined, everything has its own "existence" and the meaning of its existence, and grass, wood, and stone can be speechless.

The second realm is the relationship between "man and man".

This kind of "relationship" between people and people or people and things, some kind of nature of meeting verbal dialogue, is a kind of complex communication system, which can be expressed, in which people keep calling the other party "you" and keep becoming "you" in the other party's mouth. It consists mainly of its formation, acquisition, maintenance and application, and especially of the corresponding human abilities.

A language is a concrete example of such a system. In addition to communication, language is a major component of a person's identity and one of the main components of a culture.

The third realm is the relationship between "man and soul".

This "relationship" of a certain nature, beyond the

encounter between man and man or man and things, is an esoteric and profound connection of words, which speaks a thousand words in silence.

In this state of interaction and mutual influence between the spirit of man and thing, we constantly sense the call and respond with any shaping, relentless reflection and diligent action. The word "you" is no longer pronounced in the mouth, but in the heart.

These three things reach or manifest themselves in layers until a "relational" connection of some nature between people and people or between people and things meets a verbal dialogue, extending the eternal "you" that intersects between things, interacting and influencing each other.

God and the Eternal You

From Martin Buber's double initial use of the words "I and you" and "I and it" to meet in a dialogical "relationship" between "I and you", we understand the relationship between "I and you", which ultimately leads to the relationship between "I and God".

However, the God that Martin Buber refers to is not God in the traditional sense, in the sense of a certain nature of encounter between man and man or man and thing, in the sense that God is not mysterious or unattainable, but can be found everywhere in the quenching of life experience.

"God" means the connection between "the total you", "the total me" and the "state of interaction between people and things" of the encounter. This concept may be a bit abstract and complex.

But we can simply understand God as the higher "you", eternal in the timeline and everywhere in the spatial coordinates. Many names have been used to call upon the "eternal You. When one sings of a saint, one is actually singing of "You".

For as people praise God and give God a good name, the "you" is always present in their hearts. According to Martin Buber, the first step in achieving the search for and conversion to God is to step out of the "I and you" category.

The first step is to get out of the "I and it" relationship, which is the state of interaction and influence between the "I and it" things, as we said before. At this point, people have self-consciousness, but they separate themselves from the things around them and cannot encounter "you".

The second and most important step is to establish the connection between "I and You", between people and people or people and things, a certain nature of meeting verbal dialogue, and to establish trust in God, that is, to convert to the "Eternal You".

This transcendence of the state of interaction and mutual influence between people and things is the transcendence of the divine world over the alienated secular world, with a strong religious philosophy.

In fact, Martin Buber's reflections on the existence of "being" in the era of crisis and the existence of human life itself are based on his unique religious and cultural background.

He was a Jewish philosopher who lived during World War I and II. In the context of Jewish thought and war, the connection between "I and you" and people or between people and things, a certain nature of encounter with verbal dialogue, was itself a religious expectation of the ideal way of human existence.

However, the philosophy of the connection between "I and you" and a certain nature of encounter between man or man and things is different from the ordinary religious philosophical thought, because this objective existence is reflected in the human consciousness, and the result of the activity of thinking is not the focus of the "heavenly God", but the earthly God.

Martin Buber. By means of this earthly God, he points to every human being, to the "being" that exists in the human being's self-life, and to the world of divine beauty.

The Self-existent Being expresses its hope through prayer to the Eternal You, and the Eternal You fulfills its mission and answers through comfort and guidance.

In this dialogue of question and answer, the dialogue of "I and You" is actually created. There is an infinite uniqueness and tolerance in it, because whether it is a stone on the land, a fish in the sea, or the vast universe, everything is integrated in the state of interaction and mutual influence between people and things.

Those who ignore and despise the world, or those who are greedy for material things, have no way to approach God. Only when you see the world as an encounter with "I" can you approach God, and then truly master your destiny and gain pure reality.

This being is able to understand its own existence, and in the state of human interaction, the "relationship" of encounter and dialogue is the most characteristic of dialogue. However, when understanding this presence, it is not understood as the here and now, but as the way of being that opens the dialogue of encounter through the apprehension of the "presence" that exists in the life of the self.

"Among the three realms, the connection between people and people or between people and things, the connection of some nature of encounter and dialogue is the most powerful and prominent in life. During this time, language completes itself by speaking and answering.

Only in between, the Word, which has the form of speech, meets the answer to it, and the words "I and you" and "I and it" meet in a verbal dialogue "relationship" that goes back and forth, both as a call, as a statement, and as an echo, as an answer, active in the same form in the same language".

For it is only in this realm that one can truly speak; it is only in this realm that one can be connected to each other through language; it is only in this realm that the initial words "I and you" and "I and it" meet in a verbal dialogue "relationship" that can come and go so often.

It is only in this realm that "you" and "I" can reside in eternal "dialogue" (interaction). This is the basic characteristic of the field of the state of interaction and mutual influence between people and things, and it is the characteristic of "existence" that exists in the existence of human ego life itself.

In the life of a certain nature of encounter verbal dialogue "relationship" between a person and a person or a person and a thing, there are only natural reactions, no response actions triggered by stimulation.

In the life that is connected with the whole body of the spirit that actually exists, or with things that have actual content, there is more than language. It is only in the connection between human beings and human beings or between human beings and things that a certain nature meets the "relationship" of verbal dialogue.

The "relationship" between people and people or between people and things of a certain nature has a guarantee of the influence and effect on people and things, because "the mutuality of observing and being observed, of knowing and being known, of loving and being loved has an inalienable reality".

Martin Buber uses language to distinguish between the three realms of life in which I am associated with nature, with man, and with spiritual entities, either below language or beyond language, and only the connection between man and man or man and things, a certain nature of encounter with the "relationship" of speech, which is observed as its natural reality in language.

From another point of view, the world appears as a contradictory unity of two properties that things have in themselves, and speech is necessarily two opposing properties that a thing has at the same time.

Martin Buber Buber argues that in the connection of a certain nature of encounter speech dialogue "relationship" between "me and you" or between people and things, this kind of speech is: "speakto"; and in the interaction between "me and it" things, this kind of speech is "speakabout...".

This distinction between the "relationship" of encounter speech and dialogue is one of the central points of Martin Buber's philosophy of dialogue. It is precisely "speakabout" that gives concrete expression to the "relationship" of encounter speech dialogue or elaborates the essence of it. The philosophical thinking of the encounter dialogue of Martin Buber.

For example, "to... say" starts with "you", indicating that you are a partner, equal, and that there is a mutual response between you and me, while "to talk about" takes "it" as the object.

It shows that the object of "talk" is "it", which is the direct reflection in the human brain through the sense organs. It is only after seeing, hearing, and touching the surface characteristics of objective things that one can talk about this object "it".

This distinction reflects the characteristics of speech in different worlds. What is important to note is the connection of a certain nature of encounter with a verbal conversation "relationship" between a basic person and a person or a person and a thing.

"I and you" is the form of conversation that precedes any real encounter. It is possible to speak of "you" while the substance is "it", or to speak of "it" while the substance is "you". The connection between "I and you" and a certain nature of encounter between man and man or man and thing, the "relationship" of verbal dialogue, is not in such superficial words, but in the innate root of the state of interaction and mutual influence between man and thing.

The second is about the understanding of the time problem.

Language is a kind of complex communication system, which mainly contains its formation, acquisition, maintenance and application, especially the corresponding human ability. The double world, the two forms of speech, means that there are two aspects of things that will only become effective, meaningful or useful in a certain period of time.

In a word, "the existence of the real is standing in the present, the existence of the object is huddled in the past", and the two things will only appear as valid, meaningful or useful for a certain period of time, clearly distinguished: the present and the past.

So, what is Martin Buber's interpretation of "present" in the context of "relational ontology"? The "present" is not the end of "passed" time, the frozen moment in the flow of time, as we see it, but the real, vivid, and abundant present.

The present exists only when the present moment, the encounter, the connection between people and people or between people and things, the "relationship" of some nature of encounter and conversation, appears, and the present will only appear when "you" become the present moment.

It does not pass away with a light touch, but remains in the connection between you and me, between people and people or between people and things, in a certain nature of encounter and dialogue.

This is because the "present", that is, the presentation of something as valid, meaningful, or useful for a certain period of time, is the knowledge of natural or social things, the meaning given by man to the object, the presentation of the true existence of the original, the initial, the best and the purest.

Further, this "present" thing will only become effective, meaningful or useful in a certain period of time, and it points to the future, which can be seen by looking at the operation of the dialogue "to... say".

Any kind of dialogue requires a response, a response that points to the future, that waits for the encounter, for the answer of the dialogue, and because of this expectation, the "present" remains, the present realizes itself in the future.

This is Martin Buber's particular approach to the "now". This is Martin Buber's particular interpretation of the "present". Although this future orientation of time is similar to Heidegger's thought, because Heidegger believed that this "existence" of the self-living being itself exists

The perception of being takes precedence over the existence of any particular being, or being of beings, however or in whatever way these beings exist, which is pre-conceptual, unproposable, and pre-scientific.

For Heidegger, therefore, a foundational theory of being should be an explanation of an understanding that takes precedence over any mode of knowing, such as the use of logic, theory and concrete existentialism, or the act of reflection.

At the same time, the existence of life itself can only be accessed through the "existence" of the self-living being itself, so that the question of the "existence" of the self-living being itself necessarily implies the question of the existence of a being.

But there is a big difference, because "it" is not a kind of plan, as Martin Buber sees it. In Martin Buber's view, "planning" belongs to the realm of "it", where the future becomes a projection of the subject.

This "present" is a parameter that changes with time in the spatio-temporal information technology, and its future orientation is the opposite of "planning", as Heidegger advocates that the only way to truly understand the "being" that exists in the self-living existence itself is to turn to a special being in the past.

Therefore, the best way to inquire into the "being" that exists in the self-life itself is inevitably a cycle of explaining the past, that is, one must rely on the explanatory act of repeating the trajectory of the past but progressing into the present, the phenomenological methodology, which is described in the sense of explanation.

Because the "being" that exists in the self-living being itself is in it and cannot decide now, on the contrary, the "being" that exists in our self-living being itself expects "you".

This means the possibility of the present unfolding of

everything. Contemporary history describes the historical time frame directly related to the present time, a certain perspective of modern history, and the "now" raises the question: "What is the present experienced by all beings at the same time?

In the Buddhist view of temporal origins, the "present" is the present life, one of the three lives (previous, present, and future).

Buddhism and many practical examples of it emphasize the importance of the existence of the self in life itself, of "being" in the present moment, so that one can be fully aware of the importance of focusing on what is happening without dwelling on the past or worrying about future realizations.

This does not mean that Buddhism encourages hedonism, but simply a constant focus on one's current place in time and space (rather than future worries, or past attachments).

They teach that those who live in the present moment are happiest. In recent years, more and more people are seeking peace of mind and a focus on their own "wellness" in life.

In the process of meditation, one practices mindfulness by adjusting one's breathing and mindfulness. Even if you think of something, you have to let go of those thoughts and just keep pulling your attention back to a certain word, so you can zero in on the brain.

So meditation is a chance for the mind to rest and a practice of letting go of thoughts, designed to help the practitioner live in the present moment.

Christianity believes that God is outside of time, and that from the point of view of His view that demands answers, or answers to questions, the past, present and future are eternally 'present', which is a form of thinking that reflects the nature of things across God of time.

The "existence" of the existence of self-life itself, the "eternal life" that meets the true existence of the "relationship" of speech and dialogue. At least since Boethius, it has been presented as an explanation of God's foreknowledge (i.e., how God knows what we will do in the future before we decide what to do).

Thomas Aquinas gives a parable of the watchmen, Isaiah 62:6-7: "I have set watchmen over your city, O

Jerusalem, and they shall not be silent by day or by night. Do not rest, O ye that call upon the LORD, nor cause him to rest, until he establish Jerusalem, and make it a praiseworthy thing in the earth".

On behalf of God, He stands on a high ground looking down on a road, which God can see both before and after. Therefore, the knowledge of God is not related to any particular day or time.

The concept of "past" refers to any moment or period of time before the present moment we are in, which can be a moment, but mostly refers to a period of time. The explanation of what "speaks of..." belongs to the interaction between "I and it" meeting the verbal dialogue "relationship".

Because the presentation of "it" as the target thing when acting or thinking is only the conclusion of the past time, "the thing that was the target thing when acting or thinking is stuck in the time that has passed".

Therefore, it is developed or carried to the final stage and no longer continues, it is closed with a seal, so that it cannot be used, passed or opened at will, it can only be presented in the act of "cognition" and "recognition" in order to confirm the knowledge, and these knowings have the potential ability to be used for a specific purpose.

It means that through the process of direct contact with objective things, people acquire, through their sense organs, the recognition or association of phenomena and external connections of objective things, and are able to become familiar with, and thus understand, something that is not really active, but only for a certain period of time, becomes effective, meaningful, or useful.

The third is the understanding of the world as a whole.

In the ontology of relationship, the first words "I and you" and "I and it" meet in a verbal dialogue about the world of "relationship" and how it appears as a state of interaction and influence between people and things.

Martin Buber This is how the philosophy of "relationship" in verbal dialogue in Buber's "I and You" answers the question of the "eternal life" of true existence: "What do we experience as "you"? Nothing, because You cannot be experienced, and we know what You are? Everything, because it is impossible to know any part of You alone".

That is to say, in the "existence" of the self-life itself, in the state of interaction and influence between "I and it", in the perception of daily life experience, in the connection between human beings and the "relationship" of a certain nature of verbal dialogue.

I understand the world as something that is the target of action or thought, but the world of "you" is definitely not a world of things that are the target of action or thought. If one perceives things only by dwelling on their surface, one thereby extracts information about their nature and acquires experiential knowledge.

They experience the nature of things. With this method of encountering verbal dialogue "relations," one discovers only the nature of things, a collection of the nature of things, and not the whole of the "eternal" existence of things as they really are.

Because there are many characteristics of the "eternal" existence that cannot be described or extracted, and the nature is no longer "you". Therefore, for the empirical world of everyday experience, "you" is unreal, inscrutable, and indescribable.

The world of "you", in a broad sense, is all, all,

everything. It is also beyond the world of experience, and therefore constitutes a conditional space-time network. The world of experience as the experience of everyday life.

The true existence is in the "world of it", where people and things interact and influence each other, just like stuffing things into the causal network of space-time capsules, so that they each have their own place, their own function, and their own way....

And the "existence" of the self-life itself, "you", the world of connection between people and people or between people and things, a certain nature of meeting verbal dialogue. I don't know what is the "stereotypical order", "when anything is transformed from our "you" to our "it", then it can be arranged".

That is to say, the root of order in the empirical world of everyday experience lies in the world of "you", the world of "you" where people and people or people and things meet in a certain nature of "relational" connection of speech, not without order, but completely different from the empirical world of everyday experience.

Martin Buber calls the world in which "it" interacts with things as "worldthatisordered", while the world in which "you" who are "you" and "people" or "people and things" of a certain nature meet in a "relationship" between them is "the world-order". The world-order.

The world-order is a world in which people and things meet in a certain nature of dialogue and "relationship". "In the dark silence, in the mystery, the world-order appears in a broad and bright way, revealing its true nature, its emptiness, its inaccessibility, but the magnificence of its true existence, which penetrates the creation of human beings and their comprehension, pours into the ordered world and disintegrates it again and again.

The difference between the two orders is as great as the difference between the clouds in the sky and the earth in the ground. From the point of view of the "existence" and life experience of the self-life existence itself, the world of connection between "you" and people or people and things, of a certain nature of meeting verbal dialogue "relationship", is impractical and inscrutable.

On the other hand, the world of the state of interaction and mutual influence between "you" and things, in a broad sense, presents the whole, all, everything, the "universality", the uniqueness of the nature of all things.

Martin Buber In the universality, one can grasp the connection, the objectification, the orderly understanding of the "relationship" between "you" and people or between people and things, a certain nature of the encounter of speech and dialogue.

It is only in the connection of "relationship" between a person and a person or between a person and a thing that one can perceive the oneness of all things, and it is only in the oneness that one can have the mind of the oneness of all things.

This is a concept that is different from the experience of daily life and is a quenching of the world of experience. It is the ability to explain the known facts and principles and principles of the world as a whole with one's own words, characters, or other symbols.

This insight can only be achieved in the connection between people and people or between people and things, in a certain nature of meeting verbal dialogue.

Fourth, the concern for the world is ultimately a concern for the freedom and destiny of man himself.

In Martin Buber's I and you" and "I and it" in the original wording of the dialogic "relationship" in which

Martin Buber encounters the objective consciousness of a certain range of freedom, and the subjective consciousness of "I and it" as the world of states of interaction and influence between causal persons and things, are opposed to each other.

Therefore, "He who makes a decision without regard to consequences and according to his own heart, he who puts away all the clothes and wealth and bears the holy face of Thee in reverence, is a free man.

Destiny seems to be presented as the opposite of freedom, but destiny is in the interaction between Martin Buber and things. On the contrary, destiny is the fulfillment of freedom of the will, and freedom and destiny are one in meaning.

The true antithesis of freedom of will is fate. If not with "you", people and people or between people and things, a certain nature of meeting verbal dialogue "relationship" between each other and the external world means not quite the same, but also very different, one is to tell their own ideas to the other to understand.

The other is to understand each other's ideas and find a way to add one's own ideas, and finally to reach agreement, then "it" in the world of the state of interaction and influence between people and things, the vicious expansion of causality, and then evolved into the destiny of dominating everything and suffocating everything.

Martin Buber In his view, in the world today, the connection between people and people, or between people and things, a certain nature of encounter with the "relationship" of verbal dialogue, the mind is caught in the world of the state of interaction and influence between "it" people and things.

We try to cultivate a belief in predestination, both in biology and in history. Inevitably, man is imprisoned in the established state of interaction and influence between people and things.

In such a world, to seek freedom of will is to be regarded as insanity, and one either submits to slavery or has no hope of resistance, bowing down in a world of interactions and interactions between "it" people and things.

Thus, Martin Buber argues that the essence of freedom of will is conversion, and that conversion to God enables one to transform the world and turn it around with quiet power. Belief in predestination, on the other hand, cuts off the "relationship" of encounter with speech and dialogue that leads to conversion.

In a world where "you" meet people or people and things, where there is a certain nature of "relationship" between them, where fate and freedom are intertwined, where the free man of will is willing to do whatever he wants, where he is uncontested, where he is infinitely unattached, and where he is not at the mercy of fate.

However, it is not the case that we are at the mercy of fate, that we are dependent on the connection between people and people or between people and things, that a certain nature meets the verbal dialogue "relationship", but that we follow the expectations of fate, respond to the desires of fate, and make the connection of a certain nature meets the verbal dialogue "relationship" real by the human spirit and human activity.

We see that in the field of "relational ontology" thought or knowledge, the world takes on a different form from everyday experience. In Martin Buber's In Martin Buber's encounter with the verbal dialogue "relation", it appears that

Only when we see this layer can we truly experience the state of interaction and influence between people and things, the connection of certain nature of encounter speech dialogue "relationship", and to put ourselves in the right position to present the real life of the meaning of life existence.

Part 3. The Philosophical Thought of Jasper

Preface

Karl Teodor Jaspers (Karl Jaspers 1946.jpg February 23, 1883 - February 26, 1969) was a Western philosopher of the European school of philosophy, existential philosophy, the Neo-Confucian school of major fields of theology, psychiatry, philosophy of history, the famous Axis of Thought era, formerly known as Jaspers, German philosopher and psychiatrist, representative of Christian existentialism. He became a Swiss citizen in 1967.

In his book The Origins and Objectives of History, he put forward the famous "Axial Age" view. Jaspers is regarded as an outstanding representative of existential philosophy, distinguishing between "existential philosophy" and Jean-Paul Sartre's "existentialism", following a certain formula of criteria for validation, without confusion or full deliberation.

He was Hannah Arendt's teacher and lifelong friend, and he had a correspondence with Martin Heidegger, which was interrupted during the Nazi rule and was occasionally exchanged after the war.

Karl Jaspers (1883-1969), a German philosopher, spent his early career in psychiatry and psychology, and later focused on the philosophical theory of the historical roots of "man" and "being. In Vernunft und Existenz (Reason and Existence), Vom Ursprung und Ziel der Geschichte (The Object and Origin of History), Der philosophische Glaube angesichts der Christlichen Offenbarung), and other later works.

Jaspers also formalized his philosophy by analyzing and studying various experiences or situations in work, study, or thought during a period of time and making instructive conclusions as a philosophy of "faith" and "transcendence".

Jasper contributed to the scientific development of psychiatry, the root, foundation, or most important part of psychiatry. His philosophical work has contributed significantly to the philosophy of religion, philosophy of history, and cross-cultural philosophy that acts or changes the behavior, thought, or nature of [people or events] in indirect or invisible ways.

Although his thought is not considered to be outside of the existentialist system of his contemporaries, Jaspers was in fact no less important than Heidegger in European academia at the time, having been rector of the philosophical capital Heidelberg University and even being known as the "intellectual conscience" during World War II because of his firm attitude toward the Nazi government.

Like the popular existentialist philosophers of his time, Jaspers rejected the idea that "man" is necessarily an eternal attribute or set of attributes similar to what G. W. F. Hegel called "spirit," which makes an entity or substance its essence and which necessarily exists, without which it would lose its identity.

Conversely, man is a "being" that is always changing, and therefore cannot be defined. Although it cannot be defined, it is still possible to express the existence of life in words and language in the context of human existence.

Chapter 1: Introduction:

On the one hand, man is born in nature, a kind of creature, the so-called "natural man" (Der natürliche Mensch), but on the other hand, man also lives in a history of his own creation and change, a "historical man" (Der Geschichtsmensch) that progresses in cycles. Geschichtsmensch.)

As Jaspers mentions in his article "Die Geistige Situation der Zeit" (The Spiritual Condition of the Age), one of the most special things that makes a "person" a person is the dissatisfaction with the status quo and the attempt to change the occurrence of variation or difference.

It means that something has changed (alteration) in form, nature, or relationship with other things. In the philosophical sense, "change" occurs mainly from a decrease in the degree of essentiality of something, and is therefore the opposite of "permanence".

"Change" is one of the fundamental concepts in the history of philosophy; in summary, its meaning includes movement, modification, becoming and growth. The status quo, the creation of new values, becomes different from the past form of existence.

Therefore, life is a process of constant pursuit and creation. Man is always pursuing his desire to get what he wants, but the desire never ends and man can never be truly satisfied. Jaspers feels that whenever man encounters the unattainable desire, he will begin to think, reflect, and switch on the search for his inner self.

Section 1 The background and content of the rise of existentialism

There are some eternal questions in philosophy that do not become obsolete because of the change of time. In every age, there are subjects that study universal and fundamental problems, including existence, knowledge, values, reason, mind, language, etc., that are serious enough to be studied and discussed, or that have yet to be solved, and they will come up again and again, offering possible different responses.

In Jasper's view, everything in the universe and the great ideas of the previous philosophers are codes that point to the transcendental realm and can answer many eternal philosophical questions about it.

Therefore, the ultimate problem of philosophy is to interpret the reality of existence as a code of transcendence (chiffre-lesen), and this is the meaning of "inclusiveness".

All people must make their own choices, communicate internally with their own choices, and immerse themselves in the realm of "inclusiveness" and "oneness of subject and object" in order to hear the words of the transcendent from the objective world of experience. The spiritual communication of the transcendent's words as interpreted by Jasper is different from the dialogue of ordinary human speech communication.

Dialogue

Jasper's "philosophy of existence" is difficult to compile in a few words, but perhaps we can analyze his wisdom in this way: the holistic, fundamental and critical inquiry into the real world and human beings is always something self-imposed, directly connected and in dialogue with the divine.

The study of universal, fundamental problems in the disciplines of being, knowledge, values, reason, mind, language, etc. Thought is always rooted in the free creation of the individual. He might have likened philosophical faith to a kind of intellectual adventure, a courageous leap into the transcendent realm beyond real existence, with the desire to know infinitely.

When Jaspers refers to the "Axial Age" (Achsenzeit) and the "Four Sacred Philosophies" in "The Spiritual Condition of the Age" and "The Origin and Aim of History," the form of thinking reflects the essential nature of the object.

In the process of cognition, human beings raise the common characteristics of things they perceive from perceptual knowledge to rational knowledge and extract the essential attributes. Confucius, Buddha, Jesus, and other wise men and women of the age of wisdom all set an example of "inclusiveness" in the form of "reverence for the beyond.

1.The Philosophy of Existence that "exists in the face of frustration

If Heidegger's philosophy began with "existence to death," then Jasper's began with "existence to frustration," roughly. "Frustration" is the obstacle that prevents people from achieving their purpose in their purposeful activities.

Psychologically, it refers to the inevitable emotional reaction to the obstruction of a purposeful action of an individual, which can bring substantial harm in the form of disappointment, pain, frustration, and uneasiness.

This is why Jaspers' "philosophy of existence" is most concerned with the position one takes in the face of frustration and failure. Because of his devotion to religious beliefs, Jaspers' philosophical system of viewpoints is not only a matter of faith, but also of faith.

Therefore, in his system of philosophical viewpoints, the transcendent or "God" has always existed independently of any conditions and has remained constant and unchanging.

Rather, we should use finite existence to dominate and control the activity of life, to chase the mysterious transcendental realm, and then throw away and reject the "Weltsein" of the empirical world, to reach the transcendental realm, and to realize the real existence.

Therefore, the basic consideration of Jasper's existentialism is a philosophy of existence, just like other philosophers of the "existentialist" trend, which focuses on the existence of the individual and the group "man", the existence of life itself. How can people live more meaningfully?

These two deeper, more thoughtful, and more fundamental activities of thought are the two bricks that can be used to explain the known facts and principles and principles of Jaspers' philosophy in his own words, texts, or other symbols, and thus lead to the ultimate prayer of his system of thought, the "transcendental world.

Jaspers called his philosophy "existential philosophy" rather than "existentialism" because he thought that the latter would be taken as a fashionable movement of ordinary thought, to be expanded in its implementation or scope of action. In fact, it is a degeneration of the spirit of existence.

"This quest is rooted in the frustration of one's life experience, or in one's own dissatisfaction with one's present situation, and the search for transcendence triggers the power and the thought of breaking out of a difficult situation.

The search for transcendence is the core of Jasper's "philosophy of existence".

2. Boundary Situation of Abbott

"People accept life when they have no choice; then they live it under the condition that they have no choice; and finally they give it back with an irresistible struggle. People live blindly in the world, living and dying in confusion, not knowing or bothering much about the problems of life.

On the contrary, if a person says that he has been thinking hard about the problems of life recently, but cannot find the answers, we usually think that it is fine and he is just asking for trouble. The reason for this reaction is that we are limited in the depth of our own thinking activities such as analysis, synthesis, reasoning, and judgment.

3. The existence of life in the boundaries of body, mind and spirit

The boundary between body, mind, and spirit, as Jaspers calls it, is the gap that each person seeks to break through and transcend, a gap that also defines the difference between oneself and others.

Jasper believes that when these three boundaries emerge in the face of life's experience of human existence, it is the time when one must make a choice, not to remain in a vain and passive attitude of avoidance, but to lose the opportunity to constantly seek to break through and transcend the boundary of metamorphosis and sublimation.

Therefore, Jasper believes that there are three kinds of boundaries in the existence of life in the universe: the physical boundary, the mental boundary, and the soul (spiritual) boundary. When these three boundaries appear, it is time for human beings to analyze, synthesize, reason, judge, and make choices.

In other words, in all activities of human life and all social phenomena encountered, such as critical illness, conflicts, pain, and death, human beings have to question the meaning of their own existence.

The individual's subjective consciousness of self-love and clinging cannot be solved, so he or she feels unhappy for no reason, because he or she is chasing after wealth, fame, and ......, and the situation of boundaries becomes more and more unbalanced.

Until finally, the precious inner self is lost. When we have something at the same time, we are also possessed by the things we have.

This world has people who are single and happy, in love and happy, married and happy, divorced and happy, because she is the person who will make herself happy. In fact, it is normal that you do not understand, because when you feel unhappy, no matter what you are given, you will feel unhappy.

Jasper believes that although the physical, mental, and spiritual boundaries of life can only be manifested through external behavior, revealing happiness, joy, and well-being depends on internal truths, not external rational pursuits.

If we attribute all problems to the outside world, it means that we have the energy to give up on ourselves. If we can show the energy to give up on ourselves, where is the real self that gives up on ourselves?

Therefore, if you want to be happy, you must first change your mindset and perspective, try to find out where the boundaries of your soul are, and reconstruct your true inner self, so that the power of transformation and sublimation can follow.

Section 2. The Moment and Eternity of Abbott

What one chooses, what decisions one makes, what one chooses. This is used in everyday life, where decisions of general direction are often made and are relatively uncommon. But it is a very important word when one is making a choice.

It represents a moment of prudence and caution, a moment of life and death in front of something important, and when a person is faced with a boundary decision, he or she often has to master a momentary flutter in a very short time.

By a momentary stirring, we mean that we are living a normal and stable life, and suddenly a momentary stirring occurs, perhaps because of an event, a person, or a scene that makes us feel very moved and our "true self" emerges, and we feel that life seems different.

It is then that we can truly experience and appreciate

a certain situation or thing. For example, it is only when we raise our own children that we can understand the hard work of being a parent. It is not until one is in the position to understand and appreciate it.

1. Abbott's code and concept of transcendence

According to Jaspers, the world is full of codes that, if unlocked, reveal the true basis of life's existence, though finite. For example, when a person is single, he may feel that he can get by, but once he starts to fall in love, he will find a different perspective on life, and at that moment, he will feel as if all the secrets of life have been solved.

That is to say, we live in the world and sometimes wonder what kind of life we want to live, but in the stage of love, in the process of interaction between two people, it seems that they get some enlightenment, through this relationship, find the key to understand the mystery of life in general.

Similarly, many people read books, make friends, and even watch movies in the process, because a code is unlocked, and the whole life is opened up. Martin Luther is a good example.

One day he read a sentence in the Bible: "I believe in

the forgiveness of sins. In that moment, he had a sudden epiphany. In fact, he had read the same scripture a thousand times before, without any epiphany, but at a certain age, in a certain state of mind, and with certain external circumstances, he had a sudden enlightenment.

It is difficult to manipulate this sudden enlightenment, and it is impossible to understand why it happens.

Christians often speak of Justification by faith - believe and you will be saved - from the experience of Martin Luther. He repeatedly emphasized that one cannot be saved by oneself and therefore needs to rely on the power of faith.

The more one can admit one's incompetence and weakness, the more hope one has for salvation; conversely, the more pride one has, the less hope one has for salvation.

The pursuit of transcendence is what Jasper calls the unifier (or encompasser). Since the world and the self are relative and finite things, they must be understood in relation to an indefinable inclusiveness.

The inclusiveness of the unifier is the source of all new

horizons, the new horizon, the ultimate reality that cannot be known through object knowledge, that is, existence itself.

2.Jasper's Four Great Philosophies (Socrates, Buddha, Confucius, Jesus: The Paradigmatic Individuals.)

After studying the major thinkers of the major civilizations in history, Jaspers selected four men as paradigmatic individuals: Socrates, Confucius, Socrates, and Jesus. These four men were not what people would consider to be successes, and one might even say that they were so-called failures when measured by the world's eyes.

However, their greatness lies in the fact that they witnessed the rich potential of the human spirit. Through the four holy philosophers as examples of inclusiveness, human beings become aware of their own dignity; that is, by seeing them, they affirm how great and noble it is to be a human being inclusively.

The so-called sublime does not mean that a person is born sublime, but that when facing his or her life and walking on the path of life, human beings must have self-expectations of themselves and what results they hope to achieve.

The paradigm of humanity is definitely not those who rely on military power and political power to dominate, so to speak (such as Alexander the Great, Julius Caesar, etc.). The so-called model of human inclusiveness should be an inclusiveness that ordinary people like you and me, who have many troubles, can follow.

They pointed out that troubles are not worth worrying about, because wisdom can be honed in troubles; death is not worth fearing, but dying without knowing why, dying in a confused way.

The common characteristic of the four sages is that they enable many people to face negative situations in life (such as troubles, pains, disasters, sins, etc.) with openness, and to refine their inner spirit through inclusiveness in these situations.

3.The Call to "Inclusive" Faith

Heidegger has experienced or acted in a certain way or situation that the path of Western philosophy seems to have gone the wrong way, the wrong way. The question of "existence" has been in prison since Aristotle.

Therefore, Heidegger's first task is to distinguish between "existence" (Sein an sich) and "existence" (Seiendes), and Jasper's philosophical thinking is almost inseparable from Heidegger's.

Jaspers' philosophical thinking is also almost unrelated to Heidegger's. Jaspers points out the metaphysics of the past history of philosophy, trying to treat "existence itself" as "existence" for analysis, synthesis, reasoning, and judgment.

In this way of thinking, "existence" becomes a passive "object" (Gegenstand) or an "object" (Objekt) that is cognitively opposed to the real world or any object, and the relationship between existence and human being is in a state of fragmentation.

According to Jaspers, as long as one is awake and conscious, this fragmentation will never disappear, which he calls "subjekt-Objekt-Spaltung" (splitting of subject and object).

Only after this division is removed can one truly leap into the transcendental realm, as Jaspers says, and the task and meaning of philosophy is to guide one as far as possible towards the unity of subject and object.

Therefore, philosophy in Jaspers' view is not a system of knowledge, but an expression of faith.

The word "faith" has two meanings: first, it refers to the attitude or belief of complete trust and dependence on supernatural things (such as God, God); second, it refers to a state of cognition or action by which one can know supernatural things.

Thus, faith does not mean conversion or submission to the authority of a doctrinal system, but rather faith in the idea that the thinker himself is one with his ideas. In other words, faith is neither merely a subjective act of belief nor an objective object of belief, but an all-encompassing reality that unifies subject and object, and in which faith is the "one" (das Eine) that unifies subject and object.

Jaspers uses the concept of "das Umgreifende" to name the state after experiencing philosophical beliefs, which is not the subject or object in traditional thinking, but the "whole" that encompasses both subject and object.

In his book Einführung in die Philosophie, Jaspers mentions that "through thinking about the symbolic, we can obtain a marker of inclusiveness that points to the non-contradictory".

This means that "inclusiveness," like "existence itself," is the totality of the whole collective or the whole thing, not a single object or object. It seems that "inclusiveness" cannot be expressed in words at all, because it contains a certain mystery in its own implication.

For the philosophical point of view of Jasper, philosophy is the belief in, worship of, and the guideline for a certain religion or a certain doctrine.

If the interrelationship between existence and transcendence, that is, the connection of a certain nature between man and man or man and things, is the fundamental idea that runs through all of Jaspers' philosophy, then the concept that expresses this relationship is "inclusiveness," and when we reach the state of inclusiveness, the door to transcendence will truly open.

Jaspers' Einführung in die Philosophie

4.. Timeless experience from history to transcendence

When Jaspers mentions the "Axial Age" (Achsenzeit) and the "Four Great Philosophers" in "The Spiritual Condition of the Age" and "The Origin and Goal of History", the wise men such as Confucius, Buddha, and Jesus and the revelation of the Age of Wisdom, they all make an "inclusive" example of "reverence for transcendence".

Jasper's "philosophy of existence" is difficult to sort out in a few words, but we can perhaps analyze his wisdom in this way: the holistic, fundamental and critical inquiry into the realm of reality and man is always a self-imposed thing, directly linked to the divine.

The study of universal, fundamental problems in the disciplines of being, knowledge, values, reason, mind, language, etc. Thought is always rooted in the free creation of the individual. He might have likened philosophical faith to a rational adventure, a courageous leap into the transcendent realm beyond the realities of existence, with the desire to know infinitely.

According to Jasper's philosophy of existence, living seems to be a tragedy for modern man, a struggle that comes from the heavy burden of the heart, where man has gradually lost the ability to control himself under the pressure of survival. Man is like a lost baby, facing the street, unable to find the way home, uncertainty, fear and anxiety are the common pressure that modern man feels.

Nietzsche (1844-1900) even declared directly that God is dead and that modern people have felt the sorrow of having no home to return to.

However, the century has just passed the halfway point of the twentieth century, and mankind has been subjected to a series of misfortunes. As material civilization continues to surge, the human soul gradually sinks downward, clinging to the natural material and losing itself. The people saw the haggardness, trembling, and uneasiness of the human heart battered by World War II.

It is a matter of urgency to save the true self. Before everything else, man is something that pushes itself into the future and is conscious of its own actions. Nothing existed before the design of the ego; not even in the wise heavens; man can only come into existence when he himself plans to be something.

Therefore, man is responsible not only for his own existence, but also for all mankind. In his self-creation, he also creates others. When he performs a conscious act of choice

He is not only an act of his own will, but also a

legislator who judges all mankind. Regardless of the size of his individual behavior, he will influence the whole universe. Therefore, man cannot escape from a complete and heavy sense of responsibility when he decides on a certain act.

Chapter 2: An Overview of Existentialism

It is well known that plants do not think; they breathe, they grow, they die, but they do not think. What about animals? At least current science shows that animals can perform simple thinking activities, but they have difficulty with more complex and sophisticated thinking. In other words, thinking should be a unique skill for humans.

And why do people need to think? Admittedly, even if a person does not think, he can still live very well, as long as the physical needs can be met. But the most important characteristic of human beings is that besides physiological needs, there are higher needs.

Maslow has already made a very insightful explanation. To prove the existence of the self is one of the major purposes of human thinking. All the pursuit of spiritual freedom is ultimately for the pursuit of the existence of the self, and thinking allows people to better perceive the existence of the self.

A person without spiritual pursuit is bound to be a mediocre person, because there is nothing that can be left in the world for people to perceive. Human life is short, but thought is eternal. "I think, therefore I am." So said Descartes.

Although it has been criticized by philosophers and is not necessarily true, it illustrates the importance of thinking. This is true not only for the individual, but also for the world at large. Without thinking, it is impossible for society to progress and for human civilization to pass on.

The unity of knowledge and action advocated by Wang Yangming is a profound reflection of the intrinsic connection between thinking and action. It is a profound reflection of the connection between thinking and action. It is also about the relationship between thinking and doing. Only in this way can people continue to move upward, and thus tend to the highest good.

There is no physical difference between people, only a gap between consciousness and spirit, and thinking widens this gap. For Jaspers, the pursuit of philosophy is the process of realizing one's true self and going "beyond". Therefore, "transcendence" is the central theme of Jaspers' metaphysical quest.

In his 1932 Philosophie, he mentioned that

"transcendence" is the process of moving from "Dasein" (160) to the real self, that is, the realization of "Existenz" (existence).

When true transcendence is achieved, one can truly realize the self and reach what Jaspers calls "true transcendence" (eigentliches Transzendieren): "transcending the object and entering the realm of the non-contradictory". The question is, how can one transcend all objects and enter the realm of non-contrastive things?

According to Jaspers, there are in fact only two ways in which man can reach himself: one is by treating man as an object of inquiry or study, and the other is by treating him as a non-object, that is, as a being with a freedom that cannot be touched by the object of study.

The former approach, as advocated by scientism, treats the human being as the result of a series of psychological processes or as a statistical item in the functioning of a group, which is the subjective-objective split of the Cogito, the subject of Cartesian thought. Thus, the latter's way of treating human beings as non-objects is also the most important concept in his philosophy, das Umgreifende.

Our cognition always has a horizon-like field or horizon, and we live within this limited field. However, there is always a strong desire within us to transcend the horizon that surrounds us and blocks our vision all the time.

It is as if we can cross the horizon and come face to face with the Absolute Reality, but in reality, no matter how hard we try, this expectation will never be realized. What we encounter is still a limited reality. As our knowledge grows and our scope of perception expands, the horizon that symbolizes our enclosure seems to recede backward.

But no matter how much this horizon expands or retreats, it remains there and can never be removed. And beyond this horizon, there always seems to be a large, dark field that encompasses our field of vision as a backdrop to all of this, a backdrop that we might call the "inclusor.

"Inclusiveness" means that it is never a limited cognitive object that appears in front of us, but an ultimate reality that cannot be cognized through the knowledge of the object. It is never a word with a fixed cognitive connotation.

In other words, the whole can never be an object of knowledge for us. Even if we understand the time and place we live in and see a spiritual principle, a social mechanism or an economic structure, we cannot say that we have understood the whole fundamentally.

In other words, we are always living and thinking in a finite realm. We are aware of this finite fact, but we are also aware of a larger context surrounding this finite existence, which is the experience of an "inclusive" situation.

This experience or perception is not in the way of ordinary rational inference, but in the way of Existenzerhellung (Existential Illumination). It is a way of "existential illumination" of being (Existenzerhellung), in which the being himself illuminates himself in order to grasp his true self-existence, or to become himself (sich selbst werden), or to become aware of himself (sich selbst bewusst werden).

In this way it is possible to understand that each unique individual is not just an aggregation of objective processes, nor is it just a physical and psychological dynamic, but a whole person including feelings, will, body and preconsciousness.

But it is not enough to know oneself, because each individual does not exist in isolation, but is coexistent with other "I's", and I can acquire the concept of myself because of the interaction with the "I's" of others.

"Existential revelation can also take place inter-subjectively, in the interaction and conversation between one being and another being, and in this way, existential revelation can produce appellieren or erwecken.

Heidegger's philosophy of being sees man as an "earthly reality", then Jaspers' philosophy is a state of being in a "situation" (situation).

He believes that "being" is a condition (situation) that cannot be separated from the existence of the I. The situation is more individual than the environment, it is the individual that surrounds the here and now, and has a deep inner relationship with the existence of this individual.

Therefore, the situation means the social, historical and cultural, political and economic factors faced by the individual, and it is a situation that each person has to accept.

But on the other hand, each person can change his or her situation in the direction of his or her own future. Thus, situations offer a wealth of possibilities.

Once a person faces the pain of death, separation, war, responsibility, etc., he or she will encounter a "critical situation" (Grenzsituation), which means that there is nothing left on that side and he or she must make a decision.

The possibility of choice is the freedom of existence, and this freedom is the freedom to choose or decide the self itself from the individual reality.

This freedom is the freedom to choose or decide for oneself from one's own reality. As long as one lives in the world, one must face choices, and therefore freedom is a fundamental quality of existence for every human being.

Therefore, "revelation of existence" is the process of illuminating one's existence and realizing one's true self. This process is not a transcendence that can be completed or realized at once, but a process of continuous efforts to elevate oneself mentally and spiritually.

Fulank often refers to the freedom of change of each individual at any moment, saying that the personality of each person is unpredictable and that the basis of any prediction comes mostly from biological, psychological or sociological conditions.

However, the main characteristic of human existence is that the individual has the ability to transcend these scientific calculations, therefore, he believes that man is capable of transcending himself, that man is human because he can transcend himself, and this is what he experienced firsthand in the concentration camps - the ability to transcend his own predicament. Clearly, he was influenced by the philosophy of Jaspers.

Section 1: Background and Content of the Emergence of Existentialism

Existentialism is also known as existential philosophy; existentialist philosophy. In contemporary philosophy (although its historical roots can be traced back to Greek and medieval philosophy), its beginnings are associated with Kierkegaard and Nietzsche. But the first known exponent of modern philosophy was the French philosopher Jean-Paul Sartre.

Other philosophers include Camus, Karl Jasper,

Heidegger, and Marcel. There are various forms of existentialism ranging from atheism to theism, from phenomenalism, phenomenology, and Aristotelianism. Different systems of existentialism. Existentialism explores the following important issues.

1.Existence precedes essence. The various forms of existentialist systems believe that existence is not always the way it is. Existence occasionally changes and exists as it has become and exists, so that existence constitutes its essence.

2. An individual has no intrinsic nature, no self-identity, other than that contained in the selective activity of the individual.

3. Truth is subjectivity.

4. The abstract role can neither grasp nor communicate the reality of the existence of an individual.

5. Philosophy itself must be concerned with human predicaments and internal conditions, such as anguish, fear, emptiness, the anticipation of death, etc.

6. The universe has no rational direction or framework. It is meaningless and absurd.

7. The universe does not provide moral rules. Moral principles are constructed by people in an environment where they act responsibly to defend the responsibility of others.

8. The behavior of individuals cannot be predicted.

9. The individual has complete freedom of will.

10. The individual cannot refrain from making choices.

11. The individual may become something completely different from what the individual is now.

The core problem of the philosophy of existence is further explained here: Karl Jasper, a German existentialist philosopher, once said succinctly that "existence" means "self-existence". He rebelled against the absorption of man due to the mechanization of the modern welfare state.

Heidegger also argued that self-existence promptly means "Potential being". When man enters the world, if he realizes the possibility of becoming himself, he is authentic existence. If one does not realize the possibility of becoming oneself, then one has an unauthentic existence.

One should strive to become an authentic being. At the same time, it is emphasized that man needs to live his own life autonomously, to express his own thoughts, and to develop his own autonomous personality. The originator of "existentialism", Kierkegaard, rebelled against the phenomenon of the disappearance of individual consciousness due to the emergence of public opinion and group consciousness.

Marcel rebelled against the increasing socialization of life, the extension of state power, and the replacement of the individual with a registration card. The Saudis also fought against Nazi oppression during the Great War.

Although these philosophers of the same generation and background expressed their resistance in different forms, their attitude of resistance was ultimately the same.

On the point that "existence precedes essence," it usually means: "Nothing has any nature or belongs to any category unless it exists.

In "Existentialism is Humanism", Scharthe explains in detail If God does not exist, then there is at least one thing that exists before its essence, that exists before its concept can define it, and that thing is "man.

What do we mean when we say that existence precedes nature? We mean that man exists first, suffers all sorts of ups and downs in this world, and then defines himself.

According to existentialists, "man cannot be confined to a certain range or category because, at the beginning, he is nothing. It is only later that he gradually becomes something, so that he makes himself into whatever he is.

In other words, there is no such thing as a "deterministic" existence, man is free, man is promptly free, man is on demned to be free. From the moment he is thrown into the world, he is responsible for everything he does. Thus, man's meanness, cowardice and sinfulness are entirely the result of his own actions. "Existence is prior to essence" implies that everything must begin with the subject and its result should be borne by the subject.

"Existentialism makes a clear distinction between subject truth and object truth, and emphasizes that subject truth does not exist in the object, but in man himself. It is emphasized that the truth of subjectivity does not exist in the object but in man himself.

Existentialists have a common belief about subjectivity: no knowledge can be independent of a knowing subject. They believe that any abstract universals are as vague as formal logic.

They do not deny that real and objective truths can be obtained through science and logic, but human beings cannot rely on mathematical or trinitarian reasoning to obtain universal truths. They do not deny that real and objective truths can be obtained through science and logic, but humans cannot obtain universal and proper truths by mathematical or trinitarian deduction; that alone makes it impossible to know the meaning of self and life.

Because of its strong emphasis on subjectivity and on the situation of the individual, Existentialism has been confused with extreme individualism.

It has been repeatedly stated that the individuality emphasized by Existentialism is that each person has his or her own individual life, and each individual life is unique. Each person has his or her own way of life, and each person is able to express his or her true individuality, opposing blind adherence and the creation of a uniform model of the human person.

We affirm the right of each person to be purchased as an individual unit. Furthermore, we understand that if we are born, we must die, and that death is inevitable.

Situation

"The term "Situation" is commonly used in Existentialist philosophy. The human condition is subject to a variety of constraints. In a certain state of mind, man sometimes feels himself not only as a prisoner of the world around him, but also as motivated by his own varied emotional responses and instincts.

As he tries to master his "situation," he encounters new and insurmountable limitations. In these limitations, he realizes that he is bound by the finite and contingent nature of his existence.

Although he can improve or control his circumstances in some way, he still inevitably admits his inability to confront (Cope) the most fundamental limitations of the human condition, such as the suffering, sin, and death that he encounters.

From the point of view of Jasper's philosophy, these limitations are indispensable to human existence, and they are the reason for the disappearance of human hopes or illusions. They are also the reason for the disappearance of human hopes or illusions.

But the real experience of death cannot be truly experienced in person, because our experience of death is only the experience of someone else's death.

As a matter of fact, we cannot really experience the death of another person. Therefore, "death" is beyond the imagination of experience.

Therefore, we understand how great is the inexplicable fear that arises in the human mind in anticipation of the death of an unknown being. But if we can really feel it in practice, feel it in action, explore it, death is only a phenomenon of life, an existential phenomenon.

Death is not an event. Existential philosophers do not want to see death as an "external" event, nor do they want to observe it from an "objective standpoint", but only to perceive it in cognitive practice, to feel it in action, to explore it, and to emphasize the individual. Instead, they want to feel and explore it in the practice of cognition, in action, and to emphasize the relationship between the individual and his or her "own death" in physical action.

Therefore, by analyzing in this way, we can see that many people in society are afraid to face their emptiness, but only those who face their emptiness and do not anesthetize their confused life with a life of fun and debauchery at night can thoroughly understand the true meaning of life. understand the true meaning of life's existence.

Only the person who empties himself of his surplus and useless things, and does not whitewash himself with lies and falsehoods, can reveal his true life.

"Existentialism" can be traced back to German "Romanticism", which rebelled against the "reason" of the 18th century Enlightenment in the name of the individual.

"It is not only a philosophy but also a way of life that permeates all aspects of social life: ideology, literature, literature, and the arts.

It is not only a philosophy, but also a way of life that permeates all aspects of social life: ideology, literature, art, etc. It can be said to be a process and response to the situation (mostly unfavorable) that human beings were in at the time, or perhaps it should be said to be an analysis from a third party's point of view, to examine the past experience and to improve learning behavior.

When the trend of existentialism arrived after the Second World War, the public interest was not exclusively in the philosophical issues to be explored, but in the new social style or trend of thought in France, which therefore exuded the special color and power that the French romantic intellectual life could produce. It is not exclusively a philosophical issue.

This means that different artistic or academic communities were associated with each other, and that artists, literary figures, and performers lived a life of freedom, of indefinite residence, and of freedom from social conventions, with habits and personalities that were alien to the outside world, or that were exiled by social values that were very different. The character of a person who has a habit and personality that is alien to the outside world or has a habit that is different from the values of society.

The Oxford Concise Dictionary defines a bohemian as "a person who is not bound by social conventions, especially an artist or writer"; the American College Dictionary defines a bohemian as "a person with artistic or intellectual inclinations who lives and acts free from conventional norms of behavior".

The Beat Generation, or the weary generation, is a small group of downtrodden writers, students, con artists, and drug addicts because of its pivotal role in the formation of post-World War II American modernist culture.

In Western literature, the Beat Generation is considered an important branch of postmodernist literature and one of the major genres in the history of American literature. It is a literary movement started by a group of American writers after World War II.

It was intended to explore and influence American culture and politics in the post-World War II era. They published a large body of work in the 1950s, which spread widely. "The core ideas of the Beat Generation included a commitment to spiritual exploration, an exploration of American and Eastern religions, a rejection of standard values, an opposition to materialism, a detailed description of the human condition, experimentation with hallucinogenic drugs, and sexual liberation and exploration.

Existentialism, however, emerged as a new and

creative force, similar to, but not surpassing, postmodernist literature in the lifeless postwar years.

Existential philosophers struggled to find a solution, but some philosophers saw it as an emotion, a post-war emotion, a statement that clearly intended to show that they were oblivious to the existence of life itself, the existence that concerns human life. They are blind to the existence of life itself.

This is because they mistakenly believe that the philosophical truth of religion can only be found within the experience of the non-existence of emotions in the process of human life experience.

After all, it is closely related to the existence of human life. "Existentialism is not a fashionable thing, nor is it a religious philosophy of post-war psychological recovery, nor is it a post-war psychological counseling for suffering from illness and pain. It is a major trend in the evolution of human thought in the mainstream of modern nature and society.

Therefore, it can be said that it has a great enlightening effect on the establishment of the concept of "existentialism". In the history of religious philosophy, there is rarely a philosophy that has such a wide range of social forms and such a clear spirit of the times.

"The popularity of Existentialism is inextricably linked to the characteristics of the context of its time. It is essential to understand the context of Existentialism in order to analyze the theory of Existentialism in its context.

After the Second World War, Europeans at that time were thinking in a state of exception. Generally, they did not respond to things consciously, making judgments and taking actions as a natural process.

Only when reflecting on the chilling experience of a struggle between two or more opposing sides, using tangible or intangible power to determine victory or defeat in order to bend the will of the other side and realize their own propositions.

The question of the meaning of life will emerge from the consciousness only when the thinking about the meaning of life's existence is temporarily stopped due to the difficulty of choosing the boundary situation, and the hardening of life experience becomes no longer easy.

It is only when people have a profound experience of their existence that they will pause to think, and the true meaning of their existence will become a clear object of reflection in their consciousness.

Reflection, however, is a higher kind of thinking. Whether conscious or not, we always respond to the world with concepts, with cognitive habits, with a bunch of preconceived notions. Even the rational and active process of reflection of the human mind on the real world or any object in the form of "inward dialogue" presupposes a more fundamental awareness.

For example, when we judge whether a proposition is correct or not, we have predetermined the criteria for determining what is right or wrong. We can't start our thinking in a blank space, we have to accept that we have to think about something first.

Everyone has the freedom of choice on many issues and has to bear responsibility for the consequences of his or her choice, which is often a choice between life and death. These states of mind and the associated freedom and responsibility have become the themes of existentialism.

The main theme of "Existentialism" is the theme of life: anxiety, death, fear, and other situations, which really coexist with people. The experience of the war changed life after the war, and Existentialism was in line with the need for a humanistic sense of freedom and responsibility, and therefore existentialism became widespread. This is why existentialism became widespread.

In the same period of history, based on economic, political, and cultural conditions, in the same difficult situation, and facing the same challenges, the philosophical ideas, attitudes, and actions of the various philosophers of Existentialism, although each with their own views and attainments, have a fundamental commonality.

But they all have one fundamental point in common - that is, they all value the state of mind in which life exists and point out the importance of recognizing meaningful mental states in the environment.

In short, they both seek the value of an autonomous self-existence. At the same time, the way they guide the correct cognition is inclined to personal experience, focusing on finding feelings and perceptions in practice, feeling and exploring in action, emphasizing the intuition and inspiration of physical action, and opposing theoretical systems, especially Hegel's dialectic and

Descartes' rationalism. It opposes theoretical systems, especially Hegel's dialectic and Descartes' rationalism.

The three most outstanding philosophers were Heidegger, Jaspers, and Schartre in France. They emphasized the need for people to live their own lives of choice, to express their thoughts freely, and to give expression to their true personalities.

And they tried to resist the status and trend of collectivization. Although their rebellion is expressed in different ways, they share a strong negative attitude, just as they rebel against the basic assumptions and conclusions of traditional philosophical conceptualism.

The ideal is a mere sublimation of animal instincts, but it stifles the search for the true meaning of human existence. In this wave of rebellion, the existentialist philosophers have established a positive proposition, namely, that "existence precedes essence.

The metaphysics of social factors, such as customs, morals, habits, beliefs, and ideas, which have been passed down from generation to generation and have a continuity of inheritance, all believe that essence has a universal, abstract, and formal character.

They all strive to explore something eternal and unchanging, but existence is a concrete thing that exists in a temporal space-time.

Section 2: The Pioneers Who Influenced Jasper's Thought

After the Second World War, "existentialism" became the most popular philosophical thought in Europe and America. In the present century, the idea of "existentialism" was developed by Jaspers and Heidegger in Germany, and by Scharthe and Marcel in France.

In fact, it was mainly through the advocacy and encouragement of the French philosopher Sartre that their doctrine became popular and spread. During the period of Existentialism, there were many philosophers of existence. Although each of them had their own insights and achievements, they all had one thing in common in terms of their basic philosophical thinking.

That is: they all sought the autonomous and authentic self. This means that in the process of pursuing the cognition of the self, they are inclined to personal life experience, to truth and inspiration, and to the ideas, cultures, morals, customs, arts, institutions, and ways of behavior that have been handed down from generation to generation and from history. The way of behavior, etc.

The influence and control of the social matrix of people, and the rejection and conflict between the philosophical and theoretical systems of thought, and the confrontation between the two, and the competition, tilting, or hostile action against traditional formal thought.

"Traditional metaphysics ignores the fact that the existence of human life is a finite time and space existence, and if life does not exist, all possibilities of life existence will be terminated. It disappears.

Life is a phenomenon of integration, and this phenomenon exists in a certain form, and "essence" is only the material that constitutes this form of existence.

We know that Jaspers' so-called "philosophy of existence" focuses on the pursuit of the realization of one's true self, a pursuit that Jaspers interprets as a "boundary situation".

This pursuit, which Jaspers interprets as "boundary situations," means that the various failures or dissatisfactions one encounters in the course of one's life lead to a transcendent motivation in one's heart.

Once we encounter these "boundary situations" in life, we will try to break through and transcend.

From the previous exploration, we can already know some of the philosophers who influenced the formation of Jaspers' philosophy, such as Plato, Augustine, Spinoza, Hegel, Kant, and Heidegger.

However, the most direct and significant influences on Jaspers are Kierkegaard and Nietzsche. Among contemporary philosophers, Jaspers is attracted to Kierkegaard and Nietzsche, who faced "emptiness" but still struggled to transcend. In this section, we will explore the formation of Jaspers' philosophical thinking in more depth.

The influence of Kierkegaard 1813-1855 and Friedrich W. Nietzsche 1844-1900 on Jaspers' philosophical thought: the emphasis on the existence of the single individual.

Although they differed greatly in their ideas and beliefs, they not only changed the current state of the philosophical world, but also had a direct influence on Jaspers' philosophical thinking. They had a direct influence on Jaspers' philosophical thinking.

After realizing the philosophical thinking of Kierkegaard and Nietzsche, Jaspers felt strongly aware of the situation of being a human being and the problems of life that he faced. The philosophical thinking of both Kierkegaard and Nietzsche has replaced him from his misconceptions.

Basically, although they had completely different beliefs in their fundamental beliefs (Kierkegaard as a theist and Nietzsche as an atheist), they were both called "existentialists".

Therefore, if they are placed under the same name, their central ideas are the same from the point of view of the existence of life alone, and they wish to view this collective, popular, civilized, and popularized They want to look at this collective, popularized, civilized, and popularized issue of "life existence" from different directions and perspectives, which is a common issue to be presented from the connotation of the meaning of life existence and the experience of life.

Thus, according to Kierkegaard and Nietzsche, the power of the social matrix of the masses overrides the subjective consciousness of the individual, who gradually succumbs to the constraints of the social matrix and loses the ability to think objectively, instead focusing on the practical enjoyment of life. The individual gradually succumbs to the constraints of the social matrix, loses the ability to think objectively, and turns to the practical pleasures of life without meaningful ideals, ethics and culture.

As a result, the meaning of one's life gradually becomes vulgar and impoverished, and not only that, but also the thinking, perspective, and noble interests that are essential to one's life are gradually lost.

Therefore, does this mean that Kierkegaard and Nietzsche believe that man has gradually lost the important meaning of the value of his life existence? Thus, the individual pursuit of truth, goodness and beauty has been determined by the good and bad of the social matrix.

This is against the basic value and spirit of the meaning of life. Therefore, both Kierkegaard and Nietzsche have made it clear that they want people to recognize and recover themselves from their deviant perceptions and to emphasize the existence of an autonomous self.

In his book "Today's Time", Kierkegaard also mentions his view on the term "the masses", saying that the masses are an abstract term for the right and reason of life existence, which consists of: how much corruption, how much sin, how much stupidity, how much impulsiveness, and how much shallowness. The reason

At the same time, he uses all the cynical words to give up the individual's future for himself, to keep an open mind, to expand the horizon and the field; to be an ignorant compromise, to talk without enthusiasm and action, to hide from the crowd, to be irresponsible or blind. Irresponsible, or blind to the challenges of the truth-seeker.

The "individual person" is the sphere through which the whole of mankind is passing in this day and age, in the whole of history, and unless one can pass through this narrow path by being a "person" oneself, it is absolutely Otherwise, it is absolutely impossible to become a human being. If one wants to live as a human being, one must stand up for oneself and be responsible for every single action.

In the concept of "existentialism," Kierkegaard emphasizes that "existentialism" respects the uniqueness of the individual rather than the commonality of the human being. Why does he emphasize the uniqueness of the individual? We can gain a fundamental insight into this term from the following example, which Kierkegaard explains.

When we say, "Kierkegaard was a Danish man, he was a philosopher, he was celibate, he was not tall, he did not have a handsome face, he was a Christian...", then our perception of a particular object or doctrine The term "Danish" does not point to a single unique characteristic of Kierkegaard.

The term "philosopher" does not point to a single uniqueness of Kierkegaard, nor is lifelong celibacy possible only for Kierkegaard, who is not tall and not handsome.

These characteristics are shared by many people, and the name "Christian" can refer to many people.

However, if we look at it from another perspective, that is, through the "history" of Kierkegaard, then we can understand that he is not only a member of the human species, but also a unique Kierkegaard. understand that he is not only a member of the human species

The point of focus here is to truly understand the importance of the distinction between the "uniqueness of the individual" and the commonality.

Why is it necessary to emphasize the existence of a single individual and to value the uniqueness of the individual?

Because, we can say that when a person appears in the world as a "member of the human species", he is only "merely living" and does not yet have the meaning of "authentic existence". (b) The world is a place where one is "merely living" without the meaning of "authentic existence".

But when a person appears in the world as "I am who I am," he does not merely exist, but exists more authentically in his autonomy.

We mentioned earlier that Kierkegaard and Nietzsche, despite their individual differences in philosophical thought and beliefs, not only had a direct influence on Jasper's philosophical thinking, but also changed the contemporary philosophical status quo. The status quo.

Jaspers believed that the very existence of life is the problem that one must face in life, and that philosophy is concerned with the most personal, if not the only, problem that one must be very careful about.

In this respect, Jaspers has indeed inherited the concern and awareness of both Kierkegaard and Nietzsche for the contemporary situation they face.

According to Jaspers, people should be aware of and reflect on the spiritual world they are facing, and the crisis and its seriousness derived from the situation, and this is the starting point of philosophical inquiry, that is, to jointly care for the fate of human beings and to seek a direction for their future development. This is the starting point of philosophical inquiry, which is to care about the fate of human beings and to seek directions for their future development.

By the same token, the problem of understanding philosophy and philosophy cannot be disconnected from the time and environment in which we live. In his book "The Spiritual Situation of the Age", Jaspers also explores the origins of the consciousness of the age and the present situation, and calls both Kierkegaard and Nietzsche pioneers of vision and awareness of the contemporary situation.

From the following cognitive insights of his time, Kierkegaard says: "The world today is trying to eliminate everything, to suppress everything, to make everyone a number or a figure, or a concept that expresses the quantity of the same documentary collection. The world today is trying to eliminate everything, to suppress everything.

In our time, we do not seek to know the process of transmission and feedback of thoughts and feelings between people, between groups of people, in order to reach unanimity of thought and fluency of feeling, but only to know that by sharing information, facts or attitudes, we are able to create a common understanding with other people or groups.

Those who seek only to recognize objects that seek to establish a common understanding and perspective with others or groups, that is, those who seek only to recognize objective things. Our age is a sad one, in which people are seeking trouble and trouble for no reason, and it is an age in which people's hearts are scattered.

Jasper pointed out clearly and sincerely that in any research, he always attaches importance to the spiritual civilization of human beings, and that the spiritual civilization of human beings is the key to the portrayal of "emptiness or enrichment" in our time.

Today, the concrete individual is buried in the abstract group, and the individual hiding in the group is indeed a spiritual self-imprisonment.

It is because we dare not and do not want to become an autonomous and independent person, and we do not have a strong and certain will to maintain our existence in this earthly world, but instead, we insist on being our own imaginary self. The regret caused by circumstances beyond control or remedy!

Section 3: Jasper's Reflection on "Science and Philosophy

Philosophy is the study of universal, fundamental questions, including the fields of existence, knowledge, values, reason, mind, and language. Philosophy differs from other disciplines in that it has a unique way of thinking.

For example, it has a critical, often systematic approach, based on rational argumentation. This means that philosophy begins with people's curiosity about everything. When people are confused about everything, some of them start to think about the reasoning behind it, not only to know what is true, but also to know why it is true.

Therefore, the ancient Greek philosophers often asked questions, and the questions they asked can be categorized into three categories, which formed the basic disciplines of philosophy - metaphysics, ethics, and theory of knowledge respectively.

Although modern philosophy has seen the emergence of philosophical theories that "do not require precise reasons," such as the "technique of essence" (the recognition of essence as unknowable), this phenomenon has increased the importance of agnosticism (the existence of a world that cannot be understood after all).

Thus, logic has often played an important role in classical and modern philosophy since Aristotle's time. In particular, his triadic theory has had a profound influence on the development of Western philosophy.

Out of human curiosity, philosophers are interested in everything, but as their knowledge grows, they are divided into different disciplines. For example, the exploration of nature gave rise to natural philosophy, which then developed into science.

Most of the other disciplines are also "divergent" from philosophy, so the doctoral degrees of many disciplines (including science) are still called "Doctor of Philosophy" (Ph. D.). This shows the relationship between science and philosophy.

The idea and spirit of science was spread from the West. "The word "science" in English and its counterpart in other European languages is derived from the Latin word "Scientia", meaning "specialized knowledge" and "individual learning". Etymologically, the word science comes from the Latin Scientia (English knowledge), which is close in meaning to the Greek Episteme (knowledge).

The Greek philosopher Plato distinguished between knowledge (Episteme) and opinion (Doxa), considering the former to be the subject of scientific research. This distinction provides two views of science: a unified knowledge and a separate dianoia.

This division also represents Aristotle's distinction between theoretical science and practical science.

Aristotle considered science to be demonstrated knowledge of the causes of things, and he distinguished three types of science, theoretical, practical, and productive, and considered theoretical science to be prior to the other two, and that science could not be contracted with each other, and that each science could be understood only in its own terms.

Therefore, a third conclusion can be drawn here: positivist science is not equal to science, and the subjective value of science should be in theory rather than practice.

Therefore, one cannot deny the close relationship between matter and mind (and even matter), and even if mind and matter are separated, mind still depends on matter. This involves natural sciences such as biology and biochemistry, and social sciences such as psychology and sociology.

Therefore, when discussing the big philosophical questions of existence, knowledge, value, reason, mind and morality, we should not forget the insights brought to us by science.

This does not mean that science can replace

philosophy. After all, philosophy is the source of all studies, and this problem involves more than science, and it is still up to philosophy to solve it.

However, to ignore the knowledge brought by science and to "think philosophically" will only degenerate into a vague theory of "thinking dialectic philosophy".

Husserl: "Philosophy is, for its historical purpose, the greatest and most rigorous of all sciences. In terms of thinking itself, philosophy has the same transcendent status as science".

The relationship between philosophy and science is often thought to be the same between Western philosophy and scientific thinking. But this is only from the point of view of the difference in the object, from the point of view of the type of thought, they are actually the same.

Although science is based on observation and proof, philosophy is also based on observation and proof, but the difference only lies in the difference of their objects.

The object of science is material things, visible things, while the object of philosophy is invisible things, conceptual things. In other words, because these objects are not purely quantifiable material things like the objects of science, their methods of observation and proof must be different.

But the fact is that both kinds of thinking are based on observation and argument on the one hand, and on the other hand, they are both constructed by thought itself based on observation in their final conclusions.

Husserl, the German philosopher and father of phenomenology, believed that philosophy should be a rigorous science, like mathematics and logic, which is based on nature, not on facts, and whose goal is to reveal all possible knowledge and, accordingly, all possibilities.

Its goal is to reveal all possible knowings and, accordingly, all possibilities, the a priori nature of the world, which is thus necessary, and not merely contingent, as is the case with the laws of the factual sciences.

Husserl asserts: "Philosophy is, for its historical purposes, the greatest and most rigorous of all sciences.

Therefore, the first conclusion can be drawn here: philosophy has the same transcendent status as science in terms of thinking itself.

Religious philosophies have been interrogated by new

trends of thought and philosophical discourses, which have emerged one after another.

From a good perspective, this phenomenon is certainly the result of the increasing pluralism of today's world civilization; however, from another perspective, it may not be impossible to say that the present situation of disagreement and confusion in the world today is also the result of But from another perspective, it may not be impossible to say that the present situation of disagreement and confusion in the world today is also caused by differences and confusion in thinking.

But the reason for this is not so simple. Jasper should have seen the beginning of the misunderstanding of the meaning of life's existence long before the career change.

Thus, he offers his professional opinion: when people are exposed to new ideas, they seek to expand our knowledge of the truth on the one hand, and to satisfy our search and curiosity for fundamental questions on the other.

It can provide a way for those who have closed themselves off from real life (scholars in ideal societies, research laboratories in universities) to contemplate the meaning of life and to understand the truth and meaning of existence.

In turn, it can provide a source of living water for the anxious and confused minds of modern people. In his book "Introduction to Philosophy", Jaspers says, "For the meaning of philosophical thinking is in the present moment of life, and the one reality we can have is here and now.

What we miss because we run away from it will never come back. If we ignore the meaning of life and live and die in confusion, then we will also lose the meaning of life.

For every day is precious, even if it is a moment, it is everything that we have ever had.

Philosophy is not about finding answers from the phenomena of our senses, but about finding explanations that go beyond these phenomena, that is, the final answers, that is, the ultimate care or transcendence, which are usually obtained in the process of inquiry or study of philosophy.

Philosophy is scientific cognition, the study of all things with the natural understanding of reason. Philosophy is the study of reflection, introspection and experience, the accumulation of wisdom in life.

But how can we generate interest and motivation for philosophical inquiry? Here, Jaspers emphasizes that the root of philosophy is wonder, which gives rise to curiosity about the world, about philosophical works, and, so to speak, to the motivation to explore philosophical knowledge.

In the philosophical process, it is more important to ask questions than to get answers, and philosophy is about facing the questions asked rather than providing the answers required by them.

Because philosophy cannot be satisfied with fixed answers, every question posed is interpreted in a hierarchical way. Therefore, it can be said that it does not settle on one answer; because everyone's life situation is different, and the problematic points they face are not exactly the same.

Even if the questions are similar or identical, the answers will be very different depending on the differences in people, times, places and things. Therefore, inquiring into philosophy, we should not expect it to provide us with solutions when we face "boundary situations" in life.

Rather, we should expect to face the problem of the meaning of our own lives and to find a solution to it with the wisdom and methods we have gained from the philosopher's own experience.

Among all of Jaspers' works, The Way of Wisdom is definitely the most fundamental and essential work to study in order to enter the field of Jaspers' philosophy of existence.

This is because it clearly describes some of the most basic and essential cognitions of all philosophical thinking, as well as the main points of his philosophical thinking that can be reached in depth. A summary of Jasper's philosophical thought on existence is as follows.

"The Value of Existence" is an exploration of how to plan and design one's own future, that is, the ideal blueprint of each person's life.

First, the ideal me is to stand on the reality of my own existence, to plan, design and implement for my own future.

Second, my ideal is to make plans that violate the social matrix and exist in spite of the facts and conditions that exist in front of me.

Third, the conscientious me is one who ignores the interference of external gossip and comments, focuses on his or her own path, discovers his or her own uniqueness, makes choices based on conscience, and clearly demonstrates an attitude of self-responsibility. This is a clear demonstration of self-responsibility.

What the existentialists have done for the public is, according to Jasper, the most useful: they have guided people to understand themselves rationally.

In guiding people to love society; in guiding them to deal with their emotions with a cool head; in guiding them to love the world and humanity with a sincere love; in guiding them to seek the way of self-help in their suffering; in guiding them to seek the way of self-help in their despair.

In guiding people to create hope out of despair; in guiding people to create a future out of autonomy. He advocates that one's destiny be reversed by one's own efforts, and that one's tomorrow be created by one's own struggle.

Jaspers was the only one who focused on science and the importance of science in the age of "existentialism".

Jasper did not start out on the path of philosophy; his earliest exposure to philosophical works at the age of seventeen was to the scientific method and practical knowledge, but he never stopped to study the universal, fundamental subjects, including the fields of existence, knowledge, value, reason, mind, and language.

He believes that philosophical thinking is not the exclusive preserve of philosophers, although science cannot solve many of life's problems.

The question he poses in the scientific discussion is in fact the question of "the meaning of the existence of life", although such a term is a relatively old one, but Jaspers wants to clarify this question from the point of view of "philosophy of existence", which requires an answer or a solution. The term is an older term, but Jaspers is trying to clarify this question from the perspective of the "philosophy of being" that demands an answer or solution.

There is no other reason why Jaspers should give this part of his book, Way to Wisdom, a special focus or emphasis on science and philosophy or ideas, because Jaspers begins his book Way to Wisdom with the relevance of philosophy and science, and his personal argument about science (which is related to his In his book, Way to Wisdom, he begins with a detailed discussion of the relevance of philosophy to science and his personal arguments about science (which are related to his having crossed over from medicine to philosophy and his medical training). He has given a detailed discussion and insight into the science of science.

Therefore, it should be easier to analyze Jasper's understanding of this issue and the extent to which he attached importance to science, and to understand it from a certain cognitive point of view. Jasper's scientific research has two points of departure.

1. Science-truth. He believes that the way of deducing reasonable conclusions by reasoning purely after careful consideration of the evidence is the method of scientific cognition, and the method of the thinking process of inference and proof.

Science and truth are mutually respectful of each other, and he believes that while the interpretation of scientific knowledge is an indispensable element in the in-depth study of all philosophies, without science there would be no science. But without science, there would not be all the achievements that exist today.

Although the precision of scientific knowledge can be completely independent of philosophical truth in its overall conception, philosophical truth is a systematic conclusion of knowledge about nature and society that men have generalized from practice, there seems to be a certain level of ideology between the two. There seems to be a certain level of difference between the two ideologies, but the relationship between factual and rational evidence is inextricably intertwined.

2. Science is philosophical thinking. Science cannot understand the reason for its own existence, cannot specify the meaning of life's existence, and cannot provide a clear path to its purpose.

Therefore, philosophical thinking, that is, checking one's own thinking and behavior, checking the wrong thinking among them, and scientific thinking have a complementary function, clearly pointing to the self, or returning to inner contemplation or meditation (this is also the reason why Jaspers emphasizes that there is an irrational thing beyond reason, showing (In the existential dimension of human life.)

In his book "The Way of Wisdom", Jaspers has pointed out the difference between philosophy and science in terms of their views on things or problems from a certain standpoint or perspective: science always has a specific target audience, and scientific knowledge is not essential for all human beings. scientific knowledge is not indispensable for all human beings.

However, philosophy is concerned with the state of interaction and mutual influence between human beings and things, the whole existence of what makes human beings human, and once the truth it seeks is revealed, it will be more moving than any scientific knowledge. It will move us more than any scientific knowledge.

For the scientifically literate, one of the most criticized aspects of philosophy is that it does not produce universally valid results; it does not provide anything that we can know and understand mentally through the activity of our individual consciousness, and that we actually possess.

In contrast, the sciences in their respective fields have been repeatedly tested and confirmed, yielding very detailed and definitive conclusions that can be universally accepted insights, while the logical justifications in philosophy, despite thousands of years of exhaustive efforts, have not yet been validated. Despite thousands of years of exhaustive effort, logical philosophical reasoning has not yet achieved such results.

This is a problem beyond common understanding; in the study of universal, fundamental problems in the disciplines of being, knowledge, values, reason, mind, language, etc., it is impossible to deny that there is no generally accepted, definitive standard of validation.

According to Jaspers, anyone who wishes to explore the mysteries of the subject must go beyond the understanding of one's ability to know, understand, think, and decide, and supplement it with the practice of daily life to gain experience and understanding. Only in this way is it more reasonable or sensible, and this is something that no one else can do except for one's own personal engagement.

For Jaspers, the holistic, fundamental and critical inquiry into the real world and human beings is the process of realizing one's true self and moving towards transformation and transcendence.

Therefore, how to overcome the "boundary situations" that bring us all kinds of things that do not go well or encounter failure and hardship, how the self encounters obstacles or disturbances in the process of experiencing countless, purposeful activities, the resulting psychological state.

This is the ultimate care (i.e., transcendence) of Jaspers' philosophy of existence, which manifests itself as disappointment, pain, frustration, and anxiety, but can still regain confidence, stand up again, and continue to march forward.

Returning to the very basic and important issue of Jaspers' idea of "the existence of life itself", we can compare the similarities and differences of several similar things to show that existence is not about forgetting our past and erasing our memories.

Becoming a human being is not based on each person abandoning his or her past, and it is not based on erasing one's conscience. Rather, it is based on the self-identity of the individual based on existence.

Jasper has always considered philosophy as a seemingly unattainable goal, a discipline that he perceives as analyzing and reflecting on the fundamental questions of life, knowledge, and values, and that should explore the fundamental questions of human existence, as the important or primary of its kind.

At the same time, he also observed that the teaching activities of philosophy in the academy were comparable to those of philosophy, which had such a high status at that time.

In fact, in his eyes, it can be said that ordinary people, doing ordinary things, living an ordinary and unremarkable life, always attached to the wind, unable to stand out, to achieve the attention of the public, because of poverty and lack of material resources, and also contains the destruction of philosophy.

And also covers the meaning of the destruction of the philosophical conscience, he does not to the status or achievements of people higher than their own recognition, in order to eliminate the individual in real life, because of failure to achieve success or satisfaction, and frustration brought about by the anxiety. He also expresses his insights in a perceptive manner.

After this, he moved from being a medical student to a pathologist, believing that the knowledge he gained at the beginning of his psychology studies was only a background knowledge of psychology.

Such knowledge could only be attained by means of a holistic approach, that is, he believed that they should interact with each other and complement each other.

Therefore, Jaspers distinguished philosophy, medicine and science into three, and here, the contents of their respective developments are summarized as follows.

"Philosophy" is the discipline of analytical thinking and reflection on the fundamental questions of life, knowledge and values. It is a discipline that is aware of its own truth and limitations in a simple way.

Philosophy declares without doubt what it is and what it should be.Science, on the other hand, takes a certain object as its scope of study, and seeks to find unified and exact objective laws and truths based on experimentation and logical reasoning.And to lead those who are willing to follow, to obey, to be students, back to themselves.

The term "medicine" (psychology) is used to deal with various psychological diseases or disorders in human physiology through scientific or technical means, and also to try to explain the role of individual psychological functions in social behavior and social dynamics.

It is a philosophy that looks at everything "as a

possible phenomenon of the human mind", and thus takes a certain position or perspective on things or problems. Karl Jaspers, The Messenger of Pfalz, 1924: "I have an impulse to save myself spiritually.

I expected "science" to be a systematic body of knowledge, which accumulates and organizes and can examine explanations and predictions about the universe, pure air and reality.

I studied philosophy for my own sake to prevent harmful things from intruding or taking effect, and soon stopped taking philosophy courses to learn about the study of universal, fundamental issues, including existence, knowledge, values, and reason.

This included the fields of existence, knowledge, values, reason, mind, and language. I turned to natural science and philosophy. "It is the exact opposite. Science, as science, is a deliberate outsider', and 'it does not indicate attitudes'.

"Science" is the study of universal, fundamental questions, including the fields of being, knowledge, values, reason, mind, and language. It is not willing to be propagated as a holistic, fundamental and critical inquiry into the real world and people, and it offers advice, not bread, to those who expect meaning in their lives.

The dynamics of the subdisciplinary system of knowledge reflecting the objective laws of nature, society, and thought emphasizes the scope of academic thought or social activity for the kind of person who wants to know the will of science, to take the lead in the front so that those who follow can arrive.

Section 4: Core Ideas of Jasper's Philosophy

Before he became a philosopher, Jaspers was a psychopathologist, and it was only around his middle age that he showed his talent for philosophical thinking. He was a professor and practitioner of psychiatry at German and Dutch medical schools.

However, he later realized that the field of medicine did not provide a thorough and satisfactory explanation of the problem of human self-existence. That is, how can one go beyond all the objects of one's self-existence and enter into the non-contrastive?

According to Jaspers, there are in fact only two ways

in which man can reach himself: one is by treating man as an object of inquiry or study, and the other is by treating man as a non-object, that is, as having a kind of inaccessibility to the object of study.

In his 1913 book Allgemeine Psychopathologie, Karl Jaspers (1883-1969) has already proposed to consider, discuss, accept or adopt phenomenology as a research method in psychiatry, which can be said to be a "phenomenological psychopathology". He was a pioneer in proposing "phenomenological psychopathology".

In his 1958 book, he said: "What I found and affirmed I had been working on was the promotion of the thing itself. This thing (the thing itself) is like liberation (them) in a world of unfair or obstinate opinions, of symbolic forms and explicit or conventional standards.

I do not consider his phenomenological approach to be a philosophical process, but, as he himself has argued

First, it can be used as a description, using various rhetorical devices to visualize the phenomenal signs of existence. The rhetorical devices included are metaphor, simile, exaggeration, double entendre, and prose, etc. Psychopathology has developed principles that can be applied in psychopathology, and the methods that can be used.

He argues that, for the clinically experienced self, human self-existence can be said to be constructed by a combination of factors such as racial genetics, body structure, and social environment patterns.

This results in a situation where everything that one perceives as one's perceived self is unreal, and the existence of one's ego seems to be manifested somewhere in a vacuum.

Jasper even spoke more explicitly about Husserl's contribution to the field of psychological research in the psychological journals of his time. Although Jaspers was the first to speak out for the existential phenomenological orientation of psychotherapy in the early twentieth century.

However, as Rollo May argues, psychotherapy is in fact not the same as psychology. However, as Rollo May suggests, there is not yet a complete connection between psychotherapy and existential phenomenology, although existential phenomenology provides the norms needed in psychotherapy.

But the question is: How can existential phenomenology propose a criterion to distinguish between a healthy or a diseased state of being? After all, many people with mental illness have very complex states of consciousness.

Irrational instinctual forces, repression, anxiety, fear, deliberate forgetfulness, unconscious problems and self-delusional revelations, etc. As Dr. Strauss once intriguingly put it: "The unconscious thoughts of the patient are usually the conscious theories of the therapist.

Thus, it seems that the relationship between existential phenomenology and psychotherapy is still indirect and must be approached through a medium, and there are still many constructive and developmental processes that need to take place.

However, the existential orientation of guided learning or enlightened cognition also helps us to go further and to explain in our own words, texts, or other symbols, the known facts and principles and principles of what is the nature of human beings. The ability to communicate with each other, to analyze each other along the lines or lines of reasoning, and to understand each other.

What is the nature of the interconnection that exists between people, between people and things, and between things and things? What is the state in which man opens or shakes the interaction and influence between the self and the things of the world?

What is the experience of the creative nature of existence through personal practice? These questions are related to the clarification and recognition of the true meaning of life existence and the contribution of the phenomenological orientation of psychotherapy to existence.

However, when we encounter the inevitable "boundary situations" of terror, pain, death, etc.; and, especially when faced with the need to choose, we immediately realize that this unreal self feels so fragile.

At this point, looking back at the relevant arguments we mentioned earlier, if the "self" is only manifested in a certain place, it will be obvious, and we can use repetitive scientific verification to explore it and describe it. We can explore him, describe him, but we cannot discover him scientifically.

It is because "he" does not exist in this space at all,

and his actions to achieve a certain purpose are expressed through some past experiences, and it is up to him to decide what he wants to be.

Here, Jaspers starts from a certain position or perspective of "science", the view of things or problems, to make some observations based on philosophy, analysis, synthesis, judgment, reasoning, generalization and other thinking activities.

Rationalizing the reasons for changes in things, the connections between things, or the laws of development of things is what Jaspers does in the field of philosophy.

This is the style and form that clearly distinguishes Jaspers from other philosophical fields, and is determined by the specific context in which existential phenomenology emerged and developed, and is unique to his clinical psychology.

As a result, his philosophical thinking on existentialism is more diverse and balanced in terms of the direction or viewpoint of the overall philosophical observation of things.

For, even though existentialists in general do not express behaviors, styles, or opinions that lead to disputes and disagreements on scientific issues, most of them still do not take science seriously.

However, instead of being incompatible, leaving or not entering, Jaspers went further and wrote many articles related to science specifically.

Among the existentialists, Jaspers has a unique insight into the study of certain objects and the search for unified and exact objective laws and truths based on experiments and logical reasoning. The most knowledgeable and well-researched person in science.

In general, scientists are limited by the subject matter they study, by their philosophical world of thought and vision, and therefore cannot span a broader field.

He thought that the real self is the one that actually exists and experiences itself, and that it is based on the existing theories, and that it can be determined through rational logic. But Jaspers ultimately believes that this is a major crisis in which man will lose himself.

According to Jaspers' philosophical viewpoint, the work of the psychological process begins with the knowledge of "oneself" and the "philosophy of being" is to make oneself believe and become one's own thinking.

Jasper's "thinking" refers to the rational and active process of reflection of the human mind on the real world or any object by means of "inward dialogue". The so-called inward dialogue is like talking to oneself without the condition of the listener, and the content of the dialogue is extremely broad, including both known and unknown.

Thinking" is the process of rational reflection, which implies that the response to reality is generalized and indirect. Generalization is an abstract activity of the mind in the living world, which, through reflection, can reorganize and summarize existing activities and materials obtained in the process of practice, and describe them to become knowledge.

Indirectness is the use of direct perceptual material to derive new ideas or concepts from existing experience. The forms of "thinking" can be divided into concepts, judgments, inferences, hypotheses, and understandings; the methods of thinking include abstraction, induction, deduction, analysis, and synthesis.

Of course, it is necessary to start from the step of knowing oneself. According to Jaspers, thinking is an intentional consciousness, which points to the process of analysis, synthesis, judgment, reasoning and other cognitive activities on the basis of an object's image and concept.They are 'phenomena' rather than self-existence; although the existence of the self is first described as a whole, it is only the development of the human brain in a 'divided state' towards a process of generalization and indirect reaction to objective things, initially through language.

Although the laws or criteria by which these words are spoken or acted upon are all interrelated. However, because of these principles, Jaspers' thinking activities, such as analysis, synthesis, reasoning, and judgment, produced a series of changes.These changes have led to an innovative metamorphosis in the content of his thought, but basically his thought still holds the original basic characteristics.

The path from the subject of the dominant consciousness to the spirit, from the divine, thinking and mental state of man to existence, from the existence and growth of living systems to reason, from the ability of man to use reason to the world. Among the many "existentialist" philosophers, Jaspers was one of the first to notice the unique situation of the existence of individual life itself. This is how Jaspers explains the "philosophy of being"

"The philosophy of being is the way in which man can return to his own autonomy by guiding the basis of deviant cognitive behavior.It is a mode of thought that analyzes, synthesizes, reasons, and judges without recognizing the object, but reveals and realizes the existence of the thinker.This is the mental process of knowing and understanding things through the activity of consciousness, which is beyond the world.

It is a philosophical attitude towards the world, and is brought into a state of flux, a way of thinking that manifests the existence of life, appealing to the freedom of will of its own existence, and through the call of the transcendent from the point of view of metaphysics, to make room for its own behavior free from the constraints of social matrix. The call to the transcendent through the metaphysical viewpoint, and the struggle for space for one's own behavior free of the social matrix.

In his philosophy, Jaspers places great emphasis on interpersonal "communication," and he derives the most authentic experience of communication from the interaction between himself and his wife, and between people and things.

He believed that individuals find their feelings and perceptions in practice, feel and explore in action, and emphasized that all truths that are practiced physically must be "communicated" with others before they can be fully established.

Jasper often uses other people's words or examples as the basis for his saying, "Truth begins with two people. It is his personal experience.

He encourages everyone to reflect on the mental activity of their past life experiences. Why does life exist and why does it live? Why does life exist and why does it strive for it? The essence of human existence is to understand one's own situation, and the essence of the human being is whether one values all one's choices, big or small.

Therefore, one must seek one's own transcendence, and only when one devotes oneself to the transcendent realm can one realize the meaning of eternity. For Jaspers' philosophical thinking, the pursuit of philosophy is the process of realizing one's true self and moving towards "transcendence". Therefore, "transcendence" is the central theme of Jaspers' metaphysical quest.

The most systematic book on the subject of "transcendence" among Jaspers' writings is Philosophie, published in 1932, in which he mentions that "transcendence" is the process of moving from the "experiential" individual (Dasein) to the real self, i.e., "Existenz" (Existence) makes the originally non-existent situation a reality.

The true metamorphosis beyond the achievement of a goal or the realization of a goal, in particular, the conscious effort, can truly make the non-existent situation a reality, and achieve what Jaspers calls "actual transcendence" (eigentliches Transzendieren): "transcendence of the object into the realm of the non-contradictory".

According to the philosophical view of Jaspers, man is a being that is always changing. The existence of human life is a continuous process of pursuing the meaning of life's existence. Animals other than human beings can only have a primitive form of reproduction and cannot change the status quo of their living environment.

However, human beings are different from animals in that they are dissatisfied with the current situation and have a strong desire to change the status quo and become different from their original state of existence.

This never-ending ambition is the process by which human history strives to find and explore the beyond, and through stimulation and encouragement, to create an inner drive for people to move toward the desired goal.

We begin to reflect on the meaning of life's existence, to contemplate the meaning of life's existence, and to begin the search for the value of our own existence. No matter what we seek - power, fame, wealth, love, or wisdom, or truth - we always hope that our goal will make a situation that does not exist a reality, and make us our hearts to be fuller and more fulfilled.

However, our search and exploration may not always be successful, and the goals we originally expected to achieve require not only our own abilities, but also our subjective efforts and the cooperation of objective circumstances. In addition to our own ability, we need to work hard and cooperate with the objective environment in order to make it a reality.

However, some social customs and habits in the pursuit of goals have often caused us to suffer from the fate of failure. The pursuit of goals → completion → new goals → completion → new goals → completion → new goals → completion → new goals → completion → new goals → completion, and so on form a never-ending pursuit process.

In the process of these pursuits, we are bound to encounter some situations that cannot be changed or surpassed no matter how hard we try. For example, birth, old age, sickness, and death are the chasm that we cannot cross or change, and from which we cannot escape. In the face of these "boundary situations", the real experience we gain again through personal experience is "failure".

"Scheitern (failure) originally meant a ship running aground at sea or hitting a reef, which is the original German meaning. But the English meaning is (failure or foundering) failure or sinking, and it is widely used as a metaphor in spoken language.

Jaspers expanded the philosophical meaning of this term by adopting "defeat" as the German translation. It is different from the common meaning of "failure". A setback is a temporary obstacle that does not necessarily lead to failure, while a failure is a setback that is a foregone conclusion.

Frustration refers to people in purposeful activities, encounter insurmountable or, since they think that insurmountable obstacles or interference, so that their needs or motivations can not be met, and the resulting obstacles. Psychology refers to the state of tension and emotional response that occurs when an individual's purposeful behavior is hindered. The main factors that cause frustration are external and internal factors.

This "frustration" is not a common "frustration", but a common negative emotional reaction, related to anger and disappointment, frustration is generated because the individual's will or goal, which I love to cling to, is obstructed and cannot be satisfied.

Frustration may increase when a person's wishes or goals are denied or obstructed, and there are two types of frustration, one internal and one external. Internal frustration may increase due to challenges in meeting personal goals, aspirations, instinctual drives and needs, or dealing with cognitive deficits such as lack of self-confidence or fear of social status.

An "absolute frustration," such as interference from others when one is competing for a goal, can also be an internal source of frustration and occur as a result of cognitive dissonance. The external causes of frustration relate to the external environment under the control of the individual. There are usually two choices in the attitude one holds in the face of frustration.

One is to choose disillusionment, to choose emptiness, but this kind of lowly choice will make us feel that life is no longer meaningful, and we will lose the confidence and hope of existence, and even the courage to live.

The other choice is to get rid of and transcend all the illusory things in the world, and to realize the existence of the real life itself, which is the reflection and practice of the human brain with consciousness, an active consciousness and generalization of the nature of objective reality and internal laws.

In his book "Way to Wisdom", Jaspers said: In the pure study of universal, fundamental questions, including thinking in the fields of existence, knowledge, values, reason, mind, language, etc., almost everyone believes that as long as one has: humanity, destiny, expressiveness, and the ability to understand the world. destiny, and experience.

It is not necessary to build on testable explanations and to make predictions about the form and organization of objective things in an orderly system of knowledge.

For example, through research, training, and methodology, one will be able to possess and structure the ability to determine right and wrong, good and bad, and to form a philosophical opinion or view.

However, in order to understand that philosophy is a discipline that needs to be accomplished by oneself, one's own philosophy, it is not only about having the three elements, but also about "communication" (communication), which is a holistic, fundamental and critical exploration of the real world and human beings, and it is also a very important part of Jasper's "philosophy of existence". It is also a very important part of Jaspers' philosophy of existence.

There are many forms of human interaction, but it is always the hope that true communication can be achieved, and this communication is called by Jaspers as "communication of being". In fact, it is the communication between the real selves of individuals. Jasper says: "Communication is the root of existence. This communication is called "communication of being" by

Jasper.

Although there is a fundamental ideological gap between Western and Chinese philosophy, such as the lack of linguistic knowledge, or the lack of historical awareness, or, most often, the lack of a sense of history. The problem is an ideological one.

Here, Jaspers offers his insight into the "boundary situation", that is, when people are faced with these unbreakable dilemmas, he offers an explanation, that is, "communication". He places communication as a universal premise of human existence, a theory that forms an important interactive bridge between Chinese and Western philosophy today, and even between modern and ancient things.

In the world direction, world philosophy, world citizenship, world consciousness, world history, etc., Jasper skillfully uses the techniques of "boundary situation" and "communication" to place everything in the world era.

And this is exactly what his "boundary context" has given philosophers This is one of the important missions he gave to the philosophers in the "boundary realm", to establish a future for those who will inherit and inspire the future.

The Meaning of Survival

Thought and free creation. It is the study of universal, fundamental questions, including the fields of existence, knowledge, values, reason, mind, and language. The truth of the self lies in the heart, and it does not need to be proved by external objects.

The process of holistic, fundamental and critical inquiry into the real world and human beings is a process of communication in pursuit of the self, which can appeal to those who drive everyone to the power of philosophy, and which has to struggle for the life of those who want to be a real person or a living person -It is the existence of life, and it is here that its value is manifested.

This is the subject that Jaspers raises in the chapter "Was ist die Philosophie?" (The Way of Wisdom), which goes into great depth, touching on the nature of things. This is only the beginning of Jaspers' philosophical thought.

Jasper's existential thinking starts from the experience of the self, which he expects to make into his unique self; and the first thing he experiences is his own weakness and impotence, that is, the state of "liminality".

Jasper's experience of his own powerlessness, due to his poor health, led him from the study of law, then to medicine, then to medicine, psychology, and finally to the various experiences and situations that led him to consider himself a philosopher. These experiences and situations, which were all the result of the countless dangers and oppressions he suffered during his life, led him to describe with emotion

I am always in a certain situation, circumstances change, opportunities come and go, if I lose an opportunity, it may never come again, I can try to change my situation, but if the situation is unchangeable.

For example, I must die, suffer, struggle, etc. All of these are facts that we cannot escape from and cannot change. The careful consideration and understanding of these situations is one of the deepest sources of Jaspers' philosophical thinking on existence.

Jaspers' philosophical thought encompasses the philosophical ideas of Kant, Kierkegaard, Hegel, Nietzsche, ancient Greek philosophers, as well as religious insights and ideas. He is an eclectic and independent philosopher.

Although some have commented that Jaspers' philosophical thought is more abstract than that of other philosophers, for example, Jaspers does not deal with as many philosophical issues as Heidegger, he is more restrained and balanced in his psychoanalysis than Schartre, and he places more emphasis on systematic structures than Marcel. He is also more concerned with systematic structures than Marcel.

But whether his ideas were accepted by existentialists or non-existentialists, he was always committed to them and worked very hard on them. Secondly, Jaspers studied Western, Chinese, and Indian philosophy extensively and deeply.

In addition to his study of Western philosophy, Jaspers also paid special attention to Asian literature. For he believed that, in addition to ancient Greece, philosophical reflection was also taking place in Asia, in China and India. This shows the breadth of Jaspers' philosophical thinking.

He believes that the "boundedness of existence" is a

theme that is common to both freedom and transcendence, so that he is free to choose the doctrine to which he aspires, to "transcend" those imperfection.

If one reads the word "transcendence" in the text, it seems that there is a term that has been interpreted in various ways, depending on its usage, resulting in ambiguity.

For example, Husserl's use and discourse on Abschattungen refers to "transcendence". First of all, it is the phenomenon (phénomène) that manifests itself as "beyond", and there is a meaning that can be dissected along the lines of a vein or a lineage: this phenomenon manifests itself to me, to a subject; but this phenomenon is not me.

But this phenomenon is not me, it is there, it is objective, and it cannot be reduced to a mere flow of consciousness. So the manifestation of a phenomenon means that it has to be beyond me, outside me. This point constitutes the basic meaning of phenomenology as transcendental phenomenology.

Moreover, apparition, as a side of the object itself, consists in the matching and arrangement of the parts of the manifestation itself that make up the whole, that is to say, the subject in our understanding of the external.

Because of the subjective innate concept, what we know is only a phenomenon, not the manifestation of the object itself, not only in the "view" of a side, but also in the "view" of the object itself. This is the second meaning of "beyond".

Chapter 3: Illumination of Existenz

Section 1: The general meaning of being is the meaning of existence.

In Heidegger's book "Existence and Time", it is stated that time is the field of view of existence. That is to say, in order to understand "existence", we have to take time as the field of view, which tells us in advance that "existence" is time.

Without perspective, we cannot understand existence; but with perspective, it limits the domain of our understanding. Thus, perspective defines a domain, and for this domain, it is called Horizont (horizon). Therefore, Heidegger argues that we must first specify the horizon of time, in which the meaning of "existence" can be properly understood

Thus, in the experience of being, Jaspers is concerned

with the question of the eternal meaning of being, of the existence of life, which he articulates in terms of a "philosophy of being," which sees the existence of life not only in relation to itself, but also in relation to the transcendent (in this case The transcendent refers to God, gods, immortals, etc.).

Jasper suggests that from the direction or viewpoint of scientific observation, he considers the philosophy of existence and science as a concept of one substance or one whole compared with another substance or another whole, or as a concept of existence or change depending on certain conditions, while science studies only one aspect of existence, dividing existence into various objects, while "man" as the object of science is also a concept of existence. The "person" as the object of science is also an object.

Whether it is from psychology (consciousness in general), sociology, anthropology (human), etc., they all study the object of "human" from a single perspective (science). It is impossible to objectify "existence".

The meaning of "life existence" is the experience of life existence. When studying the topic of "existence", it is always inseparable from its unique inner life experience.

Therefore, the method of research is to grasp the meaning of life existence in its entirety, that is, to grasp the world, that is, to grasp the meaning of life existence, according to the life experience of individual life existence.

If we look at the subjectivity (as opposed to the "absolute") that exists under certain conditions and changes with certain conditions, then it is a creative activity that starts from the freedom of the individual. The philosophy of existence of Jaspers can be said to have the same starting point as Scharthe's existentialism, that is, the freedom of individual will.

In his book "The Spiritual Condition of the Age", Jaspers explains that the book was written in 1930. Although the author knew a lot about Fascism at the time, he knew almost nothing about National Socialism.

While the author was still rejoicing over the completion of the manuscript, he was shocked to hear that the National Socialists had won the initial victory in the 1930 elections. The manuscript was put aside for a year. I did not want it to appear in my three-volume Philosophy. Philosophy was published in 1931. A few weeks after its publication, this book was also published.

In order to illustrate the period, the author used only factual material from those particular years, and thus the book in many ways infected the atmosphere of the time. In spite of all that has happened since its appearance, the author believes that it is as valid now as it was then, if one considers the philosophical situation and world scenario today."

The creative activity of the point of departure. But Jaspers' emphasis on the freedom of the will is a call to a "transcendent", i.e., God, and what Jaspers calls "freedom" is the freedom of dialogue with God, in which he is similar to Kierkegaard and very different and far from Schart.

In another direction of analysis, synthesis, reasoning, and judgment, Jaspers and Schartre share something in common, that is, they emphasize that human existence is only a possible existence, that is, they understand "human existence" as the "self-design" and "realization" of "future possibilities". The philosophical view of Jaspers is that "human existence is only possible.

The philosophical view of Jaspers is that "existence is not so much existence as possible existence". That is to say, I do not exist, but I am a possible being. I do not have an autonomous self, but am in the process of reaching the stage of self-realization.

What Jasper conveys is a kind of abstraction and generalization of the common nature of things perceived by human beings in the process of cognition, from sensual to rational cognition: the state of purification of the self through the transcendent. Without the experience of life existence as a subject, "life existence" cannot show its integral and complete meaning.

It can only remain in an object form that is forcibly separated by a whole or connected things. Through this personal perception and understanding, the idea of "personal life existence" arises, which concretely manifests the theory of existence or expounds the essence of the meaning of life existence in it.

Personal existence" is the experience of life experience and the source of creation, and is the rational and active process of reflection of the human mind on the real world or any object in the form of "inward dialogue". The so-called inward dialogue is like talking to oneself, without the need for the actual center and direction of the listener's condition.

From Jasper's book "The Spiritual Condition of the Age", he clearly defines the "being of life": it uses expertise and transcends it.

It does not recognize objects or objects (Object), which means anything that can be perceived or imagined, both things that exist objectively and can be observed (such as people, trees, houses, abstract ones such as prices, freedom) and things that are imagined (such as deified figures).

The existence of the self-life itself is the result of the thoughtful activity of the human consciousness to explain the profound truths and to realize the objective existence reflected in it. As it transcends the social matrix that prescribes the worldview of existence, it is unpredictable and unpredictable, appealing to its own freedom to elucidate "existence", to the call of the transcendent, and to create a range of academic thought or social activity of absolute activity.

In any case, when a person's freedom of will is entirely his own, he recognizes the existence of life and the possibility of choice. Therefore, his behavior will not be one of giving up some of his opinions, principles, etc. to each other in order to eliminate disputes and seek harmony.

He also understands that in order for life to continue to exist, it is necessary to have an attitude of pure resignation to God, and he recognizes that yielding to the self is a sincere failure that can make a situation that does not exist a reality of its existence.

Jasper explores the "philosophy of existence" in which the existence of life itself is an abstract but absolute feeling of existence, a cognitive feeling of someone or something, and "existence" refers to "the existence of human life". The "existence" refers to the "existence of human life", which is related to the people, things, and objects that are touched by all human activities:

1. man and the world: Jasper, because of his own personal experience and feeling of life, feels that the free choice of his will, together with the spirit of self-sacrifice, can truly understand the meaning of suffering, which is man's knowledge of natural or social things, the meaning he gives to the object, the spiritual content that man transmits and communicates in the form of symbols.

All the spiritual contents that human beings communicate in their communication activities include intentions, meanings, intentions, perceptions, knowledge, values, concepts, etc. Therefore, all the meaning of existence in the material world is only for the use of man in self-realization, even in all cases of the physical body, is only for the spiritual life.

2. man and man: every man is seeking to have his personal needs satisfied, and to produce long-lasting joy, and wishes to keep the present mental emotions, not equated with happiness, pleasure, convenience, but happiness is not readily available. In Jasper's own life experience, he did not care to grieve for his own illness, but to be able to forget himself and think of others.

Through his experience of communication with his family, wife, and friends, he came to the conclusion that he wanted to sacrifice himself and make others whole in order to achieve the value of self-existence.

3. Man and himself: The value of man's existence lies in his ability to give, present, and contribute himself in a timely and respectful manner. According to Jasper, the existence of life itself is an abstract feeling, a cognitive feeling of a person or an event, and its connotation is not broad, but limited to a particular person's perception of a person or an event. Connotation is not something

superficial, but something internal, something hidden in the depths of things, which needs to be explored and excavated to be seen.

The definition of the scientific point of view by Jaspers is: the soul, the temperament, the personality, the spirit in the subject is the sum of all the attributes created by our concept of emotion, and if the meaning of the existence of life is suffering, then the affirmation of the value of one's existence.

If the meaning of life's existence is suffering, then the affirmation of the value of his existence lies in his ability to achieve the greatest happiness for the world and for humanity. Therefore, Jasper emphasizes that the interconnection between man and himself, between man and things, and between things and things is meaningful devotion.

4. Man and God: Because of his devotion, Jaspers saw the dawn of theology in his philosophical thinking. He illustrates a way of presenting the life of an individual in terms of the position or starting point from which the theist observes things.

It is by virtue of one's belief in, and reverence for,

some kind of divine proposition, doctrine, or religious ritual that one takes as an example or guide for one's words and actions, and for one's interaction with God.

It transcends all feelings or experiences gained in the course of contact with external things, and it transcends all explanations of known facts and principles and principles that can be made with one's own words, texts, or other symbols.

It is through the power of God, through the freedom of one's own will, that man is able to live in this world and feel the invisible hand of God, which gives him the power to reach beyond the realm. We feel that the invisible hand of God gives us the power to reach beyond the realm, and affirms the value of our existence.

It seems that the existence of human life itself is not as simple as one might think. First of all, in terms of the form of life existence, man is a thing that belongs to nature as an object of action or thought.

It is an object that thinks, acts, and creates in history. Then, man combines nature and history in his own life existence. This situation of man is unique.

As long as the quality of a person's accomplishment of

a goal or a task is within his or her reach, he or she will be able to finish something or do something with a feeling of pleasure or success for what he or she has done.

It is through the sum of nature and human social activities that we recognize ourselves as living beings with bodies, without which there would be no existence of life itself.

Transcendental Enlightenment

We feel the limitations of this life existence deeply in our daily life experience; in this activity, we not only experience such a physical body as part of myself, but also consider the self and this body as two seemingly different things, but actually the same.

However, if we think of ourselves as evolving from matter and life, as the existence of life itself. Then we lose the awareness of the self. For, when we consider the existence of our own being to be the same as our own body, we have not yet become a complete self.

We plunge into the depths and sources of self-consciousness through the freedom of our own will to act internally and externally. However, we do not grasp the existence of our freedom of will, of life existence itself.

Because we do not create the existence of our own being: we are not born with the existence of our own being, nor is the freedom we grant in the free action of grasping our own self, self-created. We do not create our own existence.

For man is the existence of life itself, which is always changing. The human being is a rational and active process of reflection on the real world or on any object in the form of an "inward dialogue" of the mind.

To "think" as a process of rational reflection implies that the response to reality is general and indirect.

Generalization is an abstract activity of the mind in the living world, which, through reflection, can reorganize and describe the existing activities and materials obtained in the process of practice to become knowledge. Indirectness is the use of existing experience to derive new concepts or notions through direct perceptual material.

Human beings also take actions to cluster into town forms of life existence; they are the ones who make tools and cooperate as a group to provide the existence needed for life existence. We cannot think of man as a finite being that is repeatedly present in these particular forms.

Man is a being that changes his existence at any moment: he cannot remain as he is. Man must constantly correct himself in all complex situations. He does not remain unchanged from generation to generation, but the form of life existence is constantly regenerated in a new environment, and the rebirth of human life existence itself is not limited to a predetermined path. It is a brand-new beginning.

Man does not deny that he is subject to the constraints of social matrixes, such as race, gender, age, culture, social and economic conditions, but he is still able to free himself from his own existence, from his freedom of will, as if he could jump out and transcend the environment in which he has been placed.

Man is able to grasp himself only through the things that are the goal of his own actions or thoughts and those of others. It is in the existence of life itself, in the comparison of image with image, that we can grasp our true self. But man cannot grasp himself through the world, through history, or even through the existence of his own being.

Man can only truly grasp himself through his own development of inner and outer awareness, thought or perception, including the conscious faculties or processes of understanding and reasoning, by which he acquires knowledge and action about feelings or ideas.

It is not possible to escape from one's own existence, one's own existent self, if it is only through the stirrings of emotions, or through moving words, etc., because these things are only transient, not eternal.

Only in his inner and outer actions can man truly grasp himself and transcend life, and only in this way can he escape from the limitations of his own existence.

There are two ways in which this mental process of the individual's knowledge and understanding of things through the activity of consciousness arises: one is through the unlimited progress of the existence of life itself in the world, and the other is through the unlimitedness of the revelation of the transcendent to it.

In Greek mythology, Prometheus is a titan who dares to confront the gods. In the poem of Aeschylus, a poet whose theme is misadventure

We can read that next to Zeus, the god of heaven, Prometheus supports the reason why human beings try to avoid the dangers (threats) of life and maintain their own state of life, while Zeus wants the poor human beings to be completely destroyed and extinguished. Zeus, however, wanted the poor mankind to be completely destroyed and extinguished. So he stole fire from the sky and passed it on to mankind, and taught them all the skills they needed to survive.

For example: building houses and boats, using gold, silver, copper and iron, taming wild cattle for farming, taming wild horses for walking, etc. He also taught man arithmetic, all kinds of skills. He also taught mankind arithmetic, various disciplines of learning and how to write. Prometheus gave life to mankind, giving him the opportunity to consciously create his own life through his own actions.

This work was not allowed to be part of the world order controlled by Zeus, the god of the heavens. Man has become what he is today thanks to the giant Prometheus, but also thanks to his own struggle to avoid the dangers (threats) to his life and to maintain his existence.

Since the discovery of "fire" and the invention of tools, man has gradually dominated the living and non-living worlds of the universe, that is, the entire material world. But in addition to the necessities of natural life, the courage to try to discover and develop various talents, as if the situation were critical, has been a matter of great importance.

For example, the unpredictable life at sea, where the situation is critical, the danger of not knowing in the morning what will become or what will happen in the evening, and the overwhelming desire to experience it, this unsatisfied ambition motivates the world's obsession to love and cling to something, someone, or something unknown. This insatiable ambition motivates people to develop something, someone or something relative or parallel in some scope or dimension.

"There is nothing more capable than man," in the words of Sophocles. Man's competence, his ability to do things, also understands, is familiar with, and uses his destiny.

One can find true inner peace only in the transcendent, and one cannot have long-lasting peace in the limited time of life's existence, unless time stops in the existence of life.

In the world, it is impossible to reach the highest level of attainment in a moment of peace, and things will always happen in succession; if a moment of fulfillment comes, the light of eternal rest will shine.

This moment is witnessed by the calmness of our inner mind, and this peace (of mind), without any disturbance, does not remain in the existential time of life. This calmness is only found in the Transcendental.

If man has not experienced this impact of life existence, and if he has not escaped from the existence of his own life existence and has not gone to the Transcendental, then he is not yet the self who has realized the existence of his own life existence. As long as man lives, he must always strive for the realization of the existence of his being.

Section 2: Conditional Existence

The philosophical doctrine of Jaspers is related to the fact that he had a congenital bronchiectasis (de:Bronchiektasen) since his childhood. This disease severely impaired his bodily functions and made him susceptible to infection.

According to his autobiography, it is confirmed that

he had to follow a strict method to maintain his health, and this was a considerable constraint on his life. During his studies, he studied the structure of the human body and the problem of disease, which made his life existence itself a matter that had to be solved, and thus, he had a deeper experience of the existence of life existence itself.

Therefore, I feel that the various kinds of knowledge of natural or social things that exist in life itself are the meanings that human beings give to the objects, and they are the spiritual contents that human beings transmit and communicate in the form of symbols.

At the same time, he feels that all spiritual contents, including intention, meaning, intent, understanding, knowledge, value, concept, etc., are communicated by human beings in the communication activities. The existence of the universe is the fact of the experience of the orbit of the universe; the existence of the self is the fact of the training of the life existence itself and the experience of daily life; the existence of God is the existence of the life existence itself and the fact of the cognitive religion.

Therefore, the existence of the universe should be studied by a certain object, based on experiments and logical reasoning, in order to seek unified and exact objective laws and truths; the existence of the self should be known by subjects that study universal and fundamental issues, including existence, knowledge, values, reason, mind, language, etc.

The existence of God should be known by the transcendental faith of human beings who are amazed and in awe of the mystery of the universe and life, which constitutes a doctrine of persuasion and punishment of evil, and is used to teach the world and make people believe.

Although each of the three kinds of existence has its own position, the human being who exists in life itself can be understood by means of a system of facts, ideas, concepts, feelings, values, and the existence of God. The process of passing on facts, thoughts, concepts, feelings, values, and attitudes to another person or group.

It is a complex process that not only transmits the content of the message, but also includes judging the meaning of the message. It is a complex process that not only transmits the content of the message, but also includes judging the meaning of the message so that the three existences can be connected. Therefore, his philosophical approach is based on the idea of

"Communication", which is a special focus of Jaspers.

The process is from the material existence of all things in the universe to the self-existence of man, and from the self-transcendence of existence to the metamorphosis and sublimation to the complete perfection of God.

This method of progression and metamorphic sublimation is jump thinking, which is a mode of thinking that does not follow logical steps, but jumps directly from the proposition to the answer (but not necessarily to the answer preset by the questioner), and then extends to other related possibilities.

Jasper believes that it is in these reciprocal encounters that individuals slowly become aware of themselves and know their own existence itself. Jaspers believes that it is only in these interactions that the individual becomes aware of himself, knows the meaning of his own existence, realizes his own existence, and fulfills the ideal of his own existence.

In other words, it is only through communication and interaction that an individual can clarify the existence of life itself and then realize the meaning of the existence of life itself.

His philosophy of mutual contact is based on the specific experience of human beings in the industrial society. He believes that the existence of human beings in the universe is like the gears cast in the gears of machinery.

Society is like a big gear, and the individual is like a small gear, turning and stopping with the big gear, and the individual has lost his own independent existence and cannot survive without the universe. The individual has lost his or her independent existence and cannot live apart from the universe.

However, the inner spirit of man is free to transcend all things in the universe and is not limited by space and time. Therefore, Jaspers advocates that man is a synthesis of material existence and spiritual life, realizing himself in the universe and in the faith of God.

The first and most concrete mutual contact is the state of interaction and mutual influence between human beings and the cosmic world, between human beings and things.

Man is the spirit of all things, successfully mastering the world according to or with confidence in thought, being able to identify a person or thing, being this person or thing rather than another world, or even partially modifying or completely renewing the original thing to make the world suitable for new needs, but due to the limits of normal emotion and reason that man has.

In the practice of daily life experience, people cannot grasp everything with the knowledge and experience they have gained, and they often encounter sudden setbacks and failures, so they must revive their spirits again and again and live by faith. To break through a certain state, limit, etc.

Therefore, life is to be diligent and serious, to make the best use of one's abilities, to be in constant contact with the world, to be in conflict with one's own limits, to tolerate many setbacks that do not achieve the intended purpose, and then to get up and do things with a positive attitude and with all one's strength.

In this way, people and the world can sharpen themselves through interactions with themselves and with people, and they will discover the various kinds of interconnections between people, between people and things, and between things and things.

In the midst of doubt and disappointment about the meaning of life, the only way to get along with others and with oneself is to believe that one's wishes and ideals can be realized.

From the state of interaction and mutual influence between human beings and things to the next level is the relationship between human beings and God, the absolute belief that human beings have and are different from other animals.

It is the basis for strengthening the meaning of the existence of life itself, as the nature of plants is directed toward the sun, so human nature is created toward God. There is a clear distinction between the creation of man and the creation of other beings. Man has a personality, that is, he can choose to love or to resist love through reason and will.

Therefore, man must be able to find the absolute You within himself, to be in constant contact with it, and to find a place of refuge from all sorrow, grief, suffering and disaster, in order to be free of defects and loopholes, and to satisfy himself.

As for the existence of individual life itself, it can never be self-sufficient, nor can everything in the material environment of the world satisfy his desires. Only the eternal, absolute, self-sufficient essence can stop the various demands of the mind to obtain something or to achieve a certain purpose.

Jasper's three kinds of interactions are to contact and communicate with each other, to find the meaning of existence in their own life existence itself.

The meaning of the existence of life itself is not isolated, but has both connotation and extension, and its connotation is expressed in the extension.

Therefore, he has always emphasized the importance of mutual contact, and the meaning of one's life existence itself is whether one can see the meaning of one's life existence itself in mutual contact.

This mission is to fulfill and realize the meaning of one's own existence, and to make the non-existent situation a reality.

He is deeply experienced in the words of the Bible: Jesus said, "The time has come for the Son of Man to be glorified. Truly I say to you, unless a grain of wheat falls into the ground and dies, it remains one grain; but if it dies, it bears many seeds. He who loves his life loses it.

And he who hates his life in this world will keep it to eternal life. (John 12). His "existence" was also about forgetting himself and giving to others. This thought was originally his experience of life, his own exceptions and loneliness, and it was only when he thought of the doctor helping his patients that he could grasp the true meaning of human relationships and truly understand that "loving people" is the will of God.

After Jasper's "elucidation of the true meaning of existence", he enters the stage of "realization of existence", where the focus is on mutual contact, and the knowledge of natural or social things by people who come into contact with each other is the meaning that people give to the object, and also the spiritual content that people transmit and communicate in the form of symbols.

All the spiritual contents that human beings communicate in their communication activities include intentions, meanings, intentions, perceptions, knowledge, values, concepts, and so on. Although there are two separate things in the "Explanation of Being" from God, from the world, and from oneself, in the end it comes down to the mutual contact with people, in caring for others, and in the action of loving people, realizing the meaning of existence of one's own life existence itself.

In the philosophical faith of Jaspers, he says that there must be someone in this world who is beyond this world, beyond the universe, and in the universe the former is called God. He reveals the term "transcendence".

In terms of "transcendental realm", all human cognition and practice, in terms of Buddhist materialism, will not go beyond the six consciousnesses, but at most the perceptions of the seven consciousnesses, the so-called "inspiration", which are not "transcendental realm".

"Transcendence" is the purest compassion and wisdom, which transcends the limitations of human beings as living creatures, to reach the realm of interrelationship with all things and the unity of heaven and man in the highest system of association.

It also includes the meaning of the "personality" of God, which is the manifestation of the existence of an intelligent being, and can be called the "center of life". Each person has one and only one personality, and so do the angels.

The personality of man is also called personality, while God has three "centers of life", i.e., one essence and three personalities, so called the Trinity. In other words, he is a theist who believes in the reality of God, in absolute moral law, in the phenomenal universe temporarily placed between God and existence, and in man's encounter with God in time.

Because the universe is the word of God, and man is incomplete, weak and incapable, and needs to rely on the transcendent God, man is in a restricted situation, in a situation of disappointment and faith, which is a good opportunity for man and God to communicate and come into contact with each other, and man is in the most painful When people are in the most painful and distressful situation, it is also the time when they can get the closest to God.

Personality of Life

The life of personality is the realization of the nature of life that exists in eternity. Then there are four types of beings with personality: first, human beings; second, angels; third, demons; and fourth, God.

The first three types of beings are created beings, and

their personality is the created personality. God is the essence of creation. God is not the creator, but the creator; all created beings are made by God, and created beings exist because of God's existence, and God's existence is self-existent and eternal, and His existence does not depend on another being.

Then God's existence is different in nature from that of the created beings. God's personality is the personality of creation, while the personality of the created beings is the personality of creation, which exists because of creation, not because it was created.

In other words, it is not "self-existent". In other words, it is not "self-existent". In the created world, only angels, demons, and human beings have a personality and can realize that their life lasts forever. The reason we are talking about the afterlife, eternal life, eternity, forever is because we have a personality.

This is an intrinsic characteristic of the higher forms of life created by God, animals and plants do not have this nature.

Angels are created to serve God's spirits, and are created to exist forever from the beginning of creation, and their number is limited. Then angels who sin and forsake God can never be forgiven of their sins, for they do not die, and this sin is carried on forever.

The devil is those angels who follow Satan in his apostasy from God, attempting to improve their position, degree or standard, but instead corrupting themselves, because they disobey God's will and wish to be equal with God.

Satan is the root of all sin and evil. "He was a murderer from the beginning, and did not keep the truth, for he did not have the truth in his heart; he lied out of himself, for he was a liar and the father of liars. (John 8:44) Although both the angelic and demonic realms are created by God in the same way as the human realm, there are differences because of the form of life and the mission God has given them.

The nature of God's own Trinity was revealed to us by God Himself through the Bible. The Son was born of the Father, and the Holy Spirit proceeded from the Father. The Holy Spirit is the Spirit of the Father and the Spirit of the Son, and has a personality in itself to do the work of revelation.

Christ said, "I and the Father are one. The unity of the Father and the Son and the Holy Spirit is a spiritual fellowship and unity, which is different from physical and mathematical logic. It is difficult for us to understand it unless God Himself reveals it.

For, having experienced firsthand the blows of illness and the life of captivity in the concentration camps of Germany under the Nazi regime, Jasper exhorted his countrymen that although man cannot understand God and know Him, he who believes in, worships, and holds a particular religion or doctrine as a rule and a guide for his actions and words, is a man of God. a rule and a guide for speech and action.

It is as if they are doing the will of God in secret, and they are following Him by the horns of His garment, and walking in the same way, having faith in His will, in order to break through all obstacles, to release their depression, and to be relieved of their inextricable entanglements, and to be finally relieved of their troubles and to be freed from their fetters. We will be free from the sire bondage, and thus gain freedom of mind and body.

Rational Criticism

The term "existence" is generally used to refer to the whole of all phenomena that continue to occupy time or space and have not yet disappeared, i.e. the so-called "universe" or "world", before it is explored repeatedly.

The focus of the question of existence is, of course, "my life existence". However, "man" is not only in a certain field or area of human activity, but is also inseparable from the world. For this reason, thinking about existence should begin with the exploration of "the sum of nature and human social activity".

While the mission of science is to explore directly the sum of nature and human social activity, philosophy is the study of universal, fundamental questions, including the fields of existence, knowledge, values, reason, mind, and language.

The first step of the work is not to supplement the facts recorded by science, but to reflect on a certain object as the scope of study, and to determine its value and meaning based on experiments and logical reasoning to obtain a unified and exact objective law and knowledge of truth; also It is to redo what Conde has done.

People in a normal state of mind in order to obtain the

expected results, have the confidence and courage to calmly face the status quo, and quickly and comprehensively understand the reality to analyze a variety of feasible solutions, and then judge the best solution and the ability to effectively implement it. The ability to analyze wrong or reactionary ideas, words and deeds with reason and justification, and then reject them.

The world is a system of objects composed of intrinsically related parts. Each component must have some kind of intrinsic relationship, or complementary functions, or common interests, or coordinated actions, etc. All possibilities are included in the existence of the "world".

The world is not only "out there", which is the modern society's term for everything, but it also refers to all its own "connotations". People may think that with a "world view" they can grasp the reality of the world, but this is not true; the most scientific "world view" only expresses my thoughts and feelings, my understanding of the world and my view of things.

It is impossible for science to reassemble the world through rectification and coordination into a whole that is completely outside of consciousness, that does not depend on the spirit, that does not depend on the will of man, and that is always in "my world" (umwelt); nor can we make all phenomena, combine the various parts and attributes of analyzed objects or phenomena into a unified whole: the world. into a unified whole.

The world is finite, but permanently expanding, so no single view of the world represents the only total reality. The only way to approach the reality is to break the tightly covered or closed mind and to permanently cast the mind into the ambition of innovation and transcendence.

Jasper points out that one cannot have a knowledge of the world that is completely consistent with the pattern, form or standard of existence and the actuality of the object, not only because this form of thinking, which reflects the nature of the object's properties, is nothing more than a concept left by the phenomenal world. concept, and

It is also because the world and man are closely connected to each other, and the world supports the situation so that it does not collapse on man, and the world and man constitute a close relationship, and the feelings are so harmonious that it is difficult to choose between them; in terms of the meaning of existence, the world and man in man are real bodies that do not distinguish between subject and object. Therefore, the "concept of the world" is also the extension and reflection of the human being.

Man is not willing to be a blind "being in the world"; he has an innate and unquenchable desire to understand himself and to think about the "world".

However, we should know that when our consciousness begins to think about the world, the world becomes an object in front of the thinker, in opposition to the subject of the thought, and the subject and the object are separated from the whole thing and from the whole (Spaltung). This objective existence is reflected in the "world" that is the result of the thinking activity in the human consciousness, which is certainly different from the world of the object.

Secondly, we usually say that this is true when things are examined as they are, independent of any personal feelings, prejudices or opinions, knowing that the object is reliable because it can be explained in terms of reason, so that the person concerned can understand it.

Finally, the object must be accepted by any thinking

person for no more than three reasons: as a logical matter of course, as a mathematical necessity, and as verified by empirical science. All three of these reasons indicate the ability of human beings to use reason.

In contrast to the concept of sensibility, it usually refers to the ability of humans to reason their way to reasonable conclusions after careful consideration of the evidence. It is related to the fact that nature exists independently of any conditions and is constant and unchanging: in other words, nature "embraces" reason, and reason embraces nature.

In the narrow sense, it usually refers to the earth, the globe, where human beings live today, but more so to space.

In a broader sense, it can be equated to the universe, which includes the space beyond the earth. Therefore, we are faced with the problem of two worlds, the objective and the subjective, and we need to know that there is a distinction between the subject and the object in our thinking, because we cannot avoid the splitting of the subject and the object in our way of thinking, but in fact the subject and the object follow each other.

According to the philosophical viewpoint of Jasper, when "man" repeatedly thinks and explores an "object", the process of analysis, synthesis, judgment, reasoning and other cognitive activities on the basis of images and concepts will be separated from "man's" thinking.

If one takes "oneself" as the object of one's own brain's generalization and indirect reaction to objective things through language, then one becomes an "object" (Object), and at the same time, one is still a "thinking self".

This "thinking ego", although thinking about "itself", cannot be considered as an "object", because the "it" of the person or thing to which all human activities are directed, determines the "objectness" of all objects.

Moreover, the relationship between subject and object is so closely connected in the individual events of the world and me that the connotations of subject and object "embrace" each other, and the process of analysis, synthesis, judgment, reasoning and other cognitive activities on the basis of images and concepts is extremely common.

It is impossible to imagine the "world" without making it the subject of it; on the contrary, in recognizing it as my subjective world, if I consider this abstract and universal idea to be a domain or class of entities, events or relationships, I have invisibly arranged it into the thinking of the objective world.

If one wants to understand the world and try to see the laws in the world, it is even less necessary to mention.

According to Jasper's book "The Way of Wisdom", "In thinking beyond "object knowledge", we are still not detached from this thing, the extent to which it has reached or the condition in which it manifests itself, and even when we are able to see through the "phenomenon", it (the phenomenon) still holds us tightly. Even when we can see through the "phenomenon", it (the phenomenon) still holds us tightly, and there is still implication in transcendence.

The opposite is also true: we cannot make ourselves stand in the objective without any condition, without any limitation.

"It is impossible for "man" to exclude himself completely, because what makes something objective is man's mind; and any experience consists of the subject world. For this reason, according to the philosophy of

Jaspers, the view of things or problems from a certain standpoint or perspective.

No matter how hard one tries, one cannot make oneself stand on the only true point of view, because the best and purest general idea, or the organization of ideas in thinking, is still connected with the position or point of departure from which I observe things, with the knowledge or skill that I have acquired from many practices. I am still connected to the position or point of departure from which I observe things, to the knowledge or skills I have acquired through many practices.

Thus, according to Jaspers' view of things or problems of philosophical thinking, the understanding of the world as a system of objects composed of intrinsically related parts can be obtained only in two ways: first, either by grasping the objective world as a whole (das All); second, by grasping the sum of the subjective viewpoints (das Ganze); however, these two grasps of the whole are obvious. However, it is obvious that it is impossible to grasp the whole in both cases. When one tries one's best to construct one's world as a philosophical system, one forms only a "cosmology" (eine Weltanschauung).

This cosmology is only one view of the world, which

constitutes a standard of value and gives life a certain limited meaning.

It expresses only one's understanding of the world, in the way or manner indicated or suggested [above]; this "cosmology" has a particular meaning only for the "man" who seeks to enter it, who wishes to live in it.

But it is not yet a scientific theory that can be universally understood and proven, and even if it is expressed in objectively common terms by philosophers such as Spinoza or Hegel, it is only an expression of some personal perceptions. even if it is expressed in objectively common language by philosophers like Spinoza or Hegel, it only reveals some personal perception. The various "world systems" are always only a specific range of knowledge that has been wrongly "absolutized" and "universalized".

For example, philosophically, Spinoza was a monist or pantheist. He believed that there was only one supreme entity in the universe (later called the Spinoza entity), the universe itself as a whole, and that God and the universe were one and the same.

His conclusion was based on a set of definitions and

axioms, and was arrived at by logical reasoning. Spinoza's God includes not only the material world (extensiveness) but also the spiritual world (thought). He considered human intelligence to be a component of the highest physical intelligence.

Spinoza also believed that this entity was the "inner cause" of everything, and that it ruled the world through natural laws, so that everything that happens in the material world has its own necessity.

Only God has total freedom in the world, while man can never obtain free will, although he can try to remove the fetters of the external. If we can see things as inevitable, then the easier it is for us to become one with God. Thus, Spinoza suggests that we should see things "sub specie aeternitatis" (under the eternal phase).

Secondly, Spinoza also argued that everything perceived by the senses exists only and only through the existence of a supreme entity, and that everything in the world in the pure sense (without reflection on the supreme entity) is only an illusion.

In his book "Ethics" he explains that "existence belongs to the nature of the entity" Spinoza gives the example of the circle. If the circle is compared to the Supreme Entity (or God), and a cross is arbitrarily drawn inside the circle to form a right angle (implying the formation and existence of everything in the world), then there are infinitely many right angles inside the circle.

But if the circle (the supreme entity) did not exist, there could be no angles, and there could be no so-called "right angles" (of everything). Although the right angle did not exist before it was drawn, the idea of the right angle itself was implicit in the circle, while the idea of everything, according to Spinoza, was originally implicit in the Supreme Entity.

Hegel points out that his concept of God can be called "worldlessness," but on the other hand, there is a close connection between the form of the concept of "world" and the technique or means of acquiring that concept.

Thus, according to Jasper, the idea that "the world is a whole that can be tested and explored" is closely linked to the unrealistic illusion that "the world can be completely and once and for all mastered and possessed".

"Only sufficient knowledge leads to "non-knowledge" that corresponds to objective facts, so that "being" that corresponds to objective facts does not lead to confident knowledge in any act of "knowing" and "identifying" a subject, and that such knowledge The "world system" that has the potential to be used for a specific purpose will be revealed within the fullness of "non-knowledge".

But Jasper argues that "non-knowledge" can only be attained through scientific cognition. And "non-knowledge" can never be separated from the process of scientific acquisition of knowledge through the formation of concepts, perceptions, judgments, or mental activities such as imagination.

It is also impossible to obtain the top of the development of knowledge before having scientific cognition. It is the point at which cognition is unable to exert itself or to solve a problem. Our "consciousness" of "existence" finds its indispensable origin or source in "non-knowledge", but only in that full, acquired non-knowledge.

Obviously, the technique of seeking unified and exact objective laws and truths based on experiments and logical reasoning with a certain object as the scope of study is the division of different things, which does not only occasionally encounter "boundaries", but is inherently included.

It can only perform its functions and effects on certain individual things "according to the laws of things", but "cannot change the laws"; it cannot create, but can only transform existing materials; it cannot make people transcend the material conditions of life It can't create, but only transform existing materials; it can't make people transcend the materiality of life.

Finally, consider whether the so-called "objective world of science" really constitutes a whole. Jasper thinks it is unlikely, not necessarily. Because he believes that there are "coupures" in the world that do not make the world a whole.

The real world shows the following four dimensions, or four "primordial worlds" (mondes originaux). Each of these four "primordial worlds" has its own nature, its own content.

First, matter, which has weight, occupies a place in space, and can be known by the senses; it is something that can be counted and measured.

Second, life: the ability of living organisms to move, is a special, complex, advanced form of material movement, is a system of proteins and nucleic acids. The phenomenon of life includes metabolism, growth and development, genetic mutation and induction movement. It is something organized and directed.

Third, the soul or mind: one refers to a non-material thing that is said to be attached to the human body as the master. consciousness to understand, it is something that can express feelings.

Fourth, the spirit: human consciousness, thinking activities and general mental state, the ability to understand and experience the content of things, it is the mind, it can create a history.

If we look more closely at the spiritual dimension, it also has many different levels of interpretation: for example, religion, science, art, and so on. However, the different levels of cognition formed by concepts must not be confused with the concepts formed by levels, otherwise they will be contradictory and cannot be justified, resulting in what Kant called "dichotomy", where "the public says that the public is right and the public says that the public is justified". Logical reasoning in the study of things can only be interpreted at the same level.

If there are two different levels of concepts, logical reasoning can only be established if they are translated into a common level through the description of each level. Logical reasoning is rational, but levels and hierarchies are equally important concerns for philosophy.

The dialectical method seeks to unify the law of opposites and must pay attention to the dialectical thinking between levels and dimensions, between levels and dimensions. For this reason, Jasper argues, the so-called "whole world" is thus torn apart.

Furthermore, exploring the world and engaging in physical or mental labor plays a productive role that can never be accomplished according to the desired goal. Exploring the world is a result that an individual or a system wants to achieve, and will plan for it, in order to try to achieve a defined world.

But this work immediately encounters two insurmountable problems: the first is the "unboundedness" of matter; the second is the unconditionality of thought, unbounded in space and time, without beginning or end.

Although we know that science will always make new

discoveries, there will always be "everything else" outside of the thinking activity of the human mind that reflects the characteristics and connections of objective things and reveals their meanings and effects on human beings.

Moreover, the existence of matter will always have infinite possibilities, which, when they differ, also testify to their "limits". For this reason, the "world as a whole" is not a completed fact, it is merely a "boundary thought".

In Kantian philosophical terms, it is an idea, which is in fact nothing, but which constantly urges and guides the spirit of man in his quest for the reality of truth.

Jasper says: "The direct consciousness of man, and the systematic work of the scientist, both coincide in the pursuit of the unchanging truth of the world. This desire cannot be complete, but it will continue to be, and will always be, the path of research into the meaning of life's existence, in terms of the position from which philosophical ideas are analyzed or criticized.

Jasper's cognition of the world as described above refers to the process of acquiring knowledge through mental activities such as forming concepts, perceptions, judgments, or imaginations, and conducting a reasoned analysis of wrong or reactionary thoughts, words, and deeds, and thereby rejecting them.

From there, a negative discourse occurs as a result of two things: first, as a result of the effort to explore the world, it is prepared to enter into philosophical reflection with the consciousness of the human mind; second, it outlines in advance this study of universal, fundamental issues of the discipline, including existence, knowledge, values, reason, mind, and language. The second is that it outlines the contours of this study of universal and fundamental issues, including existence, knowledge, value, reason, mind, language, and other areas of inquiry.

We all know the holistic, fundamental and critical inquiry into the real world and human beings. The true meaning of philosophy is as a way of inquiry, not just as a specific, specialized body of knowledge.

In other words, the most important spirit of philosophy is to "break through the sand", to inquire into the whole world of existence or into human beings themselves, and this inquiry is not fragmented, for it must be done in the face of the whole of reality and the whole of human beings.

Therefore, it is not an "objective knowledge", it is not something that one "has" to accept, and it has no connection with the mood or meditation of one's life.

However, philosophy cannot use objective facts, reflected in the human consciousness, to produce the results of thinking activities, otherwise it will fall into the violation of the most basic human view of life, morality, values, to show the cruelty and violence of society, uncivilized and irrational things.

Therefore, it is the result of thinking or the mental process of cognition. It is the key to the deviation of cognition caused by human viewpoints or social consciousness, but through it, the objective existence is reflected in human consciousness, and the results or viewpoints formed through thinking activities can have the opportunity to understand the true meaning of life existence, metamorphose beyond and sublimate to the realm of "unthinkable".

Section 3 Unconditional Existence

Generally speaking, the question that requires an answer must have a purpose for the existence of the thing itself, and it is also a factor that influences the existence and development of the thing, which is sufficient to attract people to study and discuss the issue.

For example, what is the "meaning of life"? For example, what is the "meaning of life's existence"? This is the purpose of life's existence, the place, the situation, or the result that one wants to achieve. This is the question that absolute immanence demands an answer or answer to.

Therefore, when it comes to the unconditional existence of life itself, one must first understand the meaning of Jasper in several philosophical points: its meaning is in reference to the enternal, to being.

It means, therefore, "absolute reliability" and "loyalty," and these properties do not arise naturally, but come from our "decision to choose. Such choices can only be perceived by going back and rethinking the past and learning from it.

Therefore, this "unconditionality" requires an "existential decision" through "reflection". This also means that it does not occur from the existence of human life itself and from the "natural state", but is generated from the awareness within the "freedom" of the will, and "freedom" is necessary and

It is not because of any "natural law" but because it has a "foundation" in "transcendence". This "unconditional" awareness determines the ultimate basis of one's life and the unconditional existence of life itself, whether it is a meaningful life or a meaningless one.

It is only in those extreme situations that it determines one's path by a silent decision. Although it often supports "life" through "existence", it can also be elaborated in an infinite way.

Just as a path extends to the depths of a dense forest (the end of life), so a person whose life is full of existence is rooted in this "unconditionality. The root of "unconditional existence" is from the nature of the self; the inner self that develops and supports the self in the dark, so that the existence of our being itself is not just "myself" in the mind.

The "unconditional existence" of the existence of our being is the "message" transmitted by the "essence of the self" to the existence of the "life experience experience" of my being. When it comes to me in my life existence, I realize that it is because of its existence that I am in the absence of my existence.

"Unconditioned existence" is not an established nature like "experiential existence". It is within the human heart, as it should be. It is only when the ego overcomes its own submission to the ego and moves towards the path of right "decision" that the existence of this "unconditioned" life itself will be realized.

In "ordinary, common life existence", this "unconditionality" is often revealed in the experience of "extreme situations" of temporal existence. When following the "unconditional" guidance of the existence of life itself, we are given a choice.

The "decision to choose" then becomes the "essence" that awakens it; in every language, goodness is usually the positive attribute of being right and desirable. Evil is the opposite of good, a negative attribute that is wrong and that one does not want. Good and evil involve a moral judgment, and the distinction between right and wrong, good and evil, is a common proposition in all human cultures.

Therefore, the being of "unconditional" life itself

chooses what it considers to be "good" in the choice between good and evil.

In short, the so-called evil is a person who lives and dies in a state of confusion, who is drunk today, and who lives in a state of flux and uncertainty, with the mode of existence of "getting by" day after day, like an animal that only seeks to reproduce and survive.

On the contrary, goodness is the kind of life that "does not reject the happiness of this society, but is governed by the norms of human behavior that distinguish between good and evil, and the right and wrong.

It is the life that "is morally permissible" as the universal law of all right conduct, and it is also "absolute" in its mutuality. Let us now compare this issue of the unconditional existence of life itself in three levels.

First, at the first level, between good and evil, "morality" is the sum of the norms of human behavior to distinguish between good and evil. In Western philosophy, morality is mostly regarded as a certain nature of communication between human beings and human beings or between human beings and things, and is included in ethics, the question is whether our "natural inclination" is dominated by a will to obey moral laws.

In terms of deontology, Imm. Kant argues that man has reason, and that it is only when he practices virtue in obedience to his own reason that he reveals his original value and ceases to be an individual subject to the laws of natural cause and effect. Virtue is something that other animals lack, and can only be accomplished by those who have reason and act in accordance with reason.

Man is part of the natural world and is subject to the laws of nature, i.e., he must eat when he is hungry and give vent to his desires, but he is also rational and will consider the legitimacy and legality when he pursues the satisfaction of natural needs.

Therefore, when man can take reason as the guide of action and follow the law generated by it as the principle of action, he has detached himself from the natural biological side and has reached a dignified and unique being.

The reason why man has morality is to show the value of his existence, and morality refers to the behavior of the actor when reason legislates itself, and is therefore a spontaneous action that is not constrained by external factors. To borrow the words of Kant, that is, "Duty is opposed to inclination.

Second, at the second level, good and evil are related by ethic: ethics (English: Ethics or Moral Philosophy), also known as moral philosophy or moral science, is a philosophical discipline that focuses on moral values.

In this context, "morality" is defined as all the norms of behavior recognized by a group of people or a culture: ethics attempts to construct a theoretical system of laws that guide behavior and to critically evaluate them.

Ethics involves defending and encouraging right behavior and discouraging wrong behavior. Together with aesthetics, the field of ethics deals with the question of values, and therefore constitutes another branch of philosophy called value theory.

Ethics aims at defining concepts such as good and evil, right and wrong, virtue and vice, righteousness and crime, to solve moral problems and to explore what is wise or foolish: as a field of intellectual inquiry, moral philosophy is also related to moral psychology, descriptive ethics and values. It takes as an element the "authenticity of our motives".

Therefore, ethics, as defined from the perspective of interpersonal relationships, is the moral code that should be observed when dealing with the interrelationships between people, families, societies, and nations, and is the moral code that individuals must follow when living in a group society.

If there is no ethical supervision, it will easily lead to conflicts and turmoil. The "purity" of the "unconditional" is opposed to the "impurity" of the inverted "power-change" relationship, because in such a relationship, the "unconditional" is only attached to various "real conditions".

Third, at the third level, the relationship between "good" and "evil" has become "mepathysical": "metaphysics" is a division of philosophy, which is the Chinese translation of the English Metaphysics.

It is the study of the real, i.c., the common denominator of all things and the properties that this common denominator possesses. Metaphysics was first introduced by Aristotle in the fourth century B.C. It is the study of the supramaterial, the supersensible, or the superpresent. Also known as "ontology," "first philosophy," and "entity theory," metaphysicians attempt to articulate the basic concepts (domains) that people use to understand the world.

For example, existence, objects and their properties, space and time, cause and effect, and possibility. One of the main subdisciplines of metaphysics is ontology, the study of fundamental areas and their interrelationships.

Another major branch of metaphysics is cosmology, the study of the origin (if any), the basic structure, nature, and cosmic dynamics, in which the relationship is based on the motives themselves, with love and hate as opposites, love enabling being and hate destroying being. Love contributes to being, while hate destroys being and contributes to nonbeing.

"Love grows in conjunction with the unconditional metamorphosis of transcendence; hate, however, shrinks to the abstract and strict adherence to the ego with the unconditional total and complete abandonment and rejection.

"Love is engaged in the construction of silence in the world, while hate is like a loud catastrophe that drowns existence in the quagmire of empirical existence and obscures the appearance of the dawn of the essence of unconditional empirical existence.

This "decision of choice" explains the sequence of the three things described earlier, each with its own different and unusual thing, and the form and nature of things from an objective point of view.

In moral terms, one wants to establish one's "decision to choose" from the beginning, arising from "thought": in ethical terms, one is "regenerated by metamorphosis" through "the will to do good in silence without wishing others to know", and one is reborn from "erroneous cognition".

In "metaphysics," for questions that cannot be answered directly through perception, the answer is deduced through rational logical reasoning under a priori conditions (which can be seen as axiomatic assumptions) and cannot be contradicted by empirical evidence. It is an awareness of being given to oneself.

Thus, "unconditional existence" chooses the "right" viewpoint and lives in the positive power of "love". Only when these three levels become one is this "unconditional existence" realized.

It seems that "to live out of love" already contains

(mostly in abstract things) all the rest, and that a genuine deep feeling for people or things can give ethical truth to various "acts of love". However, we human beings cannot live by the power of this highest level of "love" alone, because we are often confused and blindly caught up in all kinds of mistakes and misunderstandings.

Since we can never blindly rely on our "love" every second of every day, we have to clarify our loyalty to people or things with deep feelings. And for the same reason, we "finite beings" need that "discipline" we use to restrain ourselves, and because of our various "impure" motives, we need "distrust" of ourselves. The "discipline" that we use to restrain ourselves is needed because of our various motives of impurity, and the "distrust of ourselves".

Only this "unconditional" characteristic of "goodness" can give full content to the mere "obligation", and can further our various "ethical motives", and can dissolve the "destructive will" of "hate" with strong feelings of hostility or dissatisfaction towards people or things.

Section 4. Freedom, Command, and "Unconditional Being."

However, the unconditional basis of love is based on the fact that love has a deep feeling for people or things, and is consistent with the will to seek the "authentic reality", which cannot be justified without the heart to love it.

According to Jasper, we become aware of our "free existence" when we accept the freedom, the commands, and the "unconditional existence" imposed on our being. We cannot seriously deny the decision that we "must choose the fact of decision" whether we practice or escape these commands, and we must decide about ourselves with this decision of choice.

At the same time, we are responsible for our own actions, for making them more obviously oppositional; "unconditional being" does not want to hide them from the world, but to let "unconditional being" be exposed to the light of day. We have the potential for good, but also the tendency to do evil.

Therefore, we must have the ability to exercise self-control and self-discipline in order to do good and avoid evil, and to change our ways for the better. We have moments of weakness, faintness, and blinded reason, so we also need some external rules and prohibitions to supplement our weakness of will power, to remind us how to stop and how not to transgress.

My will is free, "in the freedom of "unconditional existence", in the detailed analysis of the rules, in a certain cognitive understanding, in the understanding of the ethical commandments that I should obey wholeheartedly. This command is tied to the understanding that I am a consciousness enclosed in "transcendence".

All men are born equal and free; but freedom must be tempered and respected in order to achieve true freedom. Therefore, the commandment or prohibition is usually meant to be instructive and preventive, so that people do not, through their own weakness or momentary confusion, do things that harm others rather than themselves, and destroy the harmony of the community.

Jasper uses love to illustrate why a truly free person can accept "unconditional existence". According to Jaspers, love is inherently uncoercive, and no one can decide for our will even if we don't want to, because freedom of will cannot be coerced.

When we are free to make decisions, and life does have meaning because of them, we know that we do not form ourselves by our own power; at the peak of our freedom, that is, in our freest activity, we feel that we really "must do this to ourselves". It is not compelled by an external and irresistible law of nature, so as to understand that "we" are "given ourselves unconditionally" by the transcendent.

Jasper repeatedly pays special attention to "existence" or the idea of "being", or puts emphasis on it, stating that "the existence of life itself" is the basic core value of human beings, and that it is not just "being", "living", etc., as is commonly understood.

Not only that, if social science can cover things, then the so-called soul, mind, spirit, ego, and body are the realms that prove all the time that modern philosophers have in their hearts In this way, these realms of what we call soul, mind, spirit, ego, body, etc., are all the time evidence of the mutual interference (conflict) of opposing, incompatible forces or natures (such as concepts, interests, will) within the minds of modern philosophers.

There is a paradoxical layer of interdependence or coexistence between existence and the world, which cannot exist independently of each other and at the same time cannot be merged into one, while the world is knowable and existence must be understood by the situation in which it is situated (mostly unfavorable situations). The Elucidation of Existenz

The Elucidation of Existenz. For Jaspers, "situation" is essentially a level of experience that encompasses both the physical and the psychological aspects of everyday life.

The human being, as the "being" of life existence itself, always has to exist in a particular situation, and as soon as he leaves one situation, he immediately enters another one.

Among these situations, there are certain situations that we can change or transform, but there are also certain situations that we cannot change, for example, I was born in a certain family at a certain time and place, and this cannot be changed.

In other words, there is an indeterminable quality to "existential situations". When the "existence" of life itself disappears in an instant, the situation ceases to "exist".

This situation, which is beyond our ability to change, is called "Grenzsituation" by Jasper.

They differ only in the way and manner in which life itself "exists". They are like a wall that prevents us from acting, and ultimately frustrates us.

Not only can we not exclude these situations from our experience, but they can happen to us unexpectedly at any time. At the level of "living experiential things" in life existence itself, we think that we can escape from boundary situations by closing our eyes.

However, in the end, we are powerless to do anything but give in to the situations that we encounter in the end, despite the fact that we have expanded our means of preserving our existence in the world.

Therefore, the meaningful way we respond to "boundary situations" is not to plan or calculate how to overcome them, but to act differently to achieve our potential "being"; we do so through a clear consciousness of We fulfill ourselves by facing boundary situations with clear awareness.

Our awareness of "boundary situations" is limited to the external, and the reality of these situations can only be clarified by the "presence" of life itself. The experience of "boundary situations" is the same thing as existence.

According to Jasper, the "boundary realm" can be said to have a double function: on the one hand, it is the most common phenomenon internal to our consciousness, and on the other hand, it opens up the hierarchy of experience towards the transcendental reality.

"Boundary realm changes our perception of the "existence" of life itself, thus allowing us to realize ourselves. It is a kind of leaping thinking, or non-linear thinking, which is a kind of jumping from a proposition to an answer (but not necessarily the answer that the questioner presupposes) without following logical steps.

It is a process of "Sprung" thinking that extends to other related possibilities. We may feel confused and desperate if we are not able to transform and ascend in a bounded situation, but we may also transform and ascend in a historical, unique, and non-replaceable way. We may also, in a historical, unique, and non-replaceable way, metamorphose from life existence itself to "being".

According to Jaspers in his book "Philosophy", the metamorphosis from "experiencing things" to "being" in the "boundary situation" can be divided into three steps.

First, because of the vagaries of all things, I metamorphose from experiential things in the world to the "substantial solitude of the universal cognizer" (substantiellen Einsamkeit des universal Wissenden).

I can exist in this world, but I can face all things ruthlessly. I do not want to interfere with the chaos of the world, but I can exist objectively in all objects and phenomena, being both inside and outside them at the same time. I can even face myself as a stranger.

This kind of overcoming of "self-existence" happens, and in absolute solitude, all the things that happen in the world that should be in the world without living in it are suspicious, and all things, including oneself, are unpredictable; but at the same time, one stands outside the world and observes the world with a cold eye.

Secondly, because I finally could not break away from the world that had frustrated me, I made a metamorphosis from thinking about things

"Erheiien moglicher Existenz" (revealing the possible existence). Because through the first step of metamorphosis to leap beyond the world, I find that I still cannot leave the level of "being" and "experiencing things" in the life existence itself, and as a possible being who cares about the reality, I still cannot leave the concrete situation of life experience.

The fact that I am always in a particular situation, and definitely not a collection of pure possibilities, is also a boundary situation. As a "possible being" I must take a second step of metamorphosis, from the solitude of self-existent awareness to the awareness of "possible being", in order to illustrate those, not so obvious, "boundary situations".

Third, the metamorphic leap from "possible existence" at the "experiential level" of life existence itself to "real existence in marginal situations" (wirkliche Existenz in Grenzsituationen).

After this metamorphic leap in the "being" of life itself, life seems simply to be there differently. The "self" has a new meaning, and the metamorphosis of the "being" of life itself does not follow some observable law, like the growth of life.

It is the unconscious and unconditional inner action that takes one from "before" to "after". This metamorphic leap originates in one's own self, and therefore one has already the possibility of "self-existence" in this source, and this metamorphic leap brings one to reality and makes me realize my own "existential" self in life existence itself.

These three metamorphic leaps are related to each other, but they are not just a series of ascensions in the same direction. They occur interactively with each other. When they lose their relationship to each other, each metamorphic leap will go astray.

The "boundary state" is a great test for each of us: if we look at it from the level of "being" and "experiencing things" at the level of life itself, the "boundary state" brings us nothingness, the boundary means that there is nothing on the other side of the boundary. But if we metamorphose to the level of "existence" of the being itself, the boundary means that what we encounter beyond the boundary is the real existence, which is "beyond the boundary".

In addition, Jaspers cites four specific boundary situations, namely, death (Tod), suffering (Leiden), struggle (Kampf), and guilt (Schuld).

The objective fact of death is not considered to be death in the "realm of boundaries," but only when one feels existential anguish over the death of one's loved one or over one's own death does death reach the "realm of boundaries. The same is true of suffering. Only physical pain or suffering from illness is not suffering in the "boundary realm.

It is only when we share the pain of others as our own, when we share the pain with others, that such pain will awaken our understanding of the "existence" of life itself and lead us to the transcendent realm of transformation and ascension.

As for the "struggle", only the "struggle of love" for the purpose of existence can enter the "realm of boundaries". If anyone can always ask himself to keep a clear conscience and avoid moral guilt, he will be able to understand the above-mentioned death, pain, and suffering.

It may be easier for him to bear the death, suffering, and struggles mentioned above. But even if a morally blameless peccadillo is willing to do the silent good he seeks at all costs, for the sake of the value of life, and without wishing others to know, he will still inevitably meet with defeat.

Guilt is an inescapable burden of conscience. "Every action in the world has consequences that the doer could not have foreseen. Even if the actor never expected these consequences, he will be shocked when he learns that he caused them.

But the guilt of this "boundary situation" can metamorphose and sublimate into the only positive force. When the ego makes a certain decision, it is aware that the consequences of the action will reach uncharted territory, and I cannot foresee the unanticipated encounter there and suffer the responsibility of being in my "boundary situation.

This responsibility is assumed by the "existential pathos" (existentielle Pathos) of the human existence in the "boundary situation", which is not directly observable in my existence (Dasein), but can be seen from the indexes issued by its situation or Situation to it. This situation (mostly unfavorable) is the manifestation that enables us to understand the existence of the Self.

Self-existence" first of all describes the situation (mostly unfavorable situation) in which one is in a "boundary situation": I am "there" (da-sein), I am in the "world" environment (umwelt), placed in a certain environment, the "existence" of life existence itself must "exist" in a situation. Existence" is the basic boundary of the existence of life.

It is obvious that Jasper's thinking about existence is based on the fact of self-experience or on the environment or context of things, which he expects to be his unique self. First he experienced the "boundary situation" from his own weak and powerless situation.

The powerlessness that Jasper experienced due to his poor health and the developmental factors of his workplace, and the various situations that led him from law to medicine, and from medicine and psychology to become a philosopher, together with the factor of his Jewish wife under Nazi politics In addition, he was subjected to repeated dangers and oppressions under Nazi politics, so that from time to time he experienced firsthand the "boundary situations" that existed in his own reality in marginal situations.

Through certain means of writing (e.g., vivid language, simple and straightforward dialogue), he depicts his appearance and the state of his inner world in concrete terms, saying, "We are always in a certain situation.

Circumstances change, and opportunities come and go. If I lose an opportunity, it may never come again. I can try to change my situation, but some situations cannot be changed; for example, I must die, suffer, struggle; I wait in the clutches of chance and guilt.

These are the "boundary situations" from which we cannot completely escape, nor can we completely change them. ...... Think carefully and understand," and these "boundary situations" are one of the most profound philosophical sources of philosophical reflection.

Jasper highlights these boundaries: the pendulum of chance, suffering, impotence, the unknowable future, the unreliability of world society, disease, aging, and finally "total failure", the inevitable death. Freedom, command and "unconditional command".

According to Jasper, we become aware of the "freedom" of our own will when we accept the fate that has been imposed on us. Whether we fulfill or evade these commands, or whether it is a decision entirely of our own choosing. We cannot seriously deny the fact that "we must choose our own decisions" and, moreover, decide what concerns us by doing so.

At the same time, we should be responsible for our own actions. In his book "The Spiritual Condition of Modern Man", he pointed out that only those who can exercise self-restraint have the right to enjoy freedom.

"The essence of freedom is the conflict and struggle between two contradictory parties, and it is not willing to make incompatible things give up some of their opinions and principles to each other in order to avoid disputes or conflicts, but rather to make their mutual hostility and rejection more obvious; it is not willing to cover it up. It is not willing to cover it up, but to let it be exposed to the light of day.

Jasper's emphasis on the existence of individual life, "being", is a very distinctive and special symbol of contemporary "philosophy of existence". "Being" is the pivot of the process of analysis, synthesis, judgment, and reasoning of Jaspers' philosophy on the basis of appearances and concepts.

But it cannot be written down or spoken about in a universal way. It is a possibility that is inherent in every person, and Jasper believes that "existence" has two distinctive features.

First, it is unique, and each individual person, as long as he or she is sincere and honest to touch others from the bottom of his or her heart and eventually gain their trust, is different from the ordinary, different from other things, and is a historical, non-abstract, non-generalized, and clearly detailed being. In this sense, Jasper uses the term "being" to refer to individual persons.

In this sense, existence is a kind of organization, structure, and pattern of things, and Jaspers, through historicity, freedom, choice, etc., uses the term "existence" to refer to the individual.

In the process of knowing, from perceptual knowledge to rational knowledge, the common intrinsic characteristics of the perceived things are abstracted, described in general terms, and visualized by using various rhetorical techniques. The rhetorical techniques include metaphor, simile, exaggeration, pun, and prose, etc. Through descriptions, people or things can be made vivid and concrete, giving people a clear feeling of it.

In addition, Jaspers often uses the term "possible existence" because "existence" in principle can never be realized. The realization of each being comes from some specific and limited creation, some objectification of the self. But "existence" is still the origin or source of things, an unconditional, spatially and temporally unbounded, beginningless and endless possibility.

Therefore, the individual as "being" is completely beyond everything he always thinks he is right, always thinks he knows or what he does. Each Being is the original, naturally arising depth of each ego, free from external influences, the will to become the true self.

"Existence cannot be grasped through a cognitive consciousness, such as sensation, perception, illusion, imagination, concept, etc., but only through a detailed explanation that is not abstract, not general, but clear in its details, so that the profound truth can be understood.

In other words, Existenzerhellung is the possibility of decision, which has its origin in time and can only be mastered in the time of existence.

Chapter 4: The Elements of Authentic Existenz

Section 1: Existence and Communication

Communication is the process of transmission and feedback of thoughts and feelings between people, between people and groups, in order to achieve unanimity of thoughts and smoothness of feelings, and also the process of behavior in which different subjects realize the two-way flow of information through various carriers to form the perception of the subject in order to achieve a specific goal.

This process includes not only verbal and written language, but also physical language, personal habits and ways, physical environment, and anything that gives meaning to information, for example, the consciousness level usually includes: emotions, knowledge, thoughts, etc.; the behavior level usually includes: actions, activities, habits, etc.; the organization level usually includes: performance goals, action plans, team atmosphere, etc.

What is communication? Communication is the process of exchanging information. Communication is to tell others what they want to know and what they don't understand, and to answer what the other side doesn't understand, according to the dictionary.

According to the dictionary: each other to provide each other with what they have; it turns out that the two words do not mean the same thing, but also very different, one is to tell their own ideas to each other to understand; the other needs to understand each other's ideas, and find ways to add their own ideas to eventually reach agreement.

Today, one of my community friends sent me a text message, "Dude, are you free tonight? There's a party at the Promenade Brewery at 7pm, you're welcome to bring your family. I double-checked the time on my phone. I was pressed for time and wanted to give an explanation.

"Thank you for the invitation, but I have to take my kids to the summer pool camp, so I'm afraid I won't be able to make it, so I'll talk to you some other time. Later, sitting on a row of chairs by the pool, I thought for a while and replied with seven words: "I'll talk to you some other time. Thank you.

Suddenly I realized that a short reply was enough, no need to explain the reason in detail, no need to talk nonsense, just express the goodwill of the other party, I feel it and express my gratitude. This is communication, communication is to understand what the other person means, and then see what you can give to the other person.

In the evening, I was about to take the kids to the summer pool camp to learn swimming, and they were having a great time with a group of kids, and the room was filled with the sound of kids playing.

So I raised my voice to attract the attention of the children and asked loudly, "To go or not to go? If so, what time do you want to go? The pool closes at 9 p.m." and without saying a word, he immediately changed his clothes and picked up his backpack to hurry me along.

Therefore, the philosophical community currently finds it difficult to define (communicate) what metaphysics is and what are the objects of metaphysical research. Ancient and medieval philosophers may have said that metaphysics, like chemistry or astrology, is defined by the seriousness of its subject matter, or by the subject matter that has yet to be resolved.

Metaphysics is the "science" of "being as such" or "the first causes of things" or "things that do not change".

For two reasons, it is no longer possible to define metaphysics in this way. First, a philosopher's denial of the existence of those things that were once considered to constitute the subject matter of metaphysics (the first causes of things or things that do not change) would now be considered to form the assertion of metaphysics as a result.

Second, there are now many philosophical questions that are considered to be metaphysical (or at least partly metaphysical) that have nothing to do with primary causes or invariable things, for example, the question of free will or the question of morality. This raises the question-is there a common feature that unites contemporary metaphysical questions?

The Stanford Encyclopedia of Philosophy cannot give

a definitive answer, but only a list of contemporary philosophical questions that are considered metaphysical, so that when one aspires to fulfill one's expectations, one can experience a gap that is beyond one's own ability to cross.

In particular, the transcendental action from "being", which is about the existence of life itself in the universe, requires first of all the establishment of "communication of being", that is, the communication between one's real self.

Then it is necessary to develop "historical consciousness", that is, the individual cannot be separated from the unique historical situation in which he or she is left in the world, and to realize existence alone.

Then, through the "free choice of existence," and through the experience of life in the boundary situation, the level of knowledge or skill is metamorphosed to the "true existence" so as to meet the transcendental interface.

Therefore, the mind gained after experiencing or observing a certain event or incident is applied to subsequent operations. These previously acquired knowledge skills are crucial for working or teaching.

In fact, most experts in various fields nowadays judge by their considerable experience. In particular, the fields of religion, education, military, travel, sports, and medicine, among others, reveal to us the fact that all of life's existence in this world is bound to experience failure.

Failure is not an ordinary event, but a matter of development and change according to the laws of reason and law, because all "beings" must be honest about the boundaries that life brings.

"Communication" is one of the most important concepts in Jaspers' view of the philosophy of existence or the meaning of life existence from a certain position or perspective. In fact, this is also the communication between the real selves of individuals.

The main reason why people look forward to this kind of real communication is that they expect to break the falsehoods and untruths of each other, and to see each other in a particular way or with a sincere attitude, as real and untrue selves.

The value of communication is not to obtain unchanging or ultimate results, but to initiate the "existence" of freedom of expression, where the "existence" of life itself is not a way or a method of expressing content, but a form of human freedom. It is a form of human freedom. "Existence" is not limited to the fact that one is what one is or can only be, but that one is a potential possibility.

Freedom means that there is a potential that is not influenced by external forces, that does not arise unconsciously and naturally, that refuses to see itself as a mere thing, a final end or a destination, and that the free person is only free in relation to others.

The free man realizes his "existence" only when he interacts with other people and things through the state of "communication". "It is only in "communication" that one becomes aware of the "existence" of other people's existence itself, and only then is it possible to understand the meaning of life's existence.

Jasper says: "It is true that I am in all the "others", that I live with them, that there is a part of me in our state of interdependence. But the familiar ones with whom I am unconditionally connected are more than that.

Those I can relate to as if they were my own, I do not

treat them as if they were other people, which makes it possible for me and these few confidants to be outside of the rest".

In Jasper's discourse on the objects of "communication," the so-called "other" is a common term in Western postcolonial theory, in which Westerners are often referred to as the subjective "self," and the colonized people are referred to as the "colonized other," or simply as the "other.

"The other and the self are opposing concepts, and Westerners regard the non-Western world outside the self as the other, and treat the two as diametrically opposed.

Therefore, the concept of "other" actually conceals a Western-centered ideology. Broadly speaking, the "other" is a reference that is both distinct from and connected to the subject.

For example, if a white person can be a black person as the "other", then the conclusion is that the white person must be civilized, intelligent, advanced, and elegant, and by choosing and establishing the "other", to a certain extent, the self can be better identified and understood.

But the implied egocentrism has serious flaws or drawbacks. A subject without the contrast of the "other" will be completely unable to know and identify the self in contrast.

In postcolonial studies, one of the most distinctive and central concepts and domains is that of the 'native' and the 'other', and the question of the nature of the connection between these two, between people and people or between people and things.

Native and the other are the comparison of one substance or a whole with another substance or another whole, or the existence or change of a certain condition. It changes depending on the location of the object of study, and the state of interaction and interaction between the things that describe it, and the other object chosen as a criterion.

Philosophically, the "other" is a form of thinking that reflects the nature of the object's properties. In the process of cognition, human beings raise the common characteristics of the things they perceive from perceptual knowledge to rational knowledge and extract the intrinsic properties.

The application of postcolonial critical theory is mainly based on the theories of Hegel and Sartre. Hegel's analysis of the state of interaction and mutual influence between things (master-slave) in "Phenomenology of Spirit" shows that the manifestation of "other" is essential to the "self-consciousness" that constitutes me.

(The behavior between the two parties (master-slave) is a deadly confrontation in which each party tries to destroy the other and uses the other as the person or thing that can be used as a communication link. Each party tries to destroy the other, using the other as the person or thing that can be used as a communication link. "Because they mutually recognize themselves.

The result of the conflict is that the strong becomes the master and the weak becomes the slave. The master puts his opponent under his own power, and through the transformation of the slave, he indirectly associates with things and "enjoys them".

The slave becomes a substanceless being whose purpose is to maintain the "existence" of the master. For the master, the slave is the "other", and it is only through the existence of the "other" that the subject's consciousness is established and authority is asserted.

Sartre takes the position of rejecting the Freudian "egoology" and proposes a related concept to explain the formation and interrelationship of consciousness and subconsciousness.

The "ego" (fully subconscious, not controlled by subjective consciousness) represents desire and is suppressed by consciousness; the "self" (most consciousness) is responsible for dealing with the real world; and the "superego" (some consciousness) is the conscience or inner moral judgment.

At the same time, it is only through the emergence of other consciousness that ego consciousness becomes visible. In other words, the "other" is a prerequisite for the "self".

In the section on "Gaze" in Being and Nothingness, he uses a phenomenological description to illustrate the process of self-consciousness. Imagine that I am peering through the lockhole at someone in the house, and at that moment my object of gaze is another person, whom I regard as an intentional object.

But if I suddenly hear footsteps in the hallway and realize that there is someone else looking at me, "What am

I doing? Shame is shame on the self, which recognizes that I am the object that others are looking at and judging.

Under the gaze of others, the fluid, empty selfhood that was "what it is not, but what it is not" is suddenly emphasized as "what it is, but what it is not".

In this example, it is because I feel that others may look at me that I will look at myself. Under the gaze of others, the subject experiences the existence of "I". At the same time, I am aware that I exist "for others".

Without the conscious "other", my subject consciousness cannot be established. I can only confirm the existence of "I" by projecting myself out and realizing the existence of the imaginary "other".

In short, both Hegel and Sartre emphasize the ontological significance of the Other in the formation of the subject's self-consciousness. Moreover, both of them consider the basic relationship between the subject and the other as conflict.

In Hegel, the relationship between master and slave is not mutual; "a one-sided and unbalanced recognition" occurs between them.

The slave is the intermediary in the relationship

between master and object, and his status is instrumental. The "other" is a means rather than an end, and the "other" itself appears as intransitive.

For Sartre, mutual gaze between subjects is impossible; 'A gaze cannot gaze at itself; as soon as I look at a gaze; it disappears, I only see the eye. In this moment, the other becomes my possession, and recognizes my free existence.

Neither of them can be seized without contradiction, neither of them is in the other, and "to the death of the other". "Conflict is the original meaning of existence for him".

This determines that the attitude toward the Other is one of conflict, not dialogue or anything else.

From this, we can observe that Jaspers does take the interaction and interconnection between subject and subject, between people and things. It is the origin, the root of the existence of things.

It was basically a rare act for Jaspers to propose the concept of "communication" in the context of the time, but only a few people could really communicate. Relatively speaking, it did not affect a wide range of people.

From an empirical point of view, man is a social animal, and cannot be separated from the group life, and all his needs in life must be satisfied through interaction with each other.

However, for Jaspers' philosophical thinking, "communication" comes from the deepest need of man, that is, the need to seek the self. However, the "existence" of life itself cannot be realized in isolation.

This also means that without real communication, there can be no realization of the true self, no real exchange of opinions or communication between each other, that is, "communication of existence" between true and real, not false, selves.

The communication in the stage of experiencing the law of things is not the real communication, in the beginning, I have not yet the ability to recognize the environment and the self and the clarity of the recognition to myself, that is, I am several kinds of things closely related to each other.

In the beginning, I was not yet able to recognize the environment and the self, and to recognize the degree of clarity to myself.

When I am able to recognize the environment and the self, as well as to clearly recognize the existence of the self, the independent "I" is separated from the other parts or the whole, the subject, and this "I" can think or judge something from a different point of view, or perspective.

This "I" can understand another "I" by thinking or judging the reasonableness of something from a different point of view, or perspective, the nature of a thing that exists independently without the influence of subjective thought or consciousness, and the content of thinking corresponding to "subjectivity".

However, in this sequence or passage of events, the "self" is not just a living entity that can be experienced, nor is it just a self-self, but also has the spirit of a whole idea. Since "communication" has a different nature from other things and a certain limit that cannot be crossed, it cannot bring an absolute satisfaction to people.

This dissatisfaction with the status quo of "communication" is the fundamental reason for the breakthrough to "existence" and the communication that elaborates the profound truths, the origin of the philosophical thinking of this breakthrough, just as all philosophical thinking starts from "surprise" and the cognition of the world starts from "doubt". The origin of this breakthrough philosophical thinking is the same as the origin of all philosophical thinking from "surprise", from "doubt", and from "experience of dissatisfaction" with "communication".

This experience is the starting point for philosophical reflection. In this description of the process of contemplating past life experiences, from which lessons are drawn, one learns that in order to achieve self-realization, one needs another "self" that cannot be replaced by others to communicate with me. This is also known as "existential communication".

"Communication of Being cannot be prearranged or imitated, and each communication is unique. It is absolutely necessary, just like our own freedom, because without this "communication", man loses his freedom, his root, his foundation, or the main part of himself.

If a person is unwilling or afraid to face a certain situation or thing, and deliberately avoids this "communication", it is not only a departure from one's original beliefs, but also a betrayal of the moral constraints, a rebellion against the interests of the public, and an unfulfilled and unfulfilled commitment to oneself.

It is a departure and rebellion from the original beliefs of others, and a departure and rebellion from one's own original beliefs. We must truly believe in the possibility of sincere "communication" between people, otherwise we will not be able to find the true path to truth through such "communication". Otherwise, we will not be able to find the true path to truth through such "communication", and we will not be able to achieve the ultimate goal of realizing our true self.

The objective existence of philosophy is reflected in human consciousness, and the root cause of the result of thinking activity includes many categories based on the nature or characteristics of things themselves; what is unusual and rare and surprising are the questions and insights that will cause a demand for answers or solutions.

People have doubts about what they have been told, and they will make justified, false and negative assertions about wrong perceptions or reactionary thoughts, words and deeds, and thus deny and confirm them.

The fear and feeling caused by being abandoned in spite of the constraints of emotion, loyalty or obligation, leads man to explore strange and new things, and to try to find the answer to his inner behavior.

Plato once said: "The root of philosophy is wonder. It is the compulsion to act of one's own volition, to examine all that man has observed, and has not yet observed, in space and time. This includes all the things in between.

The scientific methods and theories that explain the totality of all "being" constitute modern cosmology. This gives rise to philosophy, the study of universal, fundamental questions, including the fields of being, knowledge, values, reason, mind, and language.

Aristotle also says: "Out of surprise, men are now beginning, and have begun, to do the doctrine of the world view, the search and examination of natural and social knowledge in general and in summary (causes, reasons, etc.).

They are first surprised by the apparent seriousness of things, which are enough to be studied and discussed, or which have yet to be solved, and then, little by little, they progress slowly, thus stating the problems concerning larger things, which are not easily solved, such as those concerning the sun, the moon, the moon and the earth.

Such as the phenomena of the sun, the moon, the stars, and the origin of the universe". Surprise forces human beings to act according to their own will to seek knowledge, and it is only when I feel that I am surprised by something very rare and unusual that I realize the poverty of my own knowledge.

Therefore, the search for knowledge and experience acquired in the process of learning and practice is only for "knowledge", not for "satisfying the usual needs". The "communication" of existence is an inspirational process.

At the same time, it is a kind of realization of one's true self. In this process and realization, one's self and other's selves are completed mutually. In his book "Philosophy", Jaspers mentions that the communication of existence is a kind of love that is very hesitant and indecisive, and that this struggle to support or get rid of it is different from the usual very hesitant and indecisive.

This kind of support or release does not seek to dominate the other party nor to overwhelm the other party, it is intended for the other party on both sides.

According to Jaspers, in this "communication", a strong emotion and attachment to a person or a thing, an emotional and psychological state derived from strong love, loyalty and goodwill between relatives, is not a blind and indiscriminate love without a choice of object, but a polished and committed love. It is a "possible existence".

It is a mutual interaction between one "possible existence" and another "possible non-existence"; it is a "communication" in which people struggle to support or resist with all their might, and at the same time struggle for their own existence as well as for the existence of each other.

In the process of "direct contact with the same objective thing, the phenomenon of the objective thing acquired through the sense organs, and the level of external connection to recognize the thing, any weapon is allowed to be used, and the motive and cunning become inevitable means to treat the other as the enemy of the "other".

But it is not the same when 'existence' struggles to support or resist with all its might. It requires an openness of complete honesty, a renunciation of any sense of power and superiority, and a concern for the realization of others as much as for oneself.

In this very hesitant, indecisive situation, both partners are willing to reveal their true selves without reservation, and to allow each other to question them. According to Jasper, although love itself is not the same as "communication," it is the root and source of knowledge, power, and affection for "communication.

As long as "communication" is in progress, the struggle for love will never end. Because love is unique and unifies everything, in love we realize our true self.

The origin of love is not in this world, but in the process of direct contact with the same objective things, the recognition of the phenomena and external connections of love through the sense organs is a mystery that is not known to the general public and is complex and transcendent.

But only in this way, love enables people to realize their true selves. As long as love is real, "communication" will not stop. "Love is the real source of self-realization in "communication".

The self-realization that it facilitates is a process of development in which love is constantly manifesting itself in changing situations, but it cannot be promoted to become the ultimate perfection of self-realization". There is also an inseparable relationship between "communication" and reason and truth.

Jasper has said: "Reason requires unrestricted "communication", which itself is the universal will to "communicate". It is the level of recognition of the phenomena of objective things and external connections that people acquire through their sense organs in the process of direct contact with the same objective things.

Therefore, "communication" is the form of manifestation that depends on the correct reflection of objective things and their laws in the human mind in time. The reason why Jaspers made Kommunikation an important concept of his philosophy.

This is because in the study of universal, fundamental problems in the disciplines of existence, knowledge, values, reason, mind, and language. Philosophy differs from other disciplines in that it has its own unique way of thinking about language.

The distinction and connection between language and speech are as follows.

For example, the process of using language to

communicate is called speech. However, in the process of deconstruction of philosophical thinking, language and speech are two very different concepts. Language reflects the psychological state of an individual or group of individuals seeking to satisfy their social needs, and is the object of linguistic study.

Speech is a psychological dialogue, and is the object of psychological research. Language is the use of language, it has two meanings: one, is a human thought, called verbal activity, also called verbal behavior; second, is to express the words spoken, written things, also called verbal works. The distinction and connection between language and speech are summarized as follows.

Language is a global, general, finite, static system (knowledge); speech is a personal, specific, unlimited, dynamic expression of all situations that can be felt (words). Specifically, there are four points.

First, language has a global nature, speech has a personal nature.

Since language exists in all members of society, it is a relatively complete system of abstract symbols, it is universal to members of society, whether from the creator of language, users, or language itself, language has a universal nature.

In contrast, speech has an individual nature, each person speaks with many personal characteristics, such as geography, gender, age, cultural literacy, social status, etc., speech is the specific application of the language form and rules of the individual.

Second, language is abstract, speech is specific

Language is the abstract words spoken to the same group of people, it excludes all individual differences, it only exists as a language communication and commonality. Language is the process and result of using language, therefore, people can only directly observe speech (external speech), linguists can only be a large amount of verbal material, abstract about natural knowledge and social knowledge of the generalization and summation, will be found from the language of various units and rules.

As mentioned earlier, people's knowledge of language usually begins with the specific phenomenon of language, and what people say is specific, either through hearing or through sight, and words often carry specific features.

Third, language is limited, speech is infinite

No two people in the world will speak exactly the same, but no one can get away from the rules of the social matrix common constraints, and to achieve the means of communication. Speech is the use of words to express meaning, an action and its result. It is impossible to calculate how much a person will say or write in a lifetime.

The sentences of any one language are infinite, and the words that each person needs to say according to the interactions and gatherings between people are many and chaotic, unorganized and various.

However, for a particular language alone, there is a limit to the number of sounds that can be identified, a limit to the number of words and the rules of word formation, and a limit to the rules for forming sentences. In an infinite number of sentences, there is a finite number of things.

Each word is like a part of a machine, which can be disassembled and assembled, and a sentence or word can be used again and again, so that the same word can be combined with different words to form different sentences.

And the rules for organizing these materials are also

limited. This tells us that the concrete, infinite speech and words that we humans face every day are speech; and that some abstract, finite system that a certain social group generalizes from these concrete, infinite verbal facts is language.

Therefore, language is a collection of finite linguistic units, which are organized according to certain rules into a system, a vocabulary system and a grammatical system, in which all the speech activities of people operate.

In a specific speech activity, as a program of behavior or development, the number of words that people can speak is infinite, and the length of each sentence is, in theory, infinite.

The length of each sentence should be infinite in theory, and any sentence can be made longer by adding additional components. The use of finite symbols and their rules to say infinite words is a special or unique feature of speech.

Fourth, language is static, speech is dynamic

In people's use of language, in terms of the language they use, the rules of language are existing, constrained, and not allowed to be in constant change, which is the prerequisite and basis for speech activities.

Otherwise, human beings would not be able to exchange opinions, emotions, and information between two or more people through language, behavior, and other forms of expression, nor would they be able to organize society. Thus, language remains static for a certain period of time. Of course, as society changes and language develops, language will also undergo adaptive changes. Therefore, the stillness of language is relative, and there is movement in stillness.

The difference between speech and language. In the speech activity is always between the speaker and the listener to start, from speaking to listening is a dynamic process. Some research shows that speech is the process of contact between each other, that is, the process of transferring information.

In this process, language acts as a code for the transmission of information. The speaker uses language to send content that reflects (mirrors) events. Events include judgmental events, action events, and other descriptions of all movements, and the listener receives information through language, which undergoes several successive processes of coding, sending, transmitting, receiving, and decoding.

For example, the origins of the linguistic critical approach, often systematic and based on rational argumentation, although in the realm of the self, doubt, and the experience of boundary situations, ultimately include all of these in the search for true "communication," which is evident from the beginning in the ideology It is clear.

For all disciplines that study universal, fundamental questions, including the fields of being, knowledge, values, reason, mind, language, etc., are eager to communicate and interpret themselves. They are all eager to communicate and interpret what they are listening to as their essence, that is, the communicable nature itself. This communicability is the purest and most realistic truth, that is, the correct reflection of objective things and their laws in the human mind. It is also inseparable from the existence of real and unchanging truths.

Therefore, only in "communication", the discipline of analyzing, thinking, inquiring, and reflecting on fundamental issues of life, knowledge, and values, usually means that the subject of behavior, according to its own needs, has influence and effect on people or things through the mediation of consciousness and concepts, and that the predetermined goals and results of behavior can be realized.

All the meanings that one wants to achieve or wishes to obtain the desired result are ultimately rooted in "communication": the realization of existence, the clarification of love, the perfection of tranquility. For Jaspers' view, the most important point is to use the general idea of "communication" or the organization of ideas in reflection in order to transcend national and cultural regionalism or regionalism in order to "obtain something common to all humanity, beyond beliefs.

The philosophical view of Jaspers is that mankind is connected and influenced by a single origin and purpose that connects, connects, and complicates things, and that his world is a conscious activity for the transformation of society and nature through a holistic, fundamental, and critical inquiry into the real world and man, and for the examination of the evidence of the facts. This is the meaning of such a statement.

Section 2: Existence and Freedom

A strong feeling and attachment to someone or something, derived from a strong feeling of love, loyalty, and goodwill between relatives and psychological states, which gives rise to a series of desires to act in order to further understand things or to control situations in which novelty or uncertainty is encountered. Each person has a separate personality, a physical body that has its own purpose of action, and a separate and distinct existence.

From the point of view of the intelligence, thoughts and emotions inherent in the human heart, all human beings are of the same kind of category according to the name, nature or characteristics of the person or thing, so that all pain and sorrow, happiness and joy, sickness and health are connected. Therefore, all pain and sorrow, happiness and joy, sickness and health are connected. No one can exist independently of others, and no one can exist independently of the earth.

When you feel a strong emotion and attachment to a person or something, an emotion and psychological state derived from strong love, loyalty and goodwill between relatives, you will naturally explore and understand the inner heart. You will naturally explore, understand the inner mind, and realize that you are part of the inner mind.

The individual will also want to face new things or situations of uncertainty, and a series of behaviors will be triggered in order to further understand things or control situations. Curiosity may stimulate exploratory drive, while uncertainty may cause tension, which leads to exploratory actions such as noticing, observing, manipulating, and studying to find out what is going on.

Through the process of exploring, the individual can remove his or her tensions and gain new knowledge and understanding of all people, things and objects around him or her.

Through the exchange of strong emotions and attachments to a person or object, from the strong love, loyalty, and goodwill between relatives and psychological states, we explore and understand each other, and slowly realize and realize that all human beings are one.

The existence of all things in heaven and on earth is the result of a strong emotion and attachment to a person or object, derived from the strong emotions of love, loyalty and goodwill between relatives, and the energy of psychological states.

At a certain time or at the beginning of the process, human beings use their sensory organs - eyes, ears, nose, tongue and body - to perceive the external environment, and human consciousness is not limited to the physical body.

The human consciousness is not limited to the limited scope of the physical body, but is always in contact with the surrounding environment and likes a certain person or a certain group emotionally, so that in terms of behavior and value standards, the individual consciously or unconsciously repeats the behavior of others.

This is a psychological process that makes the individual consistent with others or groups, and also recognizes that he or she is part of the surrounding environment.

As a result of this strong emotion and attachment to a person or object, derived from the strong feelings of love, loyalty, and goodwill between relatives and the perception of psychological states, one becomes a part of the other when looking at something external to your actions or thoughts, as a target or specifically referring to a loving partner, etc.

It allows a person to no longer be limited to the sum of his or her narrow personal stable psychological characteristics, which include personality, interests, and hobbies. It is on the basis of human physiological quality, the existence of certain social things, the development of the influence of factors.

Through social practice activities, education, etc., the formation and development of a relatively stable, with a particular nature or special character. This enables us to connect with other people's hearts and minds, linking ourselves with others who are our targets when we act or think.

Thus one no longer feels alone, no longer feels the loneliness of life, and one's individual psychological characteristics, including genetic and learned qualities, are surrounded by a greater sense of identity.

In the awareness of a strong emotion and attachment to a person or object, an emotion and psychological state derived from strong love, loyalty, and goodwill among relatives, a person becomes fully aware of his or her own personal qualities that distinguish him or her from others in terms of thought, character, qualities, will, emotion, and attitude.

He is also fully aware of the consciousness behind the "existence" from the smallest to the largest, and feels that he is part of the consciousness of the group, part of the consciousness of heaven and earth, and part of the consciousness of the universe. All this is the result of a strong emotion and attachment to a person or a thing, the result of the presentation of the energy of emotions and mental states derived from the strong love, loyalty and goodwill between relatives.

Each living entity is immersed in a series of strong and positive emotional and mental states, ranging from the most sublime virtues or good habits, the deepest interpersonal relationships, to the simplest pleasures. Such emotions and attachments drive those who feel them to seek physical, intellectual, and even imaginative proximity to the object of their love.

All human beings achieve in the cooperation of treating with sincerity a living being or an object (it can be a person, an animal, an object, a deity) to make it happy as a whole, and in this feeling they come closest to the essence of all things.

Therefore, the nature of love can include love of the soul or mind, love of laws and organizations, love of oneself, love of food, love of money, love of learning, love of power, love of honor, love of others, and so on, to name a few. Different people attach different importance to the love they receive. Love is essentially an abstract concept that can be experienced but is difficult to express in words.

The essence of everything is "imperfection in perfection", and all evil, ugliness and imperfection are processes of life, that is, life is a combination of these good and bad factors. That is to say, life is a combination of these good and bad factors, and it is in the experience of life that one has to refine and

In the process of creation, you can never escape from the pain of tormented internal emotions [the joy of success and the pain of failure].

When a person, through the activity of consciousness, comes to know and understand that he or she is an autonomous creator, he or she is bound to live in the joy of creation in each moment, you create your own reality, you create your own vitality, or successful health and abundance, and you create your own joy, anger, sorrow You create your own joy, sorrow, happiness, and peace, or you choose to create your own misery, wood, and ashes. These are the values of one's autonomous self-creation.

The universe (English: universe, Latin: universus) is the unity of all time, space and its contents, which has neither a beginning nor an end.

Life's existence, that is to say, is articulated from one stage to another. From the past to the present, and from the present to the future, from the defective, imperfect, and unsatisfactory to the complete, perfect, and gradually fulfilling.

However, for questions that cannot be answered directly by perception, it is the answer deduced by rational logical reasoning under a priori conditions (which can be seen as axiomatic assumptions) and cannot be contradicted by empirical evidence.

It is the search of human reason for the most universal aspects and ultimate causes of things. The truth of the matter is that the past, present, and future exist simultaneously. Thus, metaphysicians try to clarify the basic concepts (domains) that people use to understand the world, such as existence, objects and their nature, space and time, cause and effect, and possibility.

Because of the freedom of will, man is able to investigate, through rational reasoning and logic, questions that cannot be answered directly through perception. Metaphysics refers to the fundamental principles of philosophy.

Metaphysics is concerned with the core issues of theoretical philosophy, such as foundations, premises, causes, first causes, and basic structures, such as the meaning and purpose of the real existence of all life, and it is necessary to seriously confront the problem of our own existence.

If one thinks that the past and the present me are bad, then I will try to create and improve to make my future more fulfilling. Because every day is the same day, and every self is the same self, self-denial will only make you more negative and depressed.

Free Will

Free will is the ability to choose and decide between

various possible options for action. It is a complex subject with no agreed upon definition. The philosophical definition of "free will" is not uniform.

There are many different views on the existence of "metaphysical freedom," and the question is whether people have the capacity to make truly different choices.

The question is whether people have the capacity to make truly different choices.

Jasper says: "Without the possibility of freedom of my own will, I cannot suggest that the matter of freedom is serious enough to be studied and discussed, or that it remains to be resolved. I could not raise the matter of freedom if I did not have the possibility of freedom, and "what makes me raise this question is the fundamental desire to have a free will.

Therefore, the freedom of my will precedes the doubt of freedom in my mind, and I ask for answers or explanations. I cannot wish to have "freedom" until after I have proved that it exists. I desire freedom because I have become aware of the possibility of "freedom".

It is clear from this that Jaspers believes that in delving into the question of freedom, one should first acknowledge the existence of things or the truth of things, the rationality of things, do I have freedom? Or is it possible for me to have freedom? Only then can I go further and ask "What is freedom?" The question of "what is freedom?

In the philosophical viewpoint of Jaspers, "existence" and "freedom" are an expression of the cognitive consciousness of the self, which is the abstraction and generalization of the common nature of the things perceived by human beings in the process of cognition, from perceptual to rational cognition.

Therefore, the two concepts are interchangeable. For Jaspers, "being" is constantly faced with the choice between "having" and "not having", and one "exists" only in the context of a sincere choice.

But for the view of "freedom" consciousness, this is not a vague inference, but a way of knowing things around us through practice. What really proves "freedom" is not the process of acquiring knowledge through mental activities such as forming concepts, perceptions, judgments, or imagination, but rather the activities of the self to achieve a certain purpose.

For "knowledge" is usually defined only as "justified true belief", which includes "perfected cognition", which means "truth".

In cognition, it also means "perfection". Cognition refers to the broad role of consciousness; belief is distinct from opinion and is the insistence on an opinion position; and knowledge refers to "what is known," the ability to see into things that are not easily perceived and known, including "knowing what" and "knowing why.

Thus, it is generally accepted that a person is responsible for his or her own actions, and it is pointed out that the person's actions are subject to the praise and blame of the social matrix. However, many people believe that the concept of moral responsibility is inextricably linked to free will.

In other words, the ability to make other choices. Thus, whether individuals are morally responsible, and why they are or are not, becomes another important issue.

The fact that "freedom cannot be recognized or thought of as an action or thought, but thought of as a goal, is the starting and ending point of illuminating freedom.

The self determines that I am free, not through thinking, but through being, not through observation and inquiry, but through action." From the compendium of Jasper's book "Philosophy", we explore how he constructs "freedom" on several points of view.

One is cognition (acknowledge). Cognition is certainly not the same as freedom, but it is indispensable to freedom because once one's cognition is restricted, one's choices will also be restricted.

Cognition is an increasingly important concept in modern psychology; however, different schools of thought have different interpretations of the term "cognition". According to perfect psychology, cognition is the internal mental process by which an individual thinks and solves problems; it emphasizes the need to understand the relationship between stimuli and stimuli in order to generate epiphanies and solve problems.

Modern scholars have adopted a broader definition of cognition, asserting that cognition is the mental process of understanding and knowledge of stimuli through the activities of the conscious mind. Therefore, cognition has two main dimensions: one is the cognitive process and the other is the cognitive ability.

Modern cognitive psychology has a detailed study of the cognitive process for reference, and cognitive abilities such as thinking and reasoning, perceptual attention, logical judgment, planning and monitoring, problem solving, memory extraction, imagination creation, and other mental skills are all indispensable abilities in the cognitive process.

That is why Jasper said, "Knowledge does not make me free, but without knowledge, it is impossible to have freedom. Therefore, the more one expands one's connection of a certain nature to the world, to people or to things, the more one is able to understand them.

Therefore, the more one expands one's knowledge and understanding of the world, of people and things, and of the interactions and interconnectedness of things through the activity of consciousness, the more one explores one's potential abilities, and the more one appreciates opportunities, the freer one becomes in knowledge.

Secondly, it is the willfulness (Willkur), the freedom to do as one wishes, which can be described as a kind of spontaneity of the self. Such a situation makes the choice, it becomes impossible to grasp the existing information on the basis of

In this case, it becomes impossible to make a choice based on the available information, to calculate future events according to certain methods and rules, to know in advance the course and outcome of events, because the choice cannot be substituted in a formulaic way, we can perhaps say that it is subject to the strongest motives that make us make a decisive choice.

Haynes at the Bernstein Center for Computational Neuroscience in Berlin, Benjamin Libet at the University of California in San Francisco, and Itzhak Fried, a neurologist and surgeon at the University of California in Los Angeles and Tel Aviv Medical Center in Israel, among others

Both have found through brain scanning observations that there is activity in the brain long before the participant develops a sense of choice. That is, things are decided before they enter the consciousness. The consciousness of decision is created after the decision is created

A study by neuroscientists Marcel Brass and Patrick Haggard, published in the Journal of Neuroscience in 2007, supports this hypothesis. They used a similar approach to Libet's, except that the subjects could push a button at the last minute to reject the previous decision.

They found that a special area of the brain called the left dorsal middle frontal lobe is excited when a person engages in this intentional inhibition: "The results suggest that there is a structure in the network of the human brain responsible for intentional behavior that is responsible for self-inhibition or restraint of intentional behavior. That is the free refusal of will.

Although randomness and spontaneity are not the same as freedom, they are an essential condition of freedom. This is because it promotes the substantive freedom of each individual. It is not only formal freedom, but also the resources and conditions necessary for its exercise.

The person who enjoys freedom has not only the right to do what he or she wants to do, what he or she chooses to do, or what he or she is morally obligated to do, but also the freedom to actually do these things.

Third, there is another sense in which freedom can be regarded as a law (Gesetz), which is freedom in the sense of self-discipline or moral regulation, a freedom that is self-disciplined and active, as opposed to the passive freedom of cognition.

For example, speaking is an art, and doing and being a person is a discipline. The three freedoms in the sense of self-discipline or moral norms - speaking, doing, and being - are to be explored and learned by everyone in one's life.

Words should not be spoken lightly

"A good word is warm in winter, but a bad word is cold in June. Words are not determined by the mouth, but by the freedom of will in the sense of internal self-discipline or moral norms.

A word spoken is like water that has been spilled and cannot be taken back. Therefore, before a word is spoken, it must be considered and thought through in the sense of self-discipline or moral regulation. Free promises made at will are absurd and unreasonable exaggerations.

It is a breach of one's integrity to make people hope and wait for something in the future or for the future of a person when one cannot achieve a goal or realize a goal.

Integrity is not just a simple matter of honesty, it is a combination of honesty and trust, something that we all must have in modern society.

Especially in Western culture, because integrity is about honesty and trustworthiness, which refers to a person's moral quality. Credit, on the other hand, means to keep one's word between people. That is to say, honest and trustworthy. So honesty is a promise of a thousand pieces of gold, as one in appearance.

Keeping promises. Credit is a bridge of mutual trust between people, groups and things. Credit constitutes the relationship network of the whole society, the relationship between people, groups, and things.

Everyone is part of this vast network of relationships, and credit concerns all of us. Therefore, it is important not to talk about other people's privacy. Once you have destroyed someone's trust, you are no longer worthy of trust.

When you are angry, angry and angry, some people are so aggressive that they can make the other person vomit blood without saying a few words. The words are too direct, especially when cursing people are unpredictable, and the words that come out are so clear that they will often make the other party half dead, so it's good to separate the two, and communicate again after the anger, or else the words will ruin the relationship.

As the saying goes, "three years without words to learn to speak, a lifetime of listening to learn to shut up, understand and do not understand do not talk nonsense, if there is really nothing to say do not say. Don't think of your mouth as your true nature! The actual fact is that you can find a lot of people who have been humiliated by a round of humiliation, as if they were buried alive, struggling to suffocate and die. The first thing you need to do is to get your hands on a new one.

You can't do what you want

Do not act arbitrarily according to their nature, honest and not pretentious or arbitrary indulgence, in order to meet their own desires, or to achieve their own kind of improper goals or obstinate sex, without fear, must act according to their own wishes or ideas, should be self-discipline or moral norms in the sense of freedom to look at the big picture, consider the long-term future, rather than limited to the mood of the moment.

The things in the world of self-discipline or freedom in the moral sense have a price, and you have to pay for what you want to get. You have to pay for what you want to get, not to say, "I can do whatever I want.

Everyone has their own identity, and everyone has their own responsibility for self-discipline, or freedom in the moral sense. Fathers are the core of the family and have a great responsibility for the family.

The teacher is a mountain on which the children can rely, and is responsible for sheltering the students. Many times self-discipline or moral code in the sense of freedom, so that we can not by their own minds, not by their own emotions to.

When anger is out of control, it can cause irreversible consequences; often, it can bring endless trouble to oneself. Emotions are always the greatest enemy of freedom of will in the sense of self-discipline or moral code, the ability to control one's own mental state caused by external stimuli or internal physical conditions.

This includes joy, anger, sorrow, fear, love, evil, and desire in order to control one's life. Do things in the appropriate limits of words or actions, know the right amount of proportion to achieve the appropriate stop.

People cannot be arbitrary

The sum of all activities in the process of human existence, for the meaning of happiness, there are always a lot of irresistible temptations, human greedy character or temperament, the most vulnerable to the influence of the surrounding environment.

But human beings are human beings because they have the ability to control their desires freely in the sense of self-discipline or moral norms. We must maintain goodness, but we must also have our own dignity and sense of right and wrong. Many people regret their lives because of a momentary mistake, and even if they escape from the law, they will still suffer from their conscience for the rest of their lives.

As the saying goes, "A gentleman does something, but does not do anything." People should have their own moral and conscience bottom line. People who do not have a moral bottom line and do whatever they can will only be respected and kept away.

People cannot cross the freedom in the sense of self-discipline or moral norms at will, but must take life seriously. If one does not realize the value of life, one may choose to go with the flow.

According to Jaspers, "I am free when I follow a law that I consider binding, because I am yielding to a decree that I find in my self and that I can in fact disobey, a decree that makes I am like a servant who must be at the beck and call of man, and who cannot escape the dictates of natural things, and the certainty of their development.

It is a norm of action, a rule of things, and a definite trend of development which man may or may not obey, and such norms are recognized by my freedom, and I take them as self-evident truths without proof.

Although the true form of these norms is widespread and common in nature, they become most explicit rather than abstract and general when the self feels close to them because of what they have in common with me. This freedom of the self, found by following old practices without altering norms or laws, is called "transcendental freedom.

Fourth is the freedom to choose (Wahl), because of the cognitive bias, and to rethink the past and learn from it, not understanding its mission at all, when you indulge in habitual thinking, you can never objectively look at your thoughts. But the individual who is 'being' is often affected by time and events that interrupt reflection.

It is not appropriate to make a decision based on

insufficient awareness. Choice is the deepest, most definite, and most intelligible manifestation of the self, and Jaspers explains it with regard to the freedom to choose.

What does it mean to choose in the face of chance and necessity?

Are our choices meaningless in the face of the contingent and inevitable events of life? Many religious groups believe that our choices are meaningless because everything is ordained by "God" (or something else powerful) and that we can only choose to accept or not accept them mentally? However, choice is a voluntary act that is taken after a person has thought about it.

This voluntary action occurs when at least one of two situations is possible, and the choice is to achieve a purpose. Therefore, there are several basic conditions for constructing "choice".

(1) A mental process of deliberation, without which the action would be mechanical or arbitrary.

(2) there is an actual action, if only thinking without specific external behavior, then it does not constitute a choice, so the consideration before the action, only to

make a decision, not a choice.

(3) can choose the object can not be only one, must be more than one, choose one of them, only then constitute a choice.

(4) It is an action with a purpose. Choice is an action taken by a person to achieve a purpose, and this action affirms that the actor is in a certain value context.

In philosophy, the discussion of "choice" focuses on two aspects: first, the basic nature of choice, whether choice is only a mental event or includes external behavior? The second is whether there is freedom of choice or not. The latter depends on the object of choice, and in everyday life, many subtle events affirm the freedom of choice.

But in the larger context, such as man being part of the natural world and bound by natural laws, is man's choice a mere illusion under these constraints? This is the debate between the Determinist and the Free Will advocates.

In the field of education, J.S. Mill (1806-1873) argued that man can make full use of his ability to choose, that this is what makes him human, and that this is what makes him dignified and valuable.

It follows from this that education should develop the ability to choose, but also the wisdom to choose, that is, the ability to discriminate, to identify the objects available before the choice is acted upon, and then to choose wisely.

Therefore, in reflecting on the meaning of life's existence, we cannot help but ask. Is everything in life really just inevitable? In the process of life experience, there is a natural inevitability in a person's behavior.

For example, raising one's left foot and taking a step forward, and at that moment, a sudden situation appears by chance, that is, the interaction and influence between people or things. Without the influence of anyone or anything, I lift my left foot and take a step forward, which is half a meter, so if I take 200 steps forward, I will definitely walk 100 meters. But this inevitability is influenced by the interaction and interplay between other contingent things.

For example, you may have made up your mind to take 50 steps forward at the same time that a car is coming at you, so that you have to change your pace. In this way, the original plan to take 200 steps forward may not be completed in time.

In other words, the more complex a person's thinking and behavior becomes, the longer he or she will experience frustration and obstruction, and the more susceptible he or she will be to outside influences, and the more his or her behavior will be affected by "chance" that appears out of nowhere. Natural inevitability will also be weakened.

From this, it can be seen that "chance" will arise when "necessity" of a certain nature meets between people and people or people and things. However, "chance" is inseparable from "necessity". In this context, it means that all phenomena that happen by chance in human society are also confined to the scope of necessity.

Chance can be divided into optional and non-optional. For example, in order to survive, whether to go to work or not to go to work in the face of a bad boss, and so on.

When there is a choice in the experience of life existence, it is the existence of life existence itself, the accident of choice. Of course, in the process of life's existence, the choice of the boundary situation may be influenced by certain "chance" events, which may lead to a preference for a certain option at that time.

For example, when a person chooses to go to work or not to go to work, a sudden tropical cyclone storm may cause him to prefer not to go to work.

In such a situation, the person has no choice but to go along with the arranged direction.

For example, if a person works as usual and punches the time clock at work, but because the boss's business strategy exceeds the specific conditions and the actual situation, the work starts too early and proceeds too fast, causing the company to close down, and the person suddenly loses his or her job before he or she expects it, this is the accident of non-optionality.

Although the occurrence of "chance" will result in a change from one form, state, or characteristic to another significant form, state, or characteristic, it is all within the limits of "necessity".

For example, death is an inevitable event that must be faced by the existence of our being itself, but the untimely death of our being itself is a contingent event within the inevitability. The interactions and interconnections between the two things are not in a state of opposition, as literally expressed, because every contingent event is prompted by the progress of the necessary event.

The contingent events of life itself cannot be predicted in accordance with certain methods and laws, based on the existing information, in order to know in advance the process and results of the development of things.

Everything has a current flow of time and changes in the boundaries of the situation. Moreover, most of the chance is a combination of several things, or by a few things that are bound to happen piled up.

For example, in a driving school, a teacher who has been teaching driving for many years is teaching a driving course, and he is concentrating on guiding the newcomers to the road driving course, when he accidentally drives onto a dividing island with his car.

In this case, there are a few things that are inevitable, that is, the teacher of the driving class, who is supposed to teach the students, and guiding the newcomers to the road driving course, is also inevitable in the course.

However, the accidental event is that the teacher drove onto the dividing island with his car. This is because it is not inevitable that a person and a car will drive on a divider island. From this example, we can see that a contingent event does not stand alone, but must be a combination of several inevitable events. On the contrary, the inevitable events are laws, somewhat similar to the immutable laws.

As in the case of normal conditions, the inevitable changes in the state of matter

(1) the three states of water: under a fixed pressure, water at different temperatures, there are three states of solid, liquid and gas.

(2) melting: pure material from the solid state into the liquid state of the process, and vice versa is called solidification. (3) vaporization: the process of pure material from the liquid state into a gaseous state, called vaporization, and vice versa is called condensation, and in general temperature occurs, it is called evaporation; hair to scissors will definitely become shorter after cutting, these repeatable scientific experiments, anyone each time the experiment, there will be the same results.

These things can be seen individually, unlike chance events, which can only be achieved by the accumulation of several events that have already happened. And inevitability is a self-evident truism of everyday life.

Although each person's experience or encounter is different, there are certain things that we all must encounter together. Things like birth, illness, aging, death, and making choices about where to draw the line. At any given time, the choices we make in our boundary situations are very personal. The freedom of the human will is explained by the choice of boundaries.

How we want to live, how we want to live and how we want to die are all matters of personal love and each person's circumstances are different.

There are many times when we have to make a boundary choice for something unknown in front of us, and the choice of boundary is full of unknown variables.

The choice of the boundary situation plays a role in pushing forward and has the power to change the future. However, the meaning behind the boundary choices is unknown, and whether it is good or bad is full of chance.

When faced with the inevitable and the contingent, the choice of the boundary situation often reflects a person's attitude toward the existence of life itself. Some people have a negative attitude when faced with the inevitable, because they think that since things are going to happen this way, they can't change them anyway, so they do nothing.

In fact, even if something is inevitable, we will have to make a decision about the boundary, although the decision about the boundary is an unpredictable inevitability for us.

On the negative side, it is true that even if we make a boundary choice, it will not affect the outcome, so why spend time making a boundary choice?

However, if we look at it from a positive perspective, even if we cannot change what is already done, we can still hold a positive boundary position and try our best to make the best of an inevitable event.

Undoubtedly, one's attitude is more persistent in the face of chance events than in the face of inevitable events in the boundary realm, because of the possibility of the unknown in the boundary realm, the level of chance.

Chance events are similar to boundary choices, and it can be said that boundary choices influence the occurrence of chance events. Since the prospect of a boundary decision is unknown and the outcome cannot be predicted, chance events are also beyond our control.

At the same time, it is beyond our control. Therefore, when faced with chance events, many people have the mindset of "taking what comes is what goes". This is an optimistic attitude.

But because of our confusion about the existence of life itself, we seldom have this kind of optimism. Often, when the outcome of a boundary decision is not as we would like it to be, we do not like this "chance" very much, and we will look back and blame ourselves for the wrong choice of the boundary decision, and cling to the decision of the boundary decision that has occurred. This is what is often said: "If I had known, why would I have done it in the first place?" and "If I could choose again in life, I would not have ....

However, when we think about it calmly, we seem to understand the outcome of our boundary choices in advance, and although our will is free, the outcome of our boundary choices is completely out of our control.

Moreover, even if we regret making a wrong decision, no one can foresee that this decision will be better or worse than another decision until the outcome is known. If it were possible to know in advance that another decision would be better, would there be any need in the world for the inevitable act of making a boundary decision?

The significance of a boundary decision is really a matter of one's state of mind and how one seems to treat one's life. The existence of human life itself is bound to have many storms throughout life, and will not always be at the peak of the extreme state, nor will it ever stay at the lowest ebb and flow.

These experiences of life itself, the hardening of life's ups and downs, also promote human growth and the inevitable happenings of life. In the presence of life itself, life continues to exist in a state of necessity and chance.

From childhood to adulthood, we have learned from the connection between one way and another that to live well, we must look at life in a certain way or with a certain attitude, and we must face it with an optimistic and positive attitude.

Even though we know that we should be optimistic and aggressive, it is not easy to maintain a common state of mind when facing different situations. It can be said that since life will eventually lead to death, even if we do something, it will be a futile effort, so why not let go of everything and leave it aside.

However, because "death" is known to be inevitable, in this predicted outcome, we value the existence of life itself as a process, and not as the final outcome of human affairs.

In the process of the living experience of life existence, the choice of the boundary situation is only an inevitable event, but the choice of the boundary situation is not a living thing, but the choice of the boundary situation is the right of each person to have freedom of will. But we are responsible for the results of our boundary choices.

We cannot put the responsibility on the choice of the boundary, it does not have the ability to bear the responsibility, because the responsibility is only on the person who makes the choice of the boundary.

Therefore, in order to be responsible for ourselves, we must respect ourselves, make each boundary decision carefully, trust the boundary decisions we make, and face all the good and bad outcomes positively. Because life is full of unknown variables.

We will never know what inevitable events will cause what accidental events, and we will never know when the accidental events will happen.

It can be seen that the collision and continuation of the result of personal choice, the universe of life, all the phenomena of the world, become so illusory and unpredictable that an inevitable "chance" appears out of it unexpectedly.

Therefore, the choice of one's boundary and situation has a great significance. The meaning is that, in addition to knowing the temporary "inevitability" that it directly causes, it may also have long-term effects, or the reasons that led to the previous situation of the choice of the boundary situation, which are the "chance" that will be brought by the unexpected.

So the seemingly irreversible "inevitable" destiny is not in the hands of God, but in the hands of each individual. It is the individual's choice of boundary and situation that gives this world its diverse power.

Although it is objectively impossible to analyze the orbit of the universe in detail, to understand it from a certain cognitive point of view, the ego is aware of it as a source of freedom of will, and in this freedom of will, the ego is directly responsible for itself, while others, from the standpoint of a third party, think that I am only responsible for the actual actions. I am responsible for the actual action.

The term "choice" (Wahl) means that the ego, through "free decision," is not only a reflection of the objective material world by the human mind, but is the sum of various mental processes, such as feeling and thinking, of which thinking is the higher form of reflection of reality that is uniquely human.

Being determines consciousness, and consciousness reacts to changes in the existence of the world around it, and is also aware that the ego is constantly creating itself in the historical situation of its own life existence, because I am here and have such a "self" nature of the "existence" of the ego life existence itself that I have to act in a certain way. I have to act in a certain way.

And in acting and deciding, the ego is at the same time the source of the ego's action and of the "existence" of the true egoic being itself.

The determination of my boundary situation allows me to experience a freedom of will in which I decide not only about external things, but also about the deepest freedom.

I can no longer be separated from the decision of my boundary situation, because I am one with the decision of this boundary situation of freedom of will. The freedom of the will is the choice of the boundary of the self, and as long as there is the choice of the boundary, there is the existence of my life itself; if I do not exist, there is no way to make the choice of the boundary.

Therefore, the so-called freedom to choose the boundaries is actually the freedom to exist in the existence of life itself, which is the freedom to choose or decide the existence of self from the individual reality.

Only through this freedom of will can our freedom be fulfilled, and only through this freedom of will can we have a dialogue with the "transcendental world" by being the personal existence of the existence of life itself.

Section 3: The History of Existence

Since neither the "freedom of existence" nor the "communication of existence" can be separated from the reality of the existence of life itself, the ego is in a spiritually unique situation for the existence of life itself, the existence of life itself. Therefore, I bear the "historical problem" (Geschichtlichkeit) of the existence of the ego's life existence itself.

For Jaspers' philosophical point of view, the "being" of the being itself cannot be an object of action or thought, nor does it have a standard form of something that is manifested or a standard pattern that one can follow, but each time the being of the being itself is manifested, it must penetrate into the person or thing.

It is inevitable that each manifestation of the existence of life itself goes deeper into the person or the thing, lays the groundwork for the choice of a unique boundary situation, and is related to a particular responsibility. The meaning of the "historical question" is mainly to point out that we cannot live alone, apart from the world or from history.

Likewise, the real self or "being" cannot be separated from the historical situation. For example, the air currents create resistance to flight, but the bird must use the resistance of the air currents, otherwise it cannot soar in the air.

I can only grasp the self and transcend the realm through the "existence" of "experiencing things" that exist in the existence of life itself. This unity of the "self" of the "existence" of the self-life itself and the "I that can be observed at the level of empirical phenomena" is my "historicity", and the personal perception of the "existence" of this historical life existence itself is "historical consciousness" (geschichtliches Künste). The "existence" of this historical being itself is "historical consciousness" (geschichtliches BewuBtsein). Historical consciousness is definitely not knowledge of history.

It is the realization of the reality that "the "existence" of our own being cannot be repeatedly thrown into the same historical situation twice to survive. Neither the existence of the "existence" of my own life existence nor the communication of the "existence" of my life existence is non-historical or surreal.

On the one hand, I am burdened with the historicity of my own existence, and on the other hand, I am aware of the historicity of my own existence in the "communication of existence" with other "existences" that also have the historicity of my own existence. The following unity is manifested.

First, the union of "experiential things" (Dasein) and "existence" (Existenz).

First of all, historical life existence itself is the union of "Dasein" (experience) of life experience and "Existenz" (existence) of life existence itself. The "existence" of my life existence itself is basically tied to the "experiential thing" level of life experience, and the latter is inseparable from the decisional situation of the historical boundary situation.

It is a multi-faceted, multi-perspective, multi-level concept of judging, evaluating and determining a thing; it represents the unity of the individual, and it also represents It represents the unity of the individual, as well as the "being" of the existence of the individual life existence itself within the empirical world.

Historical consciousness makes the "experiential thing" of the life experience of the self-life itself to be extremely important for the realization of the "existence" of the self-life itself, but at the same time, the "existence" of the self-life itself becomes worthless before the transcendental world. The consciousness of historicity is torn between this tension of importance on the one hand and irrelevance on the other.

Second, historicity consists in the combination of "freedom" and "necessity".

"On the one hand, the decision that has been made seems to make me feel limited; on the other hand, the opportunity to choose quickly between situations makes me feel free in the root, the foundation, or the main part of things.

The "experiential things" of life experience, as something that appears, are limited by the series of necessity, but the "existence" of "self-life existence itself" breaks through the limitation of this objective law (as distinct from "freedom") that does not depend on one's will, by the possibility of freedom of will.

If I determine the "existence" of my own existence, I do not regard the "existence" of my own existence as a purely empirical experience; the existence of the "existence" of my own existence is the possibility of the choice of the boundary for me.

The possibility of the choice of the boundary situation belongs only to the "existence" of the existence of the self-life itself. I am free as the fundamental cause of the creation of things, but my freedom of will is always limited by the environment, and I cannot start over.

Therefore, the "existence" of the existence of the self-life itself is still a temporal history. And finally, I must admit that I have already enjoyed the freedom of will given to me by the "existence" of the self-life itself.

Third, the unity of historical "time" and "eternity".

The "existence" of the self-life itself is neither a purely timeless thing nor a purely temporal thing, it is the fullness of a moment that bears the past and contains the present moment of the future.

In this moment, I can realize the eternal truth, and I can recognize an event that is equally significant in all ages, such as the Christian religion. This moment of union of time and eternity (der Augenblick als die Identität von Zeitlichkeit und Zeitlosigkeit) is called by Jaspers the "eternal present" (ewig Gegenwart).

It is only in this historical depth that the "being" of the self-living being itself can communicate with other "beings" of the self-living being itself, but when this communication is broken, it is possible to face the transcendental realm.

The so-called "eternal present" refers to the moment

when the "being" of the egoic existence itself makes the final choice of the boundary realm, and the consequence of the choice through the boundary realm is also eternal.

Fourth, truth itself has a historical nature.

Philosophy is the study of universal and fundamental issues, including existence, knowledge, values, reason, mind, language, and other fields. Philosophy differs from other disciplines in that it has a unique way of thinking, such as a critical, often systematic approach, based on rational argumentation.

This view contradicts the claim that "truth is universal, eternal, and total". For the Jasperian view of philosophy, philosophical thought, if true, facilitates a process of transmitting facts, ideas, concepts, feelings, values, and attitudes to another person or group. It is a complex process that not only transmits the content of a message, but also includes judging the meaning of the message.

It is also a dynamic process that, like time, cannot be reversed or repeated after it has occurred, so it is important to communicate effectively and in a timely manner; and it is clear that inferential thinking will never achieve a universally true understanding of the "existence" of the existence of the self.

At most, we can only obtain a view of the "existence" of life itself. The history of the correct reflection of objective things and their laws in people's consciousness represents a kind of cognition, a thinking activity in which the human brain reflects the characteristics and connections of objective things, and reveals their meaning and effect on people.

In a broad sense, cognition includes all cognitive activities, i.e. perception, memory, thinking, imagination, understanding and production of language, etc., collectively known as mental phenomena. In a narrower sense, cognition is sometimes equated with the limitations of memory or thinking, and also represents the one-sidedness of a person in acquiring knowledge.

Whether an objective "existence" reflected in human consciousness is true as a result of thinking activity cannot be separated from the thinker, because the environment and the context of the time in which the thinker lives can determine whether he can clearly identify and grasp the essence of the existence itself, whether he can observe, think, analyze, etc. in such a thorough and profound way. Obviously, the philosophical truths understood in this way are different from scientific truths.

The study of universal, fundamental issues, including truths in the fields of existence, knowledge, values, reason, mind, language, etc., is, as Kierkegaard said, "a truth for which I can live and for which I can die".

It is also the truth that is recognized by a being with a unique consciousness and a unique personal experience, or by another entity that is external to itself and interacts with other things, or the "truth of being".

There is no question of a similarity in nature, role, position, or number to the object, or to one of the two systems, in the order in which the things follow each other, nor is there the possibility of universal truth.

"Being" means that there is no objective criterion of truth. Every "being" that exists in itself is unique, special, and will never be the same again, and no one else can take its place.

Even at the level of the "existence" of the egoic being itself, there is no protection of that proven clarification of the true concept of the "existence" of this one being itself.

And the "existence" of another egoic being is equally

true. The truth may be ultimately one, but this unity does not appear directly, for the "truth of being" is based on action, more than on the content.

The meaning of this true and unchanging truth is, in fact, a philosophical belief, the "existence" of the existence of the self in itself, and the recognition of the relationship between itself and the transcendent world.

Section 4: The Expression of Encompassing

Jasper's holistic, fundamental, and critical inquiry into the real world and human beings begins with "our own inclusiveness," which is articulated through the "being" of the existence of the self in itself, and leads directly to the "transcendental world" and "existence itself.

It is a discipline that explores and reflects on fundamental questions about life, knowledge, and values through analytical thinking. The emphasis on a subjective way of thinking does not exclude the human ability to use reason. In contrast to the concept of sensibility, it usually refers to the component of reasoning that leads to reasonable conclusions after careful consideration of the evidence.

It is only Jaspers' view that "reason" alone, by means of mental activities such as concepts, perceptions, judgments, or imagination, is unable to grasp the existence of the existence of the self as such, nor can it achieve the transcendence of the existence of the self as such.

Some philosophers have criticized the philosophy of existence as a kind of irrationalism, but at least in Jaspers' philosophy of existence, the so-called "irrational" does not mean "counter-rational", but it can be said to be "super-rational". It can be said to be "super-rational," although it is super-rational.

Although it is said to be super-rational, it definitely does not mean to exclude reason, but to transcend reason itself by means of reason. The basic idea of inclusiveness can be said to be the creation of Jasper.

Basically, it can be said that it is a way of unification and remedy designed to transcend the dilemma of "subject-object division" caused by rational cognition.

Jasper's inclusiveness originally refers to "existence itself" or "total existence"; "existence itself" cannot be an object of cognition because it is an "inclusiveness" that is neither a subject nor an object, but covers both the subject and the object as a whole.

It cannot be an object of cognition because on the one hand it is the condition and basis of cognition of all objects, and on the other hand it cannot be divided, because it is the whole of subject and object.

Inclusiveness" is a concept without content or impractical content if measured in a secular way, but it is the form of our realization of existence. It opens up an infinite number of possibilities, allowing the functional role of these existences to become visible, and making all existences more explicit.

Therefore, Jaspers suggests that if we want to analyze in detail and understand the meaning of "inclusiveness" from a certain cognitive point of view, we can understand it in two ways: on the one hand, it cannot be the object of action or thought, and on the other hand, it can be the object of action or thought. On the one hand, it cannot be the object of action or thought, the process of acquiring knowledge or exchanging opinions or debates on an issue through mental activities such as forming concepts, perception, judgment, or imagination; on the other hand, it is a thought that appears in our mind whenever we think about it or talk about it.

It is a term that includes a variety of concepts, and its meaning refers to the mental activities such as sensation, perception, thinking, memory, etc., in which an individual is able to analyze, synthesize, judge, reason, generalize, etc., by using the mental activities of sensation, perception, thinking, memory, etc., and by integrating awareness and knowledge of his or her physical and mental state and changes in people, events, and objects in the environment.

"Inclusiveness" and "existence" are also a whole and cannot be treated as objects. "To think philosophically about "inclusiveness" is to explore "existence" in the life of the self.

It is not a content that can be expressed or taught through exploration or research, but a change in our consciousness from one form, state, or characteristic to another.

And a new attitude to the mental process of knowing and understanding things through the activity of consciousness. When we think about "inclusiveness", we are also thinking about the existence of life itself, and we are learning through observation and reading, discovering problems, collecting data, forming explanations, obtaining answers, and communicating, examining, and inquiring into learning.

Therefore, the way of grasping "inclusiveness" is not the way of reasoning and deducing reasonable conclusions after careful consideration of various evidence, but a way of "existence" clarification of the existence of life itself.

It is no longer a way of thinking about something that is the goal of action or thinking, but a way of thinking that is new in analysis, synthesis, judgment, reasoning, and generalization. It must be a dynamic, dialectical way of thinking.

On the one hand, it does not give up the rational and active process of reflection on the real world or any object by limiting the human mind to an "inward dialogue", but on the other hand, it does not allow itself to be confined to analysis, synthesis, reasoning, judgment, and other thinking activities, but must start to oppose itself and deny itself. Such clarification of cognition can only clear the confusion and confusion, and the recognition of the existence of self-life itself.

When we analyze "inclusiveness", we can also say that it is an explanation of the interaction and interconnection between the subject and the object, where the subject refers to "the inclusiveness of the existence of the self" and the object is "the inclusiveness of the existence itself".

The inclusiveness of the subject is associated with the modes of experiencing "experiential things" (Dasein), "consciousness itself" (BewuBtsein), "spirit" (Geist), and even "existence" (Existenz) of the self-living being itself, while the inclusiveness of the object is the "Transzenden" (Transzenden). Transzendenz" (beyond the boundary).

However, Jasper also mentions that in terms of the elucidation of the "existence" of the ego-life being itself, one can observe oneself from several perspectives.

First, Jaspers sees man as the "being" of the existence of the self-living being itself

"He is a living being in time and space. He has instincts, needs and impulses, and his actions are for the satisfaction of these things. At this level, the human being can be the object of action or thought in various sciences, such as psychology, sociology, and anthropology.

However, these studies take certain objects as the

scope of study, and seek to obtain unified and exact objective laws and truths based on experiments and logical reasoning. It is not enough to grasp and understand the whole, the whole self.

Second, person is a collective term that includes various concepts.

Its meaning refers to the individual's use of sensation, perception, thinking, memory, and other mental activities, the state of his or her body and mind and the environment of people, things, and changes in the comprehensive awareness and understanding of itself.

According to Jaspers, from this level, human beings as consciousness itself can produce the mental process of knowing and understanding external things through the activity of consciousness. Almost everything is under the extensive coverage of our consciousness.

Thirdly, man is a spirit that desires wholeness, perfection, and fulfillment.

According to Jaspers, human consciousness, thought activity and general mental states express the synthesis of life experience, experience and consciousness itself. Through the usage and meaning of the word Dasein by

Jaspers and Heidegger, it denotes a considerable difference in the form or content of the degree.

For Heidegger, the German word Dasein, generally translated as "this being," is used specifically to refer to human existence, and he defines Dasein in terms of such domains of existence as tethering, freedom, and historical degradation.

Thus, Heidegger's meaning of the word Dasein encompasses the two words that Jaspers uses to reflect the results of his thinking in words, sounds, tones, expressions, and gestures: namely, "experiencing things" (Dasein) and "being" (Existenz) in a general sense. Existenz.)

In the context of "spirit," which is the composition and structural form of several or many things with relatively distinct differences, man and the universe can be "included," and in the idea of the whole collective or the whole of things, man is no longer seen as an individual, but as a part of the whole. It is a part of the whole.

It is only through the 'inclusiveness of ourselves' that the 'inclusiveness of being itself' can be explored in the existence of self-life. "Existence itself never appears independently as a physical and cognizable thing.

It only develops through him in the "inclusiveness of ourselves" of the self-living being itself. We perceive the "existence itself" of the self-living being as the existence itself of the self-living being itself, which we seek out from our own situation.

It is not that we form a concept expressed in words or phrases from the many attributes of the same thing based on perceptual knowledge of two or more forms of thought that reflect the nature of things.

The concept is abstract and universal in nature. The act of associating in a certain way and subjectively creating something that is objectively and universally accepted to achieve a certain purpose.

It is not a way to analyze something in detail, to understand it in a certain cognitive way, or to act or think about it as an object. But it is the ultimate goal of life that attracts us and never stops searching for it.

From Jasper's philosophical viewpoint of "inclusiveness" to the Chinese philosophy of Laozhuang, the novelty or uncertainty of the situation, the further understanding of the thing or control of the situation, and the series of inquisitive behaviors that are triggered. The purpose is to achieve a state of oblivion, forgetfulness of subject and object, and unity of heaven and man.

Jasper has explained and elaborated on the essence of the core idea of Laozi (Li Er), "The Tao is inclusive. "The Tao is not an object of human cognition, it has an inexhaustible value orientation and evaluation scale, and is the mechanism of evolution of everything in heaven and earth, one of the beliefs of Laozi's philosophy.

The "Tao" is also both intrinsic and transcendent, and is composed and structured in the form of a four-dimensional up-and-down relationship, filling the nature of the greatest and most rigid between heaven and earth.

Both Jaspers' concept of "inclusiveness" and his philosophy have a characteristic that he would never consider his set of ideas to be ultimate and absolute.

If we can grasp the concept of "inclusiveness" of Jaspers, it will be more helpful for us to grasp his whole idea of "existence" in depth.

Jaspers famously said: "Existence" is inclusiveness: Sanil (the author of Jaspers' biography and the publisher of his book) expresses the content of Jaspers' thought in words and phrases: this phrase has at least two different meanings This statement has at least two different meanings.

One is that "inclusiveness" is entirely about the image of "things" and

One is that "inclusiveness" is a term for the image of a "thing" and the use of various vivid rhetorical devices to visualize and elaborate on things.

For example, imagine it as some kind of round, invisible, or some kind of shell-like thing, thus forming a finite, inclusive imagination, which must be replaced by an infinite "inclusive" abstract thought.

Secondly, since "inclusiveness" is not in a state of division, "inclusiveness" is unknowable, it is that indeterminate one (das unbestimmte Eine) that exists. Should we then be silent about it? Such a desperate conclusion was not reached by Jasper.

Rather, he says that if one is equally unable to recognize (erkennen) "inclusiveness", one is able to articulate (erhellen) the deeper truths. "Inclusiveness" is a kind of unexplained utterance and ideation, both of which are free of the need for specification, in order to achieve clarity.

It means thinking, exploring, and making silent speculations and debates about what comes up in order to make decisions. It is a kind of Vergewissern that cannot be clearly understood.

How Jaspers articulates "inclusiveness" is a complex question that demands an answer or answer.

Jasper cites the book The Great Philosopher to suggest a shared relationship or causality between things or signals: to think about "inclusiveness" in a holistic, fundamental and critical inquiry about the real world and human beings means to enter into the very existence of the self-living being itself.

And this can only be done indirectly, because as soon as we talk about it, it becomes the object of our thinking.

We must use the process of analysis, synthesis, judgment, and reasoning on the basis of appearances and concepts in order to get the "inclusive" non-objects that others can't think of and to inspire thinking.

The book "The Great Philosophers" is a way of understanding the best things that Jaspers has revealed by making the history of philosophy realistic and examining the way in which "inclusiveness" has been revealed in different periods of history and in different regions. Or a way of thinking based on observation that is felt with the heart.

Section 5: The Concept of Transformation "Beyond" the Present Situation

The metamorphic "transcendental" situation that Jaspers speaks of comes from his concept of "inclusiveness" of the subject-object unity, which is Jaspers' study of the central idea that cannot be answered directly through perception, but must be answered or answered by inquiry through rational reasoning and logic. Jasper's metamorphic concept of "beyond" the present has two directions of meaning.

First, it is a transcendental journey that is open to no conditions, no restrictions, and no limitations.

The first is a transcendental journey that is open to all conditions and without any restrictions, that is, it includes the transformation of the world into a specified direction, including the directionality of things, the behavior of animals that actively adjust the spatial position of their bodies or parts of their bodies, and the existence of metamorphic "transcendental" situations that can not be obtained directly through perception by rational reasoning and logical research.

These transcendences allow one to move from imaginative to non-imaginative thinking, to analyze, synthesize, judge, reason, and generalize, and to distinguish between something in oneself or one who is bound by certain conditions, which may be artificial or natural, and which cannot be exceeded as if there were rules.

It is an objective argument, not a subjective test, and a quantitative indicator of the probability of the occurrence of various things, contained in things, and predicting the trend of their development. It is the transcendence from empirical existence to real existence.

Secondly, there is no condition, no restriction, no limitation.

The relationship between man and the transcendental realm is in a state of mutual hostility, rejection, and conflict between two things, which can only be interpreted through a code. The relationship between the two can only be interpreted through the cipher.

In particular, the great philosophers of the history of philosophy have explored and reflected on fundamental questions of life, knowledge, and values through analytical thinking. Their writings, and the disciplines in which they embody the study of universal, fundamental questions, include the fields of being, knowledge, value, reason, mind, and language. Ideas, too, can serve as coded texts, a springboard to the transcendental realm.

As we have mentioned before, the existence of the self existent itself is paid to the individual by the transcendent, and without the transcendent, there would be no freedom. It is also a process of future-oriented metamorphosis "beyond" the present situation.

In this sense, it is necessary to analyze in detail and to understand from a certain cognitive point of view that freedom is not as arbitrary as we think it is.

In this sense, it is necessary to analyze in detail, in accordance with the rules, and to understand from a certain cognitive point of view that the understanding of transcendence is not aimless and directionless. Freedom and transcendence are justifiable, a process of gradual freedom from exceeding the prescribed limits.

The result is a collective term that includes a variety of concepts, the meaning of which refers to the individual's use of sensory, perceptual, thinking, memory and other mental activities, the state of his or her body and mind and the environment of people, things and changes in the comprehensive awareness and understanding of less and less constraints. At first, human existence is limited by the external environment and conditions, but in the transcendence of the external limitations, human beings gain the inner freedom.

The existence of the self exists in the existence itself, and the process of existence exists in the special functions and activities of the human brain, which is a reflection of the objective world in a state of anxiety, annoyance, and fear that is unique to human beings, expressing a spiritual level of being bound by restrictions that do not go beyond the scope.

But the further transcendence makes people aware of the interactions and interconnections between people and the world, the existence of many invisible codes, and the content, structure and development of the spatio-temporal world itself.

This also refers to the objective world that exists independently of human consciousness. It is the sum of various processes, such as celestial evolution, geology, meteorology, physics, chemistry, and biological evolution, which are not influenced by human activities, and is called "innate nature.

All phenomena that existed before the emergence of human beings are eternal and infinite, indicating a certain kind of mystery and mystery, usually complex in origin and not known to the general public.

In the end of his book Wissenschaftder Logik, the 19th century German philosopher Georg Wilhelm Friedrich Hegel (1770~1831) says: "The idea, in its own absolute truth, determines its own particular aspects, and in its own absolute truth, determines its own particular aspects. In the end of his book [Wissenschaft der Logik], Hegel says: "The idea, in its own absolute truth, determines for itself its particular aspects, or its original prescriptions and its alien aspects, and the idea of immediacy, as its reflection, freely externalized into nature.

In discussing the philosophy of nature it is also said that nature is the idea in the form of "otherness" (Anderssein); nature is the spirit of self-alienation. Hegel argues that in the idea all indirectness is abandoned and all oppositions are unified, so that it is independent and self-contained, unifying itself and itself with each other.

This ultimate absolute immediacy or absolute unity is a simple fact, a ready-made thing that does not need to be stated through any indirect medium.

In this characteristic of the idea, it is the intuitive thing of feeling, and the intuitive idea is nature. In fact, Hegel has recognized "nature" as an objective, ready-made fact.

Therefore, in Jaspers' "transcendental concept", the deepest code of life is that he who loves material life will lose spiritual life; he who sacrifices material life will preserve spiritual life.

The true self receives spiritual comfort in the depths of the heart. Therefore, the "I" in the depths of the heart is more clearly aware of its own limitations, an invisible and insurmountable gulf.

This condition may be artificial or natural, like a rule

that cannot be crossed, especially in the consciousness of death, which makes one aware of the limits of one's own existence, the limits of one's choice of situations. According to Jasper, there are four ways of transcendence.

Jaspers' analysis of the current state of metamorphosis "beyond"

According to the philosophical viewpoint of Jaspers, philosophy is the study of universal and fundamental issues, including the fields of existence, knowledge, values, reason, mind, and language. Therefore, it is the philosophical thinking of the changing and developing situation, which is constantly in search of the existence of the self-life itself.

According to Jaspers, "Our search for existence leads us back to the question of the seeker itself. The seeker itself is not just existence, that is, empirical existence, because an empirical existence will no longer seek the existence of the self-life itself, it can already be satisfied from itself.

For a seeker, the reason for what is eagerly awaited and expected to be sought, the existence of the self-living being itself, is the 'possible reality', and this seeking is philosophical contemplation.

The holistic, fundamental and critical inquiry into the real and human world differs from other disciplines in that philosophy has a unique way of thinking, such as a critical, often systematic approach, based on rational argumentation.

The traditional philosophers have two interpretations of philosophy: they have always regarded philosophy as a kind of learning and experience acquired by man in the process of study and practice, a kind of organized and orderly.

However, Jaspers sees philosophy as a personal interpretation, which has two interpretations, one of which is the process of repetitive reflection to explore psychological explanations, and one of which is the process of continuous transformation "beyond" the present situation.

"Encompassing" is the center of Jaspers' metaphysics, which reflects the form of thinking about the nature of the object's properties, while transforming "beyond" the present is the action developed by human beings in accordance with this central concept. For Jaspers, what he calls "philosophical thinking" is in fact an action of transforming "beyond" the present.

After understanding the importance of exploring and studying the concept of metamorphic "transcendental" reality in Jaspers' philosophy, it can be interpreted from another aspect that Jaspers' philosophy is a "philosophy of being" and a "philosophy of transcendence" that explains the metamorphic "transcendental" reality of human beings.

It is a philosophy of thought, culture, morality, customs, art, institutions, and behavior that has been passed down through history. Most of the very old customary religious philosophies on the metamorphosis of the "transcendental" present see the metamorphosis of the "transcendental" present as a "transcendental thing" that has no direct relationship with human beings.

However, Jaspers' detailed and in-depth explanation and presentation of the metamorphic "transcendental" situation is a further interpretation, in which he takes traditional religious philosophy, which has no influence or control over human social behavior, and isolates human beings through "inclusiveness. Through "inclusiveness" he transforms the transcendent that is isolated from human beings into transcendent actions that are closely related to them.

From Jasper's point of view, although these transcendental things are objects that metamorphose "beyond" the present situation outside of human sensory experience, their manifestation is still an "inclusive mode" related to the subject, and they are "inclusive" in juxtaposition to the subject.

While transforming the meaning of the "transcendental" present as such a change, Jasper's thinking also derives the concept of transforming the "transcendental" present and sublimating it to leave the "transcendental realm", using the "transcendental realm" as the "foundation of existence" for human beings.

In order to realize the action of transforming the "transcendental" reality, one must receive the "code" from the "transcendental realm" and explain it in detail in order to realize the "possible reality" of one's own existence.

From this, it is clear that Jasper analyzes the metamorphic "transcendental" situation in detail and understands it from a certain cognitive point of view. The metamorphic "transcendental" condition is an action of the free will of man, and this action must be realized through the "transcendental realm".

To summarize Jaspers' interpretation of the present situation of metamorphosis "beyond", this paper will briefly explain the meaning of the present situation of metamorphosis "beyond" from the following levels, so that the original intention of the present situation of metamorphosis "beyond" under Jaspers' philosophical thinking can be more clearly interpreted.

First, the so-called metamorphic "transcendence" of Jaspers is beyond all objectivity and objectiveness. "The meaning of the true metamorphic "transcendental" state is to go beyond objectivity into nonobjectivity.

According to Jaspers, in the past, when philosophers talked about the metamorphic "transcendental" situation, they often limited it to the "transsubjective" aspect, but the real metamorphic "transcendental" situation should be "beyond allobjectivity of the metamorphic "transcendental" situation".

Secondly, the essence of reason is negation and doubt. When Jaspers points out that it is impossible to truly transform the "transcendental" present by relying on existing theories and the results obtained through rational logical deduction, he also states that the true transformation of the "transcendental" present should be the realization of the process from "empirical existence" to "actual existence".

From Jasper's point of view, the metamorphic "transcendental" condition is not only a human-specific action, but also an action that human beings must perform (what they have committed themselves to do or should do).

"Not only can a human being choose to transform "beyond" the present when there is a boundary situation to choose in life, but he can also restrain himself from transforming "beyond" the present. But at the other boundary of choice, Jaspers is more forceful in his desire for the fulfillment or realization of specific wishes or conditions for the metamorphosis of the "transcendent" present.

"Not only does man have to transform "beyond" the present situation in the choice of the boundary of his existence, but he must either transform and sublimate or become so depressed that he is deprived of the opportunity to transform "beyond" the present situation again.

It is clear from this that the "transcendental" present that Jaspers is talking about is not a given fact that exists in the existence of the self-life itself, but a chance of freedom of the will. Therefore, he must transform "beyond" the present situation.

But the choice of whether to transform "beyond" the present is still his own. He can choose to transform "beyond" the present or not, but if he chooses not to transform "beyond" the present, he will lose the opportunity to transform "beyond" the present again.

Thirdly, metamorphosis is an activity to achieve a certain purpose, not a destination for the existence of the self. According to Jaspers, "the metamorphosis of the "beyond" is a movement in the "spirit" of real existence, and this activity for a certain purpose is a movement of reflection, and the first philosophical thoughts are those that accompany each metamorphosis of the "beyond".

"Transcendental philosophy is a choice between the boundaries of life existence, it is not a search for something to act or think about that is outside the boundaries of the choice.

From these two sentences taken from other articles, we can see two main points: one is that transforming the "transcendent" present is an action, and the other is that transforming the "transcendent" present is also an action of thinking.

Judging from the overall situation, the questions that people ask for answers or solutions can be divided into two kinds: questions about the "direction and goal of the scientific world" and questions about the overall, fundamental and critical inquiry into the real world and people.

The former can be used to observe things as they are without adding personal opinions. In the latter case, the way to sort out and make a decision is to transform "beyond" the present situation, and the result of the latter is not an accumulation of knowledge but a change of consciousness.

The knowledge obtained from "the direction and goal determined by the scientific world" has universal validity and can be confirmed through experiments based on experiments and logical reasoning to find unified and exact objective laws and truths with certain objects as the scope of study.

However, this is not the case for the holistic, fundamental and critical inquiry into the real world and human beings. The method used to transform the "beyond" present situation in solving philosophical problems is to transform the "beyond" present situation, which is the same objective existence for everyone.

Therefore, the question of holistic, fundamental, and critical inquiry into the real world and human beings must be distinguished from the question of "the direction and goal of the scientific world". Jaspers thus distinguishes philosophical problems into three main areas: "the direction and goal of the philosophical world," "the elucidation of reality," and "metaphysics.

According to Jaspers, there are three modes of transforming "transcendental" action, which are "transcendental in world-defining directions and goals," "transcendental in actual explication," and "transcendental in metaphysics," depending on the field of application of the transforming "transcendental" action.

As we can see from the above account or the detailed

explanation of what happened, the solution to the problem of holistic, fundamental, and critical inquiry into the real world and human beings is not the same as the solution to the problem of objective laws and truths based on experiments and logical reasoning with a certain object as the scope of study, but the solution to the scientific problem must have a definite object as its answer.

In order to solve philosophical problems, philosophical thinking must be carried out, that is, metamorphosis "beyond" the present situation. The solution to the problem of a knowledge system reflecting the objective laws of nature, society, and thought can be carried out in two ways, one is in thinking and the other is in action.

The transformation of the "transcendental" status quo must be toward the "transcendental realm". The greatest difference between the holistic, fundamental and critical inquiry of Jaspers and other atheistic philosophical realms of existence and human beings is that Jaspers recognizes the existence of the "transcendental realm" or the reality of "transcendental" existence.

And he takes the "transcendental realm" as the "foundation of existence" for the existence of human ego life itself. According to Jaspers, "the ordinary existingconsciousness of the egoic being itself does not metamorphose into the "transcendental" reality, but the freedom of the will of the egoic being itself provides the opportunity for the egoic being itself to do so.

The realization of this opportunity is completed when the actual existence of the ego being itself opens up to its 'transcendental realm'. The real transformation of the "transcendental" reality must be realized in the existence of the "possible reality" of the egoic existence itself, and the reason why the person who is the "possible reality" of the egoic existence itself has to transform the "transcendental" reality.

The main reason is that man has the freedom of will, and Jaspers believes that the freedom of self-existence and the "transcendental realm" are very closely related and cannot be separated. "Only a person who is truly aware of his or her "freedom" can attain the certainty of "God", which is so closely related to "freedom" that it cannot be separated.

Why is that? Because in the freedom of the will of the ego being itself, I do not exist through the ego being itself, but I exist through the freedom 'given' by the ego being itself.

"What is important is that the human being, who is the actual being of the Self-existence itself, should experience the fact that the freedom of the will of the Self-existence itself is given to him by the "transcendent world".

The freedom of the will of the human being is the center of all the potentialities of the existence of the self-life itself, and through the Beyond, through the One, the existence of the self-life itself is led to its own inner unity.

As we can see from the above quoted articles and books, Jaspers believes that as man becomes more certain of the freedom of will in his own being, he will also become more certain of the "transcendental realm".

Basically, Jaspers sees the relationship between the existence of the self-life itself and the "transcendental realm" as a kind of "existential care" which is used to compensate for the deficiency of the "formal metamorphosis of the "transcendental" present" in thought.

The interplay and interconnection between "existence"

and "transcendence" can be said to be more concrete and direct than the "formal metamorphosis" of the "transcendental" present.

When a person realizes the limiting nature of the boundary decision, including the individual's use of sensory, perceptual, thinking, memory and other mental activities, the integrated awareness and understanding of his or her physical and mental state and the changes of people, events and objects in the environment, a limiting barrier is constructed.

When the transcendence of the boundary situation is chosen toward the "transcendental realm," one becomes aware of the difference between the "real" and the "transcendental realm," that is, the gap that cannot be crossed over the "transcendental realm," which is Jasper's "transcendental realm" or "God.

In the choice of the boundary, Jaspers mentions that God is only the ultimate concern of human consciousness, a personal, pure and free field of consciousness.

Therefore, Jaspers believed that there are three kinds of boundaries in the existence of life in the universe: physical boundaries, mental boundaries, and soul (spiritual) boundaries.

When these three boundaries appear, it is the time when man must analyze, synthesize, reason, judge, and make choices; that is to say, in all the activities of human life and all the social phenomena encountered, such as critical illness, conflict, pain, and death, man must question the meaning of his own existence.

I. Bodies' Boundaries

The "bodily boundary" refers to the limit of what each person can tolerate to be touched by others. It varies depending on the person, time, age, and gender, but it is up to the individual to decide.

Most people only begin to think about the meaning of life when they are faced with the threshold of physical collapse, such as a car accident, injury, aging, or when they feel their days are numbered. At this point, many people begin to ask: Why have I come to this point? How should I go on in the future?

Life is so short, what choices should I make to make it meaningful? But these people are lucky. What is really sad are those who do not think about these questions even when their bodies are on the verge of collapse.

The so-called human knowledge of natural or social things is the meaning given to the object, the spiritual content transmitted and communicated by human beings in the form of symbols, the process of choosing the possibility of becoming oneself and realizing oneself.

Many people like to ask what is the meaning of life, however, the meaning of life can never exist in a certain place or on a certain thing. The meaning of life is when one decides to do something, and in the process of this life experience, a power of self-affirmation arises.

That is to say, the ideas and truths contained in the things of life can only come from within, not from outside.

2. Psychological Boundaries

The so-called "psychological boundary" (boundary), as the name implies, is the limit of what is psychologically acceptable to each person. Beyond a certain limit, there will be a feeling of being forced and compelled.

The human psyche is the ability of the self to acquire knowledge through mental activities such as forming concepts, perceptions, judgments, or imaginations, for example, I have a normal psychological condition, so I am emotionally stable when interacting with others; I am happy when people praise me, and I am sad when people criticize me.

Many people normally think of themselves as decent people, but when they are faced with a difficult test, they suddenly have a dark, inexplicable impulse, and only then are they alerted to the fact that they are not as stable and calm as they normally think.

That is to say, one may seem healthy on the surface, but when faced with a difficult situation, it is then that one realizes that one is not so stable and reliable.

At the same time, we may notice some thoughts that we do not understand, or even blind spots that we do not usually notice.

3. Spiritual boundaries

The soul represents the spirit, which is related to the question of meaning. Whether life has meaning or not is not a psychological issue.

Most of the people who come to me for treatment of mental illness are upper class people who are physically healthy and mentally normal, but not happy. In other words, there must be something wrong somewhere, and it is not in the body or in the mind, it is called "spirit".

If we agree with Jung that it is possible for a person to be physically healthy and mentally normal and not be happy, this means that there must be a third factor that determines whether or not people are happy, and this third factor, for the moment, is called "spirit", which can be understood as the spiritual dimension.

However, what belongs to the spiritual level, we can't see and touch, only the mental and emotional feelings. When we don't feel happy, the alarm is already ringing inside, it has not been happy for a long time.

So what is the spirit? Western texts already reveal that people believe in the existence of spirits: Body represents the body, Mind represents the mind, and the last one is called Soul or Spirit.

It refers to the spiritual state of a person. The last one is called Soul or Spirit. You cannot enter the Soul." -Note: "They are all referred to as the mind. Also: 心靈 (refers to the inner heart, spirit, mind, etc.); 靈明 (refers to "heart", i.e. subjective spirit)

Therefore, Jasper believes that there are three kinds of boundaries in the existence of life in the universe: the boundary of the body, the boundary of the mind, and the boundary of the soul (spirit). When these three boundaries appear, it is the time when human beings must analyze, synthesize, reason, judge, and make decisions about the boundaries; that is, when all activities in human life experience and all social phenomena encountered, such as critical illness, conflict, pain, and death.

The choice of the boundary situation questions the meaning of the existence of the self-life itself. If there is no transcendence, the existence of one's own being will lose its original selfhood.

In other words, the transcendental realm cannot be reached through dialogue, but can only be experienced in the form of "freedom of will" and "metamorphosis" of the existence of the ego being itself. The present situation".

For Jasper's transcendental realm, "freedom of will" and "transformation of the "transcendental" reality" are inseparably related.

Jasper says: "I myself am certain that in freedom I do not exist through the existence of my own life itself, but I am given to myself by the social matrix because I may lose myself, but therefore this 'unconditionality' requires an 'existential determination' of the existence of my own life itself through 'reflection'.

This means that it does not occur from any "state of nature", but is born within the "freedom" of the will to exist that exists in the self-living being itself, a "freedom" of will that is necessary and not due to any "law of nature" but because it The "freedom" of this will is necessary, and is not due to any "law of nature" but has its basis in the "metamorphosis" of the "beyond" present situation.

A freedom of will that cannot be forced upon oneself. The true self is recognized as such, which means that it does not exist through the existence of the life of the self itself.

I experience the highest degree of freedom in being free from the constraints of the social matrix, a freedom that is profoundly connected to transcendence. And the true meaning of the existence of the being of the self is the freedom of the will, and the source of this freedom is what Jaspers himself calls "the transcendental realm or God".

He believed that belief in God is the guarantee of the freedom of the will that exists in one's own being, because to deny God is to deny the freedom that exists in one's own being.

Schartre holds the opposite view. He denies God, but he also believes that man is free. Jaspers strongly opposes this because he believes that if there is no God, then there is no freedom in the existence of the ego itself.

To think that the ego exists through myself is a kind of self-deception, turning freedom into a synonym for helplessness and emptiness, because man's belief in this freedom of will without God is simply a false and arbitrary assertion without foundation.

One should not give up one's freedom of will by yielding to the authority or power of the world's social matrixes and constraints, but one should be responsible for the existence of one's own being, and especially not give up the freedom of one's own being in order to pursue one kind of freedom over another.

One should learn how to control the choices of one's own boundary situation and the choices one makes in one's own hands, and then face the problems, positive or negative, arising from these choices, and then strive to overcome them and solve them. Learn to be responsible.

When one tries to understand the "transformation"

beyond the "present" in the time of one's existence, the experience of daily life will inevitably encounter "frustration".

In Jasper's thought, Scheitern is a very important concept, not only as a concept, but also as a code for transcendence itself, and as the key code that enables the existence of the self to leap into the "transformed transcendental state".

Only the symbol of the intuitive nature of the root can serve as a code for the transcendental realm. The symbol of the main purpose and intention of self-consciousness cannot be considered as a code if it is not transcendental, because all codes are codes of the transcendental realm.

For Jaspers, the existence of the self-life itself is the existence of existence. But there are different levels of "frustration". Jasper describes the nature of the cipher as follows: "The cipher is the language of existence that exists in the self-life itself when it transcends the realm, not the transcendent itself. It is not the transcendental world itself. It is a difference on the conceptual level.

Human thought is inevitably frustrated, and the interpretation of the cipher, including the interpretation of the "existence" cipher, is a mode of thinking, and therefore is predetermined to be frustrated beyond human will or human power. Jasper distinguishes between "frustration of thought" and "frustration of existence.

The "frustration" of existence includes the "frustration" of freedom of will, the "frustration" of the relativity of the choice of the boundary situation, and the "frustration" of the guilt of conscience condemnation. In the context of boundary situations, there are obviously two ways of thinking about the interpretation of the term.

First, it is the nature of existence that treats each other, such as big versus small, beautiful versus ugly.

Secondly, it is the existence that depends on certain conditions and changes with certain conditions (as opposed to "absolute"): for example, the most valuable and the least valuable.

Therefore, there are many different levels of "frustration" that people feel, and when we face "frustration" with our I-love persistence, whether it is "frustration" at the level of "experiencing things" in our daily life or "frustration" in our own existence, we will adopt different attitudes. But most of the time we avoid the fact of 'failure'.

Human beings, after careful consideration of the evidence, reason their way to a reasonable conclusion. We think that we can overcome it if we enrich our knowledge and experience in terms of the structure of our thinking and our activities to achieve a certain goal.

However, this attitude of inevitability is the accidental process that leads to the failure of everything, in fact, the inevitability of expecting success also breeds the accident of unexpected failure.

According to Jaspers, "The real and obvious 'failure' is not in the defeat of any boundary choice, any destruction, self-abandonment, or failure. It is only when I am unwilling to 'fail' and dare to face 'failure' that the code of immortality in 'failure' becomes clear.

A true "failure" cannot be prearranged or planned, so it becomes neither a "failure" nor a password.

Furthermore, when it comes to the 'defeat' of the boundary decision itself, can those fearful or worrying crisis situations, suggesting that decisive or final consequences will follow, be the most crucial code for the 'existence' of the existence of the self?

The seriousness of this matter is enough to attract people to study and discuss, or to demand answers or answers, from the "existence" of the ego's life existence itself, to realize the close relationship between the ego and the "transcendental realm", and to realize the ego through the boundary situation, because one must transform "beyond" the present situation and anticipate the impossibility of the life "existence" process. It is because one must metamorphose "beyond" the present and anticipate the impossible possibility of the "existential" process of life.

From Jasper's philosophical point of view, the desire for fulfillment and the expectation of frustration are in conflict with each other, and the existence of the ego's life itself "exists", resulting in the "frustration" of the choice of the boundary situation. It is a prerequisite for the real frustration of the desire for fulfillment.

Therefore, the 'defeat' in the dilemma of boundary decision is, for the transcendental view of Jasper, as if "the 'defeat' itself is just an impractical, inscrutable nothingness, and is no longer a code.

Therefore, the 'defeat' that dares to face the defeat of the 'existence' of the self-life existence itself, but does not deliberately seek to choose the boundaries of the situation, makes the 'existence' of the 'existence' of the self-life existence itself free of will, and has a new aspect of the meaning of life existence.

Therefore, as a possible encounter with the "existence" of the self-life existence itself, and as the freedom of the will to choose the boundary situation, a perceptual or sensory experience, the experience of perceptual or sensory resistance, the "existence" of the self-life existence itself "resists" absolute "frustration", and even when all possibilities and freedom cease to "frustrate", the "existence" of the self-life existence itself is the most manifest realization of the self The essence of self-realization is best revealed by the "existence" of the self-life itself, even when all possibilities and freedom cease to "fail.

But the person who is the "existence" of the existence itself is a mode of life existence, not an impractical, inscrutable nothingness of life existence.

The experience of encountering the "frustration" of the existence of the self and the impractical and inscrutable nothingness of that frustration makes one experience that the "frustration" of the freedom to choose one's own will in a boundary situation not only reveals nothingness, but also reveals the existence of the transformation "beyond" the present situation.

The frustration of revealing this emptiness has two aspects.

First, it is the level of the master's motivation to move forward, which leads one to transform "beyond" the present situation.

The second is the level of escapism and depression, which makes people's fundamental attitudes and views on life

The questions that we are asked to answer include: why we live, the meaning, value, purpose, ideal, belief, and pursuit of life, etc. Toward destruction and nihilism.

From the perspective of the choice of "defeat" in the boundary situation, it seems impossible to survive the "existence" of one's own life existence. However, for the sake of the existence of all living systems and the maintenance of their existence and development, the "existence" of human life itself is still struggling to get rid of the fear, and even though it knows that it is impossible to succeed, it still tries to transform "beyond" the present situation.

"The transformation from fear to calmness is the greatest transformation that one can achieve.

All the codes of the transcendent realm, including the codes of "existence" and "frustration" of the choice of boundaries of the existence of the self, ultimately lead to the "frustration" of the psychological state of the individual in the process of purposeful activity, which encounters obstacles or interference. Only "transcendence" itself does not "fail".

Finally, through the "defeat" of the existence of the self, we can see the condition of existence towards the "transcendental realm", and it is in the "defeat" of the defeat that we can experience the "existence" of the true meaning of the existence of life.

Defeat" can certainly bring one a great blow or disappointment, or even complete despair, and lead one to the disillusionment and emptiness of the meaning of life existence, but the existence of self-life existence itself can also bring one the opportunity to transform "beyond" the present situation.

It can lead us to a new code for the transformation of

the "transcendent" status quo, allowing us to reaffirm the "existence" of our own existence and to grasp the transcendent realm towards eternity.

Chapter 5: Conclusion

It has been said that "man accepts life without choice, then lives it under conditions of helplessness, and finally surrenders it in an irresistible struggle.

Some philosophers believe that philosophy should clarify the phenomena of cosmic interpretation of the world and life, such as Hegel's establishment of an all-encompassing philosophical system. Other philosophers tend to provide science with the basic cognition of life experience in order to prevent displacement of scientific theories.

There are also philosophers who try to integrate various academic fields to provide human beings with a comprehensive and progressive knowledge of the world as a whole.

The task of philosophy, as proposed by Jaspers, is not to claim to be able to know the universe and to recognize one's own world, but rather to help people to recognize the value of their own existence and to make an autonomous and positive choice, out of the confusion of being lost and sunken and unable to satisfy themselves.

It is because of people's deviated cognition of the meaning of the existence of the self and the existence of life itself that they are unable to attain any given cognition of the existence of life and are unable to understand the quenching and confusion of the experience of life.

Thus, Jaspers' philosophy of existence guides one to seek the possibility of solving the autonomous life of the individual in the process of unblocking the existence of life, when one cannot obtain the clarification of the existence of life itself through the formation of concepts, perceptions, judgments, or mental activities such as imagination.

According to the philosophy of existence of Jaspers, if one wants to help the philosophy of life existence of the self, in the so-called "uncertain environment" where one does not know what to do because of doubts.

In other words, the "being" of the self is unable to know the outcome of its actions and the probability of various possible situations, while the being of the self is mostly in a situation of boundary decisions. It is necessary to study modern man's concept of the existence of his own being.

We propose how to recover the value of the existence of self-life from the cognition of the existence of self-life itself, so as to avoid the unrealistic and inscrutable destruction of nihilism and the path of failure and frustration.

On the one hand, by studying and using the existence of objective things and their related laws to achieve effective, convenient, low consumption, high output, etc., the methods and means of specific purposes, indeed, bring further significant development to human production, providing various aspects of human life But the rapid progress of material civilization

However, the rapid advancement of material civilization has only seen the dazzling glory of technology, which cannot really help all mankind to achieve harmony and happiness, and may even lead to disaster and destruction. Everything seems to be in a state of lack of change like a mechanical operation, which makes people completely lose the crisis of autonomous cognition.

On the other hand, from the viewpoint of the inner world of thoughts or feelings, because of the large variety or quantity of conscious thoughts, mental states, and the world of thoughts and feelings (material wealth, intellectual experience, etc.), human emotions (types of things, threads, etc.) become more and more diverse and complicated, and the wisdom, thoughts, and feelings inherent in human hearts become more and more responsive, and they become very sensitive to a certain thing or a certain kind of The human being is very sensitive, quick to perceive, and can quickly judge or react to something.

The human being has the consciousness to think, to think, to reflect the nature of the objective reality, the internal laws of the nature, indirectly and in general. It is increasingly open, liberated, unrestricted, not so much constrained.

In the process of contact with external things, people get more and more feelings or experiences; the stage of success and joy, often fall into boredom, boredom, no reliance on the mental barrier, leading to fall into the unrealistic and elusive spiritual emptiness.

Mental expectations do not achieve the intended

purpose, the physical or spiritual feeling is very painful and deep, often leading to the inner search for stability and normalcy, without fluctuations; urgent or intense, so that the rhythm of life in a state of high readiness of the spirit, often make people feel crowded in the inner world.

A peaceful, unsettled, calm and quiet life often makes people feel very monotonous and lacking in interest and excitement, and does not allow them to be energetic.

As mentioned above, from the perspective of Walther's pessimistic criterion: the experience of life in the existence of the self is, so to speak, a loss of confidence in the existence of the external image or environment of the world, which is revealed without hope, and unhappiness because of the failure of hope.

It is often accompanied by confusion (Verwirrung) about the inherent qualities of the world of people or things, and is overwhelmed by confusion. Here we explore the influence of Jaspers' philosophical thinking on modern man and its meaningful insights through the balance of his thinking on the benefits of the Waldensian pessimism criterion.

The Wald pessimistic criterion considers that for any

action plan, it is assumed that the worst state will occur, i.e., the state with the least benefit value.

Then, the decision principle is to compare the results of each action plan after implementation and take the action with the greatest benefit value as the best action. That is, it finds the worst outcome of each action, and then finds the best one from the worst outcome as its choice.

Here we explore the influence and significance of Jaspers' philosophy on the choice of boundaries in an uncertain environment for modern people.

(1) Pessimistic criteria.

It means that for any action plan, it is believed that the worst state will happen, that is, the state with the smallest value of return occurs. Then, comparing the results of the implementation of each action plan, the action with the greatest return value is the most optimal first action decision principle. That is, the principle of "taking the big from the small", that is, the most conservative value to estimate, from which to choose the largest reward scheme.

(2) Optimistic criterion.

It is to find the best result of each action, and then find a better one from the best result as the choice.

In other words, when using the optimistic criterion, the decision maker starts from the most optimistic point of view and considers only the most favorable state of loss and gain for each decision principle. In other words, the principle of "taking the biggest out of the big" means that the most optimistic value is used to estimate and choose the most rewarding solution.

(3) Regret criterion.

This is the principle of choosing the smallest of the maximum regret values for any action plan as a backup for the highest priority decision.

This is actually an application of the pessimistic criterion. The pessimistic criterion is the "smallest of the big", which is based on the value of earnings. The regrettable criterion is the principle of "taking the smallest of the large", that is, estimating the maximum extent of the regrettable, and selecting the option that minimizes the opportunity cost of the regrettable or counter-utility shown.

(4) Subjectivism criterion.

It is the subjectivist view that we believe that reality is real and that there is no potential real reality independent of perception for any course of action. One would think that consciousness is reality, not subjective idealism.

This contrasts sharply with objectivity and realism, which holds that there is a potential "objective" reality that can be perceived in different ways.

The claim that "the activity of our minds is the only unquestionable fact of our experience" is not shared, is not public, and has no external and objective truth.

Without knowing the probability of occurrence of various situations and assuming equal chances of their occurrence, the most rewarding solution is selected from among them.

The choice of boundaries under uncertainty is indeed an experience of the existential experience of life, emphasizing the "communication" between people, which is not only necessary, but inevitably realized.

Jasper's book "Philosophy of Existence" explains that the "self" first understands the "self" that exists in the life existence itself, is gifted to itself, and creates itself freely with its own will. In the philosophical life of existence, in addition to self-reflection, it is also necessary to have "communication" with others in order to realize the truth.

Jasper takes a more optimistic attitude towards the establishment of interpersonal relationships. Everything is done in practice, in feeling and feeling, in action, in exploration, and, above all, in physical action.

Therefore, Jasper repeatedly emphasized that "truth begins with two people. Therefore, Jaspers repeatedly emphasized that "truth begins with two people. We use the concepts and techniques of Jasperian communication as a way to make amends and try to rescue or redeem.

Although we cannot insist on the expected satisfactory result for the person or thing that guarantees the effect, we believe in the possibility of positive thinking benefits under the Wald pessimistic criterion of benefit thinking, and the chance of achieving or realizing a certain value scale of things or events, and thus the expected result, will be relatively greater.

Jasper has always been deeply and genuinely concerned with the fact that people exist in a time of immediate facts and conditions.

He believes that if modern people abandon the social matrix of ideas, cultures, morals, customs, arts, institutions, and behaviors that have been handed down from generation to generation and from history. The influence and control of invisible constraints on human social behavior.

The person will feel overwhelmed by the confusion. The person may realize that he or she is in a lonely and helpless predicament and can only wait for death in an impractical and unpredictable way while feeling the meaning of life.

The internal emotional or psychological conflict leads to irrational feelings of worry or fear. If the mind is caught in this negative mood, it is up to the person to help himself.

In his Man in the Moderrn Age, he presents the following crisis facing modern mankind that he wants to express.

"No security", in the context of that era, means, in the present view, the limited support and support of some kind of interaction dynamics between the members of the society, between the interactions and interconnections of affairs. In the present view, it means the limited support and support of some kind of interaction dynamics between the members of the society.

For example: basic survival, basic living, basic medical care, employment, unemployment, free and compulsory education, basic old age, housing conditions, safety, reasonableness, and freedom of speech. It needs to be built on the civilization and wealth of the whole society, gradually increasing and building the rule of law, and gradually improving to realize.

In the age we live in, the following state of affairs is manifested: he is in rebellion against the Nazi regime; he is in the nihilistic view that the world, life (especially human beings), exists without objective meaning, purpose, or comprehensible truth.

In ethics, the term "nihilist" or "nihilism" is used to refer to a person who completely rejects all authority, morality, and social convention, or who claims to do so.

Either by rejecting all established beliefs, or by extreme relativism or skepticism, the nihilist believes that those in control of power are ineffective and should be confronted.

For nihilists, the ultimate source of moral values is not culture or reason, but the individual itself in despair; although postmodernism has been ridiculed by some as nihilism, to the extent that nihilists tend toward defeatism, it does not conform to the nihilistic formula described above.

In the midst of the kind of distress with which so many are dissatisfied, the postmodernist philosopher seeks to find the forces and causes that celebrate the unique human relationships he explores in all their forms. Skeptics do not have to draw any conclusions about the reality of moral concepts, nor do they have to discuss questions about the meaning of existence in the absence of knowable facts.

They are in the pursuit of those who have abandoned the final goal and followed the wrong path. Post-modernist thought has taken cognitive and ethical systems to the extreme of relativism. This is particularly evident in the work of Jean-François Lyotard and Deschutes.

These philosophers have attempted to deny the truths, meanings, historical processes, humanist ideals, and foundations upon which Western civilization was built. Although in principle postmodernism is considered a philosophy of nihilism, it is noteworthy that postmodernism accepts the criticism of postmodernism.

It is noteworthy that nihilism embraces postmodernism. Nihilism is a claim to the truth of the universe, which postmodernism rejects; the masses are constantly and impetuously shouting "there is no God".

And because of the loss of the ego's faith in God, man loses the value of the existence of his own life, because the ego feels that it has no reason to explain itself, and therefore the existence of the ego itself is slaughtered as if it were at will.

Therefore, Nietzsche's late works are mainly concerned with nihilism. A volume of The Will to Power consists of a selection of Nietzsche's notes from 1883 to 1888. He named it "European Nihilism" and considered it the main problem of the 19th century.

Nietzsche defined 'nihilism' as the idea that the world, and especially human existence, is devoid of meaning, purpose, intelligible truth, and intrinsic value.

In philosophy, Jaspers used the fundamental fact that the way of cognitive activity of analyzing, synthesizing, judging, and reasoning about external appearances and concepts is a concept of "context" that is unique to human mental activity.

The so-called "boundary situations" are the unavoidable facts, that is, the situations themselves, the contradictions, conflicts, sins, sufferings, deaths, etc., which have the existence of self-life itself, and are unavoidable, and all these "boundary situations" will occur in the process of life experience in one's life.

To face and overcome the seriousness of the "boundary situation", which is a problem that has been studied and discussed, or has yet to be solved, Jaspers presents his understanding and thoughts on the matter: he believes that the "situation" is one in which we can "change the original thought" or "modify or change the original thing".

But there are other 'situations', such as the existence of the self in a particular time, place, or family, that cannot be changed. These are the common "situations" that all human beings cannot intentionally avoid because they are unwilling or afraid to face a certain situation or thing, such as birth, death, pain, struggle, aging, and guilt. These are the common "situations" that all human beings cannot intentionally avoid because they are unwilling or afraid to face a situation or something.

They are like a wall that stops us from carrying out activities to achieve a certain purpose, and ultimately makes us feel frustrated.

These situations, which we cannot exclude from our daily experience, happen to us all the time, everywhere, from time to time. Although we try in different ways to avoid protecting the ego so that life itself continues to exist, at the end of the day, when we are not able to do so, we are not able to do so.

But in the end, when we encounter these "situations", we are helpless to do anything but compromise with the external pressure and give up fighting against it.

Therefore, to overcome these "situations", Jaspers proposes to change and change the purpose of our activities in order to achieve the existence of our potential self-life itself. The understanding of

Through the use of our senses, perceptions, and memories, we become aware of our state of mind and body and the changes of people, events, and objects in the environment.

In his book "Philosophy", Jaspers says, "Every action in the world has consequences that the actor did not anticipate, even if he never expected them. Even if the actor never expected these consequences, he will be surprised when he learns that he caused them.

In this world, even a person who lives together in a social matrix, and who is free from personal faults or defects in the rules and norms of his behavior, will inevitably experience things personally (the "life" of a person).

Inevitably, one will still experience the frustration of things (mostly suffering, disasters, etc.), the guilt of responsibility, and the conscience that one cannot escape. But the guilt of choosing the "boundary situation" can be transformed into a power.

When a person makes a decision in a "boundary situation", he or she realizes that the consequences of the action will reach an unknown realm, and therefore the situation that he or she personally experiences there (mostly suffering, disaster, etc.) becomes the responsibility of the person in the "boundary situation". The situation that one experiences there (suffering, disaster, etc.) becomes one's responsibility in the "boundary situation".

One must bear the burden of all the problems that arise from the "boundary situation" in life, which is a manifestation of the duty of responsibility. In his philosophy of existence, Jaspers places great emphasis on the responsible choice of "boundary situations".

According to Jaspers, "We become aware of the freedom of our own will when we accept the ups and downs of our lives and the course of our lives, which we cannot seriously deny, and the fact that we must choose our decisions 'in the realm of boundaries', and that we must use them to We have to use this "boundary situation" to make decisions about ourselves, and we should learn to be responsible.

One must learn to have the insight to make correct "boundary decisions" and to strive for such insight, not to shirk one's responsibility because of traditional dogmatic knowledge.

In Jasper's mind, the most valuable spiritual legacy in human history is the achievements of the West, China, and India. Jasper argues that human civilization began in certain regions of the world.

It was only after the topic of the metamorphosis of the celestial-human relationship was first raised for discussion and study that several major civilizations of human society slowly emerged, including the Chinese Taoist prophet Laozi (Li Er), the Jewish prophets (Abraham (Ibrahim) and Moses (Moses), the Indian prophet Buddha (Shakyamuni), and the Christian (Moses). Shakyamuni), Christianity (Jesus), Islamic prophets (Muhammad), ancient Greek philosophers (Socrates, Plato)

During these developments, the meaning of the existence of human civilization began to emerge.

Taken together, the three issues described by Jasper are, in Jasper's view, shared relationships or cause-and-effect relationships between things or signals. The metamorphosis "beyond" the present in "world orientation" suspends our existential consciousness in an infinite number of possibilities.

The metamorphic 'transcendental' condition in 'existential enunciation' holds 'existence' together in a state of suspension, appealing to the freedom of will of 'self-existence' (Selbstsein). In the metamorphic "beyond" condition, the "being" of the ego-being itself calls for the "being" of the ego-being.

Each of the three metamorphic 'transcendental' situations may be met with different resistance and must therefore be supported by the 'existential dynamic' (existentielle Antriebe). This dynamic can be explored in three directions.

1. The dynamics in "world orientation" is the desire to know the world and to search for the "being itself" that exists in the existence of one's own being.

2. The motivation of "Being Explained" is the desire to realize self-realization through communication with the world and with others.

3. The motivation of "transcendence", which is the pursuit of "God" or "the Absolute" by the "being" of the existence itself.

These three dynamics are necessary for the pursuit of true philosophy, and they are indispensable. The three ways of metamorphosing "beyond" the present must also be integrated and coordinated with each other in order to realize the true self.

"World Orientation, Existence Explanation, and the Quest for Transformation Beyond the Present are all interdependent, and only when they are pursued simultaneously can we move toward true transformation beyond the present.

When one realizes the "existence" of one's own life existence, and realizes the finiteness and transience of one's current life existence, and thinks about the meaning of "existence" of one's own life existence, one must strive to pursue the true meaning of one's own life existence.

Once a man does not know himself, he will lose himself and not find himself. In the end, he will lose himself in the unpredictable stage of life.

On the contrary, if man can face up to the true meaning of his own existence and know the importance of himself, he will be able to get closer to himself and set a direction to strive for the true meaning of his own existence.

Metaphysicians try to clarify the basic concepts

(areas) that people use to understand the world, such as the existence of life itself, the objects of objective consciousness and their nature, space and time, cause and effect, and possibility.

The first is: What is there ultimately in the existence of life itself? (What is ultimately there?); secondly, what is the self of life existence? (What is it like?): What is the content of each person's "self" within the existence itself?

It is a question that cannot be answered directly through perception, and the answer is deduced through rational logical reasoning under a priori conditions (which can be regarded as axiomatic assumptions), and cannot contradict empirical evidence. It is a paradoxical question of human reason's search for the most universal aspects and ultimate causes of things, which can be described as a matter of opinion.

For example, primitive Buddhism in India interpreted the "emptiness of origination" from the perspective of "this exists, therefore the other exists; this is born, therefore the other is born; this is not, therefore the other is not; this is not, therefore the other is not", which means that there is no such thing as "I".

The top number of human beings can only be regarded as a product of the temporary existence of the "five fetishes" (i.e., color, subjection, thought, action, and consciousness). However, sentient beings are unable to understand and always think that they are physical beings in the cycle of rebirth. Sakya means accumulation.

In the harmony of one's own body and mind, a sense of self arises, corresponding to the characteristics of I-love and I-slight, and opposing him (called falsehood). This is a delusion that does not exist at all - sakhya vision.

Whether it is oneself, another person, or an animal, there is a body and mind that are in harmony with each other, and all of them can be said to have a worldly false self (received falsehood). For people, there is the "bhakti" I-ness; for oneself, there is the "bhakti" I-ness, and there is also the "sakti" I-ness. There are two kinds of "I" existence: one is the "Patna" I; the other is the "Sakya" I. The meaning of the word "tantra" is "numbered", which means that one is constantly suffering in birth and death. Not to mention the fact that human beings have a "soul" within their bodies and minds as a "consciousness".

In Western humanistic thought, some people put the question of whether or not the "self" exists, and if so, what is its content, in the context of "personal identity". Such issues are discussed in the context of Personal Identity.

Respect for the "identity of the person" is perhaps the most important ideal. Contemporary humanism, in its attempt to replace Christianity, has succeeded in separating the concept of the human person from theology and associating it with autonomous ethics, or with the concept of a purely existential philosophy, with respect to the dignity of the human person.

Thus, although personhood and the "oneness of personhood" are widely discussed today as a noble ideal, no one seems to have identified the concept of personhood as inseparable from theology in terms of history and existence.

Within the very narrow confines of this study, an effort should be made to show how deeply and indestructibly the concept of personhood is linked to patristic theology and ecclesiology.

Personality, as a concept and as a living reality, is a mere product of patristic thought. Without understanding this, the deepest meaning of personality cannot be understood or proven.

Chapter 6: The Meaning of Life's Existence

1. "Stubbornness" is the essence of life's existence.

It is not easy for people to live their own life, knowing that they will die one day in the future, no matter how rich or poor they are in this life, but they still have to live unconsciously for the sake of realizing a certain ideal or achieving a certain purpose, regardless of the consequences.

Living in a society with various and often numerous interconnections of parts, factors, concepts, aspects or influences, which are difficult to analyze, answer or understand, we cannot see the actual connotations hidden inside the human heart, and we miss the hang-ups because we cannot rest assured.

We can't forget the great achievements and

accomplishments of yesterday, we can't finish our busy day, we can't imagine our life in the doldrums, we can't realize our ambition of tomorrow's aging, we don't know which day we will disappear in the unexpected, this is the reality of life.

We have always understood clearly that there is an old saying: "Those who, after hearing others' opinions or attacks on their shortcomings or mistakes, will first review themselves will definitely develop in a better and better direction".

However, no one likes to be emphasized to point out the negative or the shortcomings as a suggestion for improvement, even if they sometimes comment on what is good or bad. Even if the comments are sometimes good or bad, they may be directed at flaws, mistakes or attacks, or they may be ordinary comments rather than negative comments, or they may just point out flaws without making suggestions for improvement. But one does not take it personally and keeps doing the same thing.

You don't listen to straightforward advice, you don't like to be told what to do, but you demand that the other person must do what you want; you hope that the other person doesn't mind your straightforwardness, saying that this is your nature, but you hate the other person, you look arrogant when you tell them what to do, and you speak too straightforwardly. The "stubbornness" of the ability to decide one's own behavior.

However, the Western philosopher Schopenhauer was able to accurately interpret natural and social phenomena as "will" and "will" as life, according to the existing empirical knowledge, experience, facts, laws, cognition and tested hypotheses, through generalization and deductive reasoning, and other logical inferential summaries.

Oriental religious philosophers interpret it as "obsession" + "delusion", which means "the state of mind that consciously strives for the realization of a certain ideal or the attainment of a certain goal".

It is impossible to understand that when we come into the world naked, it means that we will also leave empty-handed, taking nothing with us, which is a warning of the "emptiness" for which we have worked hard all our lives, insisting on our own opinions and refusing to adapt.

However, what is even more saddening is that we see every objectively existing thing and situation in front of our eyes, and we see every species, including people, stubbornly, but we think that there is nothing special about it, and we are not surprised that something happens. This is the nature of life that cannot be experienced at all.

Therefore, as long as a person has not yet joined the "will", life is like a blank sheet of paper, and it depends on how one's "will" will paint one's life in the future.

Life can be very beautiful or very dark, depending on how you face it. Since you have come to walk, you should definitely let yourself live a meaningful life and do something that you feel is meaningful. The existence of their own life itself, the life of the full and meaningful. The first thing you need to do is to be clear and open-minded every day.

As a person's life is a conscious effort to realize a certain ideal or achieve a certain purpose, the amount of money in material life, the size of power, the level of ability, these things that will exist temporarily as life is born, live, change, and die, cannot represent the meaning of the life experience of quenching one's life.

It cannot represent the value of life. To say so is

certainly to hurt the self-esteem of countless people, because this is what we want in our life, is our life existence, the ultimate goal of our life to become angry and strong.

So, what do people live for? What is the meaning of human life? This is a question that only Homo sapiens (scientific name: Homo sapiens, meaning "modern, intelligent human being") with higher intelligence would ask since ancient times. First of all, let's explore what is the purpose of human life? What is the reason for living?

What do we live for? From our daily life, we always feel that we live for others. When we were young, we lived for the "will" of our parents before we joined the "will". In our parents' "will" world, we were a treasure for them.

We only hope that you can grow up happily and carefree. We did not join the "will" when we were young, so we laughed and played naughtily, which satisfied their (parents') happy expectations. This is because there is a hope or dream that continues in our parents' "obsessions" + "delusions".

As we grow up, we begin to live by consciously working hard to achieve a certain ideal or purpose. We need to acquire knowledge, including what people know, how they know it, and exactly what it means to "know something".

The definition of knowledge is an important theme in the theory of knowledge. A belief alone does not constitute knowledge; there needs to be a good reason to support the belief in order for it to be considered knowledge.

So, in school, you listen to your teachers, you live for your classes, your assignments, your exams. You are walking on the edge of one's own feelings, thoughts, beliefs, or other mental states, school and social knowledge, and standing at the point of life's choices.

This is because partial knowledge is being explored. For the most part, it is impossible to understand an area of knowledge in its entirety, so knowledge is always incomplete and partial.

Just as in school when solving mathematical problems, all the information is known and it is assumed that the solver has a complete understanding of the formulas needed to solve the problem, this is not the case for real-world problems, where partial knowledge of the context of the problem and the problem data is needed to solve the problem (false consensus effect).

As your wings grow fuller, your self-life will be lived with a new attitude to meet the next goal. When we enter society, we "will" to start living for work.

First, you have to decide to achieve a certain purpose, and the psychological expectation to fill your stomach is often expressed in words or actions. If you want to find a job to make ends meet, you have to do physical or mental labor.

You must work hard at night to get more and better pay, and status, you must fight.

This process also includes falling in love, getting married, and establishing a family. In order to realize a certain ideal or achieve a certain purpose, and consciously work for it, some of the psychological state, for the relatives, for the marriage and blood-based social units, including parents, children and other relatives living together, and live the goal of struggle.

When our children grow up, we start to live for them again, to create the best family environment and work environment for them. The sunset shines on the tops of the mulberry elm trees, and from the moment we close our eyes and enter heaven, we have completed the whole meaning of "existence" in our life.

2. The meaning of "existence" (source: mindhave)

In addition to the above, human being is the will to consciously work for the realization of a certain ideal or the achievement of a certain purpose. Then, is there any meaning left for the existence of the self? When you think about it, it seems that we do not feel that we are living for ourselves!

When we really don't know what we live for, let's backtrack and imagine what would happen if we consciously work hard to achieve a certain ideal or a certain goal, but unfortunately we die with regret halfway through.

For those who care about you, who care about you, it is undoubtedly a painful blow, and may even make some people lose the confidence and courage to continue living. At that time, you will suddenly realize that living is also a responsibility that you need to help and that you cannot shirk because it is your duty.

Therefore, our aspirations, our ability to make our own decisions, always feel like we are living for what others see in us.

As an independent individual, we are born with an inexplicable desire to achieve self-affirmation in order to realize a certain ideal or to achieve a certain purpose, and this recognition of the existence of things or the reality of things comes almost entirely from external sources.

All success factors, in the end, come from the closest to your sincere, honest, to touch others from the heart, and eventually gain the trust of others. If someone has an opinion about you, it's because they want you to see themselves.

Who do we live for? In a realistic sense, no matter how great human beings are, they cannot escape from the dictates of reality in the end.

In fact, when we begin to understand that coming into this world is just a learning process, we can grow through learning. We see the things that we don't normally do as we would like as positive energy in our lives.

For example, the advice that "honest and upright advice is often harsh and not easily accepted," think of the expression "harsh advice" in the sense that there must be someone around you in your life with whom you have a brief conversation or whom you don't even know.

He is just a passerby, talking on the phone, buying something. Whether you know them or not, everyone and everything, they appear unexpectedly, as if they are there for themselves, staring at you, making comments or attacks on flaws, mistakes, uncomfortable conversations, as if they want you to see and teach you something.

Therefore, don't have too narrow stereotypes about the wisdom of "learning", and examine life deeply with a reflective attitude, because each of our hearts is like a mirror that reflects the side of the world we see, so that if we want to see the most real world, we need to erase all the troubles that bother us on top of the mirror in order to see the most real world.

Just as they are teaching us something, we are not able to understand in the moment what kind of revelation and association they are trying to send us, and naturally we are not able to realize: "What is this person and this thing teaching me.

It may take us some time, perhaps one night,

tomorrow, a month later, or even a year, five years, or even longer, or even at the end of our lives, to realize that when we unexpectedly encounter someone or something again, we will remember that the person or thing was trying to teach us the truth of the existence of our own life.

As the saying goes, "When we see a wise person, we should think of the same thing, and when we see an unwise person, we should think of ourselves". We don't know whether we really understand it or not at the moment, because everyone can use the wisdom and cultivation, but when we encounter a problem, it's still the same hideous, ugly face.

It will be seen in the next event you encounter, when you are faced with the choice yourself. Who among us has not wanted to get rid of most people, to live a free life alone, to think that this is the more appropriate and right way to live, to live a very different life, but must face loneliness and boredom from time to time, and painful loneliness and suffering for no reason.

Therefore, the true meaning of "love" is never "living for others". Similarly, there is no excuse for parents and children to "live for each other". Even Confucianism, which respects filial piety and ritual in the East, follows the principle of "harmony as precious, harmony as different", that is, respect for each other, but does not require that each person be "regulated", "obligated", or "deserving".

For example, don't we often hear parents say to their children, "Son! What we do is all for you! These words not only add to the children's mental burden and stress, but they are also too false, too heavy, and too untrue.

We ask ourselves, "What is the meaning behind these words and what do they teach us? What is missing in the existence of life at this moment when we reveal our grievances and sadness, and why do we feel so miserable? Are we really living for others?

When you see the foul-mouthed, rude and impolite people, this allows you to learn to respect others and self-love; when you see the cowardly, weak, closed and inferior people, this allows you to learn to compassionate embrace and give.

When you see the treacherous and tricky villain, this allows you to learn loyalty, integrity and trust; when you see the arrogant and stubborn and proud people, this allows you to learn respect, kindness and humility; when you see the frightened and helpless people, this allows you to learn courage, commitment and face ....

Don't we often hear wives or husbands say, "Everything I do is for this family! It's all for you! And for the children!" These words also sound awkward. Can we bring happiness to the family and to our "self" if we are not happy?

We ask ourselves the same question: "What is the meaning behind these words and what do they teach us? At this moment when we reveal our grievances and sadness, what is missing in our lives, and why do we feel so miserable? Do I really live for others? Is it really for the sake of others? Or is it the addition of "distinction" behind "clinging" and "delusion"?

Therefore, the realization of learning wisdom happens all the time, every day, as long as one is attentive, it is everywhere. These truths may seem simple, but that does not mean they are relatively easy to put into practice.

The growth of daily life experience is invisible and progressive, and so is the reduction to mediocrity. Since we always feel that we are living for others. Why should we continue to live when we feel that life is full of pain, boredom, and never-ending suffering?

Let's ask the question of the meaning of the "existence" of the existence of the self in life, citing the philosophical viewpoint of the French novelist and philosopher Albert Camus. Albert Camus is sometimes called the hero of absurdity or the philosopher of absurdity, because "absurdity" is the central concept in his philosophical thought.

In Camus' logical thinking, "absurdity" refers to the attempt to find out what is the meaning of "existence" in the very existence of one's own life in this world.

The result is an attempt to find the wisdom of the past in a group or society that has been handed down in tradition, in beliefs or behaviors that have symbolic or special meaning (folklore), in philosophies that originated in the past, but to no avail.

According to Albert Camus, life has no reason and no meaning at all, and the search for the existence of the existence of the self in itself gives rise to a feeling of "absurdity".

This "absurd" feeling of extreme error, of a very unconscionable "absurdity", may sometimes arise from the helplessness of knowing, through observation, the transience and impermanence of life, or from the feeling that there are many things in life that one cannot control.

It may also arise from the feeling that there are many things in life that are beyond one's control, or it may be a state of mind in which one consciously strives to achieve a certain ideal or purpose in life, and suffers from a setback or failure that prevents one from recovering from a purposeful activity.

01. Sense of Absurdity

But Albert Camus personally believes that the most damaging sense of absurdity comes from the mechanics and purposelessness of everyday life. Albert Camus believes that this is a real feeling that many people, especially in the labor force, have experienced firsthand.

As Albert Camus points out, our daily "life" consists of getting up, getting on the bus, going to work or to school, eating, going to work or to school, going to work or to school, going to work or to school, going to work or to school, eating, going to bed; all the days of Monday, Tuesday, Wednesday, Thursday, ... go by in this mechanical and numb way One day after another.

In any case, one's care for self or existence often does not appear until one day when one is at a loss or confused about one's life, because one is less likely to feel one's existence when one is focused, busy, or happy or blissful; but one is clearly aware of one's existence in situations of emptiness, anxiety, or difficulty. In a situation of emptiness, anxiety, or difficulty, one becomes clearly aware of one's problems.

Therefore, it is often when one is faced with a difficult situation that one becomes more conscious and aware of one's self and existence, "Why? This question of "existence" comes to the surface.

According to Albert Camus, when we try to respond to this question, we find that there is no objective human existence in the world for us to find things, places, or truths and borrowings that others have never seen before.

There is no reason or meaning for being in this world and surviving to this day. When people discover this fact, they choose to avoid it because they are unwilling or afraid to face a certain situation or thing, to distract themselves with work or various forms of entertainment, to avoid the problem, and to continue to live numbly.

But Albert Camus (in French: Albert Camus), who is interested in the surface characteristics of objective things, directly reflected in the human brain through the sense organs, believes that since human existence has no knowledge of natural or social things, and gives meaning to objects, but is only a spiritual content that humans transmit and communicate in the form of symbols.

So when one is honest and courageous, when one faces the world and oneself, one cannot help but think why one continues to live. Thus, Albert Camus profoundly and gravely states that there is only one philosophical question that is truly serious: suicide. (There is only one really serious philosophical question, and that is suicide.)

In the face of this dilemma of life, Albert Camus argues that people should not commit suicide. But Albert Camus does not want us to live and die in a state of confusion, nor does he think, as some ethicists do, that suicide is an immoral act.

Albert Camus believes that one should not commit suicide simply because it is a compromise and surrender to "absurd" external pressures.

According to Albert Camus, although there is no

objective human business in this world, people's ability to recognize their environment and themselves, and their clarity of perception, can give value to their lives through their actions.

One should live a tragic and heroic life, face the absurdity bravely and directly, and live in a "rebellious" manner, which is the only way to save the existence of one's own life, the dignity and value of life.

The "rebellion" that Camus refers to here is not the ordinary teenager's dissatisfaction with old rules, things, and views that no longer apply to the present.

While recognizing that the new has its imperfections and that it is not easy to verify its specific superiority to the old, the priority is to try the new in the face of dissatisfaction with the old. The rejection of the old is more one-sided and blind, and often tacitly recognizes the old as useless, obsolete, decaying, and other derogatory terms.

Therefore, the best way to understand his rebellious attitude of "rebellion for the sake of rebellion" is through the story of "pushing the stone up the mountain" mentioned in "The Myth of Xerxes".

02. The Myth of Xerxes

In The Myth of Xerxes, Xerxes is a powerless, lowly man who lives under the authority of the gods. Xerxes was punished by the gods for offending them, and he was told to keep pushing a huge rock up the mountain.

But every time he pushed it up the mountain, the boulder would roll back down the mountain and Xerxes had to push it up again. This action was repeated over and over again, without end. In the eyes of the gods, there is nothing more terrible than this eternal despair, this futile punishment.

One day, when Xerxes returned to the bottom of the mountain again, he was well aware of his absurd fate. However, he decided to lift the boulder again and go back up the mountain, thinking to himself, "Yes, let's do it again! . Since the gods wanted him to keep pushing the stone up the mountain because it was the most painful punishment, he had to bear the suffering with his own will and "enjoy" it, and then the meaning of punishment would be lost on him.

The Myth of Sisyphus Punishment The Myth of Sisyphus

Photo Credit: Titian Public Domain

According to Albert Camus, this sense of absurdity can strike anyone on any street corner. It is unbearable in its nakedness, it is a light without light, it is inscrutable.

But the difficulty itself is worth contemplating the tragic fate of the eternal return. Instead of choosing to kill himself or to live, Xerxes, through a gesture of "rebellion," despises the gods, sees the process of punishment as an act of his own will and initiative, destroys the meaning of their punishment for him, and "exists" unyieldingly.

Likewise, we should face the absurdity of life without the comfort of religion (the illusory and non-existent gods) or the distraction of the pleasure of entertainment or the desire for fame and fortune, and so we face the absurdity and the oppression of fate.

As a story, Sisyphus is only an allegory for our courage to face and rebel against the absurdity of life. But when we put this allegory into the context of human business, the question of the meaning of "existence" in the existence of our own lives? The question remains.

For, Camus, to Xerxes, this futile process must be repeated again and again. This myth, proposed by the philosopher Camus at a time of existentialism, had a great impact on the thinking of the 1950s and 1960s.

According to Camus, the constant pushing of the boulder up the mountain symbolizes the "life process" of human beings - birth, struggle and struggle for survival, and finally death - a process that has been going on for generations without end. What is the meaning of such a life?

Camus analyzes the tendency of the modern subject self to think about perceptual objects, to synthesize particular, unconnected perceptual objects, and to associate them into a regular natural scientific knowledge with an innate cognitive ability, and to interpret human existence and the world as "absurd".

Broadly speaking, it means all, all, everything, and the concept of "absurdity" is interpreted through philosophical discourse, literary criticism, and art, where it seems to presuppose that the suffering in our lives, as if it were hidden within the substance of things, has the capacity to produce other things or phenomena, and that the cause of this is the gift, punishment, or mockery of the self-will.

But if the actual situation is only the "will" of the ego (the mental state that arises from the decision to achieve a certain purpose), there is no such thing as the mockery of fate.

There is no so-called mockery of fate, we just come to this world because of our own will, in order to realize a certain ideal or achieve a certain purpose, and consciously work hard for it, and must bear the pain and annoyance and the negation of no understanding when the will is not perfect, then what should we do?

In fact, the power we have is much more than we know; our willpower for the resilience of life is also much stronger than we imagine. If we start from the idea of realizing a certain ideal or achieving a certain goal.

We live to pursue our own value in life, we live to be our true selves, life is a gift from nature, and we really have no right to waste our lives.

In fact, in the end, you will find that the love that is like glue, sensational, and intense is over, and the hate that is engraved in your heart is over, leaving only yourself in the mirror, or so truly exist, even if you do not really agree with the "existence" of that once self, life.

Since we are all here to learn to grow up, everyone who appears in front of us is our life teacher, whether they are older than us or later in life, their stories of growth have reduced our pain and shortened our groping time, and finally made us mature and learn to take on responsibilities.

Thinking or judging the reasonableness of something from different viewpoints or perspectives, the perspective of the nature of a thing that exists independently without the influence of subjective thoughts or consciousness, endlessly thinking about ourselves and living for what seems to be a very foolish behavior.

But the doubt that each person consciously works for the realization of a certain ideal, or the achievement of a certain purpose, always exists. Therefore, those who can observe are able to investigate the relationship of karma, and those who can observe are able to deeply understand the meaning of "existence" in the existence of their own life.

3. What is the meaning of living?

A man who had lost faith in life once approached the

ancient Greek philosopher Antiphon of Ramnos (480-411 B.C.) and asked him with a sad face, "Master, what is the meaning of living?" Antiphon said, "I have not yet thought this question through, so I will live!" By contemplating the self and existence, we experience that the self is unique, and that man is in the position of being the contemplator and the creator of the essence of his existence.

Being is individual and particular, and the consciousness of being is a subjective, felt awareness. This is what Martin Buber meant. As Martin Buber says: "Everything else exists under the contemplative and profound examination of life by the self".

To be unique and distinctive is the most noteworthy, important and precious fact of existence in this world. It is also the absolute meaning and ultimate value that I can give to myself, because my existence is different, important and unique.

But at the same time, we also lose faith or feel unhappy because our hopes are not fulfilled, because my existence has no weight and the world does not necessarily need my existence, while my disappearance cannot be prevented from happening in a certain situation, and someone can always fill up the insufficient things or objects with substitutes afterwards. At any time, someone can fill my vacancy with substitutes.

In the orbit of the universe, in the flood of past events and activities of human society, and in the systematic recording, study and interpretation of these events and actions, I will be forgotten and everything will be quiet again.

Does man have absolute value, or will life eventually return to worthlessness? It depends on how the individual lives out his or her life. The meaning of "existence" from the awareness and realization of the existence of the self is to know the unique and unique state of the existence of the self from the awareness and consciousness of the self.

And to realize that the existence of the meaning of "existence" of the ego life existence itself has its own predetermined goal and result of the behavior of the subject according to its own needs, through the intermediary of consciousness and concepts, that is, the meaning of "existence" of the ego life existence itself is the purpose, not for other purposes, nor should it exist for other purposes. It does not exist for other purposes and should not exist for other purposes.

Otherwise the meaning of "existence" of the self-life existence itself, the life existence itself, would become a means for other purposes, so that the meaning of "existence" of the self-life existence itself, the way of existence, would lose its way of existence as a human being, but would exist as a thing. For example, real existence is not determined by how much life one has, but by what is the meaning of "existence" in the existence of the self.

People often affirm the value of their own existence by what they have, they affirm their existence by having a house, money, and fame, but all these things are subject to change and loss. What is the meaning of the "existence" of human life and existence itself, and what can existence truly possess? What can others not deprive or take away? What is the meaning of "existence" in the existence of human life itself, and how to show the real value of oneself?

We must consider ourselves as human beings to realize the meaning of our own existence, the purpose of our own existence, and treat our own existence as the purpose of our own existence, no longer as a tool to obtain a degree, fame, or wealth. It is no longer a tool to get a degree, fame, fortune, but a valuable existence. This is also the meaning of "existence" of self-life existence itself, existence in a human way.

In the face of the meaning of "existence" of the existence itself, the anxiety and anxiety of the uncertainty of life, and even the loss and confusion, when you want to find the meaning of "existence" of the existence itself and the way out of life, you are thinking about how to settle your body and mind, how to settle your body and mind, how to establish the direction of life. To establish the direction of life.

Through thinking about the meaning of "existence" and the existence of the existence of the self, we can affirm the need to have an autonomous life.

That is, to choose how to achieve the meaning of "existence" in the existence of the self. In creating one's own self and one's own nature, one is taking responsibility for one's own form of life, facing one's only chance in life with sincerity, and living the life one wants to live through one's own choices.

By thinking about the meaning of "existence" and the way of existence, we can understand and master our own existence and determine the direction of our existence. To further establish oneself.

To find the meaning of life and the value of existence for the meaning of "existence" of one's own existence. To realize the uniqueness, purpose, and autonomy of life, to avoid being materialized, instrumentalized, and instrumentalized, and not to let one's existence and life fall into a state of being manipulated, used, and traded.

From the awareness and understanding of the meaning of "existence" of one's own life and existence, and the affirmation of one's own self and existence, from consciousness and autonomy to freedom, one not only determines the meaning and value of one's own life, but also gives and creates the value of life and existence.

Therefore, the phrase "It cannot be said! It cannot be said!" This means that it is the closest thing to the original reality of the "truth", and it is immediately enlightening for a person who wants to realize the "Avalokiteshvara" for himself.

What was known before was all false distinctions, and when one truly understands the true connotation, there is no such thing, then one is truly "aware" of it. Therefore, when I see this "I cannot say! It cannot be said! No matter what you do, in terms of the true meaning of victory, it cannot be found.

Therefore, it is only in this state that it is "correspondingly" convenient to say that for the individual, it is the truth, but for the whole, it is not yet seen as the "truth reality.

4. The true path of "the way of the ancient ancestors".

Why is it that so many people are like pachyderms, repeating the essence of the gleanings of others, but are unable to realize it for themselves? The "mind and action are destroyed and words are broken", "color is emptiness and emptiness is color, so there is no color in the air", "a name can be a name but not a name", and "a path can be a path but not a path".

This is always through one's mental activities such as sensation, perception, thinking, memory, etc., one's comprehensive awareness of one's physical and mental state and the changes of people, things and objects in the environment, and one's understanding of the meaning of life's existence.

For a person who wants to personally realize Avalokiteshvara, the face of truth can be multifaceted, that is, for questions that cannot be answered directly through perception, it is deduced through rational logical reasoning under a priori conditions, and cannot contradict empirical evidence.

This explains why Western culture has always been "suspended" in the framework of truth. Similarly, the thinking of philosophers from generation to generation has always been unable to break away from the confusion and disorientation of the "ancient path of the ancestors" to personally realize the true "Avalokiteshvara".

Therefore, those who claim to be knowledgeable and wise are like carp passing through the river, but only a few can really understand the true meaning of the existence of their own life.

Therefore, it is obvious that the emergence of the enlightened person of the Truth is too important for human beings, and if the enlightened person of the Truth does not emerge, human beings will not be able to see the true nature of the Truth of the universe.

The higher wisdom reflects the illusion of the objective world according to what is already known. People believe that the supernatural and superhuman mysterious realms and powers dominate nature and society, and thus generate infinite awe and worship.

To imagine what is not known, or to seek or establish rules and evidence to support or judge a belief, decision, or action, to fool people into believing, worshiping, and holding as a rule and guide for words and actions the complex psychological history of a religion or a doctrine.

This kind of mentality, in which the family has a broom and enjoys a thousand pieces of gold, is already contrary to the Buddha's original intention of "Avalokiteshvara".

In the following, we seek to interpret the meaning of the existence of the universe and to achieve the meaning of the existence of liberation [total will] from the existence of life, based on the viewpoint of analyzing and reflecting on the fundamental issues of life, knowledge, and values.

From the inevitable "nihilism" as a guide to the Western understanding of the meaning of life existence, we continue to understand the other side of the truth, transforming it into the ontological "existentialism" generation, and the metamorphic transformation into the process of achieving the meaning of life existence of liberation from the [total will]. This is a general explanation of the deconstruction.

Reference Source

Wikipedia

Education Encyclopedia | Education Cloud Online Dictionary

Dictionary of Buddhism

H. Newton Malony (ed.), A Christian Existential Psychology: The Contributions of John G. Finch, University Press of America, 1980, p. 168.

Citation error: no reference provided for Ostenfeld's reference Ronald Grimsley. Søren Kierkegaard and French literature : eight comparative studies. Cardiff: Univ. of Wales Press. 1966. ISBN 9780708302088.

Jon Bartley Stewart, Kierkegaard and Existentialism, Ashgate Publishing, Ltd. 2011, p. 204.

Liang Shiqiu, ed. The Far Eastern English-Chinese Dictionary, February 1960.

Qi Keguo, The Integration of the Masterpieces of Christianity Through the Ages (Part II, Vol. 22), translated by Tse Ping-tak (Hong Kong: Southeast Asia Theological Education Foundation & Fu Kiu Christian Publishing House, 1963), 13

Ibid, 13-4

Tian Lik, The Academic Library of Christian Thought Through the Ages - A History of Christian Thought, translated by Yin Da Yi (Hong Kong: Chinese Institute of Christian Culture, 2000) Ibid, 576-78

Roger E. Olson, The Story of Theology, translated by Rui-Cheng Wu and Cheng-De Hsu (Taipei: Campus Books, 2002), 676.

Roger E. Olson, The Story of Theology, 673.

Tian Lik, 581-2

Roger E. Olson, 677

Tallick, 583

Zickgo, A Collection of Christian Masterpieces Through the Ages (Part II, Volume 22), 15

Roger E. Olson, 678

Kilgore, "Conclusion of the Non-Scientific Follow-up of Philosophical Fragments," 215

Ibid, 215

Roger E. Olson, 679-80

Zhou Lianhua, "Dao Sheng Renren Series, Vol. 2, No. 18 - Existence and Faith," 24-5

Tien, Rick, 592-93

Bretall, Robert (ed.) (1946). Kierkegaard Anthology. Princeton, NJ: Princeton University Press. ISBN 0-394-60303-6

Evans, C. Stephen (1999). Kierkegaard. In R. Audi (Ed.), The Cambridge Dictionary of Philosophy (Second Edition). Cambridge, UK: Cambridge University Press. ISBN 0-521-63722-8

Gardiner, Patrick (1998). Kierkegaard, Søren Aabye. In E. Craig (Ed.), Routledge Encyclopedia of Philosophy. London: Routledge. Retrieved November 04, 2004.

Jansen, F.J. Billeskov (1996). SØREN KIERKEGAARD - Life and Work

McDonald, William (2001). Søren Kierkegaard. In

Edward N. Zalta (ed.), Stanford Encyclopedia of Philosophy (Winter 2001 Edition).

1. Copleston, F.C. Existentialism. philosophy. 2009, 23 (84): 19-37. jstor 4544850. doi:10.1017/S0031819100065955.

2. ^ See James Wood's introduction to Sartre, Jean-Paul. nausea. london: Penguin Classics. 2000. isbn 978-0-141-18549-1.

3. ^ Tidsskrift for Norsk Psykologforening, Vol 45, nummer 10, 2008, side 1298-1304, Welhaven og psykologien: Del 2. (Page archived for backup in the Internet Archive)

4. ^ Lundestad, 1998, p. 169

5. ^ Slagstad, 2001, p. 89

6. ^ Seip, 2007, p. 352

7. ^ Stanford Encyclopedia of Philosophy, Existentialism, 3.1 Anxiety, Nothingness, the Absurd (page archived in the Internet Archive)

8. ^ Bassnett, Susan; Lorch, Jennifer. Luigi Pirandello in the Theatre. Routledge. March 18, 2014 [26 March 2015]. (Archived from the original on 2021-02-05).

9. ^ Thompson, Mel; Rodgers, Nigel. Understanding Existentialism: Teach Yourself. Hodder & Stoughton. 2010 [2017-08-19]. (Original content archived 2021-02-05).

10. ^ Caputi, Anthony Francis. Pirandello and the Crisis of Modern Consciousness. university of Illinois Press. 1988 [2017-08-19]. (Original content archived 2021-02-20).

11. ^ Mariani, Umberto. living Masks: The Achievement of Pirandello. university of Toronto Press. 2010 [26 March 2015]. (Archived from the original on 2021-02-05).

12. ^ Jean-Paul Sartre. Existentialism is a Humanism, Jean-Paul Sartre 1946. marxists.org. [2010-03-08]. (Archived from the original on 2011-06-14).

13. ^ E Keen. Suicide and Self-Deception. psychoanalytic Review. 1973 [2017-08-19]. (Original content archived 2018-09-18).

14. ^ E Keen. Suicide and Self-Deception. psychoanalytic Review. 1973 [2017-08-19]. (Archived from the original on 2018-09-18)

METAMORPHOSIS:
The Reality of Existence and Sublimation of Life
(Volume 3)

蛻變：生命存在與昇華的實相（國際英文版：卷三）

出版者/美商 EHGBooks 微出版公司

發行者/美商漢世紀數位文化公司

臺灣學人出版網：http://www. TaiwanFellowship.Org

地　　　址/106 臺北市大安區敦化南路 2 段 1 號 4 樓

電　　　話/02-2701-6088 轉 616-617

印　　　刷/漢世紀古騰堡®數位出版 POD 雲端科技

出版日期/2023 年 2 月

總經銷/Amazon.com

臺灣銷售網/三民網路書店：http：//www. Sanmin.com. Tw

　　　　三民書局復北店

　　　　地址/104 臺北市復興北路 386 號

　　　　電話/02-2500-6600

　　　　三民書局重南店

　　　　地址/100 臺北市重慶南路一段 61 號

　　　　電話/02-2361-7511

全省金石網路書店：http://www.kingstone.com. Tw

定　　　價/新臺幣 2400 元（美金 80 元/人民幣 500 元）

CPSIA information can be obtained
at www.ICGtesting.com
Printed in the USA
BVHW052205230123
656965BV00009B/65